SOUTH CAROLINA REFLECTIONS

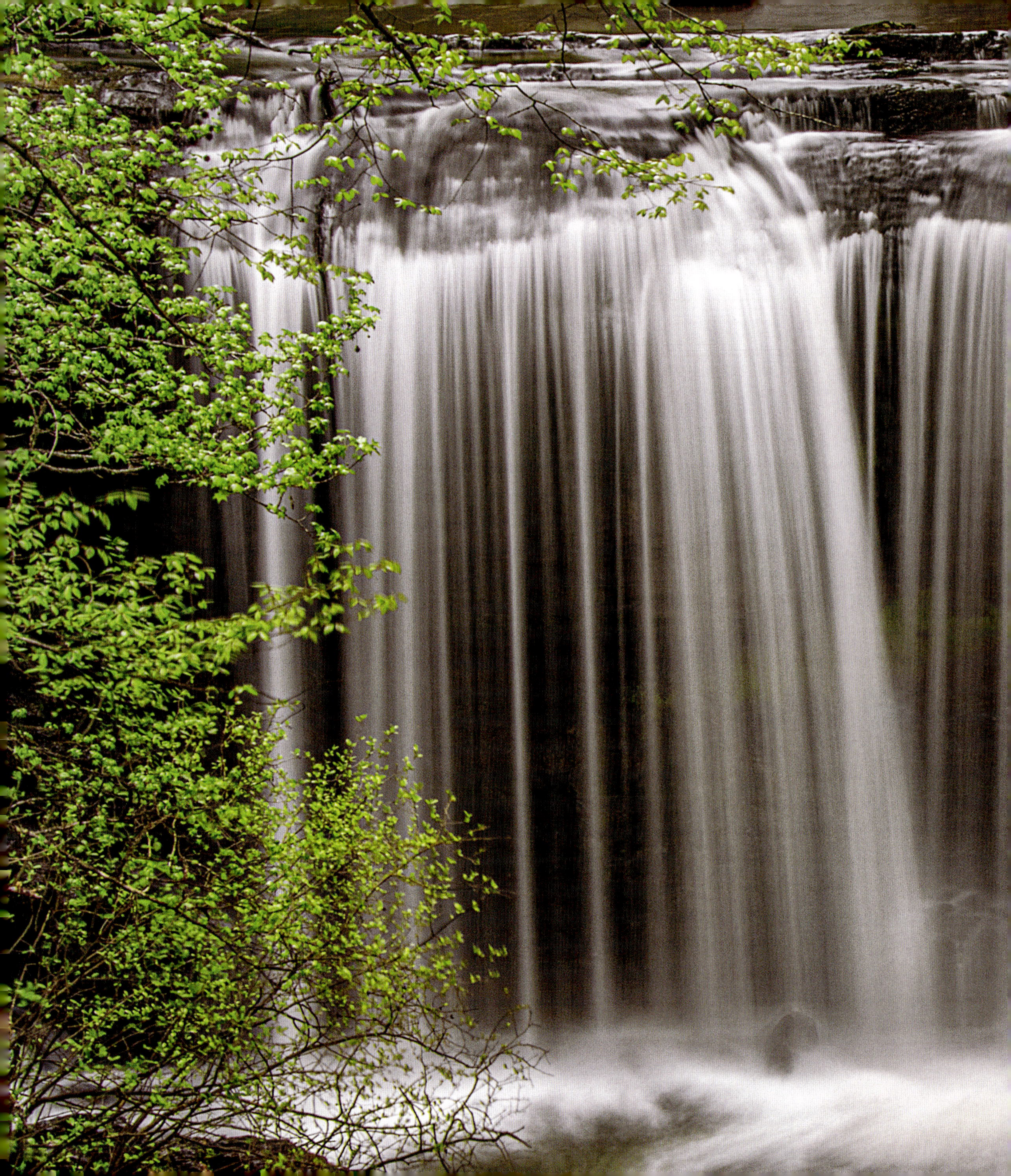

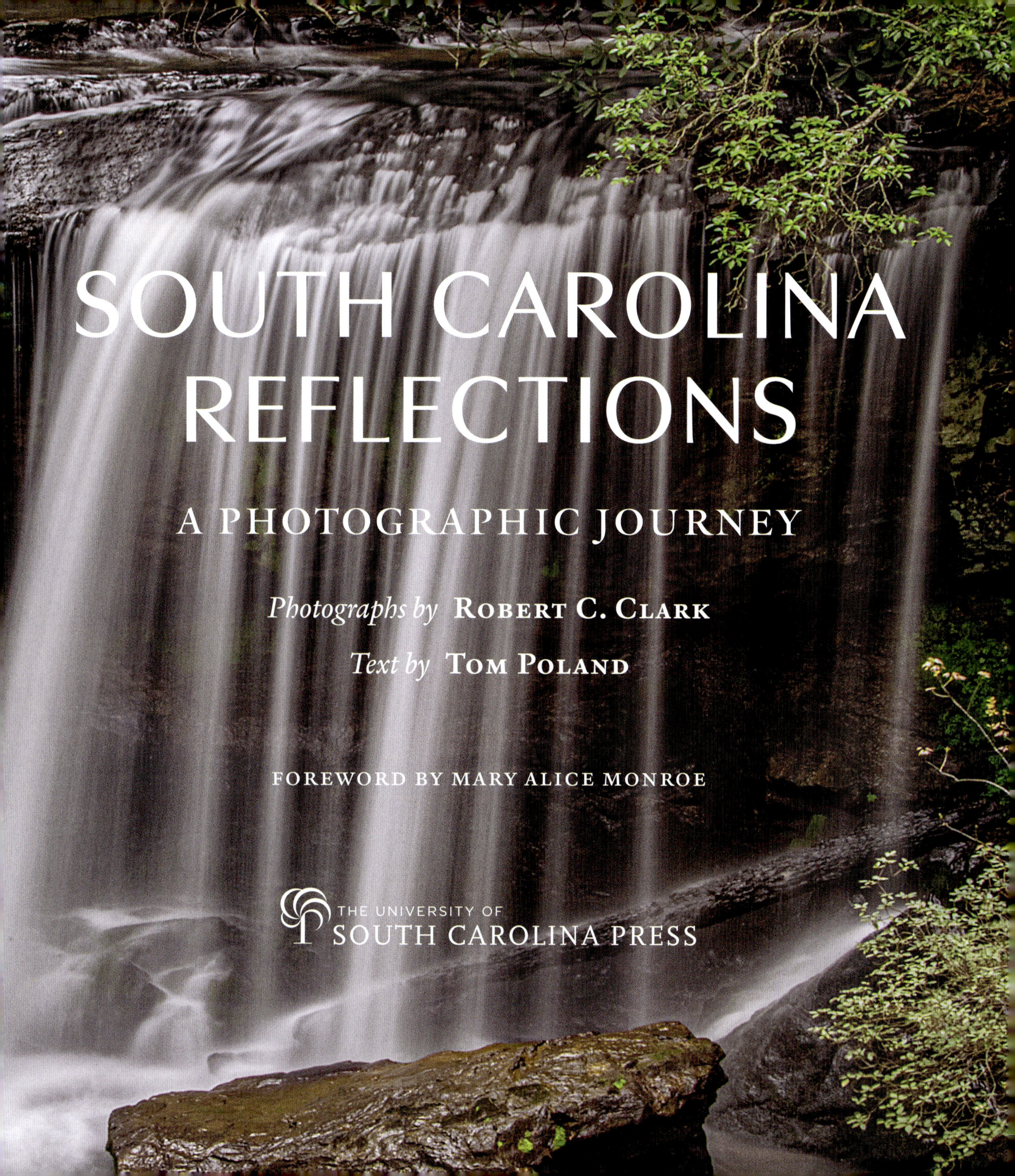

SOUTH CAROLINA REFLECTIONS

A PHOTOGRAPHIC JOURNEY

Photographs by ROBERT C. CLARK

Text by TOM POLAND

FOREWORD BY MARY ALICE MONROE

THE UNIVERSITY OF
SOUTH CAROLINA PRESS

Published by the University of South Carolina Press
Columbia, South Carolina 29208
USCPRESS.COM

Designed by Nathan Moehlmann, Goosepen Studio & Press
Printed in China

Library of Congress Cataloging-in-Publication Data
can be found at http://catalog.loc.gov/.

ISBN: 978-1-64336-556-5 (hardcover)

TITLE SPREAD: Brasstown Falls

Consider Oconee County's Brasstown Falls four waterfalls in one. Tucked away in the southern edge of Sumter National Forest, it tumbles 120 feet in three dramatic drops. An observation platform gives visitors a commanding view of cascading Brasstown Creek.

ILLUSTRATION PAGE VI: Lawson's Fork Creek

Lawson's Fork Creek runs into the Pacolet, which joins the Broad, Congaree, and Santee before their waters spill into the Atlantic. During the Civil War, the Glendale Mill made shoe soles and cloth for the Confederacy. Long before that Native American hunting parties pursued wildlife here.

CONTENTS

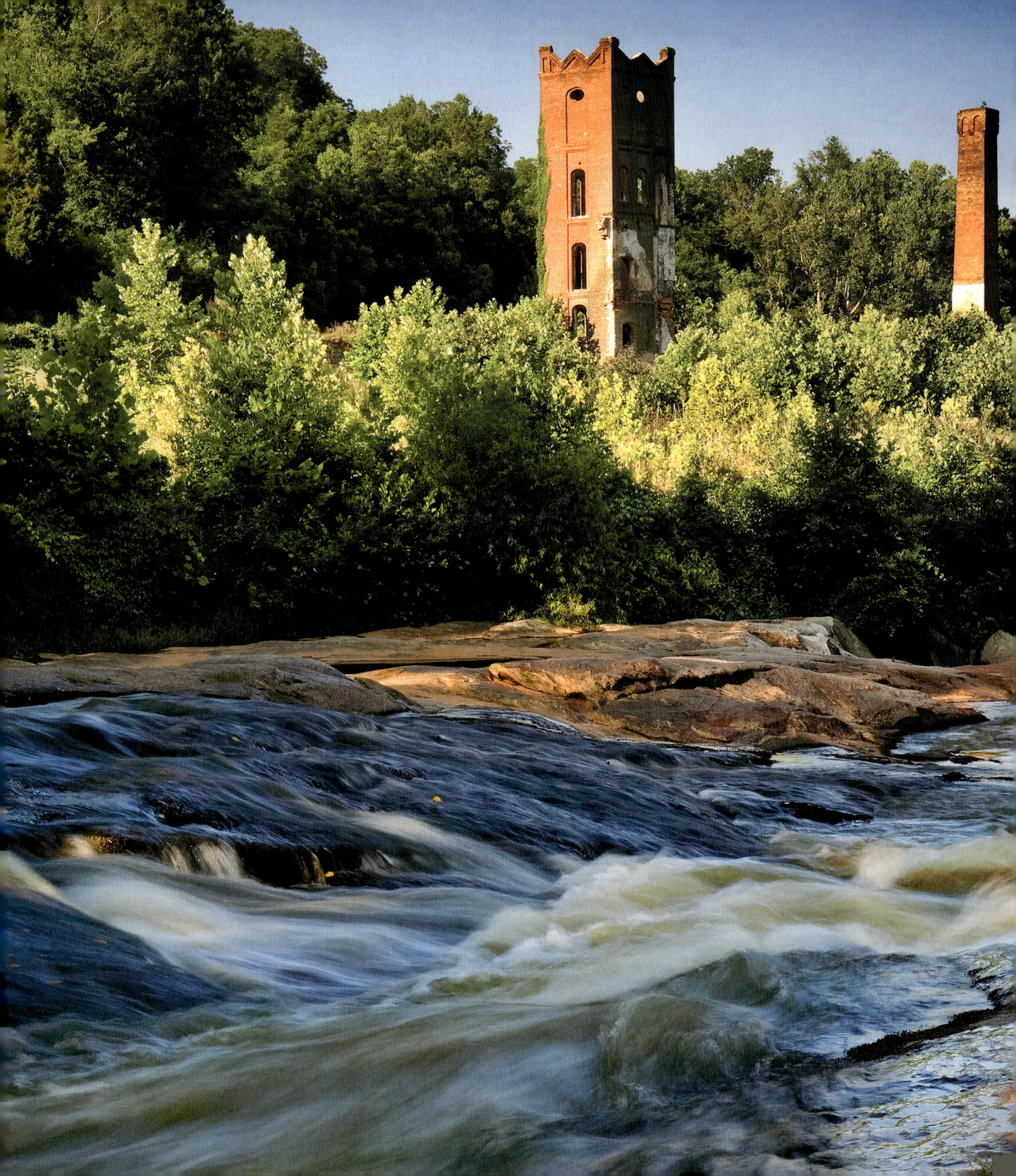

FOREWORD

A STATE OF AWE AND WONDER

South Carolina is an ancient land, born of rock and sea. Rivers, spawned high in the mountains and fed by rain and melted snow, gush over boulders and between rocky ridges, cascading down to form even more rivers and sets of streams that flow lower into the state's watershed, the Atlantic Ocean. We gave these terraced landscapes names: the Piedmont, foothills of an eroded mountain chain of sedimentary rock; the Sandhills, the beach dunes of a prehistoric coastline; the flat and fertile land of the Coastal Plain; and the Coast, the seductive and sultry Lowcountry where the sea caresses a vast carpet of swaying marsh grass and warm sandy beaches.

Life teems in this rich ecosystem, breathing in and out with the tides, living and decaying to form the soul-stirring sights and pungent scents of what South Carolinians associate with *home*.

Not only our geography but also our history is tied to the sea. The graceful, tall ships brought the first visitors to South Carolina's shore. The port city of Charleston became a glittering jewel of wealth and culture unparalleled in the original thirteen colonies. It was also the port of entry for 40 to 60 percent of Africans brought to America during the slave trade. Their African culture and the sweat of their backs formed the great rice agriculture and plantation history that helped shape the people, society, history, economy, and culture of South Carolina. The warships of the War for Independence, the American Civil War, and two World Wars, as well as the nuclear submarines of the Cold War, slid through our waters like so many sharks and marked South Carolina's significant and important role in American military history.

Ours is a *living* history. It surrounds us. Wherever we turn, we run into a monument, trip over a historical marker, or face some clue as to who we are and from where we came. Living here means having one foot in the past and one in the present. We hold our history dear, our traditions close. But we also carry the burden of our past. This is a land that suffered military and economic defeat and the legacy of racism.

But, in the fullness of time, all histories fade, and nature prevails. Travel along our coast, and witness how the sea rises and pushes back. Dynamic sand spits—Bay Point Shoal, Crab Bank—shift and are swallowed. At Castle Pinckney rocks crumble, and the wild pushes up through the stones, determined to survive. Hurricanes baptize the land with wind, and the wheel of time turns round and round, all proving that change is a part of nature. As our state's population rises along with sea levels, our challenge is to revere the past without falling into the trap of nostalgia, lest we ignore the urgent, pressing questions facing our future. Faulkner stated, "The poet's, the writer's, duty is to write about these things. It is his privilege to help man endure by lifting his heart, by reminding him of the courage and honor and hope and pride and compassion and pity and sacrifice which have been the glory of his past."

South Carolina is a state of inspiration. Our rich and complex history and the power of our landscape form the palette of our state's meaningful and profoundly inspiring culture, traditions, and values. Poets, writers,

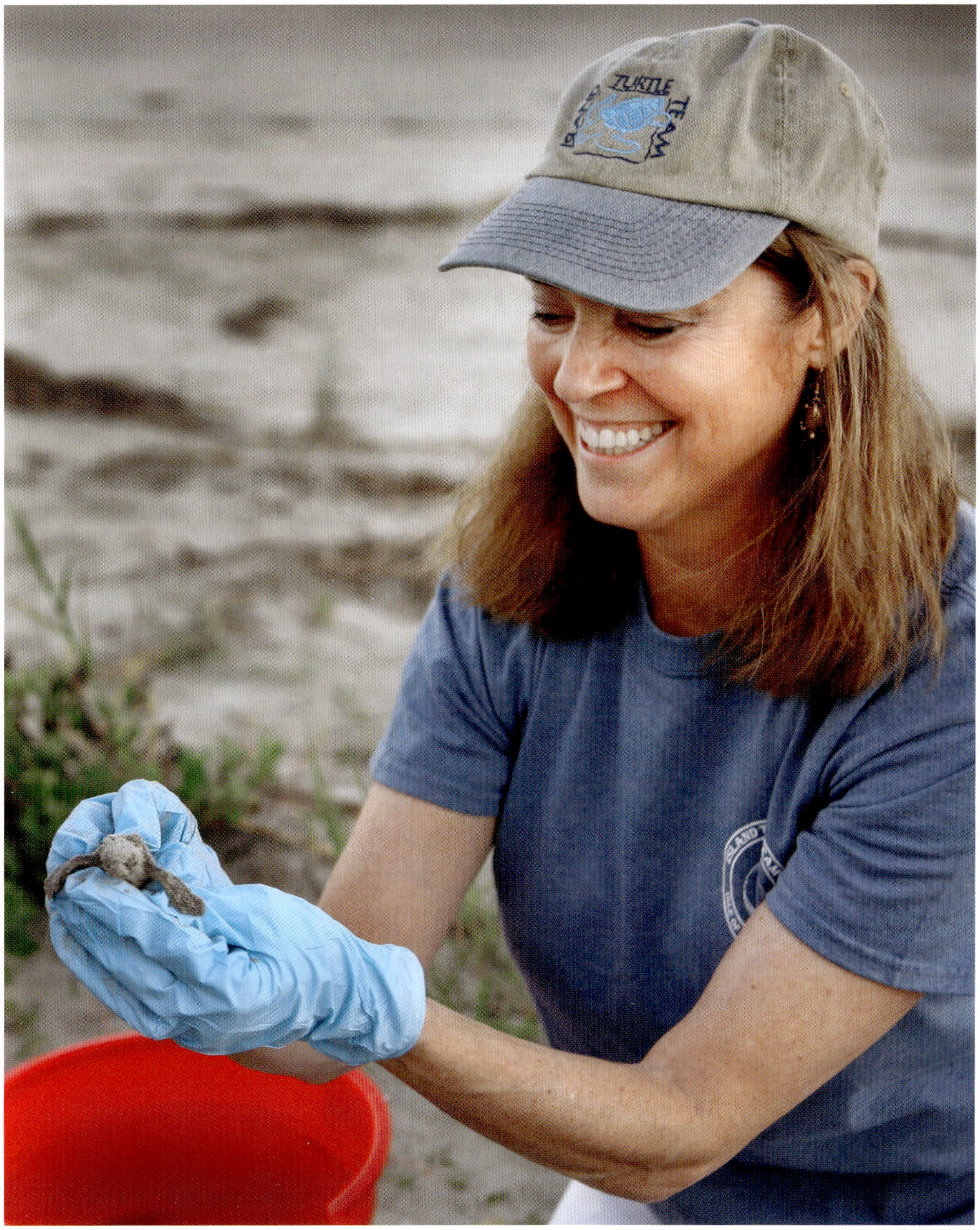
TURTLE
TEAM

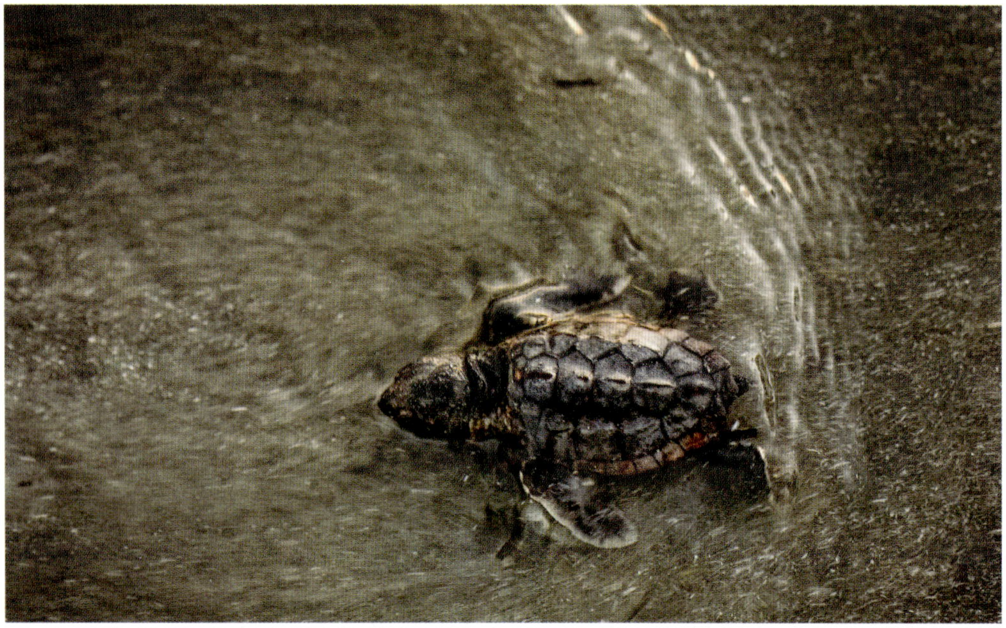

artists, and craftsmen flock to our storied cities and breathtaking landscapes, each desperate to capture in words and color the source of an exquisite revelation. We all feel it. We stare, mouths agape, at a vast sunset of hallucinatory colors. High on the Blue Ridge Mountains, we witness a vista that dares to touch the hem of the angels. Standing at the shoreline, we look out to where the sky joins the sea to blend into a seamless horizon. In the face of infinity, we feel miniscule yet undiminished. We lift our faces to the sun. We resonate to a higher power, a universal knowing that binds us all, human and beast.

These are the gifts of South Carolina. The land and sea offer even the poorest of us a king's bounty. Yet with these gifts comes the notion of noblesse oblige. The noble spirit seeks to preserve and protect, not for gain or recognition, but simply because it is the right thing to do. Marjory

Kinnan Rawlings wrote, "The earth may be borrowed, but not bought. It may be used, but not owned. It gives itself in response to love and tending, offers its seasonal lowering and fruiting. But we are tenants and not possessors, lovers, and not masters."

In South Carolina we put great value on our landscape, history, traditions. We hold them in our work-worn hands to protect, care for, and preserve them, so that we in turn may pass them on to our children, and they to their children to enjoy for generations to come. Thousands of acres of woodlands, wetlands, farmlands, urban parks, and historical sites have been conserved. We must continue the good fight. When we talk about protecting tourism, outdoor recreation, and quality of life, we are discussing conservation. *Stewardship and service.* These are not merely our call to action—they are our privilege.

I've sat on the beach beside a sea turtle nest with tourists and residents alike while the moon and stars shone overhead, the surf rolled in and out, and the mosquitoes hummed, waiting for a sea turtle nest to emerge. People asked countless questions, not idle curiosity but born of a sincere desire to learn. As I crouched near the sand to check the nest, I turned my head and looked up to see a child watching me, eyes as wide as saucers. Farther up I see the eyes of the mother, father, and grandparents, every bit as full of awe and wonder. Nature makes children of us all.

I hope this book of reflections with Tom Poland's words and Robert C. Clark's photographs offers the opportunity to discover and learn more about South Carolina's historical charm, her out-of-the-way vistas, unsung secrets, community festivals, art, and endangered species. And more, her proud history of stewardship and service. With knowledge comes commitment and an awakening of our moral imagination. This is our watershed moment.

Conservationist Baba Dioum tells us, “In the end we will conserve only what we love. We love only what we understand. We will understand only what we are taught.”

I believe in my heart that whether we are “come-yahs” or “been-yahs,” we all hear the state’s siren song. We all come *home* to South Carolina.

Mary Alice Monroe
Isle of Palms

PREFACE

OUR UNENDING JOURNEY

In 1987 Robert C. Clark and I assigned ourselves a feature to see how it might be to collaborate. We didn't realize it, but we were about to embark on a long journey. We struck out on a summer morning, looking for something we both might find worthwhile. On our drive westward on Highway 378, we found it—the lovely ramshackle shacks of the South, tenant homes.

Robert's images and my narrative came together in "Tenant Homes—Testament to Hard Times," a feature that chronicled the hardscrabble era when making do meant everything. As a tenant himself, the Georgia writer, Harry Crews, wrote, "Survival was triumph enough," and he was right as rain.

Our feature made the rounds. Warren Slesinger, an acquisition editor at the University of South Carolina Press, read our feature, picked up the phone, and called me.

"If you fellows have other stories like that, I have a contract for you."

We did, and he did. An introductory lunch at Columbia's old Carolina Inn led to a contract and a book, another book, and later still a third book, *Reflections of South Carolina* (1999), which led to *Reflections of South Carolina, Volume 2* (2014). And then that rocky river, time, rolled on.

A tad over twenty-five years later we present *South Carolina Reflections: A Photographic Journey*. Born of tenant homes, white- and blackwater rivers, green-gold salt marshes, bluegrass, granite outcroppings, and a thousand things more, it's the crown jewel of our *Reflections* series, produced during our fiftieth year as a photographer and a writer.

Throughout our journey, we've worked as both individuals and collaborators. Premeditated and spontaneous, the inventory of our work includes Carolina bays, back roads, dying and abandoned churches, a photo of the week series, and magazine features devoted to railroad villages, rocky shoals spider lilies (*Hymenocallis coronaria*), waterfalls, Americana, old barns, peach orchards, and more.

Robert and I met at the South Carolina Department of Natural Resources. I first worked in film there, later becoming the managing editor for *South Carolina Wildlife* magazine. Robert remembers his second day of work as a photographer at *SC Wildlife*.

"My editor told me I'd be traveling with two historians to visit Hampton Plantation State Park. From the back seat, I marveled at my introduction to South Carolina: live oaks, Spanish moss, and marshlands. I knew I'd love experiencing South Carolina.

"I treasure the memories I've gathered as a photographer. I've experienced why so many people love living in the Palmetto State. Beautiful nature preserves, wildlife, history, and, of course, the people who make the character of this state so unique."

In the early 1990s, Robert's interest focused on the backroads, barns, tenant homes, and the struggle to make a living off the land. Today, few of those places exist.

"Over the decades, Tom and I have documented South Carolina on our own time and dime. Nobody hired us to write and photograph our vision of this unique state. Tom is from Georgia, and I am from North Carolina. We met in the 'middle' and have enjoyed working together all these years. Our journey continues. We can't wait to see what's around the next curve."

Robert's right. We've seen South Carolina in many lights, from dawn to midnight, and in her many moods and colors. Autumn's palette . . . mountain mists . . . sunsets over lakes, peaches holding their share of sunshine . . . an old church campground . . . basket weavers . . . work boats . . . ruins that rival Rome's . . . feathers aplenty—laughing gulls, great blue herons, egrets, and painted buntings. And colors from blue crabs, boneyards, and indigo bottle trees to pink and fuchsia spring finery and red–green pitcher plants.

Meeting our readers has been rewarding. At book events some ask, "How long did you work on this book?"

Our answer surprises them.

"All our life."

We present a book you'll treasure. We believe it casts the best reflection yet on South Carolina. As for the future, Robert puts it in perspective.

"I hope another team carries on the tradition of photographer and writer. South Carolina deserves it."

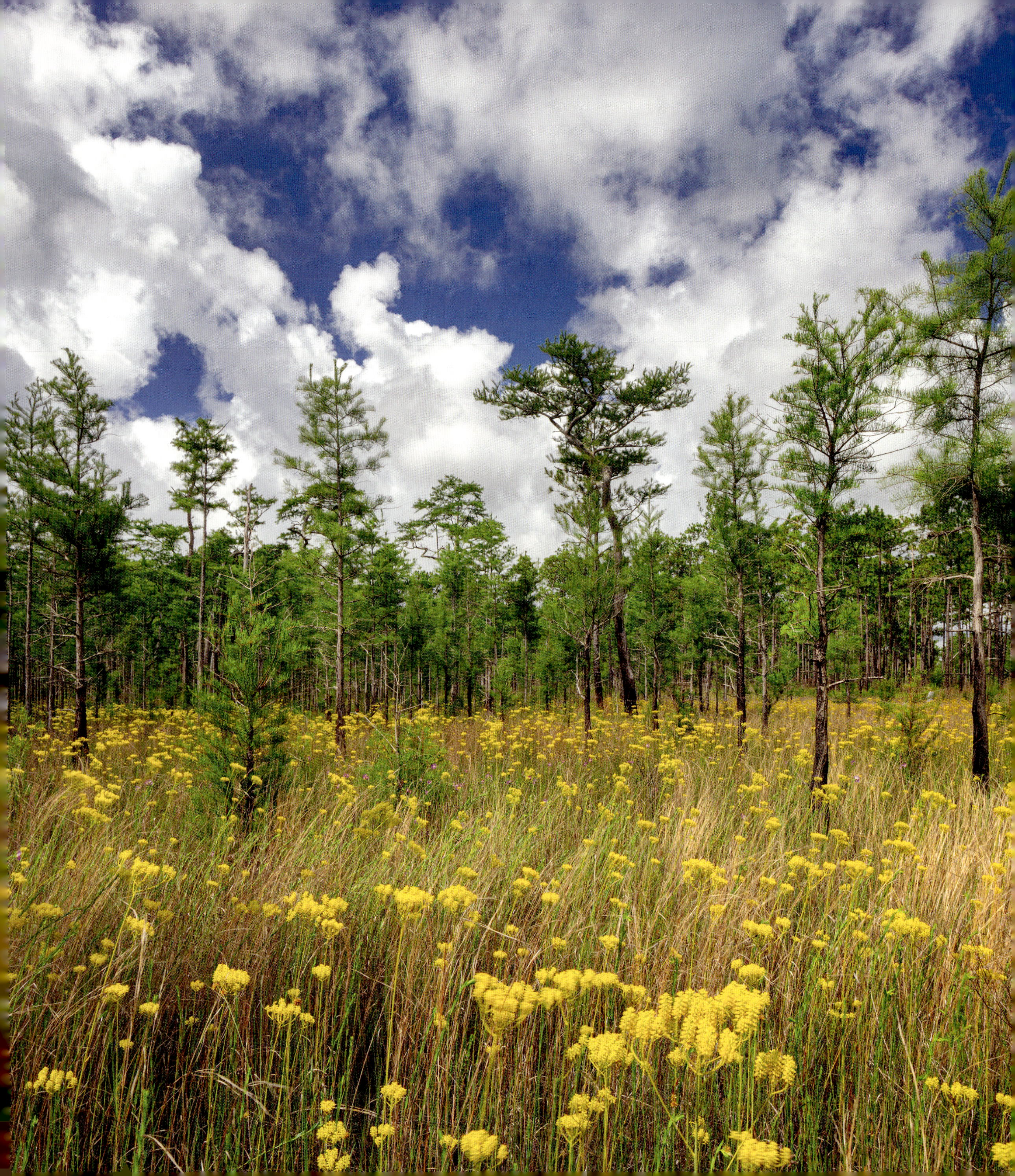

ACKNOWLEDGMENTS

We thank those who helped with our first two *Reflections of South Carolina* volumes, including Warren Slesinger, the University of South Carolina Press, readers, and the people and organizations that hosted our presentations and signings. We thank Helen Clark, Jack Clark, Theresa Clark, Mary Clark, Jay Browne, Joey Frazier, Henry Clay, Emily Clay, and Margaret Clay. We thank Mary Alice Monroe for her foreword, and we thank the libraries, museums, garden clubs, colleges, and civic groups who invite us to speak as well as the magazine editors and journals and newspapers who keep us busy between books.

AUTHOR NOTE

Six broad geographic provinces comprise South Carolina: Blue Ridge, Piedmont, Sandhills, Inner Coastal Plain, Outer Coastal Plain, and Coastal Zone. Culturally, we have the Upcountry, Midlands, and Low-country—the last, commonly identified as Beaufort, Berkeley, Charleston, Colleton, Dorchester, Georgetown, Hampton, Jasper, and Williamsburg Counties. Geographic and cultural overlap influence where certain sites fall in this work.

Tall Pinebarren Milkwort, Wambaw Bay

The blooms of tall pinebarren milkwort splash gold across Wambaw Bay's savanna.

SOUTH CAROLINA
REFLECTIONS

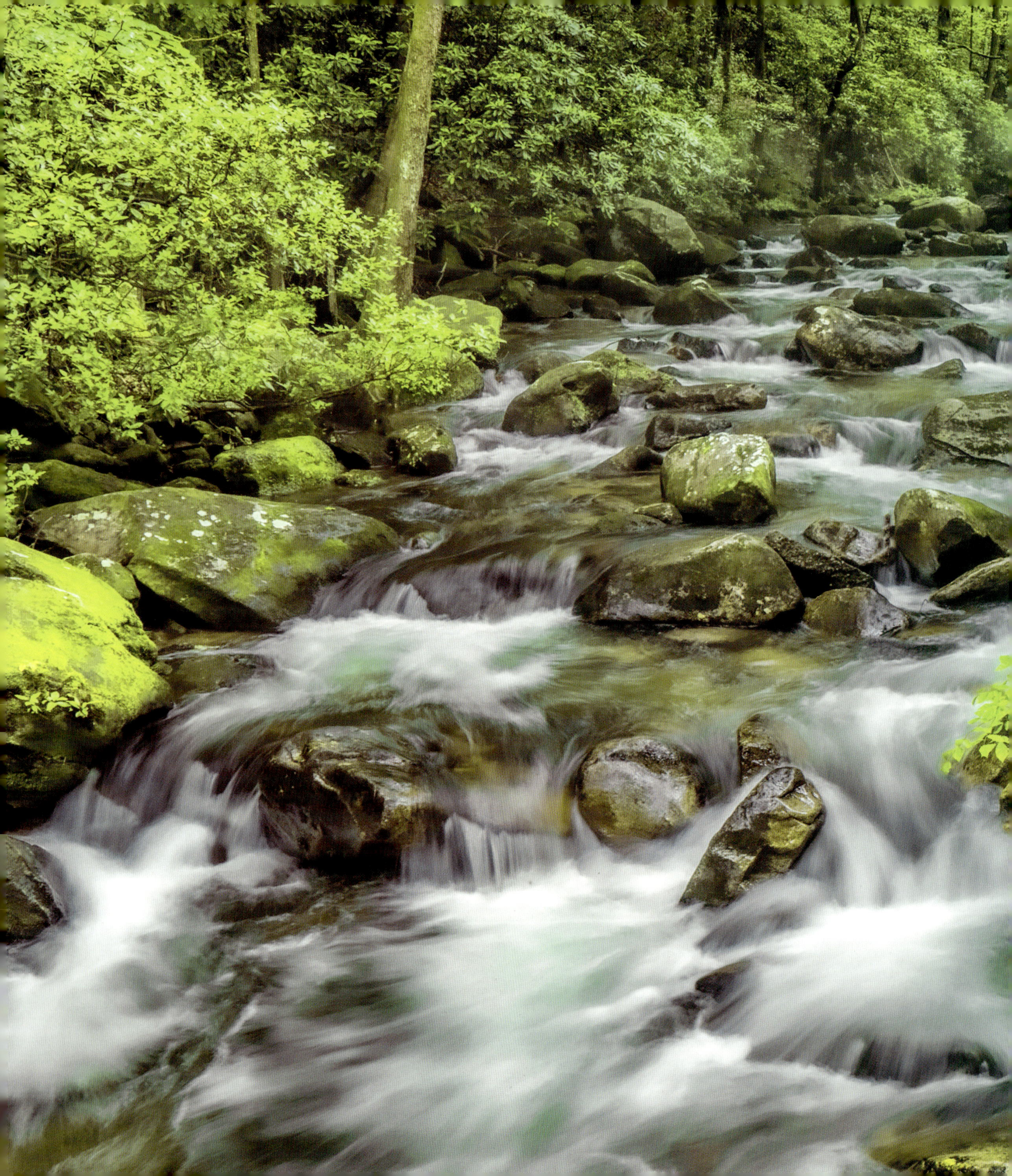

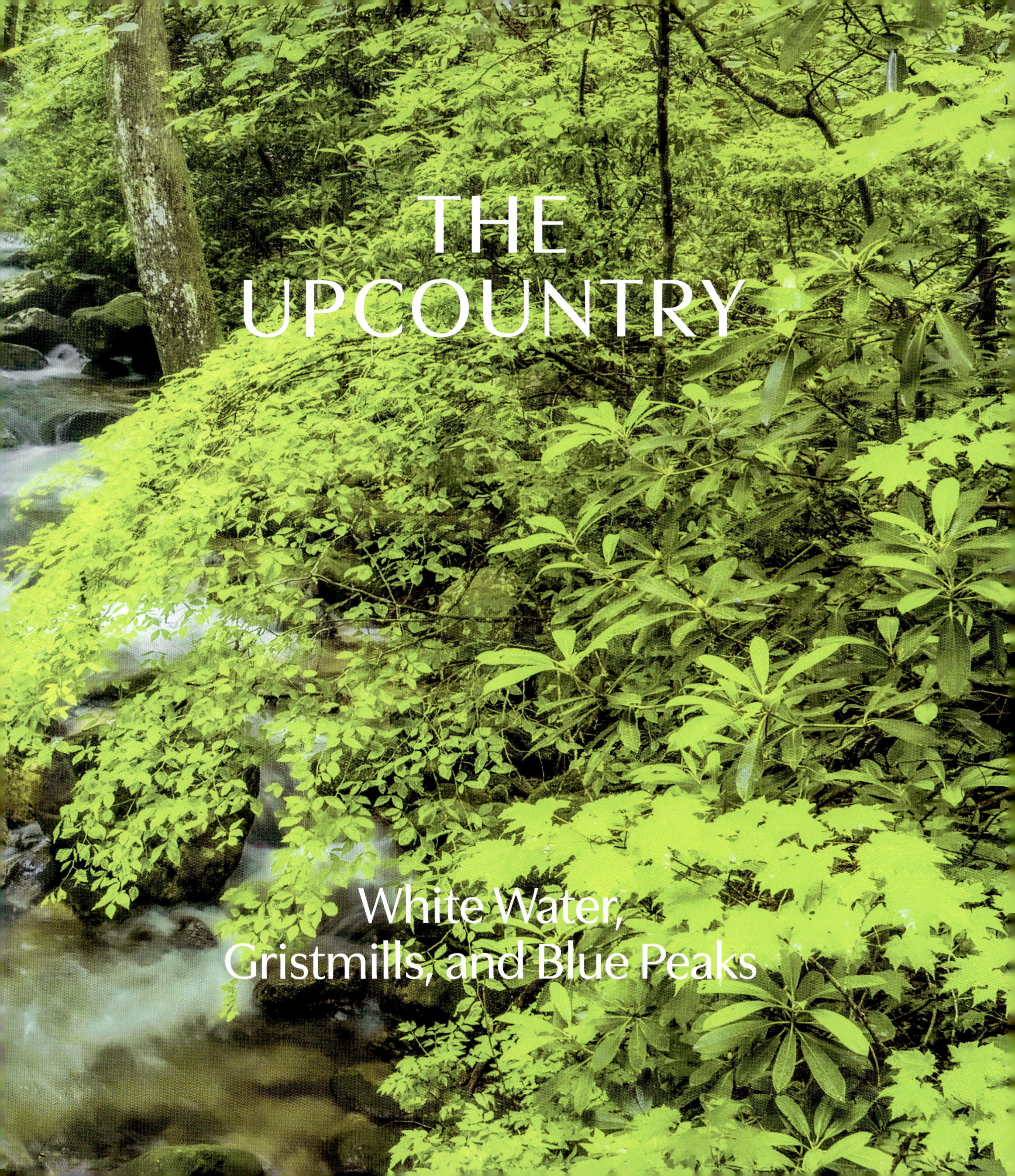
THE UPCOUNTRY
White Water,
Gristmills, and Blue Peaks

OVERLEAF

Middle Saluda River

The first river protected under South Carolina's 1978 Scenic Rivers Program, roughly five miles of the Middle Saluda and its major tributary, Coldspring Branch, benefit from a 600-foot-wide scenic corridor that runs from US 276 to one mile upstream of the Cleveland Fish hatchery. Running through Jones Gap State Park in northern Greenville County, the Middle Saluda drops about 1,000 feet in four miles. The river's clear, cold water supports self-sustaining trout populations.

Five Ridges

Like a watercolor within a frame of trees and western clouds, five smoky ridges in the northwest corner roll like waves.

After a continental collision thrust up the Blue Ridge Mountains, rain, sleet, snow, ice, heat, and wind went to work cutting drops and gorges, forging a land destined to surprise those who love hills, wild rivers, waterfalls, and scenic vistas. In these ancient hills things change quickly. Your senses switch to high alert. A rock wall cuts off the world, then just around a curve a drop-off reveals a stunning valley.

In the Upcountry's crumpled, carved land you'll see raging rivers, green summits, rocky gorges, and silver shoals. Stunning sunsets balance early morning fog banks and haze-covered mountains. Come autumn, colors paint the hills where legends like the Great Spirit dined at Table Rock. Fall colors, you divine, are one of Earth's better performances. The Sumter National Forest cloaks the hills with green-wooded slopes where tangled footpaths lead to pebble-strewn trout streams.

The Upcountry is a curious mix of manmade and natural attractions. Greenville has one of the country's top urban waterfalls, a series of cascading stair steps on the Reedy River aptly named Falls Park.

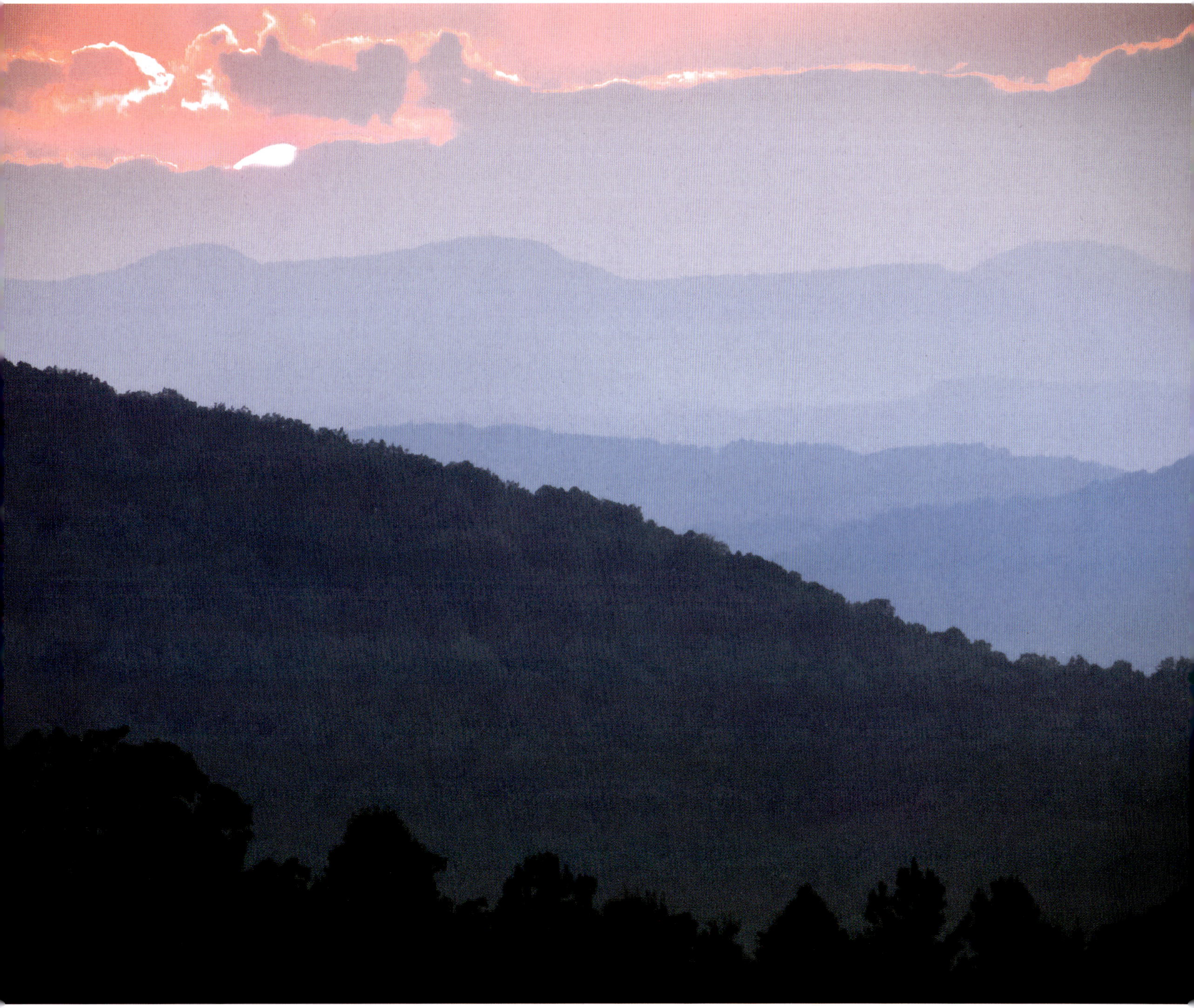

The Upcountry blesses South Carolina with rocky cliffs, gorges, rare flowers, and silver shoals, and add to that list orchards; cold, clear lakes; whitewater rivers; and gristmills. Weave along mountain flanks through thick ranks of rhododendron, mountain laurel, and descend into and back up ravines. Challenging hikes to waterfalls reward exertion.

Textile magnate Roger Milliken's love for trees led him to create an arboretum in Spartanburg, his place of rest. Witness the Middle Saluda River in Jones Gap State Park. In the Dark Corner's heart, you'll find an an old bridge that looks like a rock fortress. Discover an old Huguenot cemetery, an old clock tower, a petite police station, potters, and greenways and gardens. Given nature and man's creations up here there's much to do and see. One thing's certain. This uplifted land uplifts the spirits of all. You just feel more alive in the Upcountry.

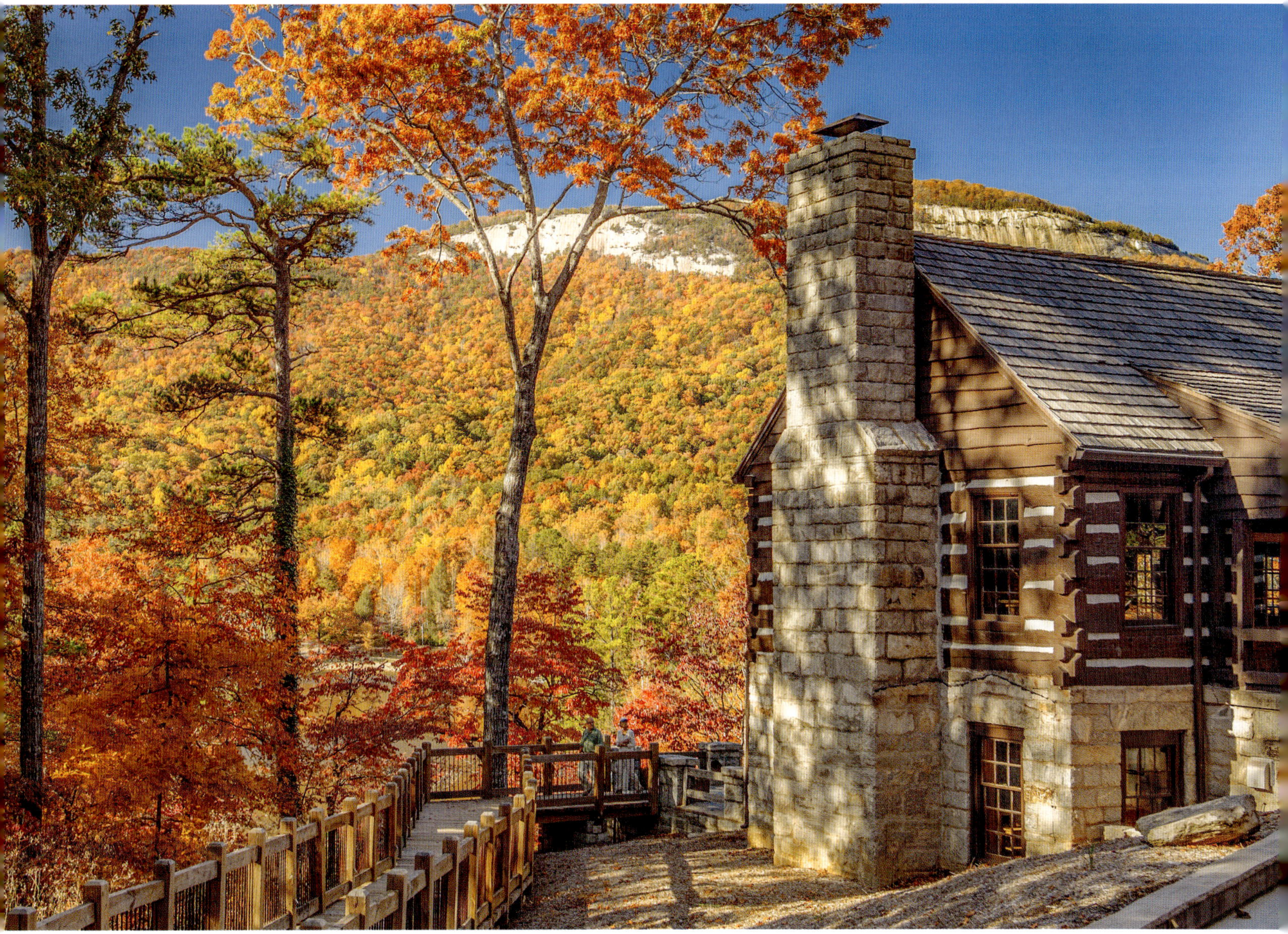

Table Rock Lodge

The Civilian Conservation Corps (CCC), a voluntary government work-relief program, built the lodge at Table Rock. From 1933 to 1942 the CCC gave work to unemployed, unmarried men ages 18 to 25. The restored Gaines Lodge provides a sweeping view of Table Rock Mountain, beautiful in autumn and throughout the seasons.

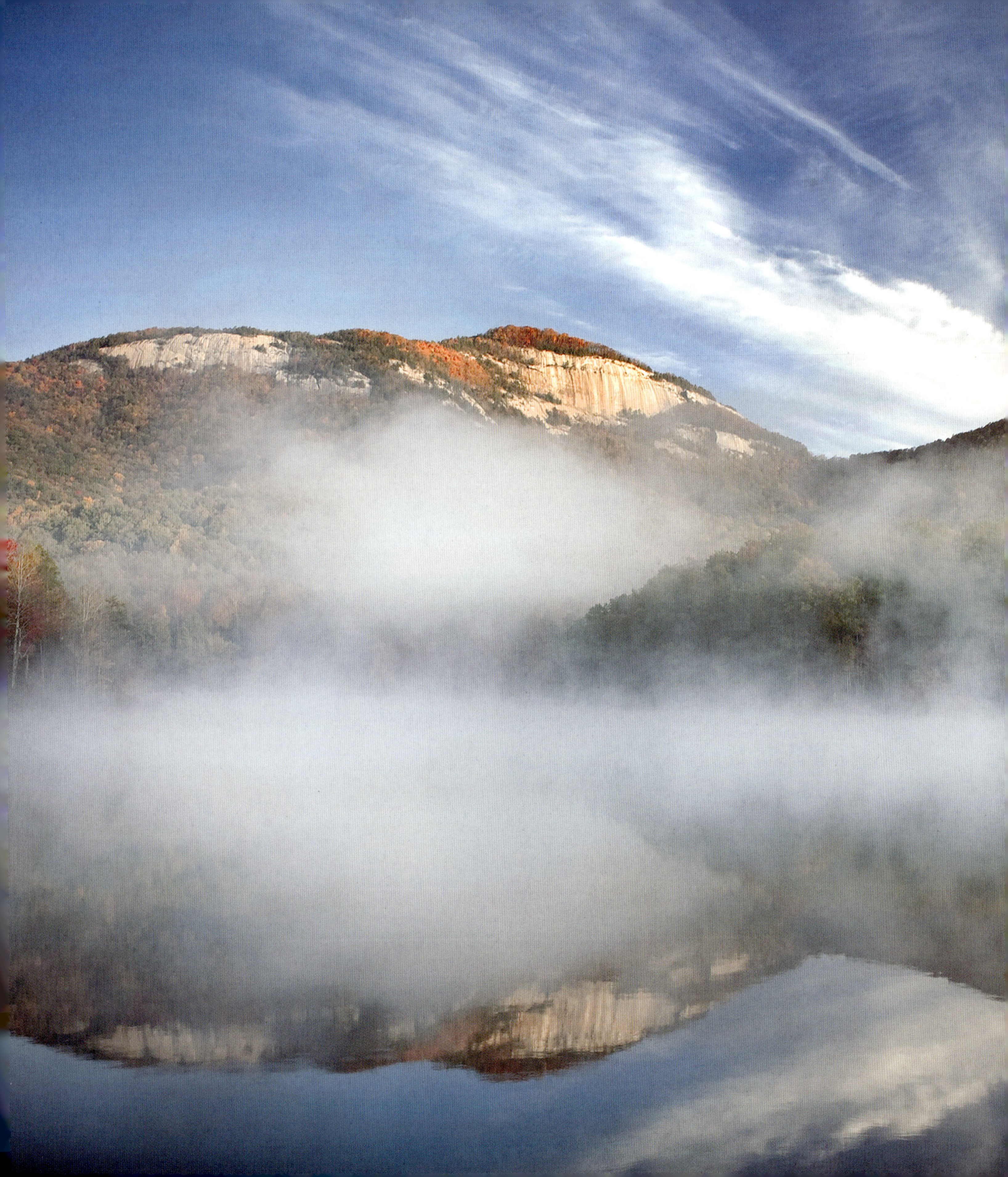

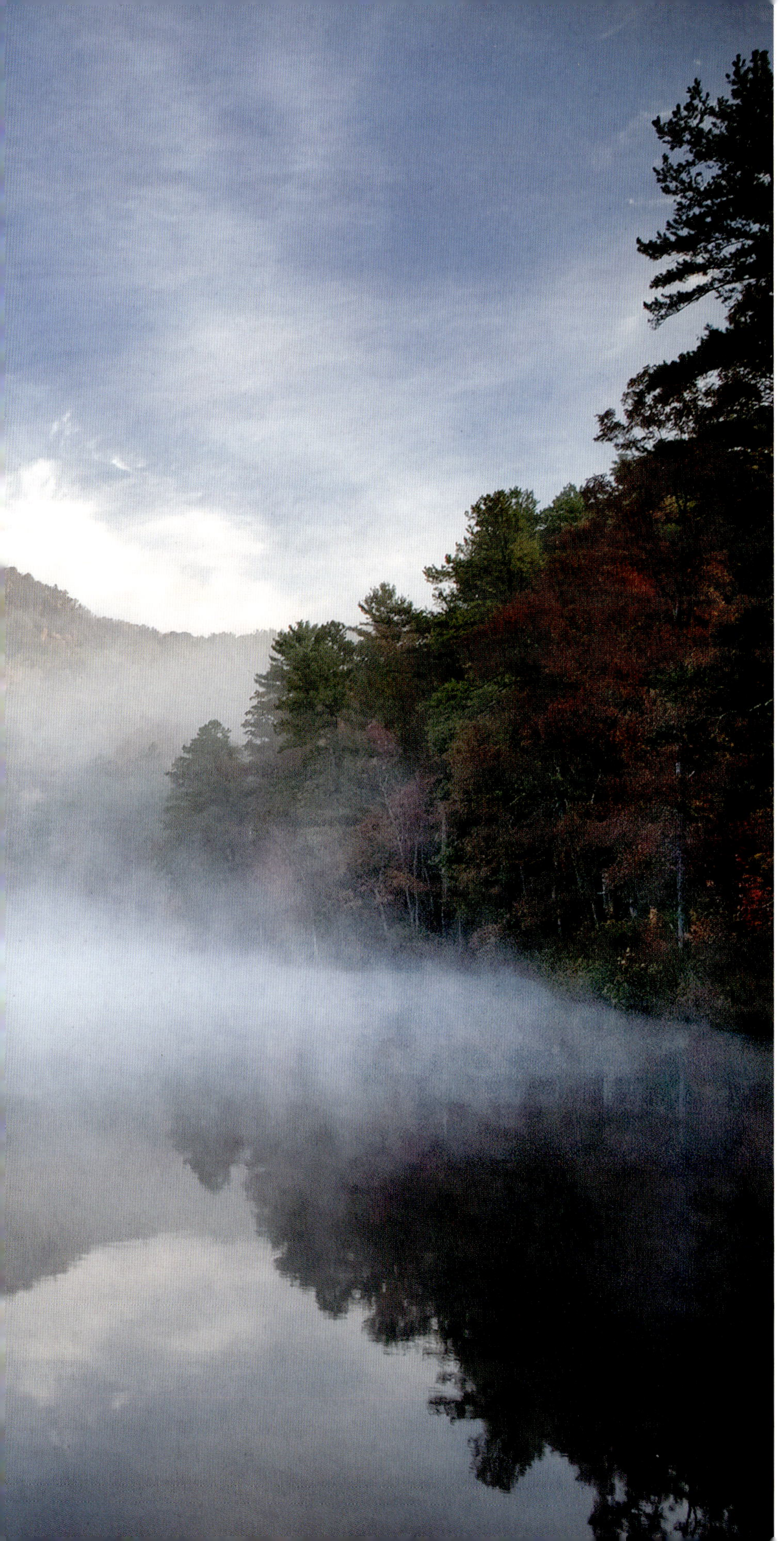

Autumn Mists

The days shorten, the air cools, and mists mute the hues of autumn. Bursts of color appear in October and spread across the region into November. The onset of autumn colors signifies a seasonal rite of passage.

Scenic Pickens County

Autumn's palette ranges from gold and red to green, rust, and orange. This photo, taken from the deck of a home, is said to be one of the Upcountry's better views.

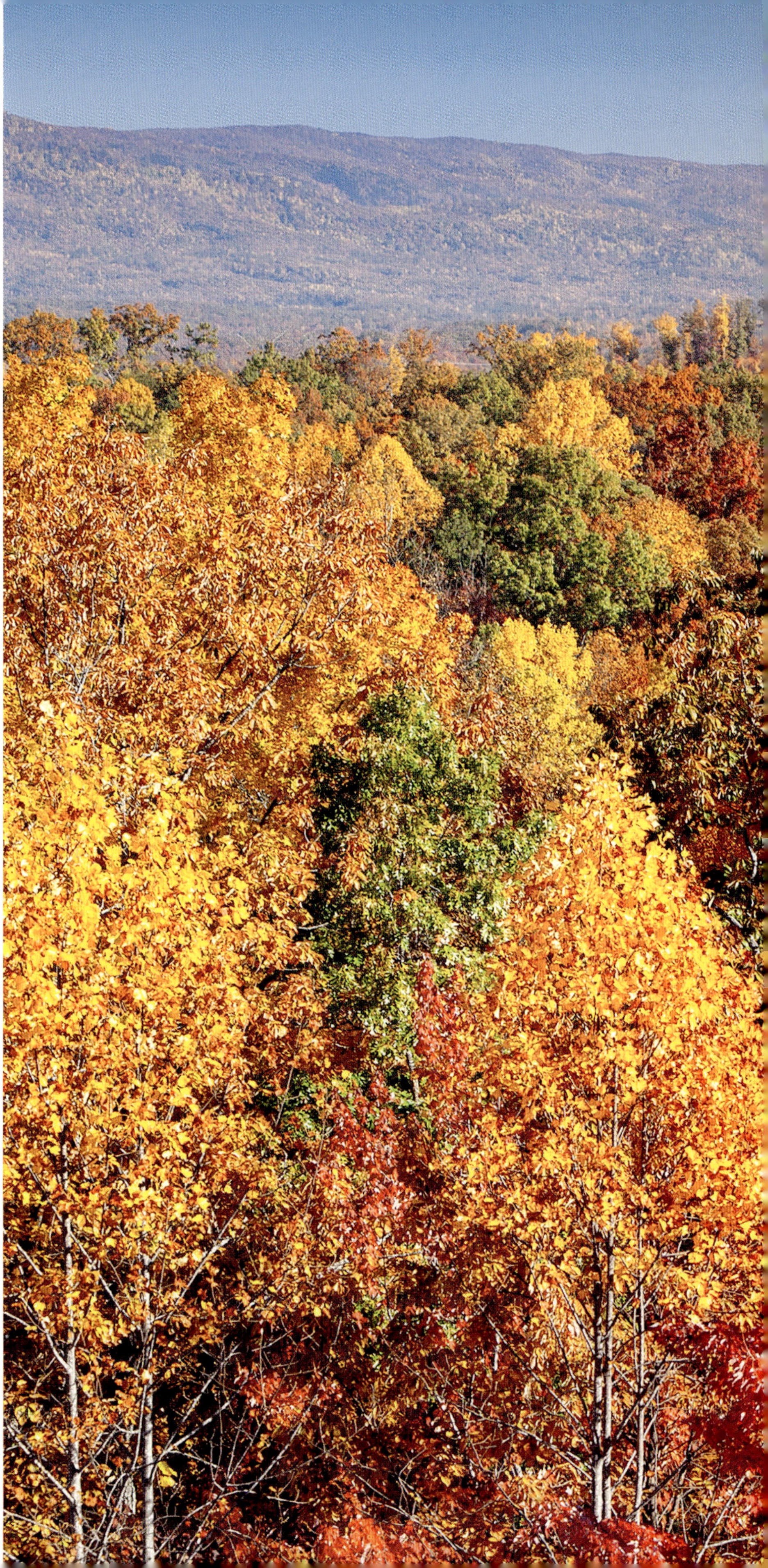

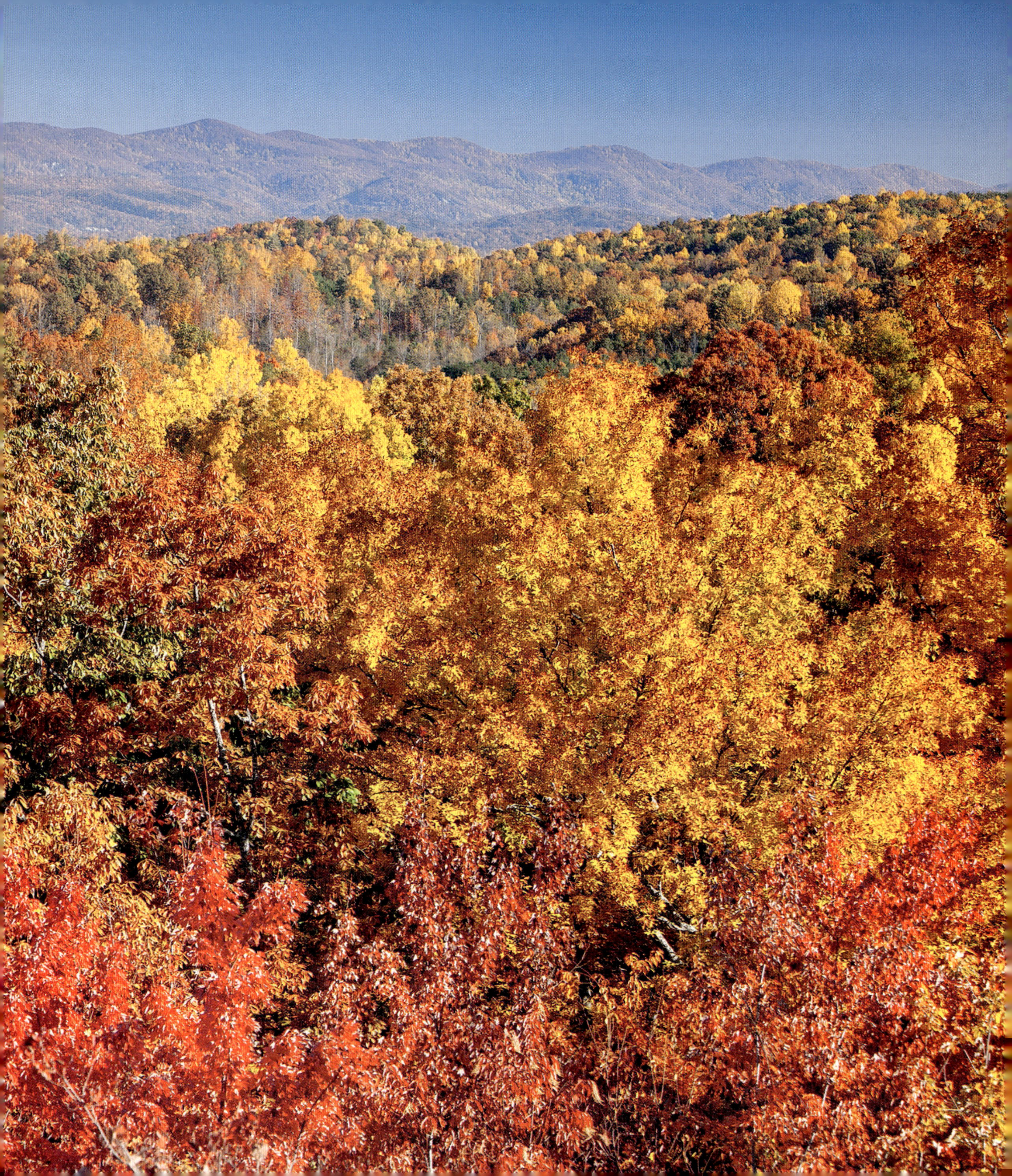

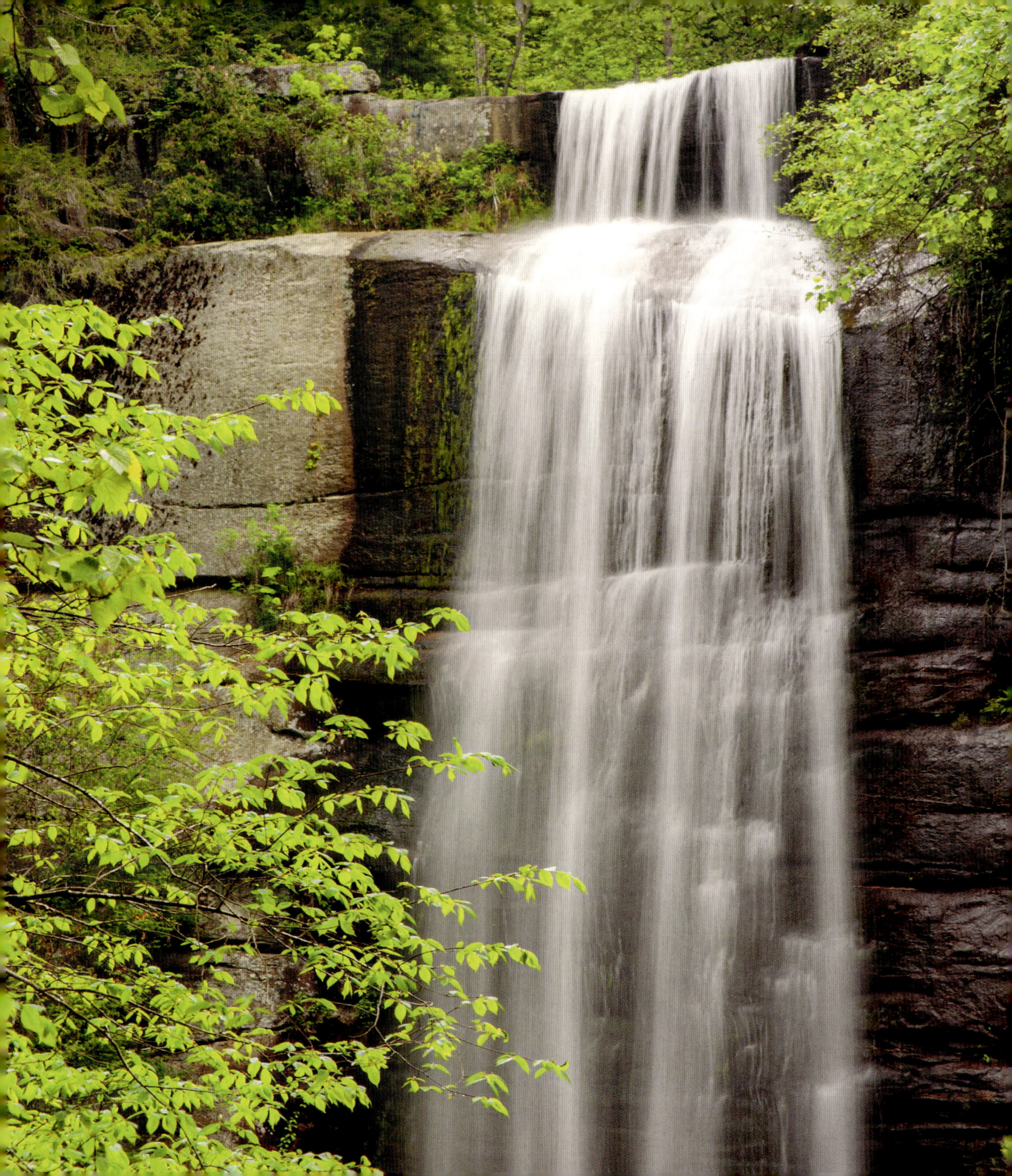

Twin Falls

You'll find Twin Falls in the Eastatoe Valley. Twin Falls also goes by Eastatoe Falls, Reedy Cove Falls, and Rock Falls. Whatever you call it, take the fifteen-minute walk to the falls, owned by a private foundation. Thanks to a partnership with The Nature Conservancy of South Carolina the twenty-five-acre nature preserve is open to the public year-round.

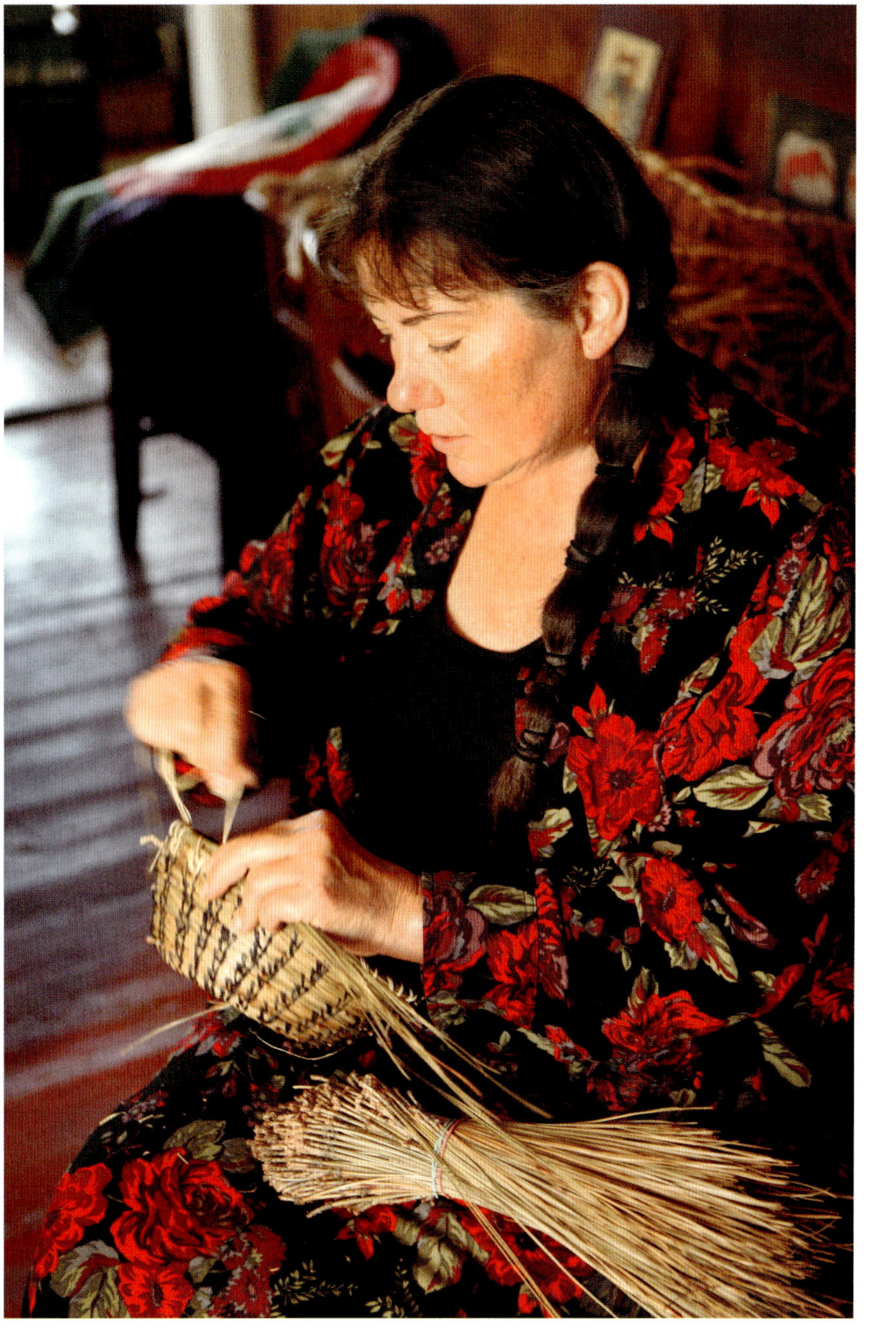

New Life for Kudzu

Cherokee Nancy Basket of Long Creek weaves baskets from kudzu, which remains plentiful, unlike sweetgrass. Kudzu's long runners prove excellent for basket making, and its beauty rivals Lowcountry sweetgrass baskets. Nancy weaves pine needles into her artistry.

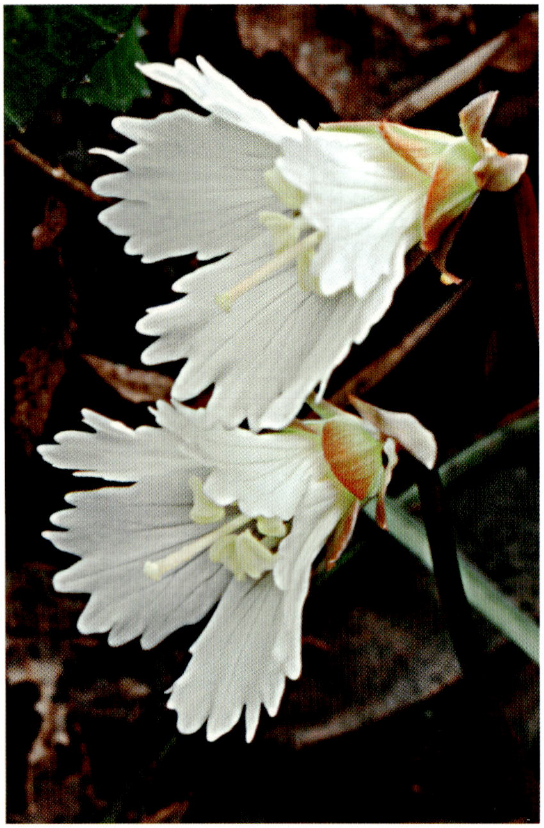

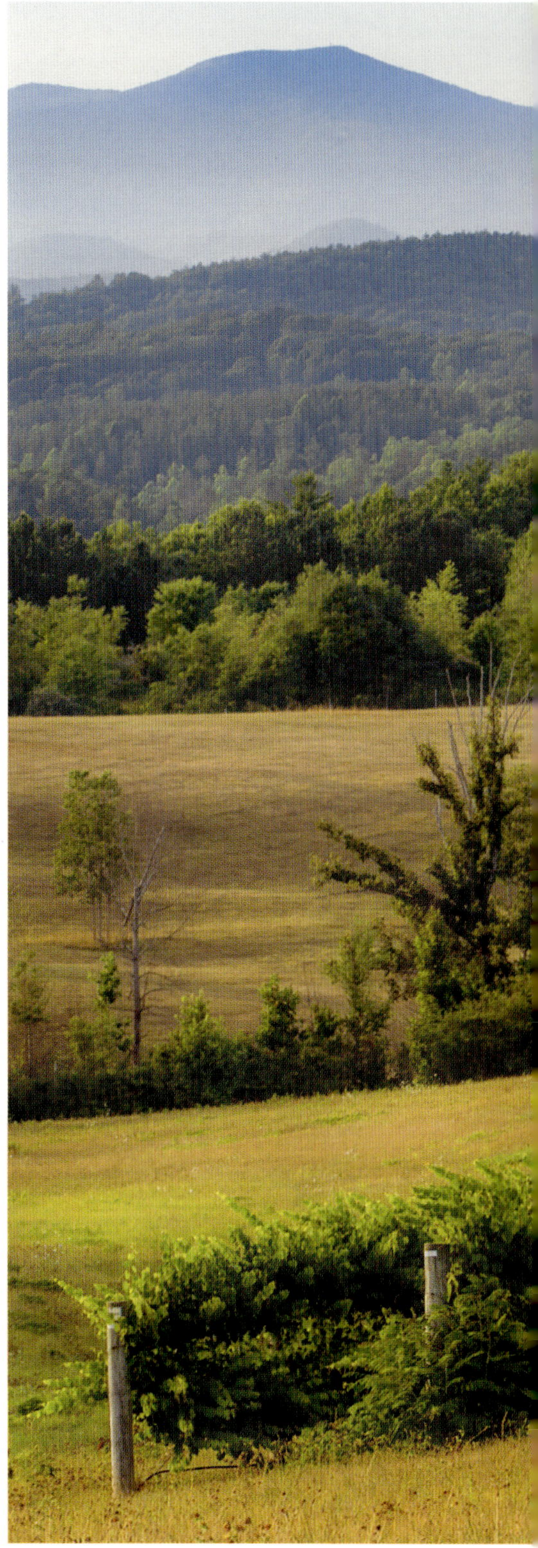

Appalachia's Rare Flower

Among South Carolina's more unique and earliest wildflowers, the Oconee Bell (*Shortia galacifolia*) blooms from mid-March to early April. Botanists describe these wildflowers as a very rare evergreen herbaceous shrub. Native habitat includes stream banks and the slopes of gorges.

Chattooga Belle Farm

At 1,700 feet above sea level, Chattooga Belle Farm, in its own words, "is a 198-acre working farm, distillery, and event barn located in beautiful Long Creek, South Carolina." The venue offers a 270-degree view of hills, vineyards, orchards, and berry patches against a backdrop of the Blue Ridge Mountains. In the background sits Georgia to the left and North Carolina to the right.

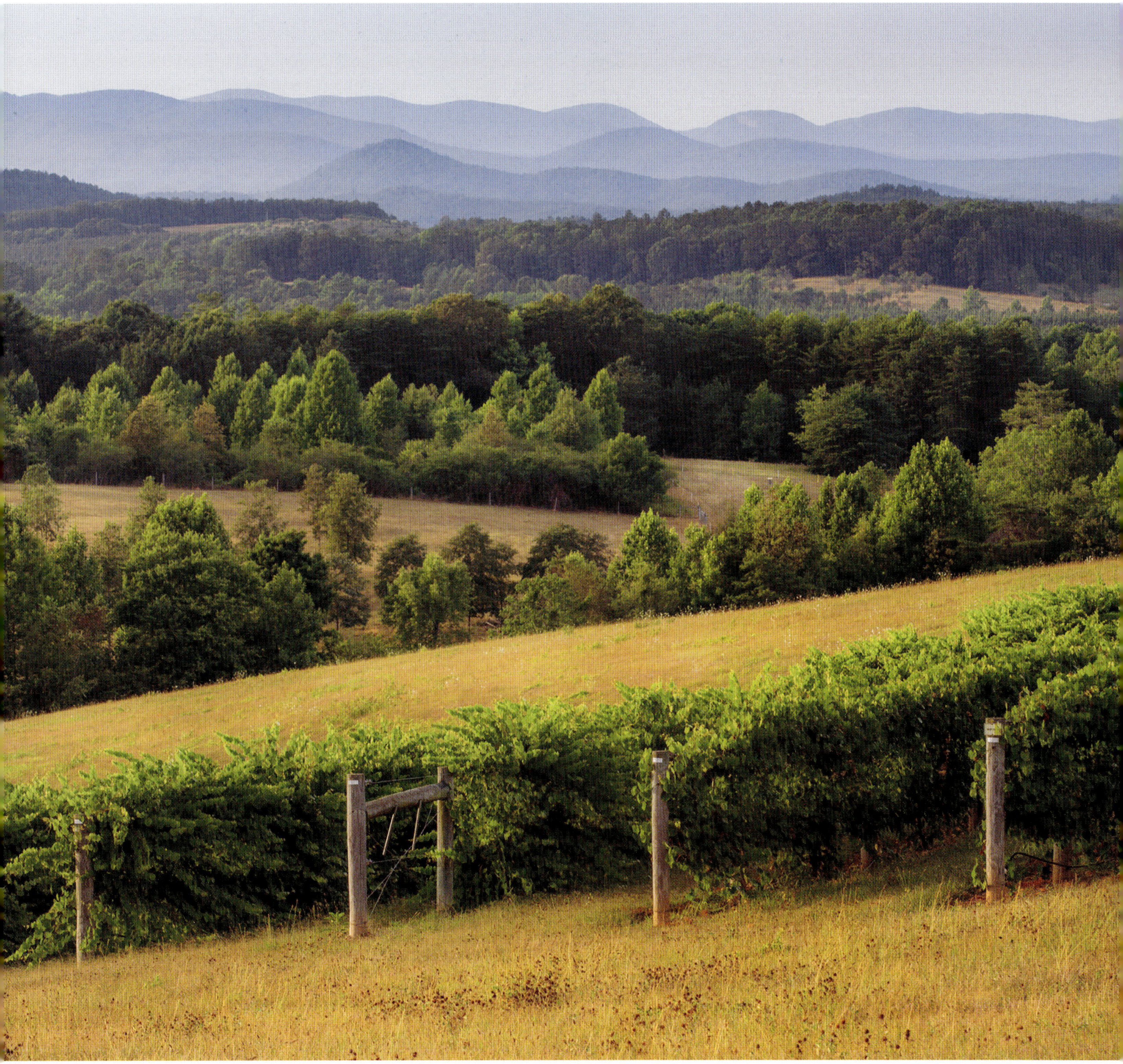

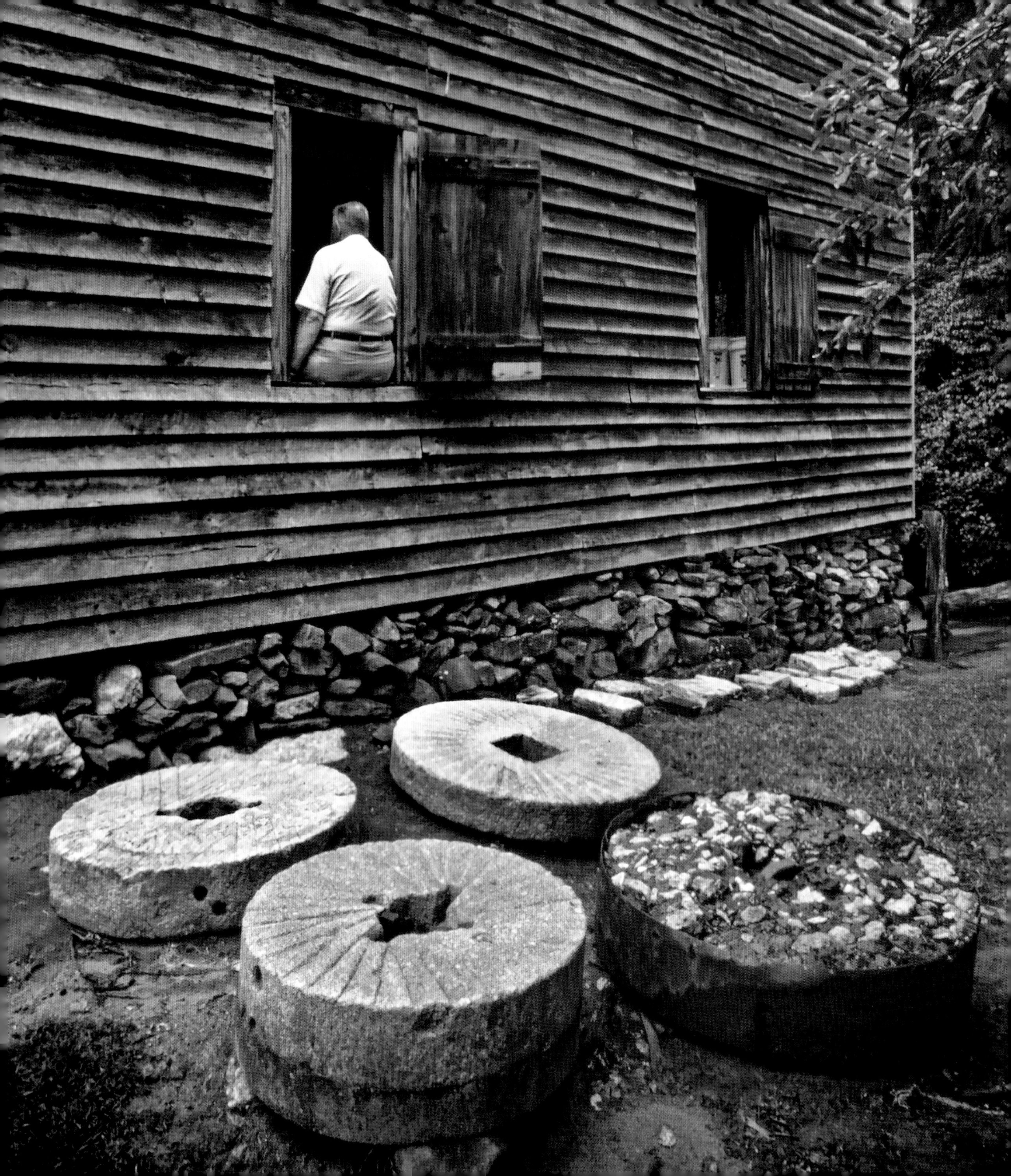

Hagood Mill Stones

Millstones work in pairs with a revolving upper millstone, the "runner," and a stationary bottom stone, the "bed." Stones weigh more than a ton, and as they work against each other, the grooves create a scissor-like action that grinds grain. Up until around 1890 millstones produced most flour. Many believe stone-ground grain tastes superior to grain ground by modern roller-milling methods.

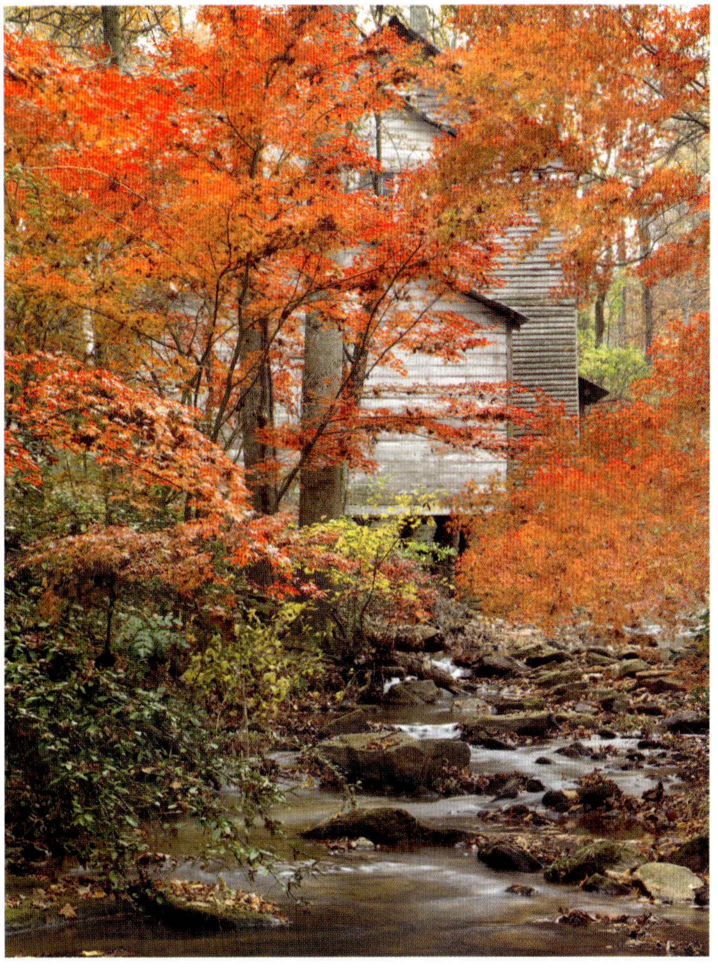

Power from Shoals Creek and Clear Creek

This mill, located near Greer, has carried several names, Bruce's Mill, Heller's Mill, and Taylor's Mill. Folks now call it Gilreath's Mill. The water wheel, apart from the mill, powered the grinding of cornmeal and flour. If you know where to go, you can still find mills that served the table and provided people a gathering place.

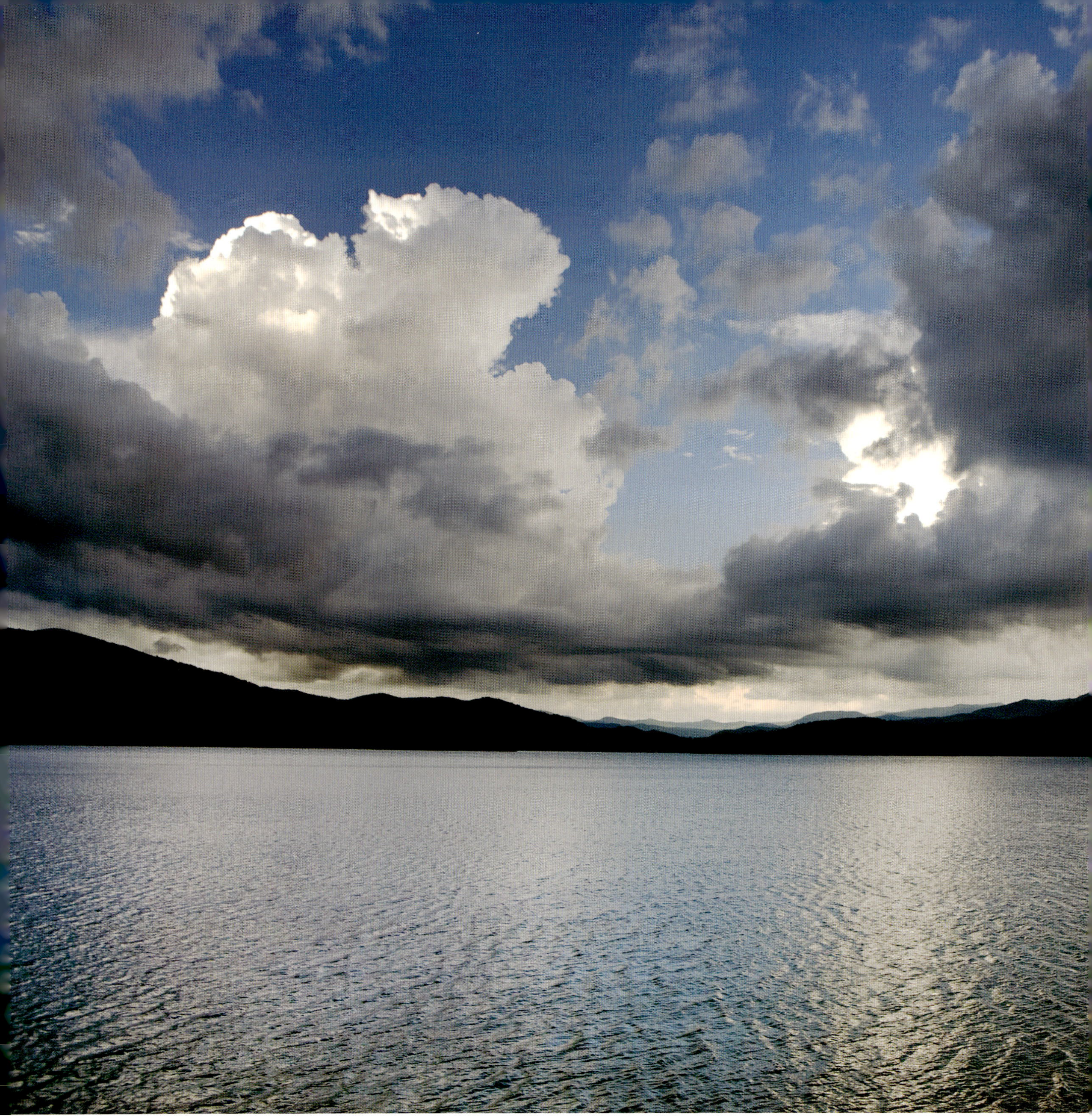

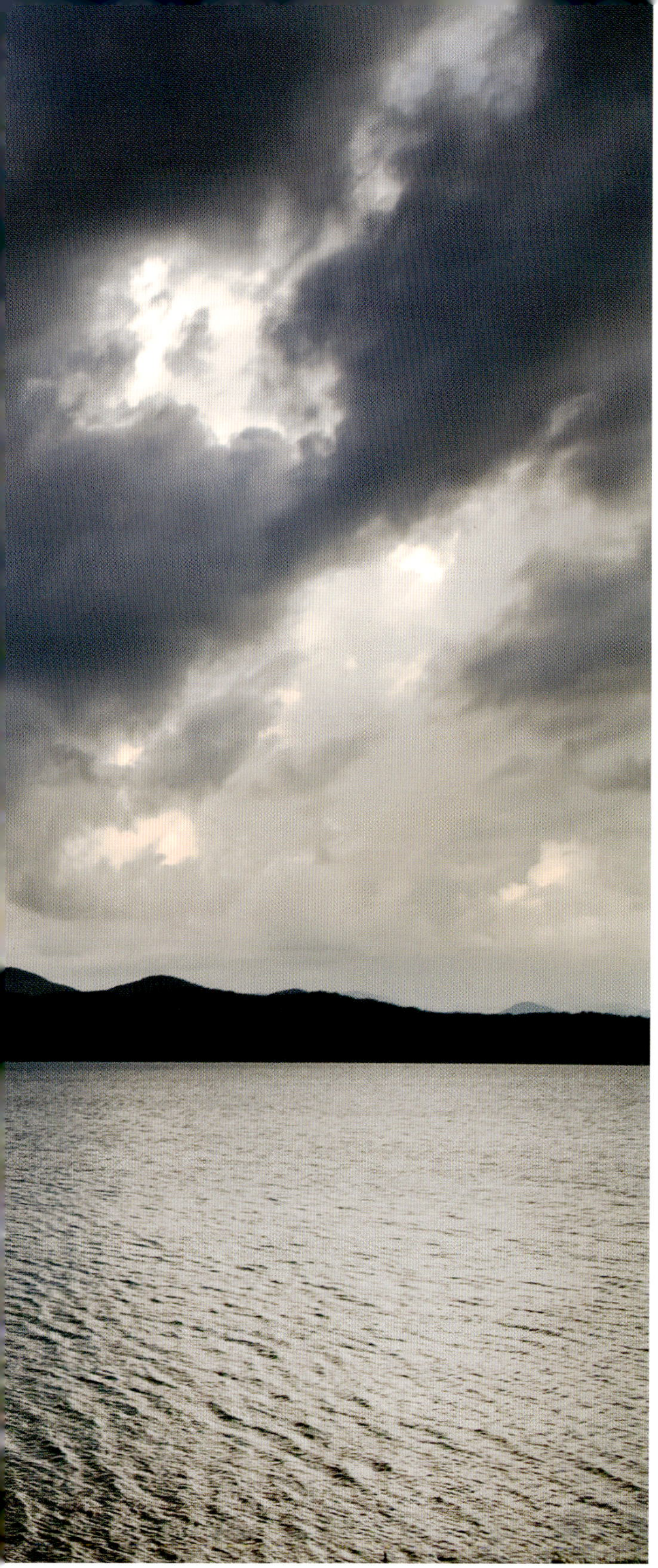

Lake Jocassee

Lake Jocassee, a 300-foot-deep reservoir, receives its clean, clear, and cold waters (just how trout like it) from Appalachian mountain rivers. Smallmouth bass (*Micropterus dolomieu*) live here too, a species other South Carolina lakes don't support. "Jocassee" in Cherokee means "Place of the lost one."

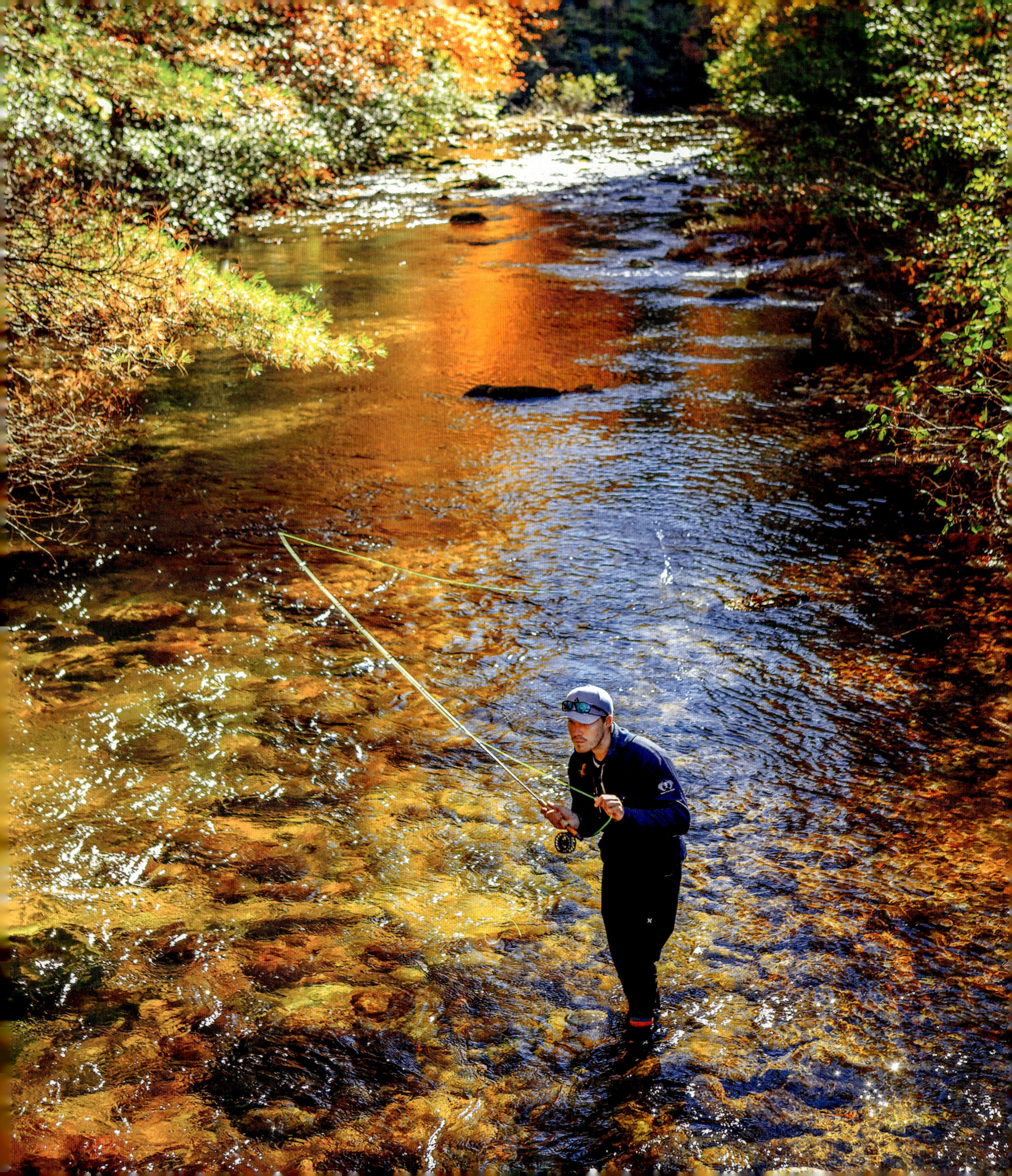

Whitewater River Trout Fisherman

One of the keys to catching trout is getting close to your quarry. While South Carolina doesn't readily bring trout to mind, as many as 50,000 trout anglers take to the Northwest Corner's cold waters each year.

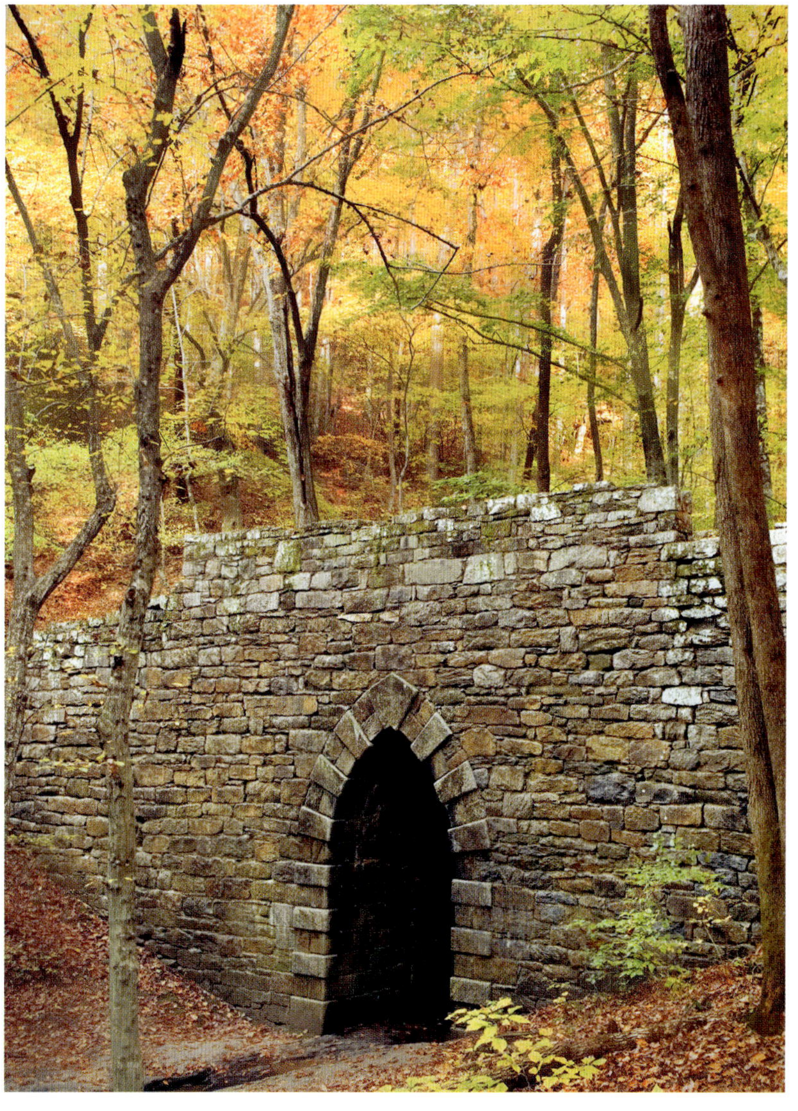

Poinsett Bridge, 1820

In the Dark Corner you'll see South Carolina's oldest intact bridge, named for Joel R. Poinsett. Little Gap Creek flows through its Gothic arch. The bridge is part of an original road, linking Greenville with Asheville, North Carolina. The Dark Corner was once a place of mystery and violence where even preachers made moonshine. In June of 2024, the South Carolina Department of Natural Resources Heritage Trust Program added 283 acres to Greenville County's Poinsett Bridge Heritage Preserve.

Spring at Table Rock

Newly minted leaves and dogwood bracts provide a soft counterpoint to Table Rock's hard gray slab.

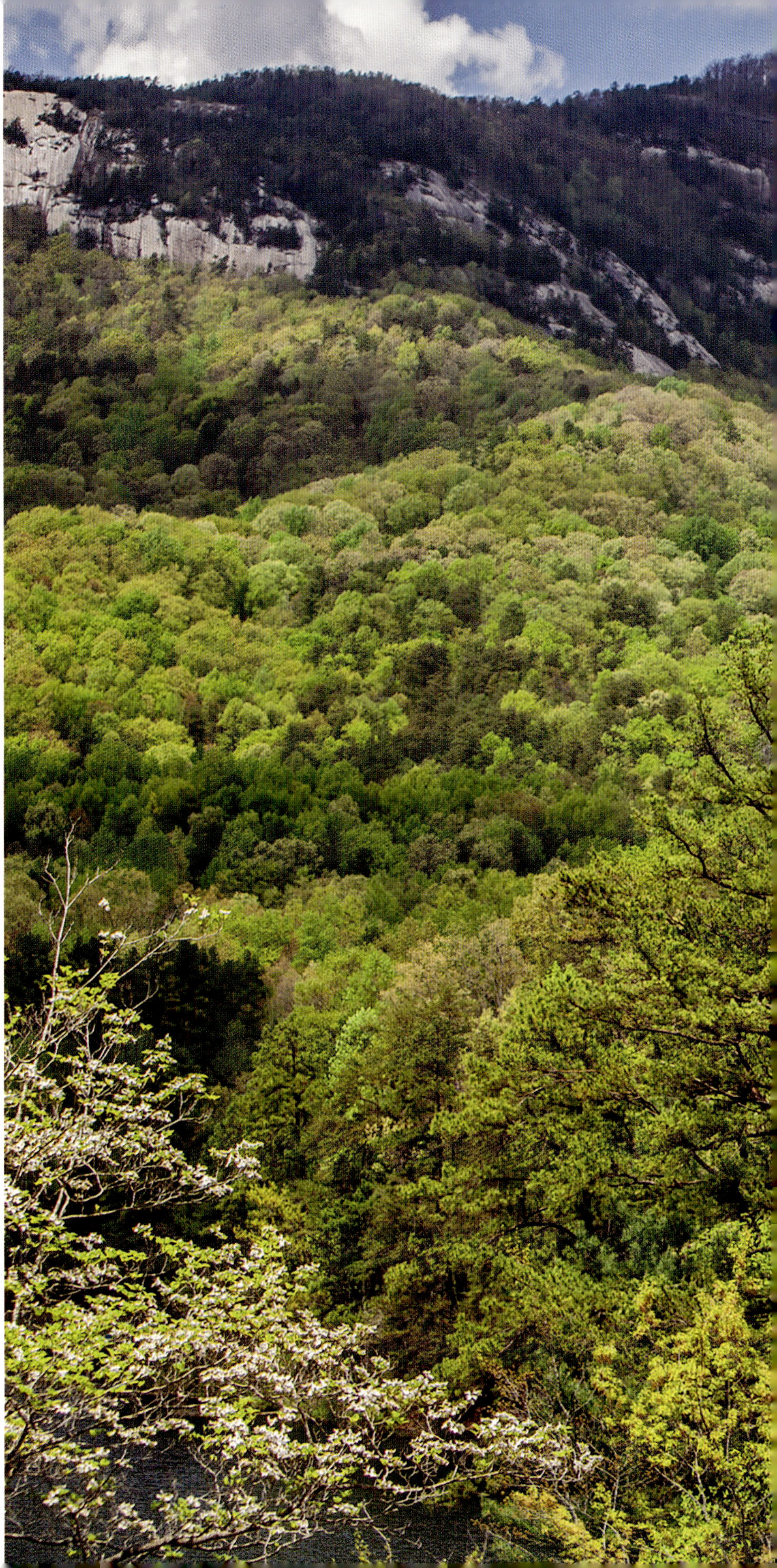

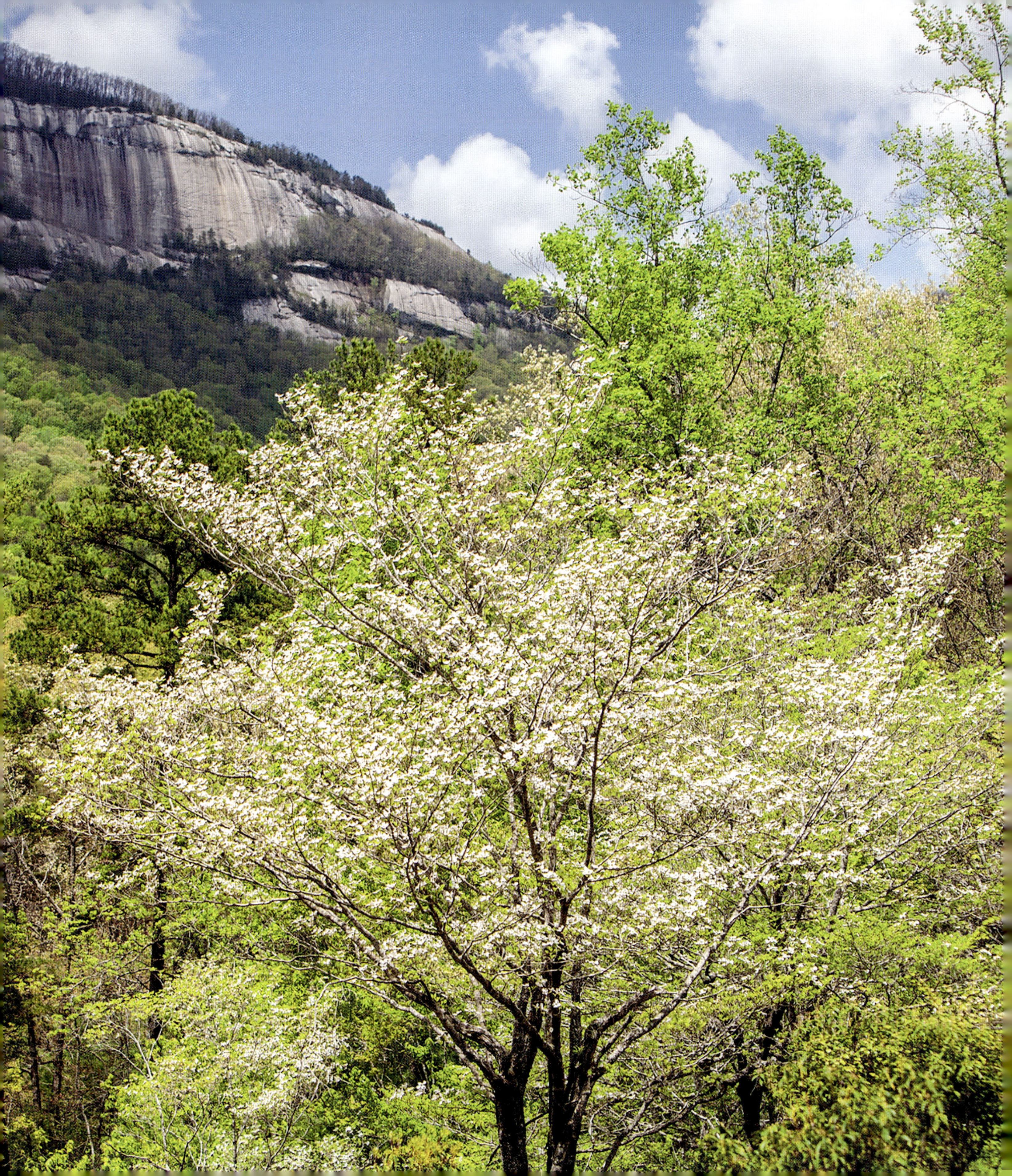

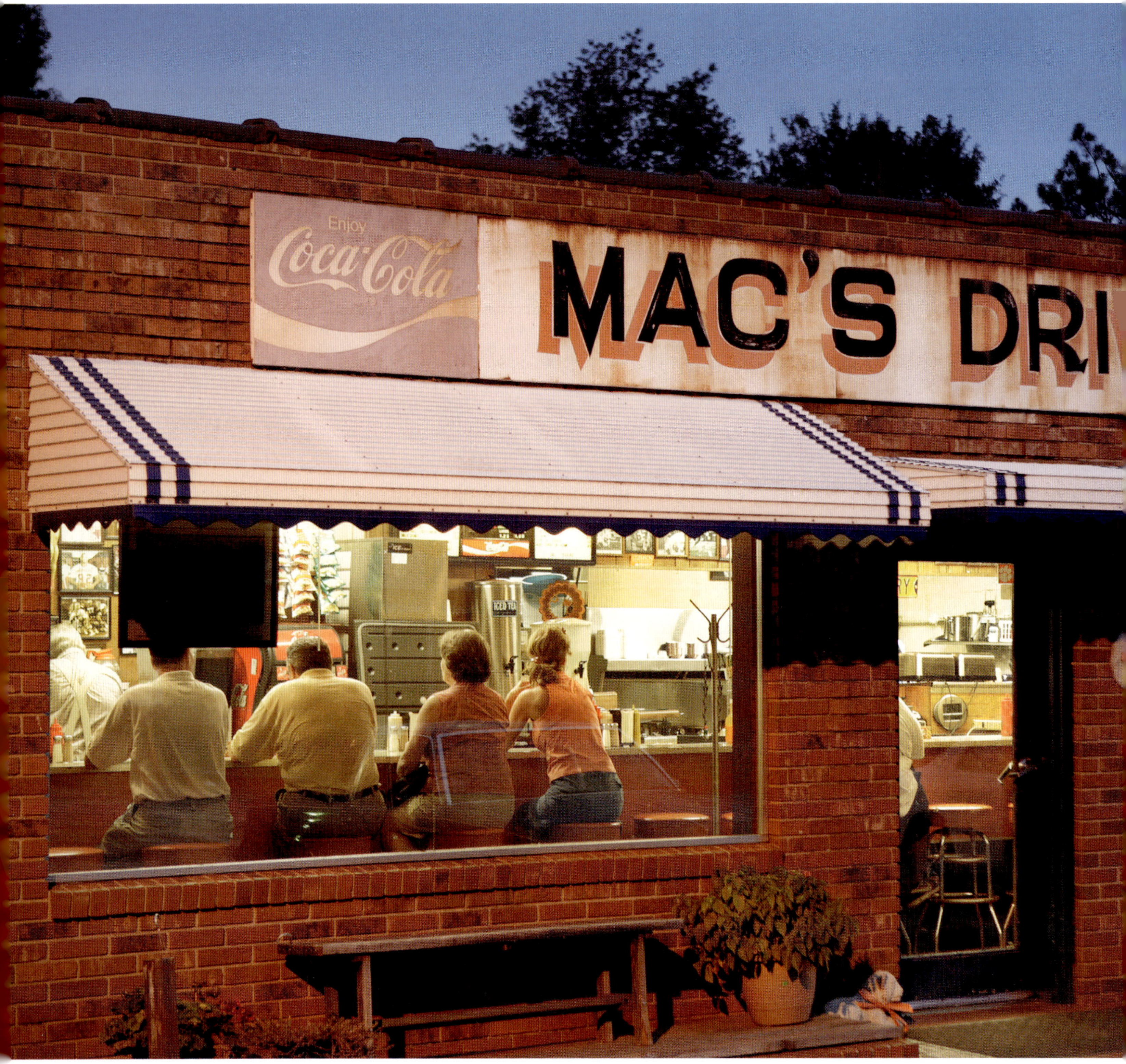
Enjoy
Coca-Cola
MAC'S DRI
ICED TEA

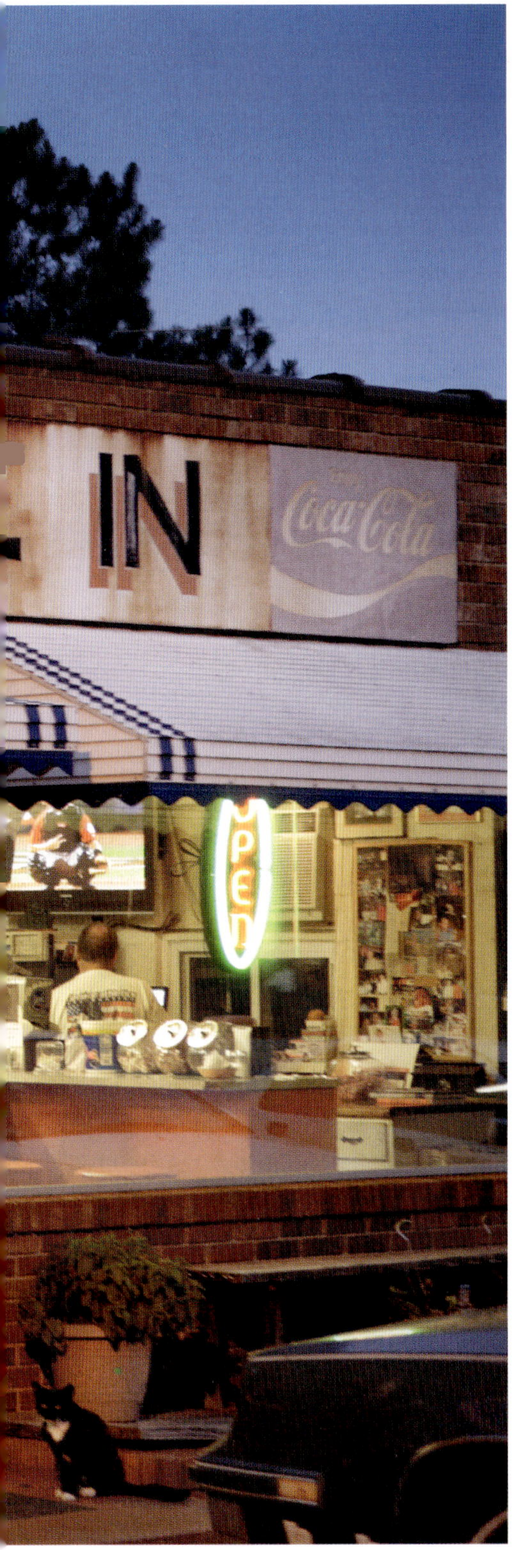

Sit a Spell

The late Harold "Mac" McKeown's iconic eatery now wears a coat of ivy and a colorful front. It even has a new sign. More than food has been served here: the offerings included charitable acts. McKeown died December 30, 2009, the very day the City of Clemson and Clemson University recognized him for his longstanding contributions to the city and university.

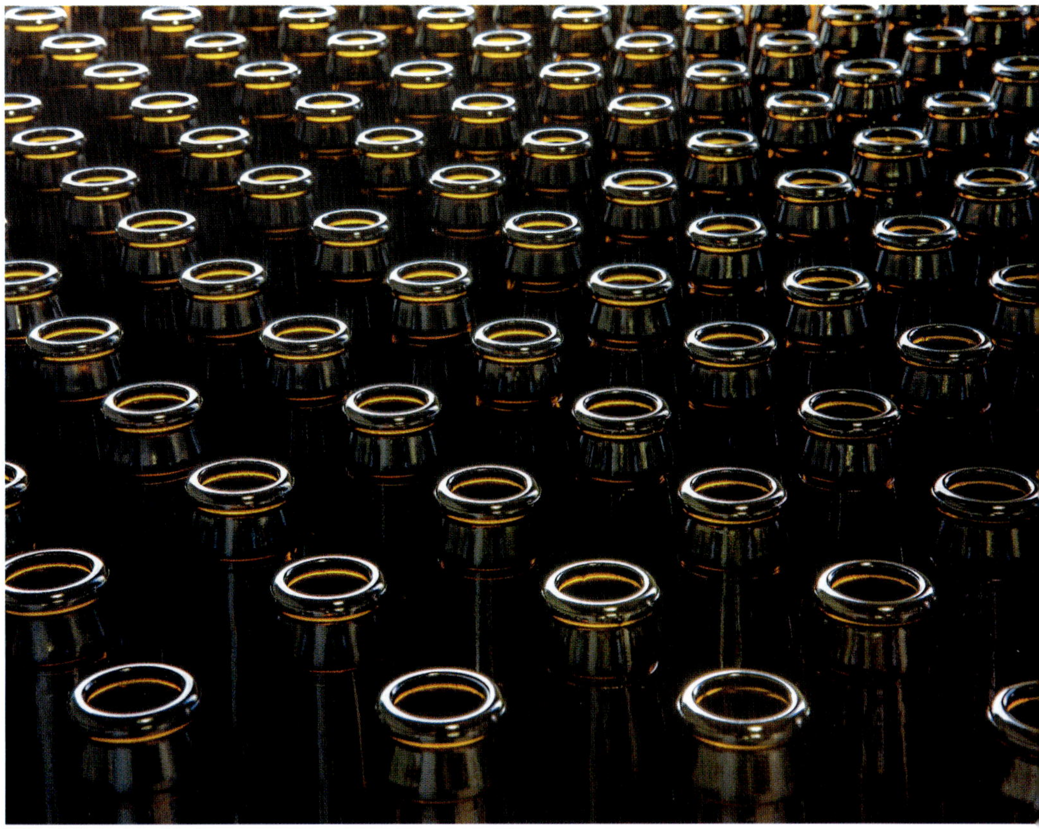

Ready for Filling

"Handcrafted, every drop, every time." That's how Rockers Brewing Co. describes its brewery magic. Rockers Brewery crafts rotating delights, such as Son of a Peach, Sparkle City IPA, Hoppy Hula, Iceberg, and Palmetto Trail Ale, among others. For an entertaining, delicious time head to Spartanburg and try some of their "crafted cookin' food" delights.

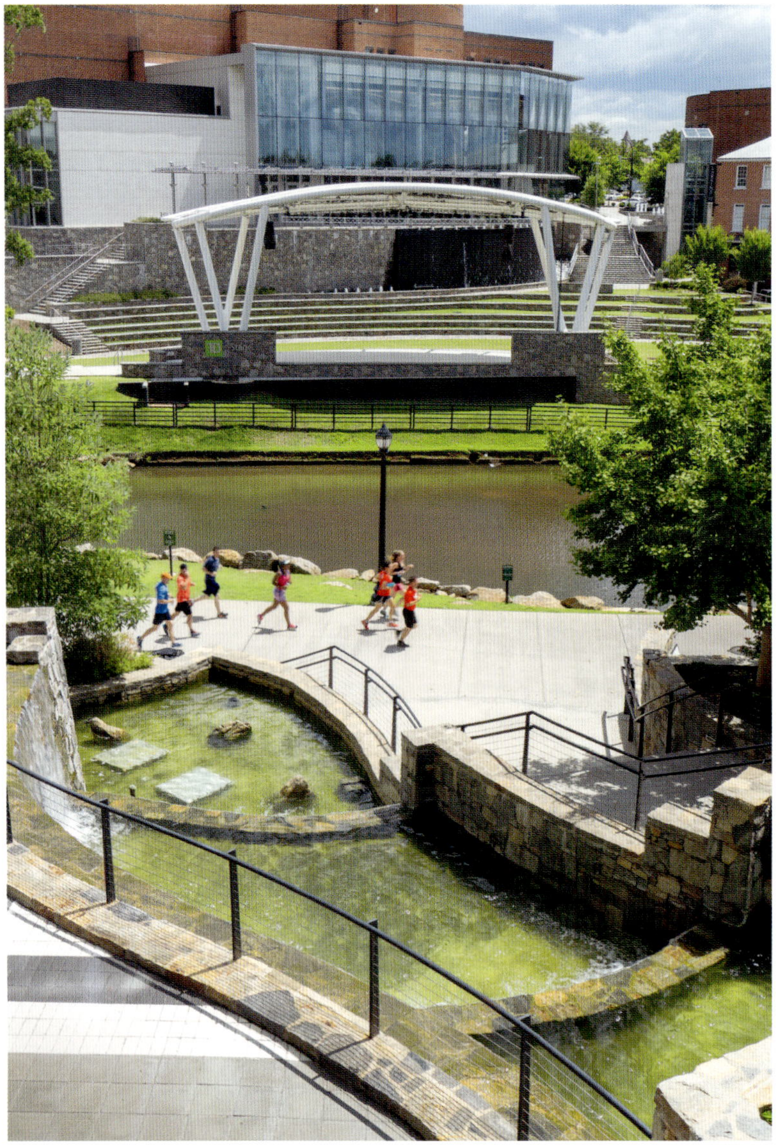

Downtown Greenville

Water drives Greenville's brand, and the Reedy River, rising in the foothills of the Blue Ridge, flows through Greenville to create an inviting environment for joggers, tourists, shoppers, and businesses. Downtown's mixed-use philosophy has led to art along the Reedy River; Liberty Bridge, an innovative 345-foot-long pedestrian bridge; and contemporary retail and residential spaces.

Twilight at Falls Park

As the day winds down, people congregate in Greenville's Falls Park. One by one and then in pairs and groups, they come. Workers, residents, and visitors gather to admire urban whitewater.

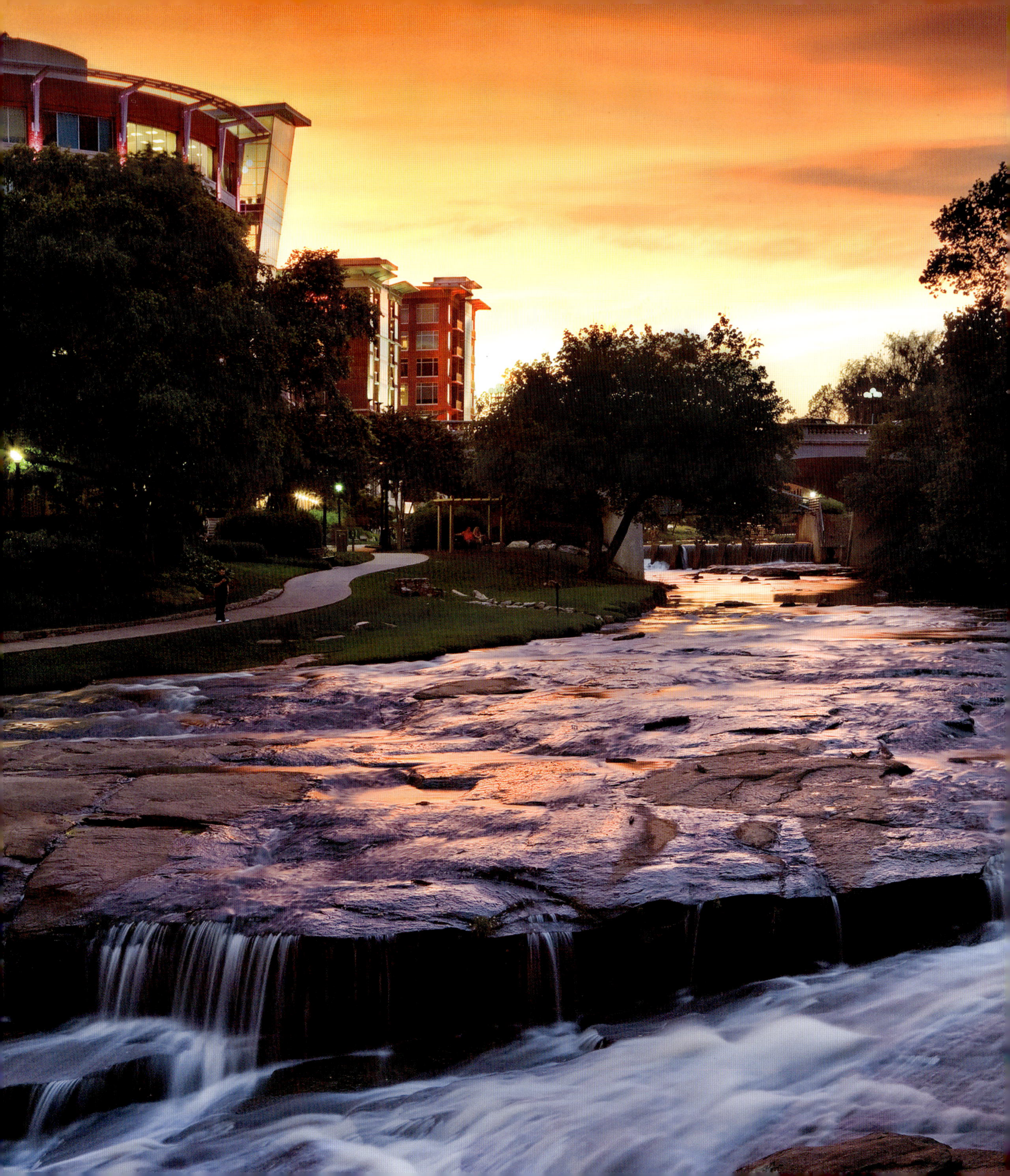

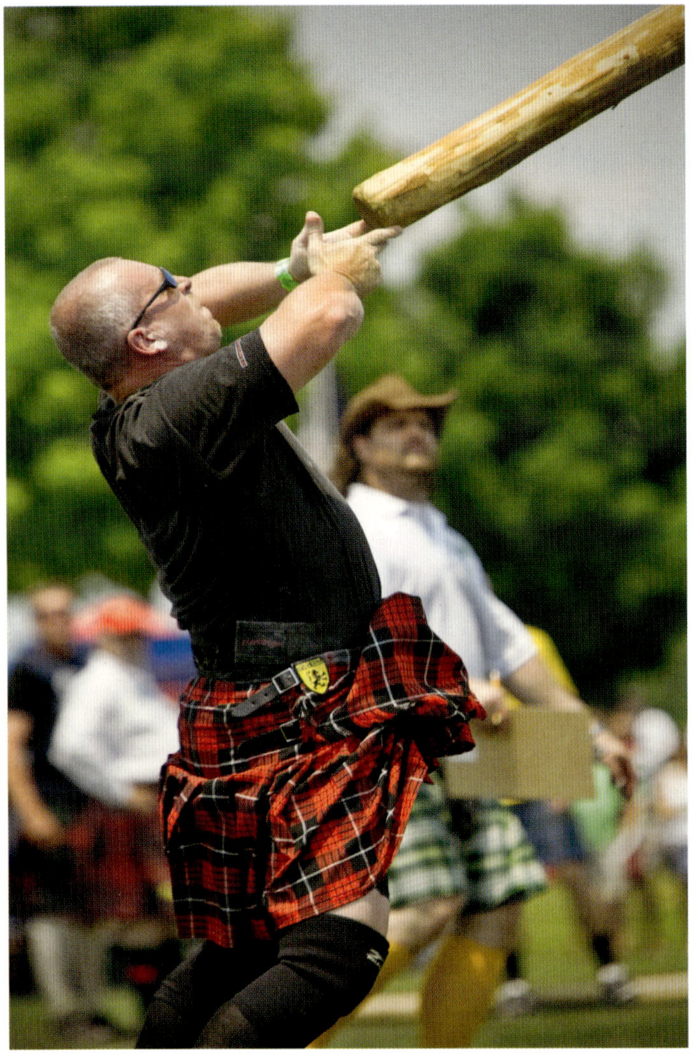

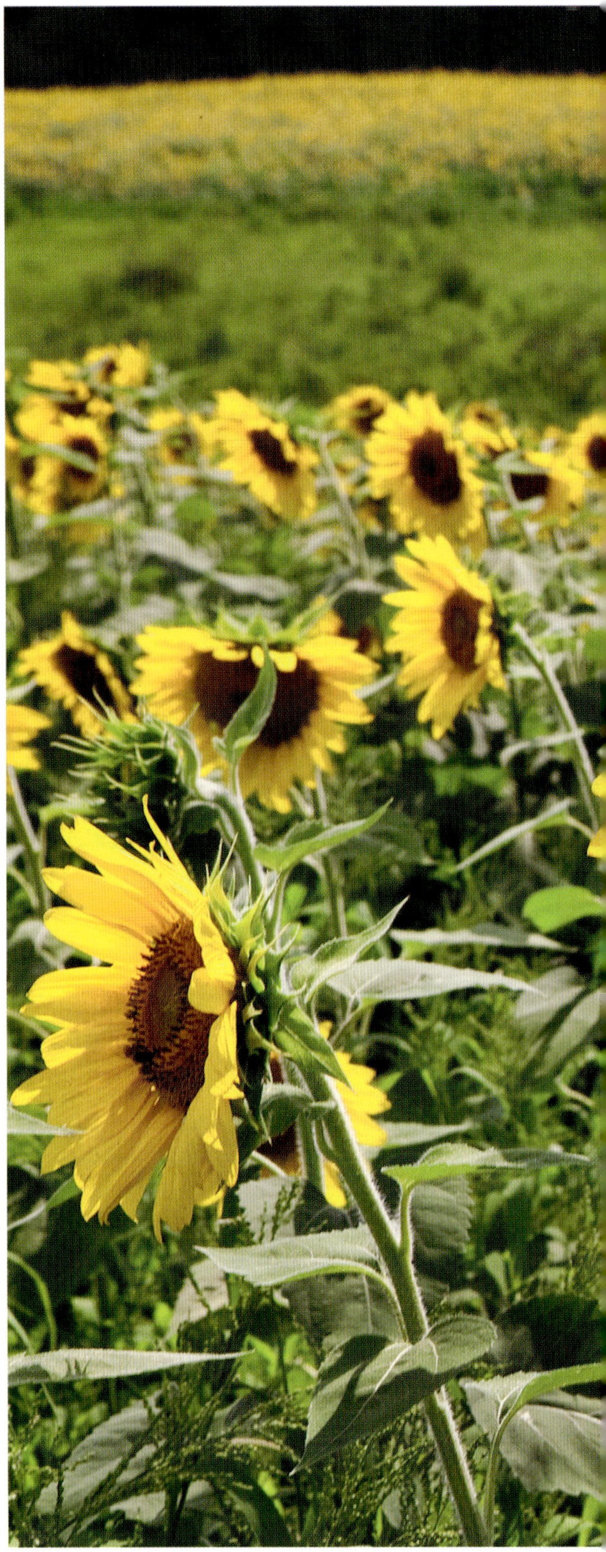

Tossing the Caber

Greenville has one of the country's highest concentrations of people of Scots-Irish descent. Its Scottish games festival, Gallabrae, features heavy athletic competition events such as the caber toss, which developed from the need to walk across narrow chasms.

Following the Sun

Sunflower heads not fully developed track the sun. As these flower heads mature, solar tracking diminishes, then ceases altogether.

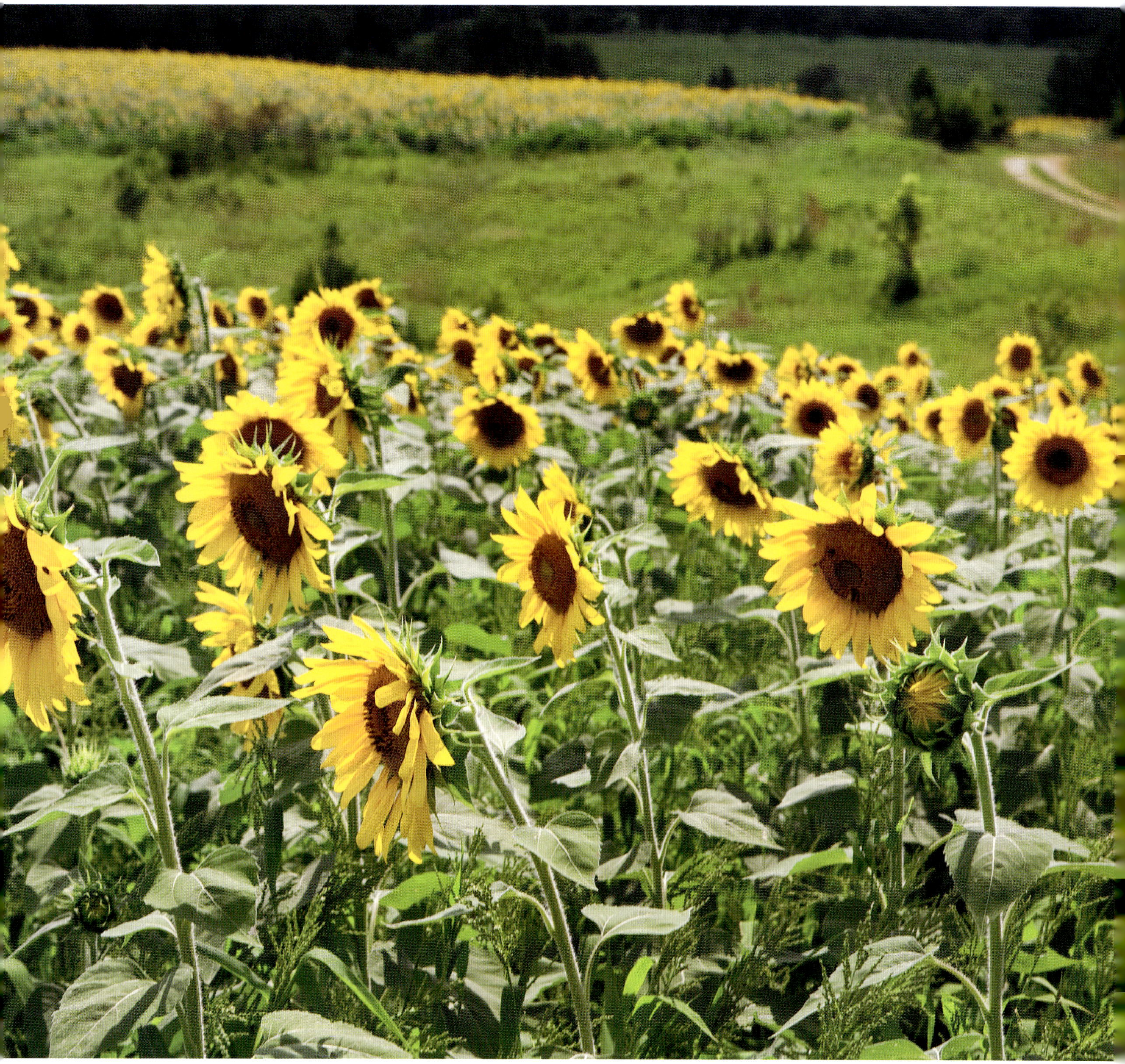

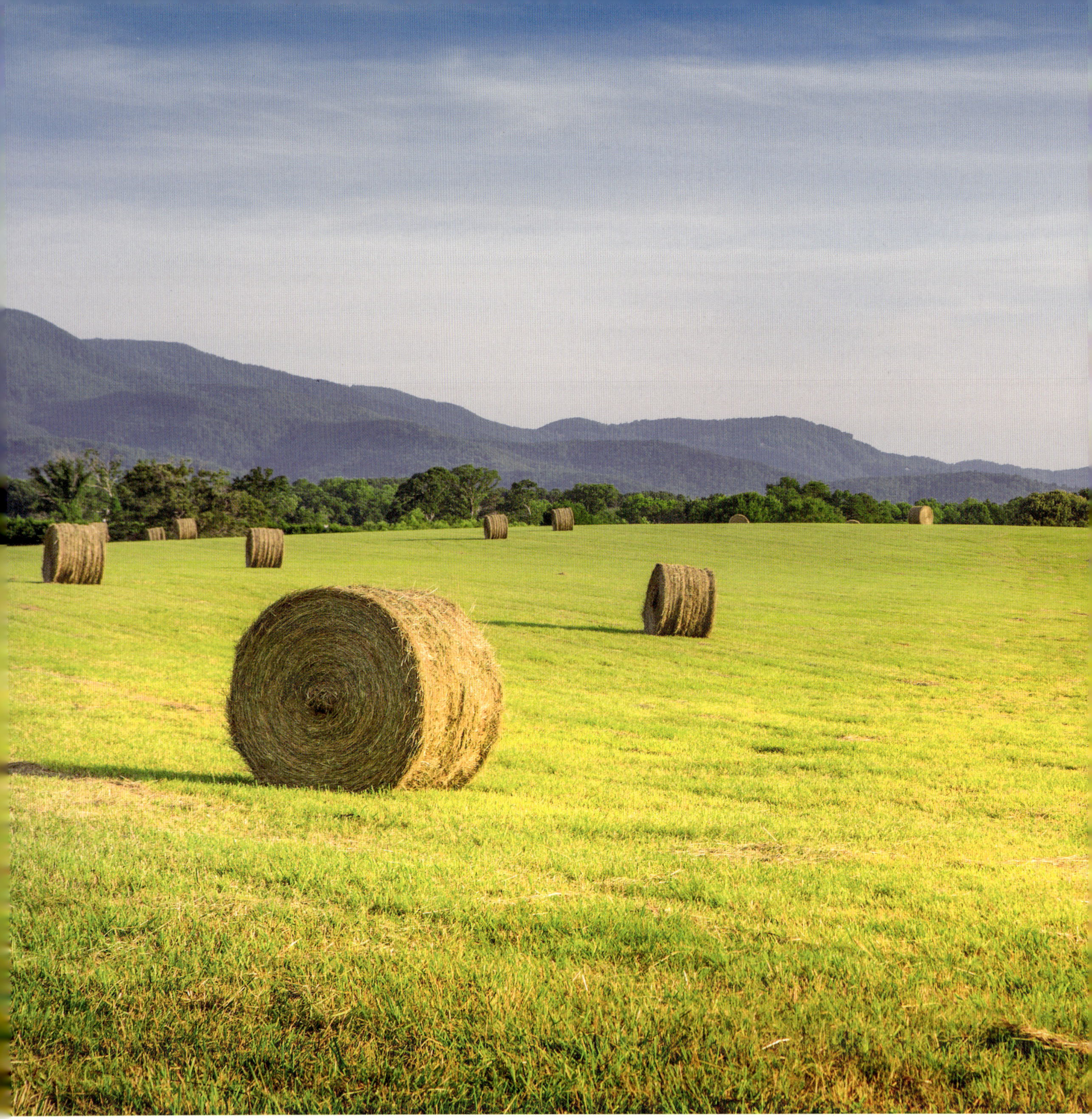

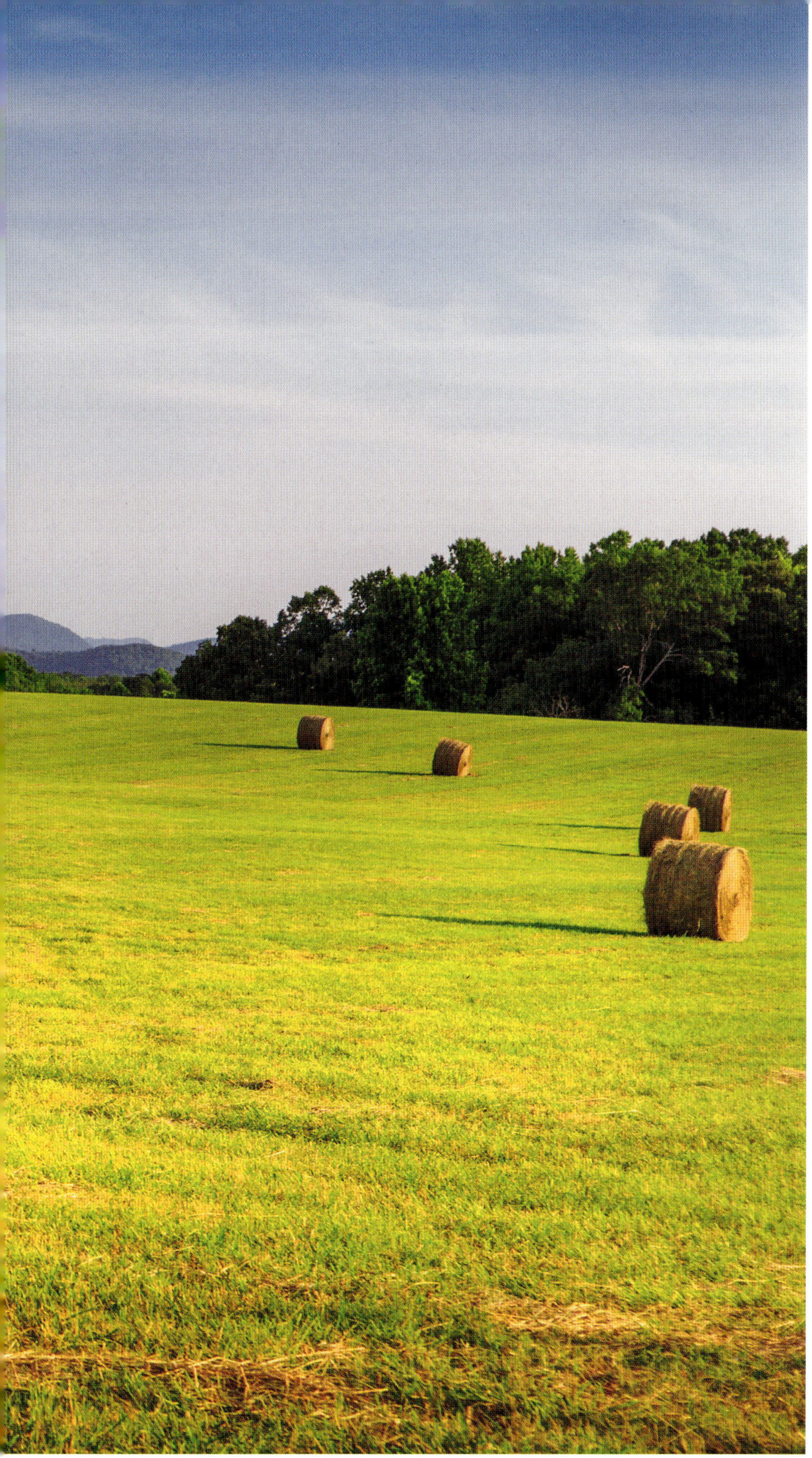

Insurance for Livestock

Near Gowensville, round bales, seeming to roll away, supplant the smaller rectangular bales farmers long stored in barns. Making hay while the sun shines is not a cut-and-dried subject. Whether round or "square" as rectangular bales are called, the toughest thing about growing food insurance for livestock is the weather. Either too much rain or not enough.

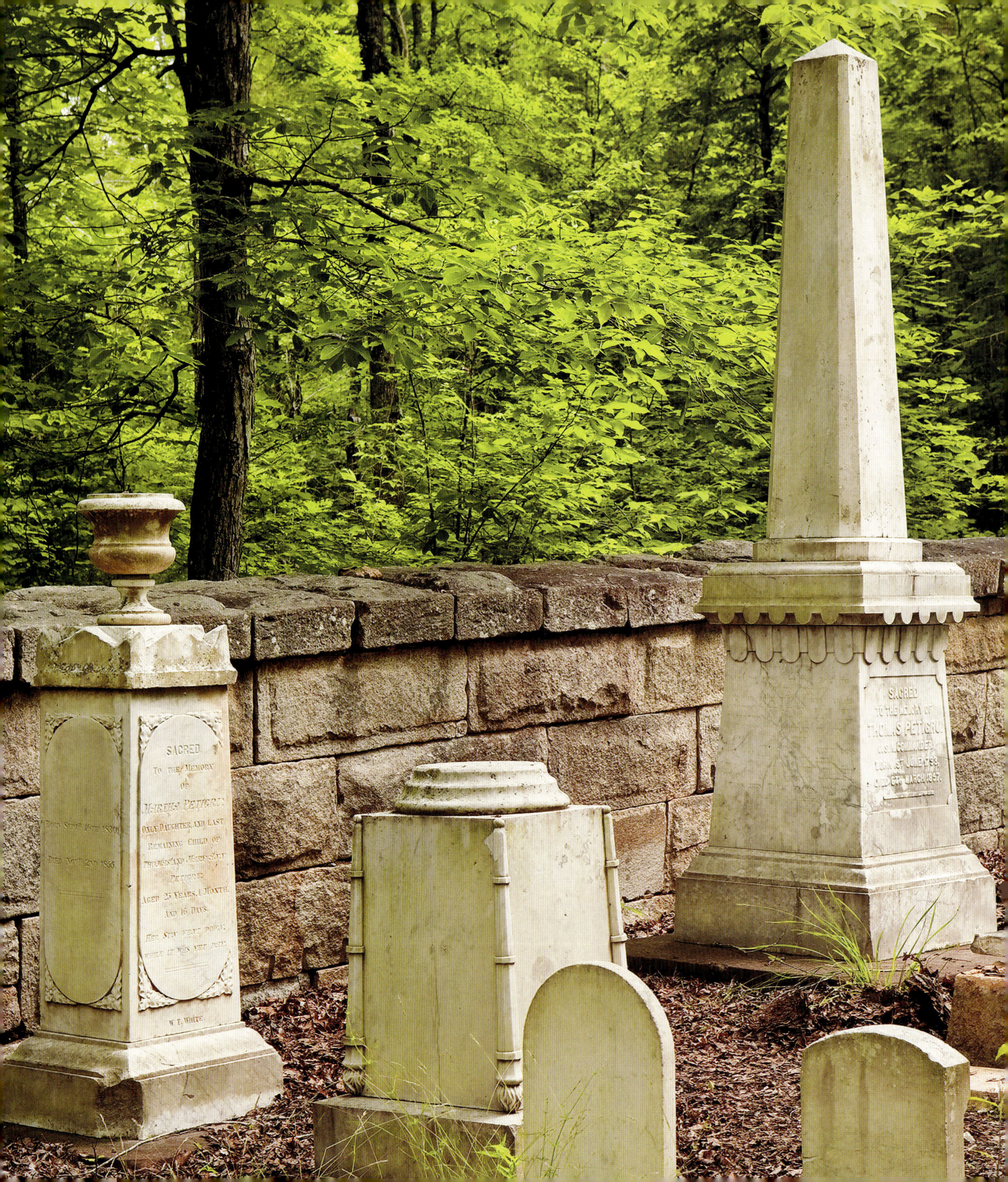
SACRED
TO THE MEMORY
OF
ONLY DAUGHTER AND LAST
REMAINING CHILD OF
AGED 25 YEARS, 1 MONTH
AND 16 DAYS
W. T. WHITE
SACRED
MARCH 1857.

Badwell Cemetery, New Bordeaux

Among the graves in Badwell Cemetery is that of Rev. Jean Louis Gibert (1722–73), who led the French Huguenot settlement established in 1764 at new Bordeaux. Gibert died at 51 from poisonous mushrooms. Legend holds that a troll guards Badwell Cemetery. Thieves twice made off with the Grim Reaper sculpture that adorned the iron door providing entry, but it was recovered each time. Today its whereabouts are unknown, and mystery, secrecy, and bureaucracy prevent opportunities to see it or to return it to its rightful place.

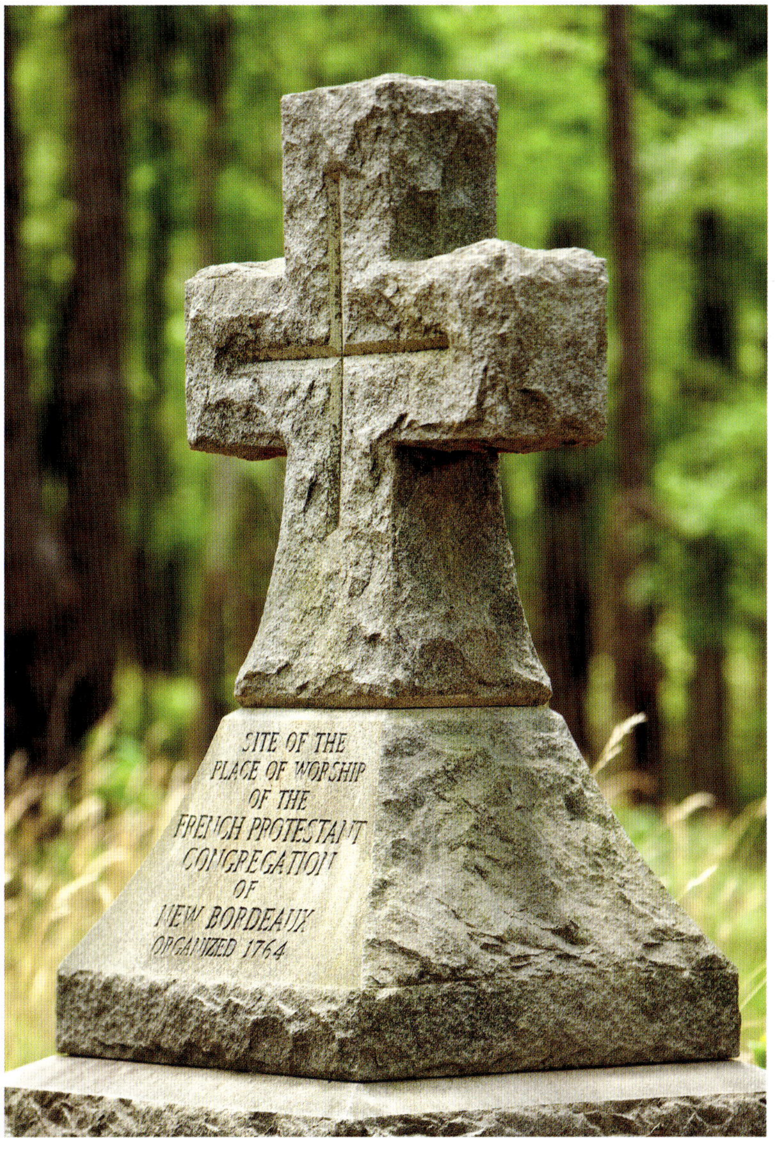

Huguenot Memorial

A Maltese cross marks the spot of the New Bordeaux Huguenot place of worship. New Bordeaux was the last of seven French Huguenot colonies in South Carolina. The French settlers brought the European model of agriculture here, and fruit trees, olive groves, and vineyards sprang up. The villagers prospered in the 1760s and early 1770s, but the Revolutionary War ruined their economy, and New Bordeaux faded.

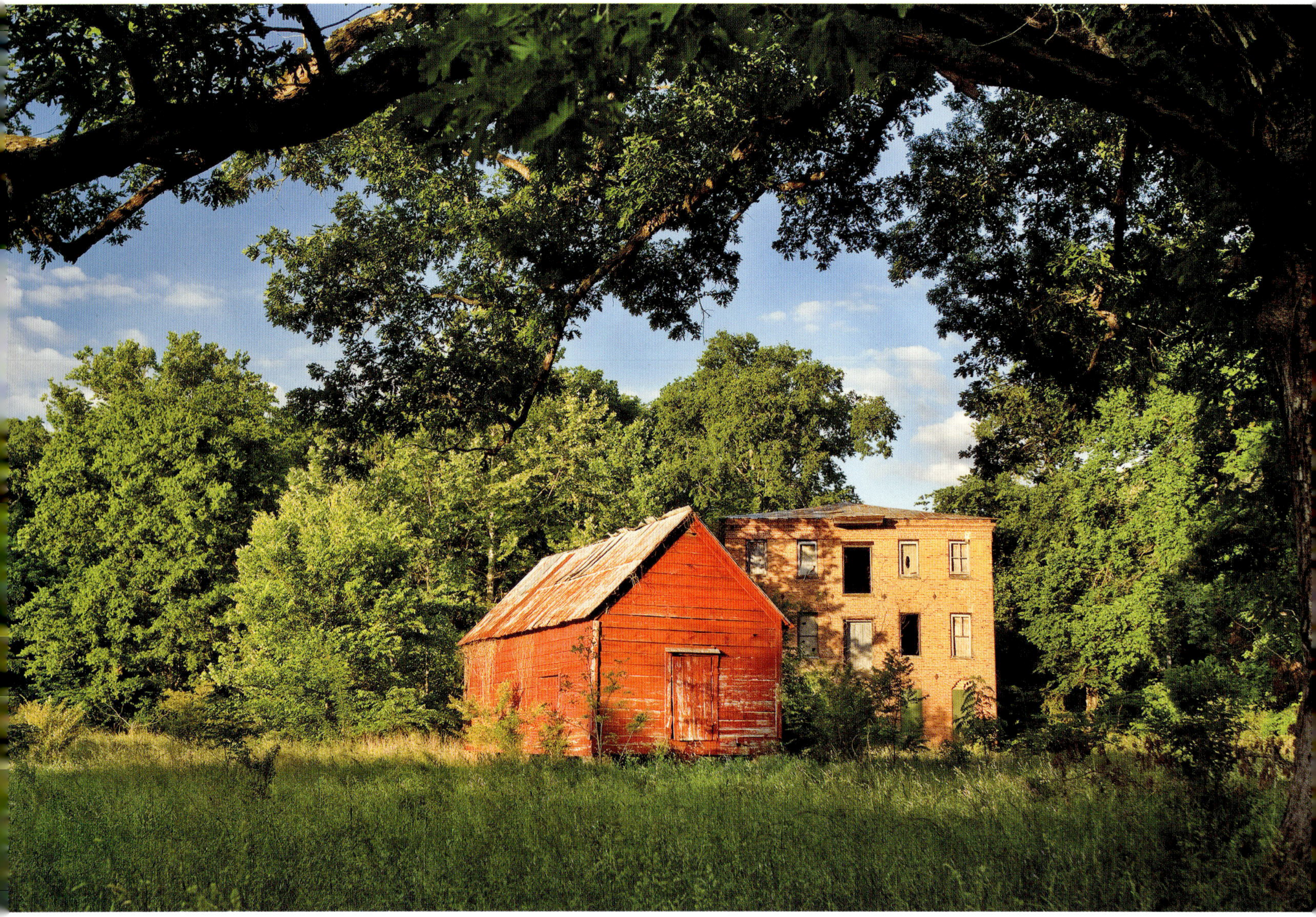

Calhoun Mill, ca. 1860

The Calhoun Mill centered a complex of six outbuildings, cotton gin included. This mill helped develop a commercial center for the Mt. Carmel area. A brick mill was a rarity; most were wooden.

Dorn Mill
National Register of Historic Places

This ca. 1898 cottonseed mill was converted to a flour and gristmill in the 1920s. Rural America's small towns depended on mills like Dorn Mill. With the arrival of more complex mill technology, small mills began to disappear.

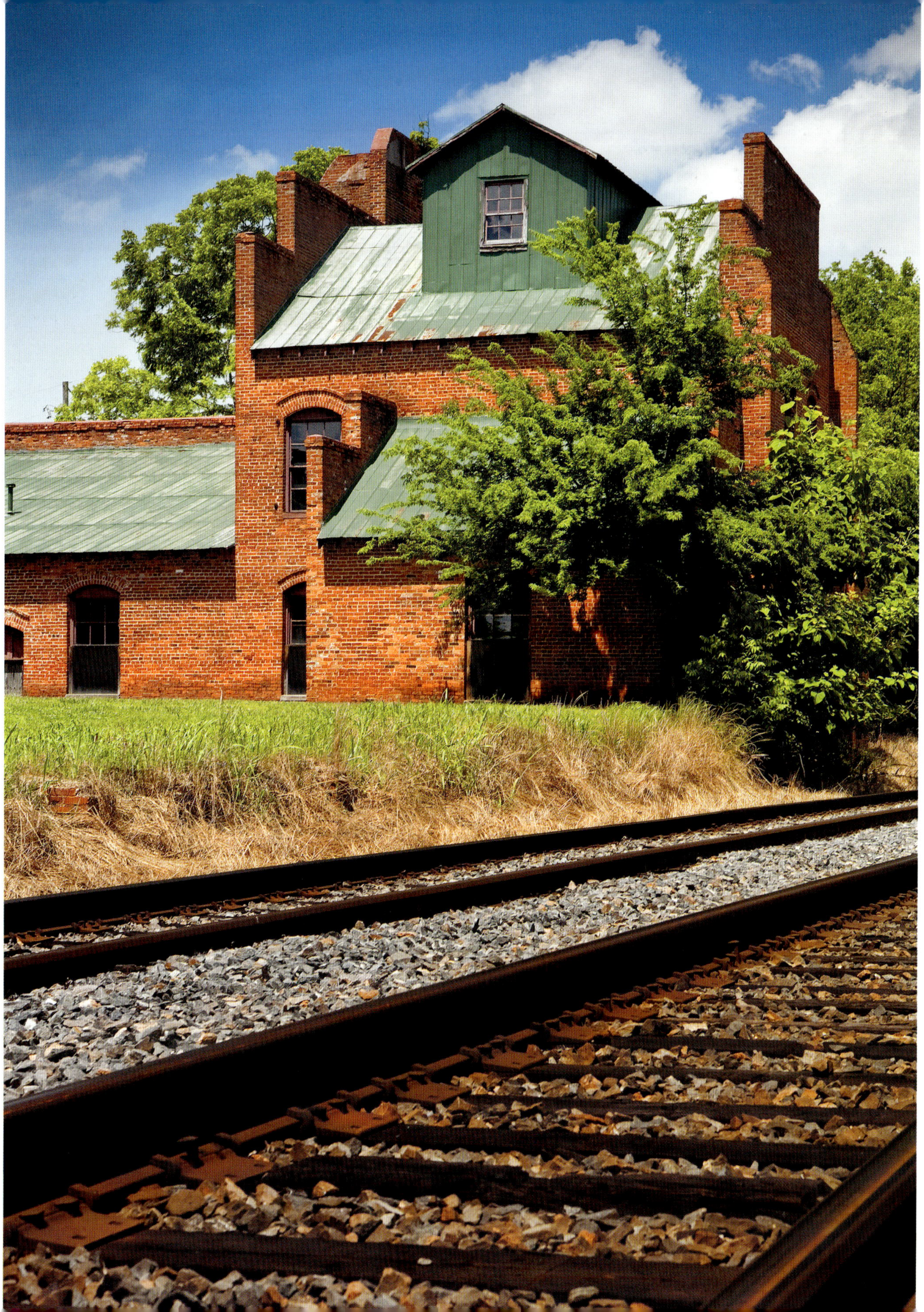

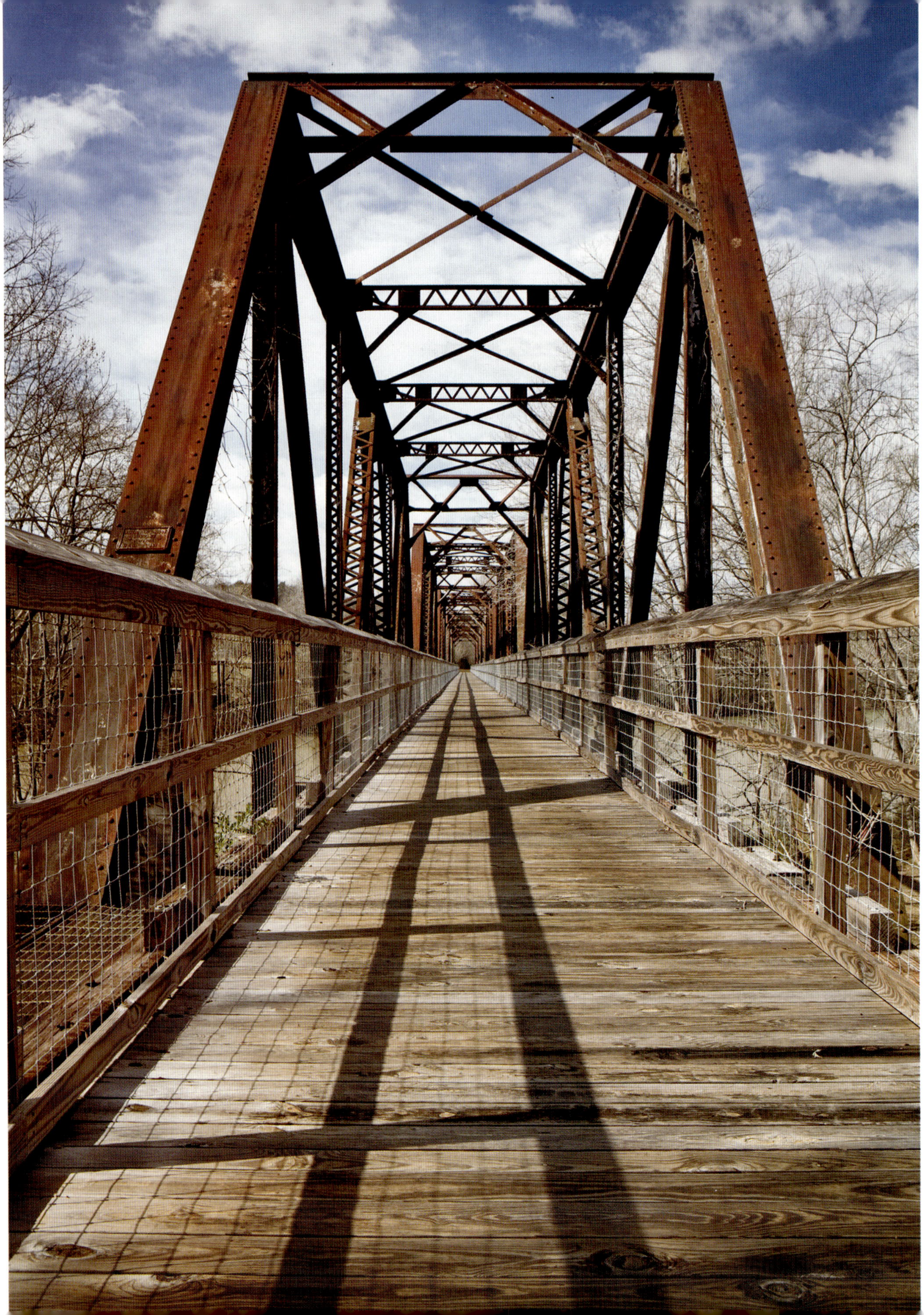

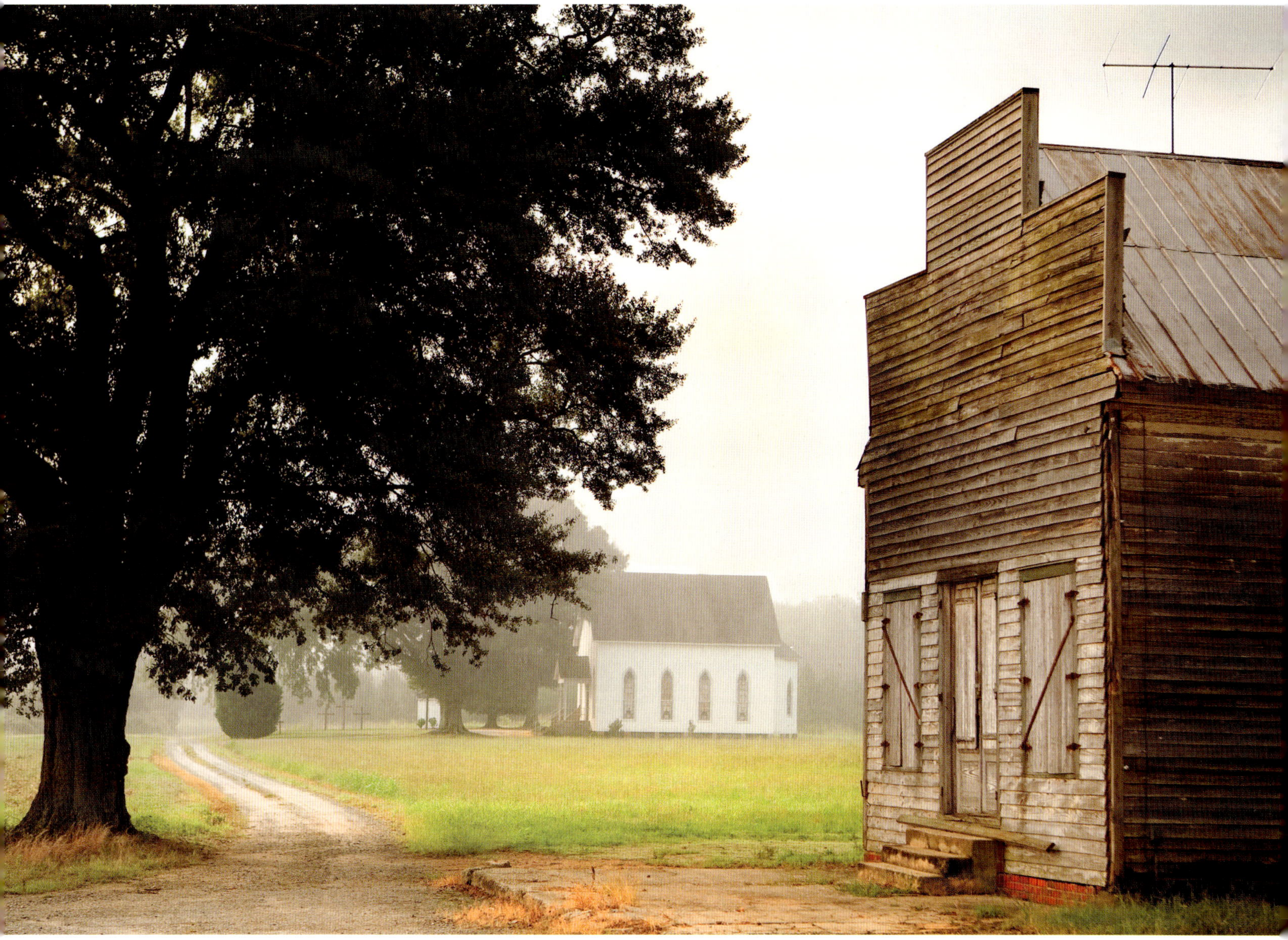

Toward Infinity

It took Palmetto Conservation years to purchase an eleven-mile-long, 200-foot-wide right-of-way from Norfolk Southern Railroad. The result? A trail that runs from the Broad River's banks in Fairfield County into Newberry County. Hikers and mountain bikers can negotiate fourteen trestles such as the one here.

The Rural South

Kinards, an unincorporated community in Laurens and Newberry Counties, sits on the edge of Sumter National Forest as well as the edge of time. Note the vintage TV antenna on the roof of the old store.

Wells Japanese Garden
National Register of Historic Places

W. Fulmer Wells designed Newberry's Japanese garden, which his father, Henry B. Wells Sr., established in 1930. The garden consists of indigenous and exotic flora and torii gate. The garden was donated to the city for public use in 1971.

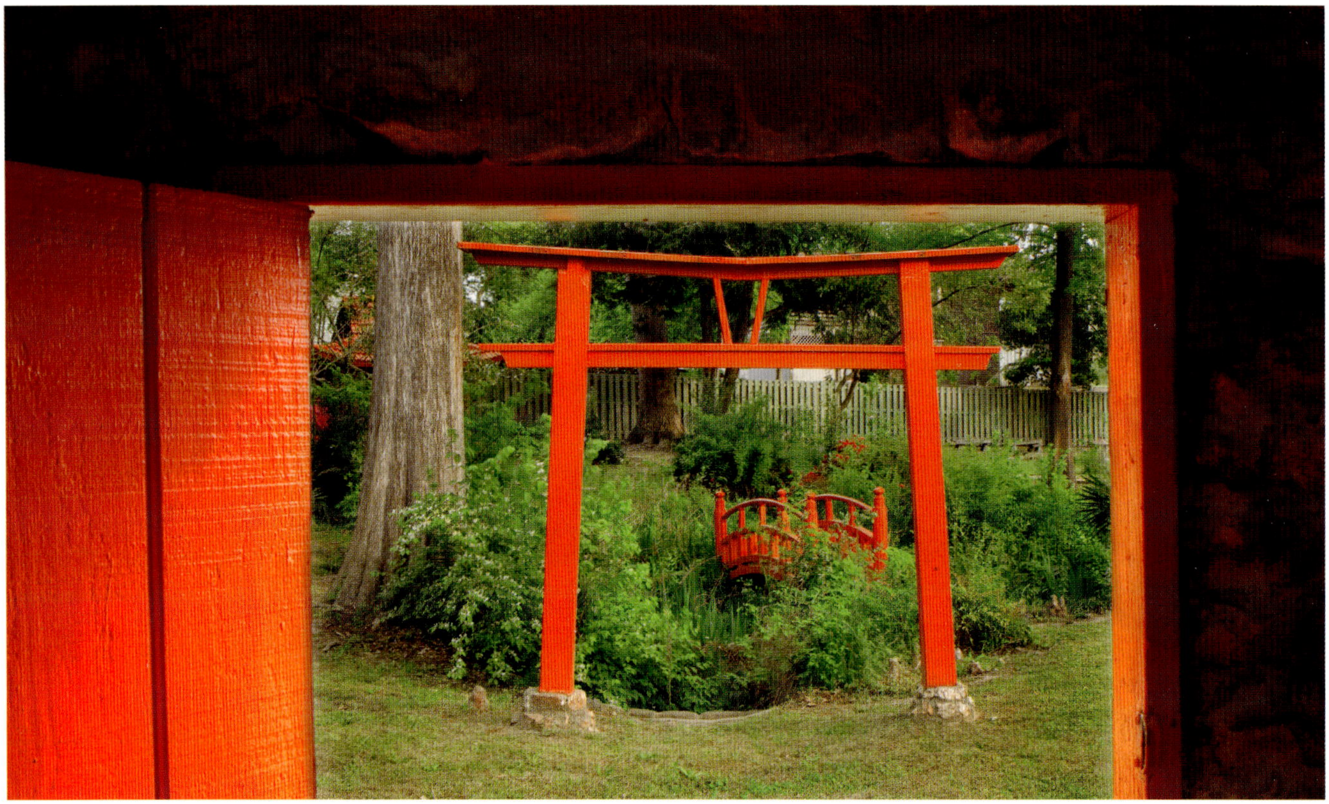

Newberry Opera House
National Register of Historic Places

Built in 1882, the Newberry Opera House closed in 1952 after showing *Day of the Outlaw*. By 1959, demolition threatened it. Public outcry saved it. In 1969, the Newberry Historical Society promoted the preservation of the Opera House, as did several other community groups. After renovation the Opera House reopened in 1998 as a performing arts center.

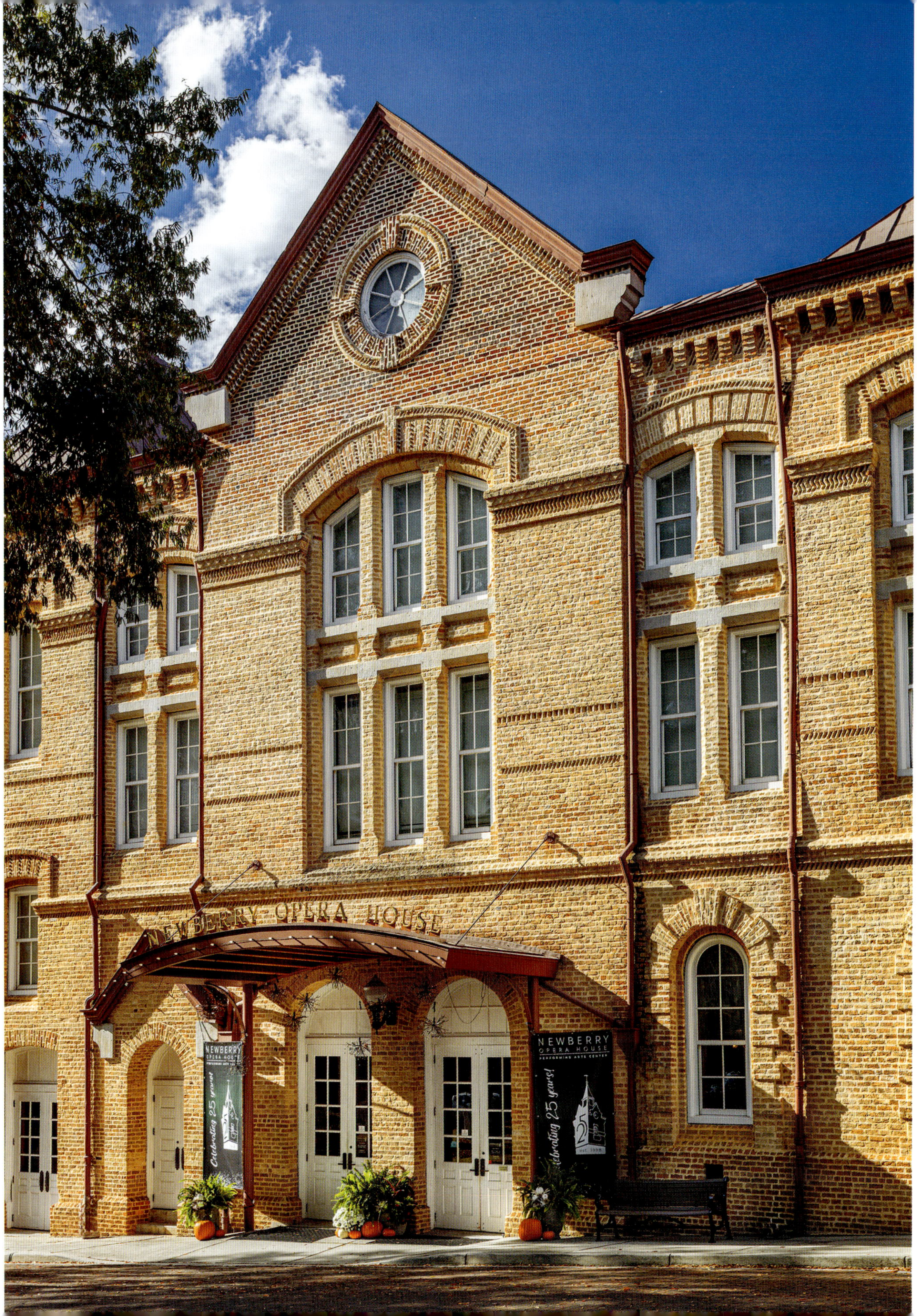
NEWBERRY OPERA HOUSE
NEWBERRY
OPERA HOUSE
Celebrating 25 years!
NEWBERRY
OPERA HOUSE
PERFORMING ARTS CENTER
Celebrating 25 years!

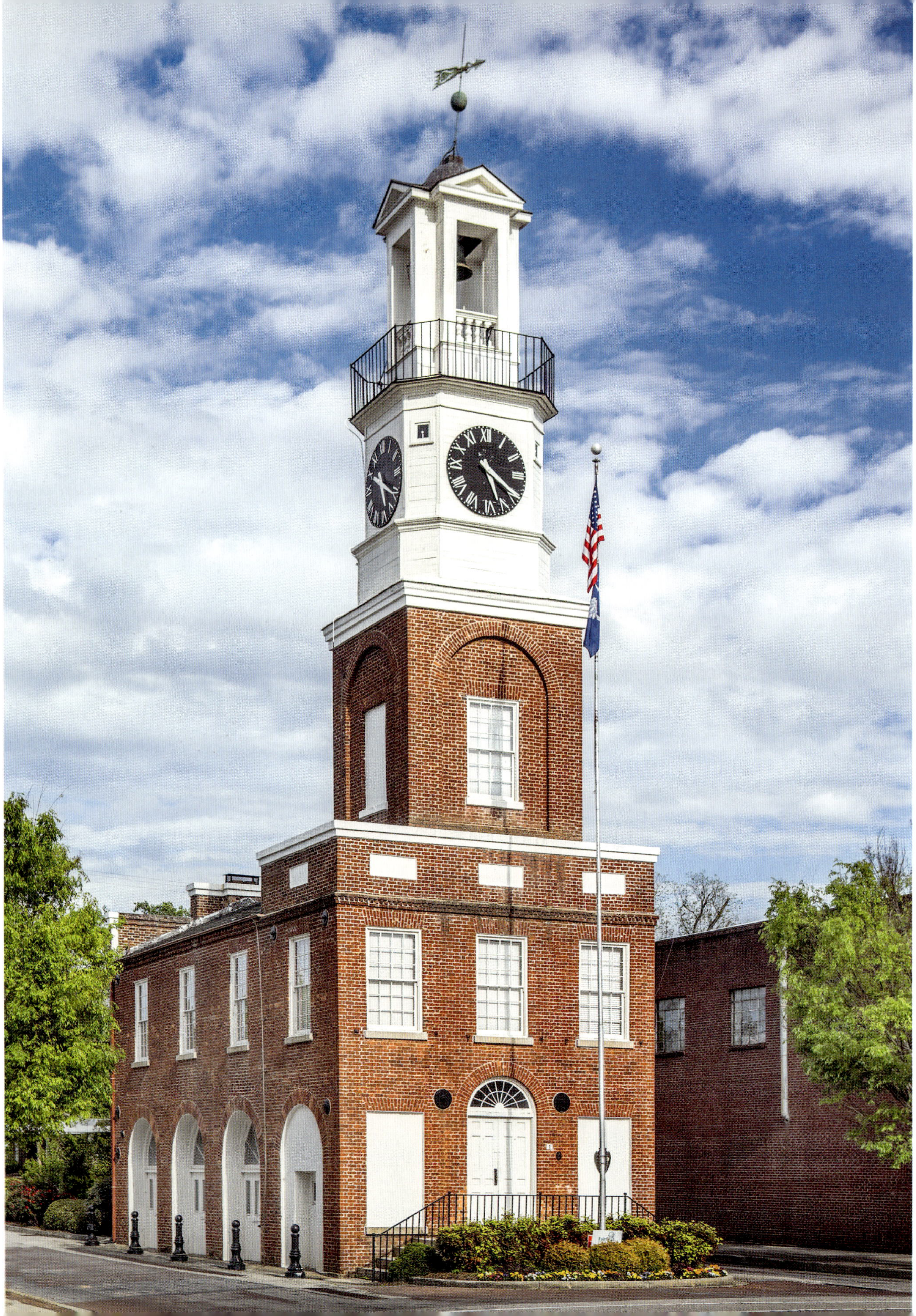

The Watch Tower

Winnsboro's town clock came from France in the 1830s. Fifty wagons hauled the works from Charleston to Winnsboro. Locals say the clock has run continuously for 100 years, making it the longest continuously running clock in the United States. The present tower went up in 1875. The tower bell, also made in France, was rung to announce the arrival of fresh meat, an old, common custom.

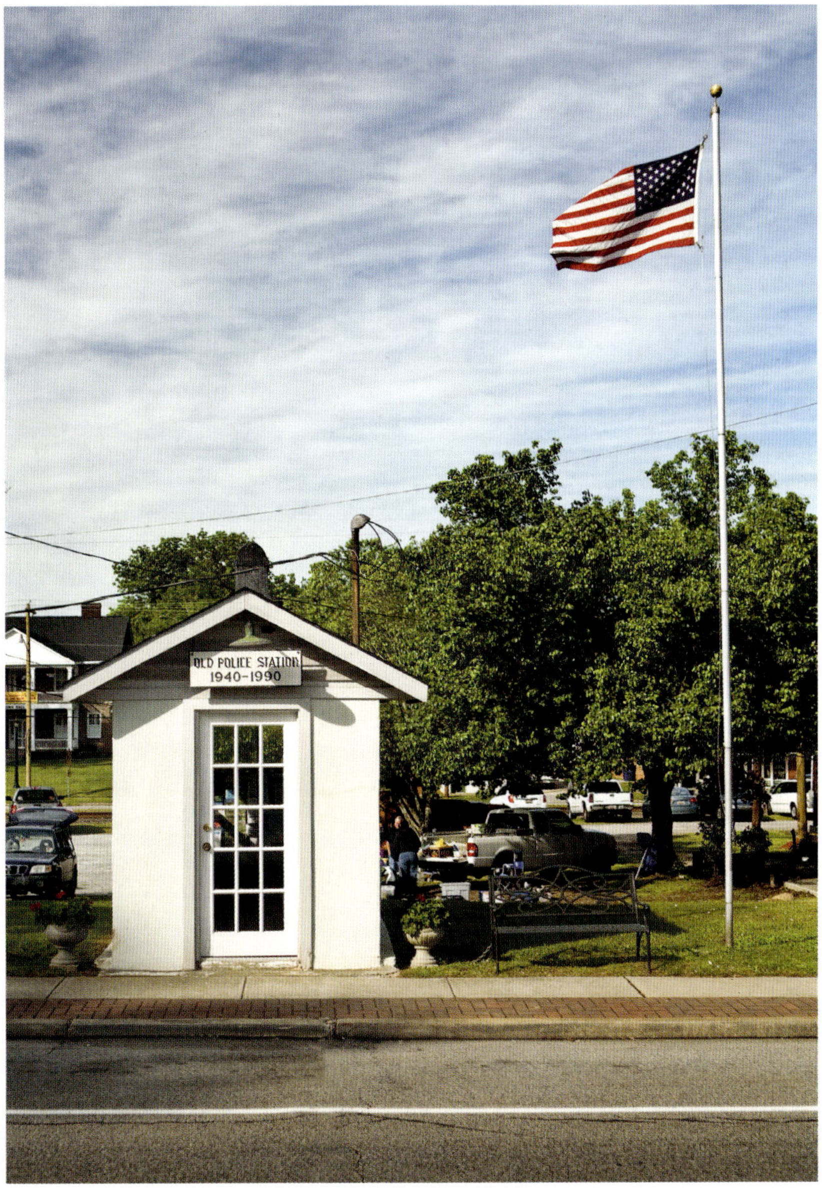

The Old Ridgeway Police Station

This compact building first served Ridgeway as the town well. In 1940, as part of a Works Progress Administration project, workers covered the well; thus the "World's Smallest Police Station" came to be. Today, the Old Police Station dispenses tourist information to the curious who arrive via US 21 to see the station and its claim to fame. It also made it to Hollywood, appearing in the 1989 film *Staying Together*.

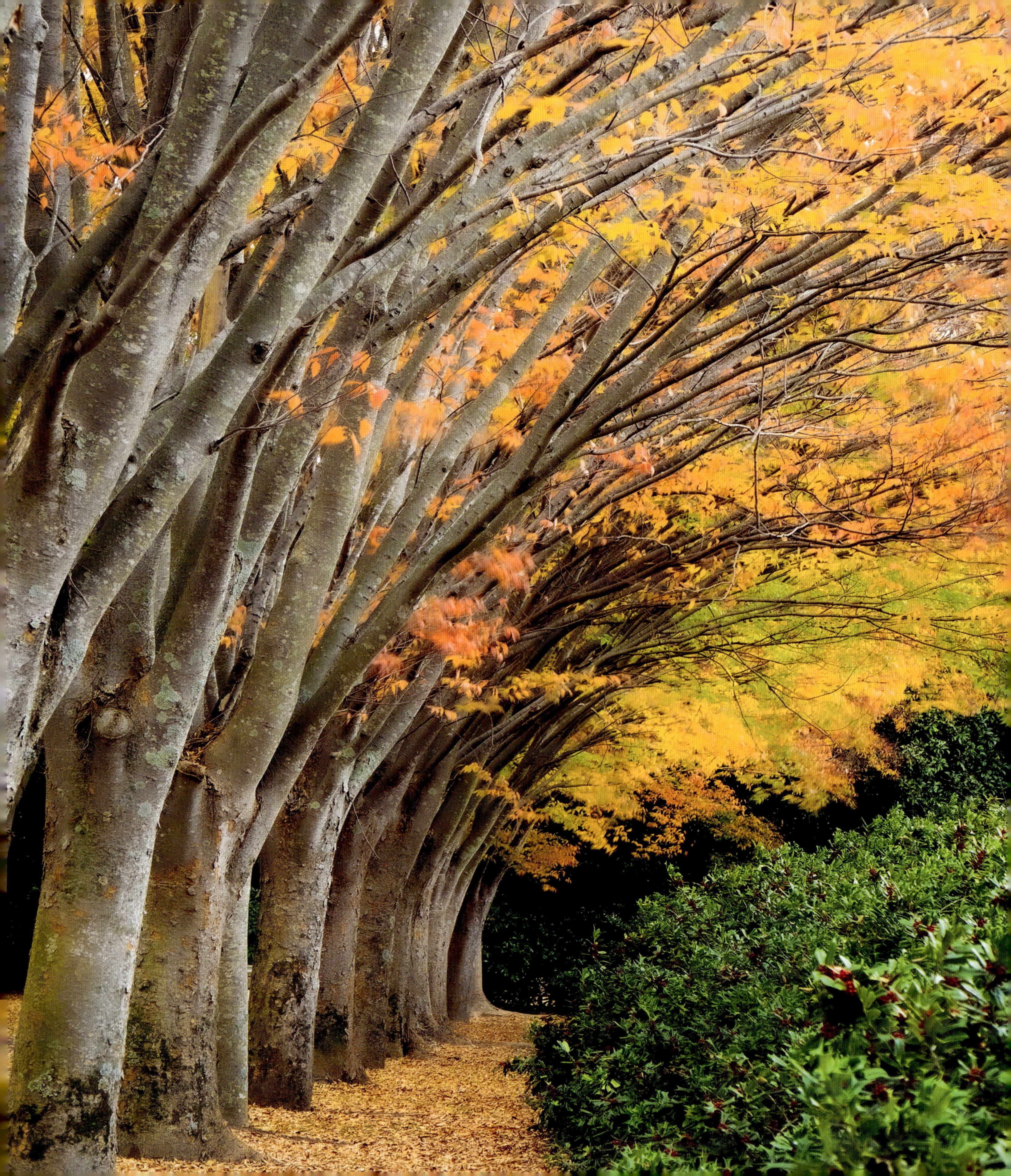

Milliken Campus Allée, Spartanburg

American textile heir, Roger Milliken, loved trees. Milliken's Spartanburg campus features an arboretum that represents decades of tree planting and cultivation. Here, you'll see wine glass trees, green vase Zelkovas, whose branches resemble the graceful curve of a wine glass. Milliken would deem the green vase Zelkova a noble tree, a tree that withstands the tests of time. In 1999 Milliken founded the Noble Tree Foundation, a 501(c)(3) organization that promotes the planting of Noble Trees that beautify the community.

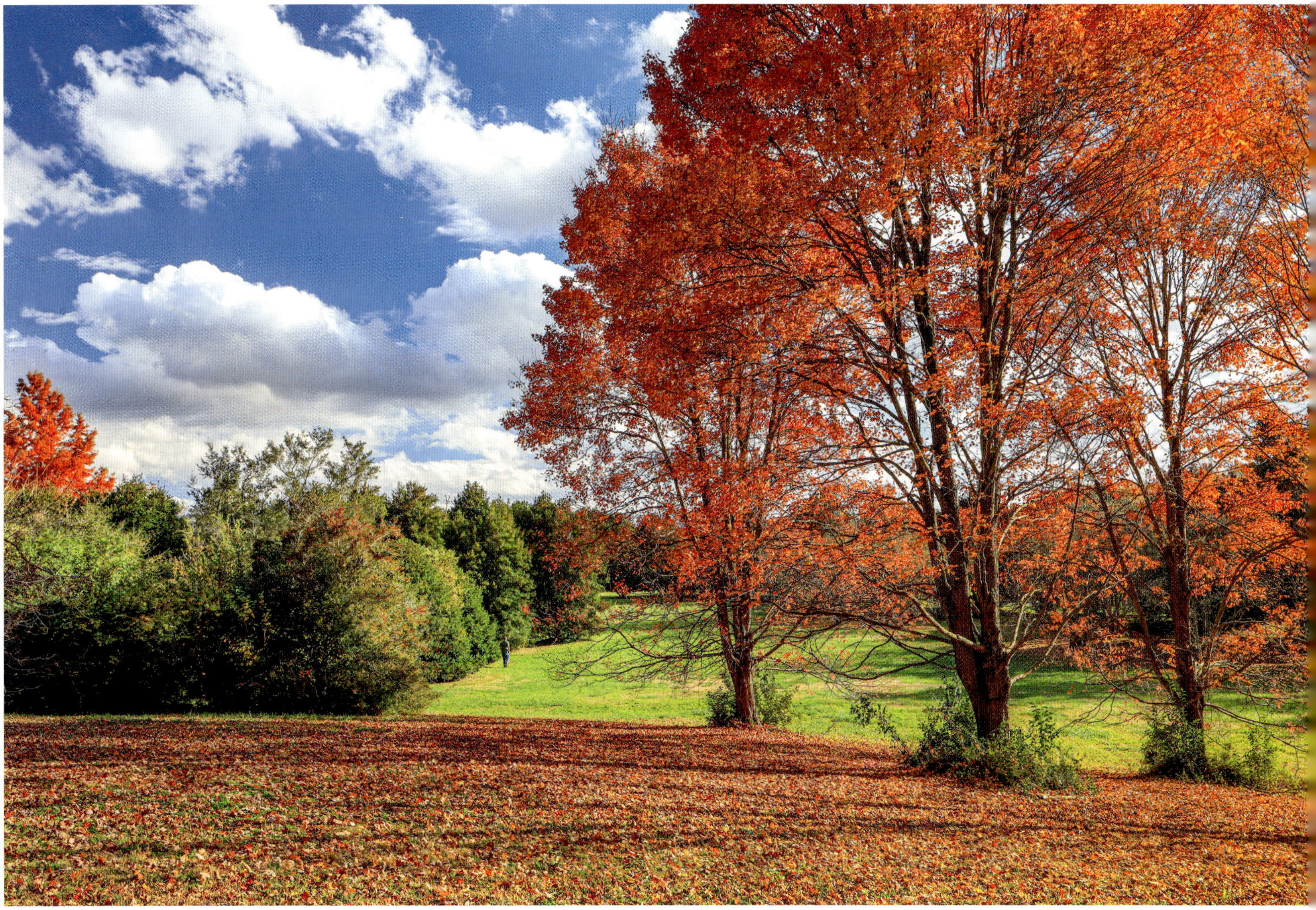

Spartanburg County's Autumnal Glory

Look closely. It's a good day for an Upcountry Carolina walk.

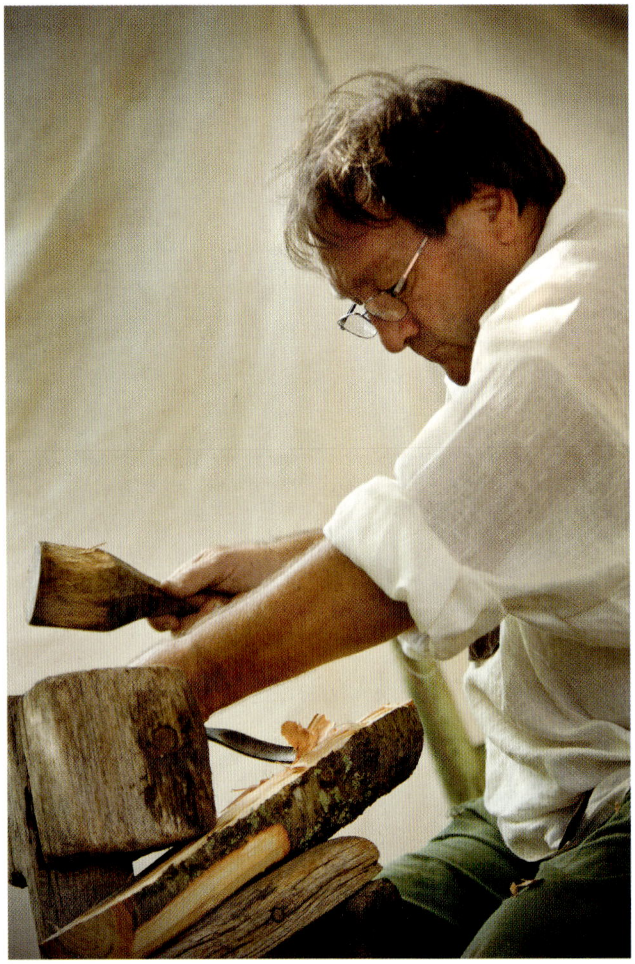

The Woodworker

Aptly named, Ike Carpenter of Edgefield County demonstrates his pioneer woodworking skills at Festifall at Walnut Grove. In early days men, as Carpenter demonstrates, shaped wood into useful tools and beautiful furniture. Carpenter's steady hand and eye for detail render oak into functional art.

Walnut Grove Plantation

Step back to pre-Revolution when King George III granted Charles and Mary Moore land in 1763. With holdings that grew to 3,600 acres, Moore depended on enslaved African Americans and his sizable family to work the land. Walnut Grove's tours and historical accounts share the stories of people who settled the backcountry, fought for independence, and in time helped a new nation rise.

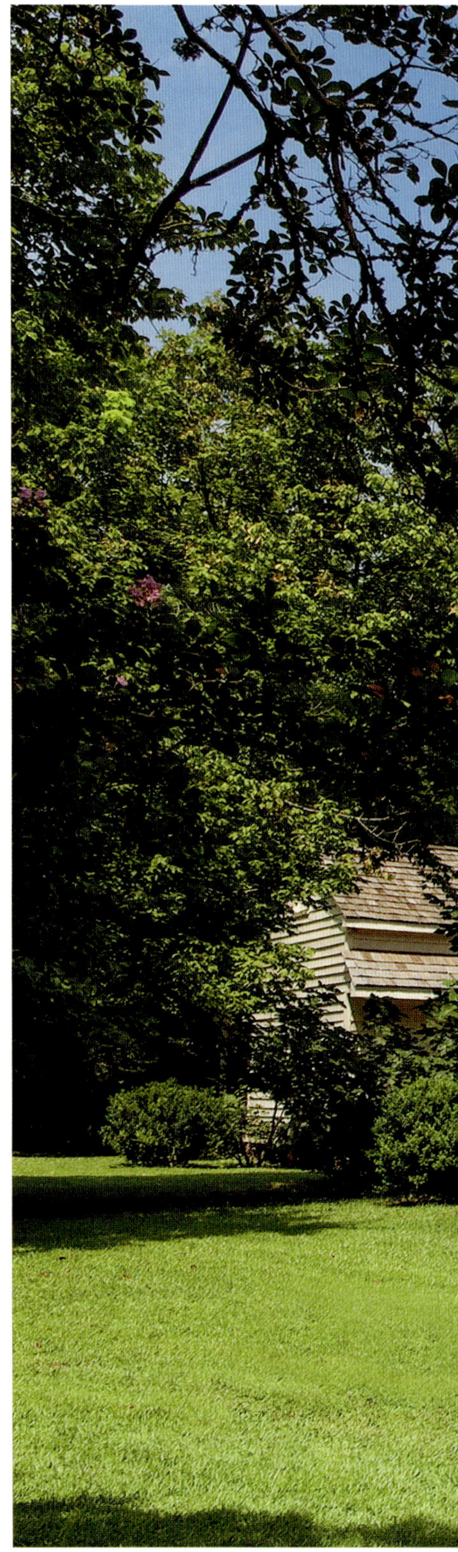

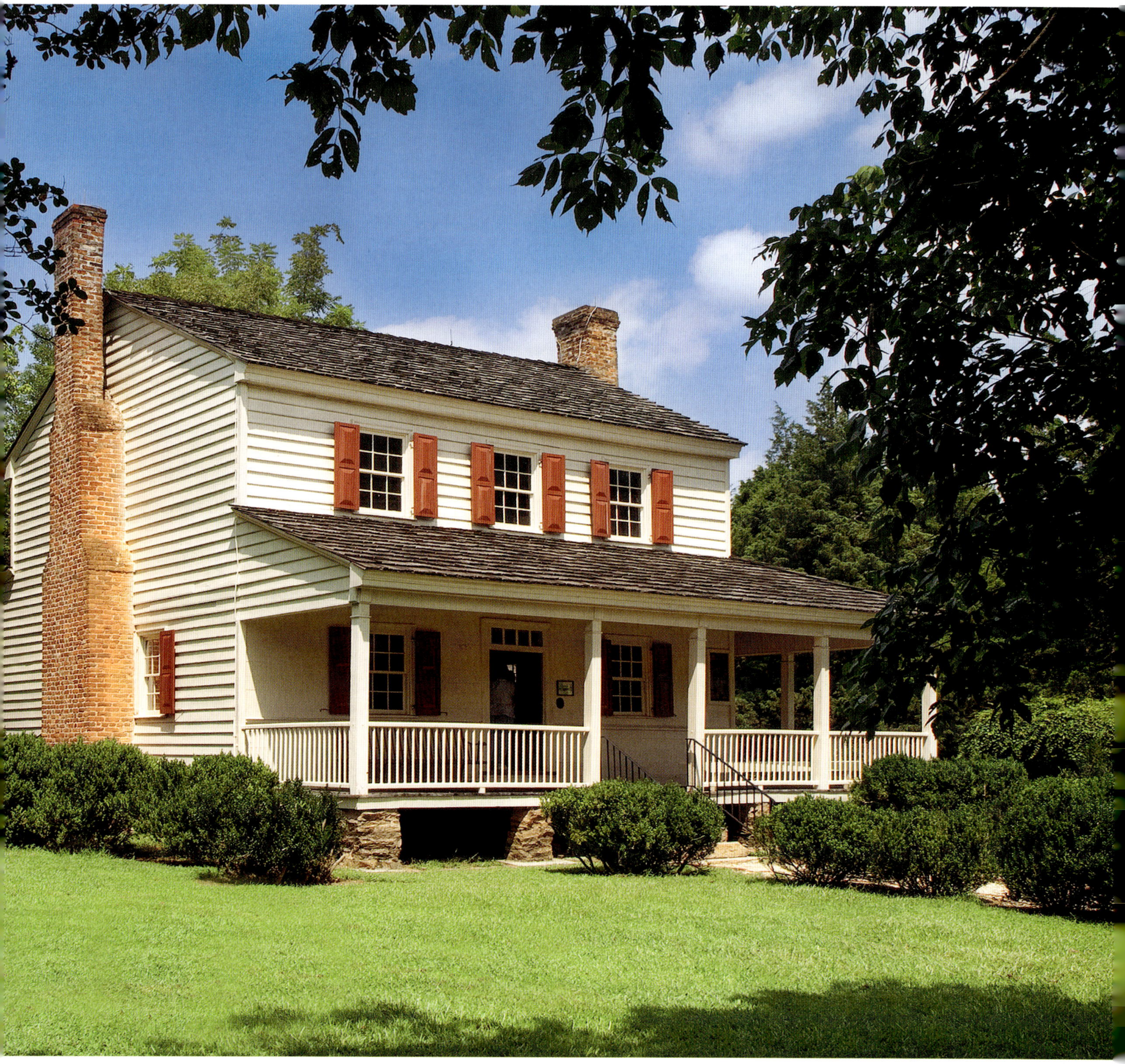

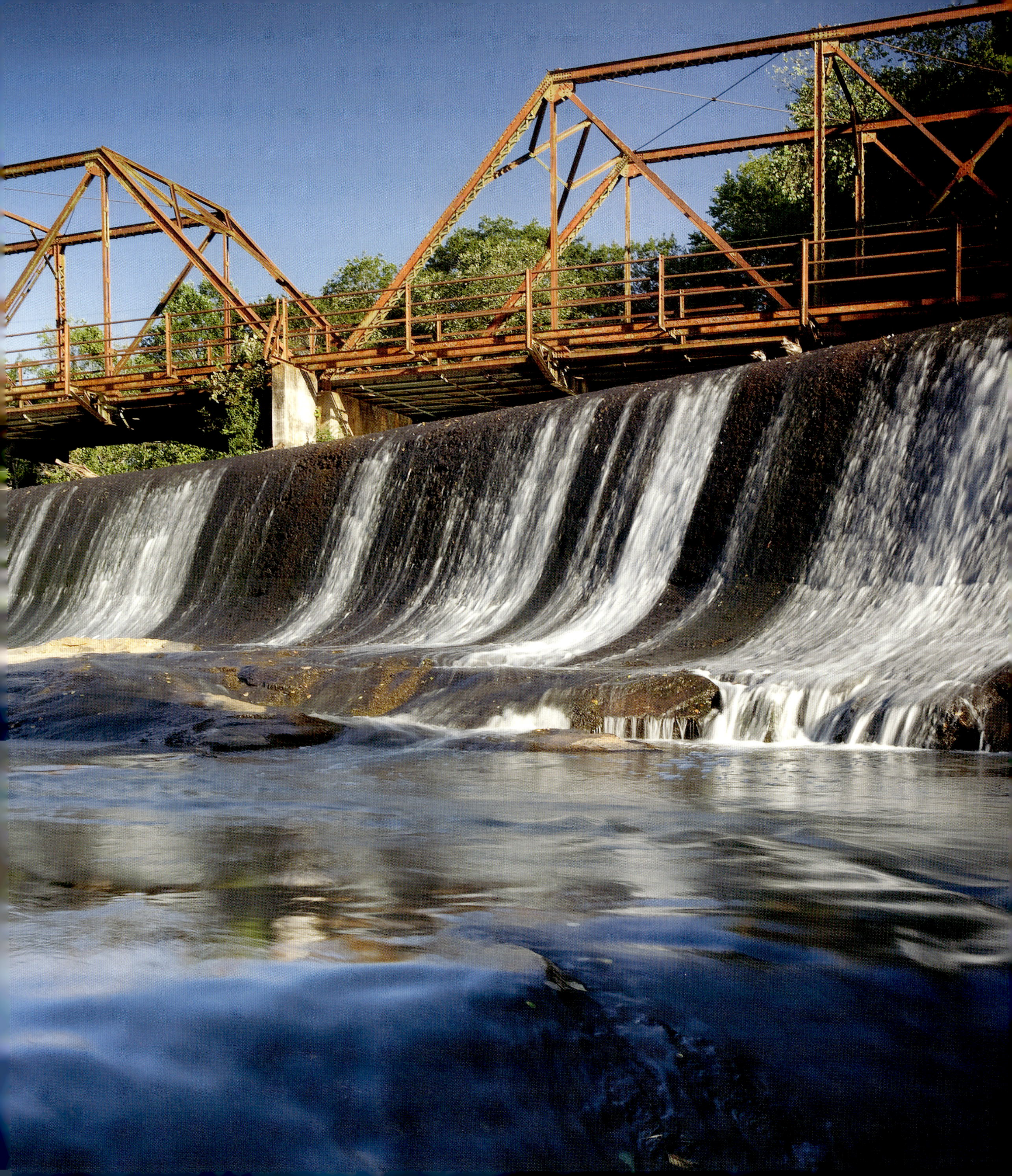

Restored Bridge

This Pratt truss bridge commands a view of the Glendale ruins. The Palmetto Conservation Fund, Spartanburg County, and South Carolina Department of Transportation restored the bridge to its ca. 1928 appearance. The Glendale Bridge connected the Glendale Cotton Mill and mill workers' homes to the community park across the creek.

RUINS AND REMNANTS

Spartanburg's Glendale Mill burned March 21, 2004. Its ruins tower over Lawson's Fork Creek, whose plummeting waters attracted the old mill in the first place. Shells, described often as Gothic, loom over people who come to the creek to relax and fish.

One can kayak to the Atlantic from here. Writer and environmentalist John Lane did. Lane wrote with reverence of the old mill after it burned. "Now it's gone. What was probably the best, most scenic example of an intact mill village in our area has now lost its centerpiece, its heart."

We can take heart in the new venue the old mill provides for outdoor recreation. People walk the graveled path through the ruins and climb the bluff overlooking the creek. Behind the Environmental Studies Center, a Bartram garden grows native species only, and a rock amphitheater brings a tiny Stonehenge to mind.

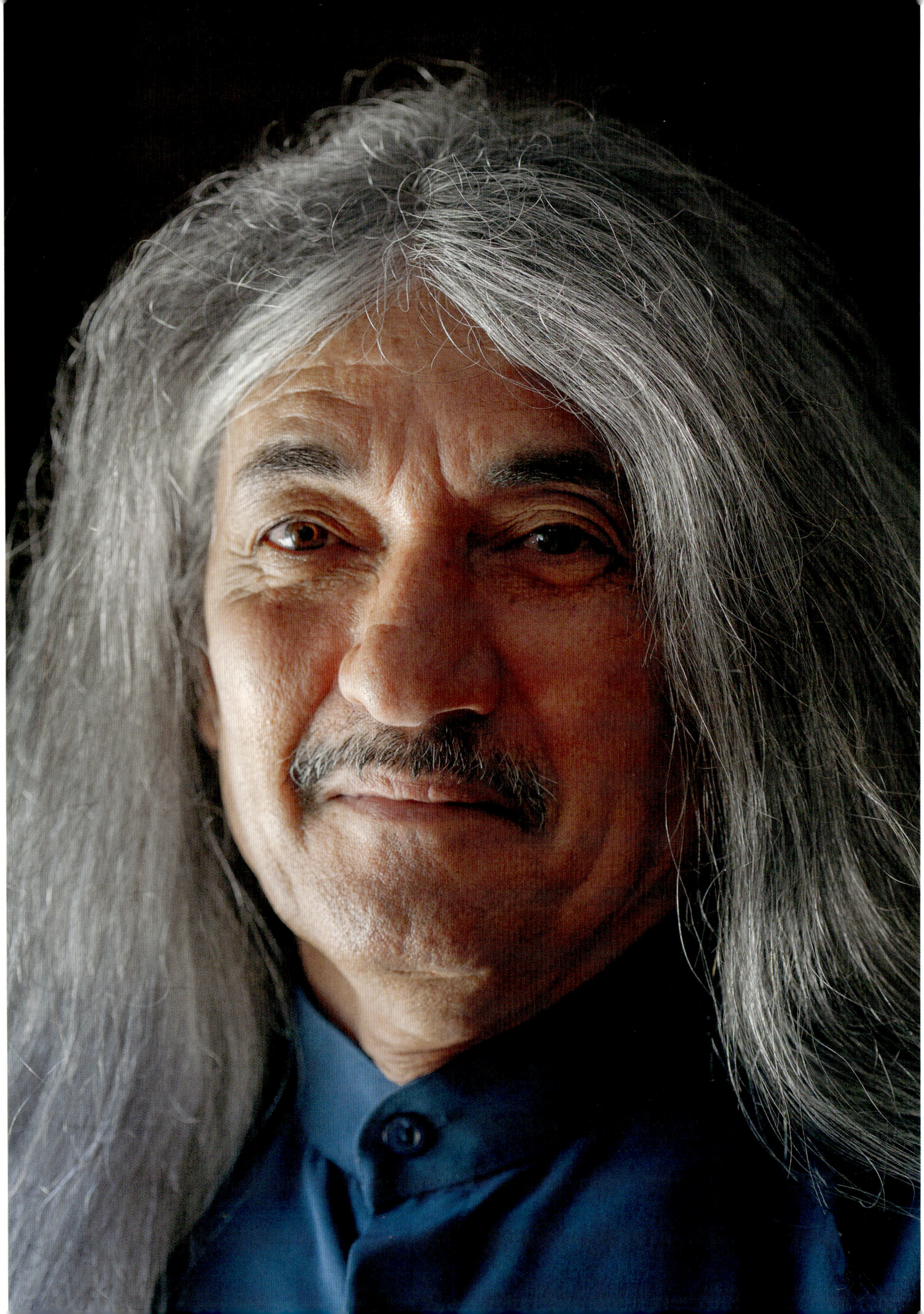

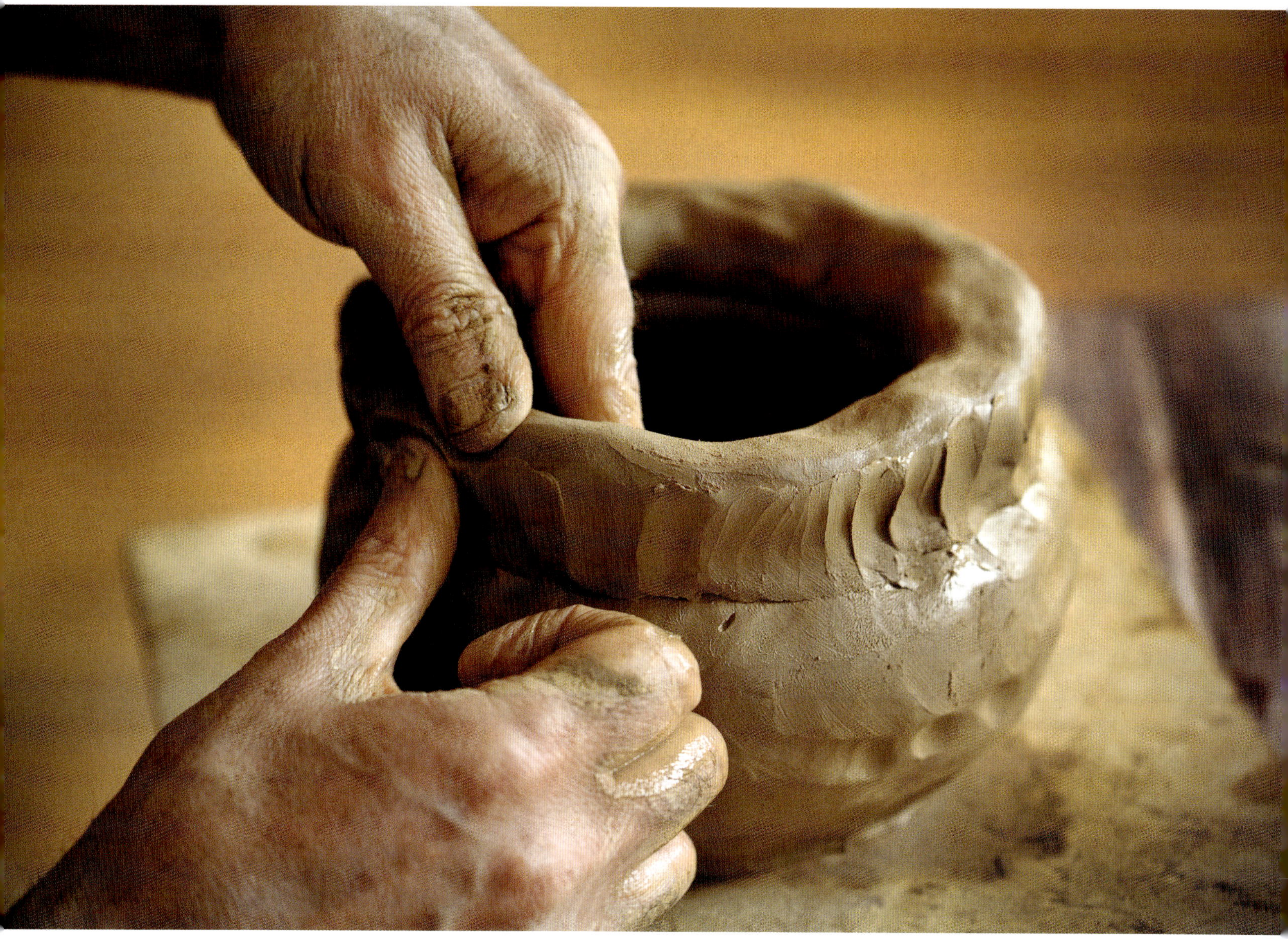

Chief William "Bill" Harris

Potter William "Bill" Harris, chief of the Catawba Indian Nation, testified before the House Interior Appropriations Subcommittee: "The tradition of pottery making among the Catawba, unchanged since before recorded history, links the lives of modern Catawba to our ancestors and symbolizes our connection to the Earth and to the land and river we love."

Shaping a Heritage

Chief William "Bill" Harris's grandfather, Douglas Harris, served as a chief of the Catawba Nation and his grandmother, Georgia, a talented potter, played a pivotal role in preserving the Catawba people's 6,000-year-old art form. She passed her love for the art form to Chief Bill Harris.

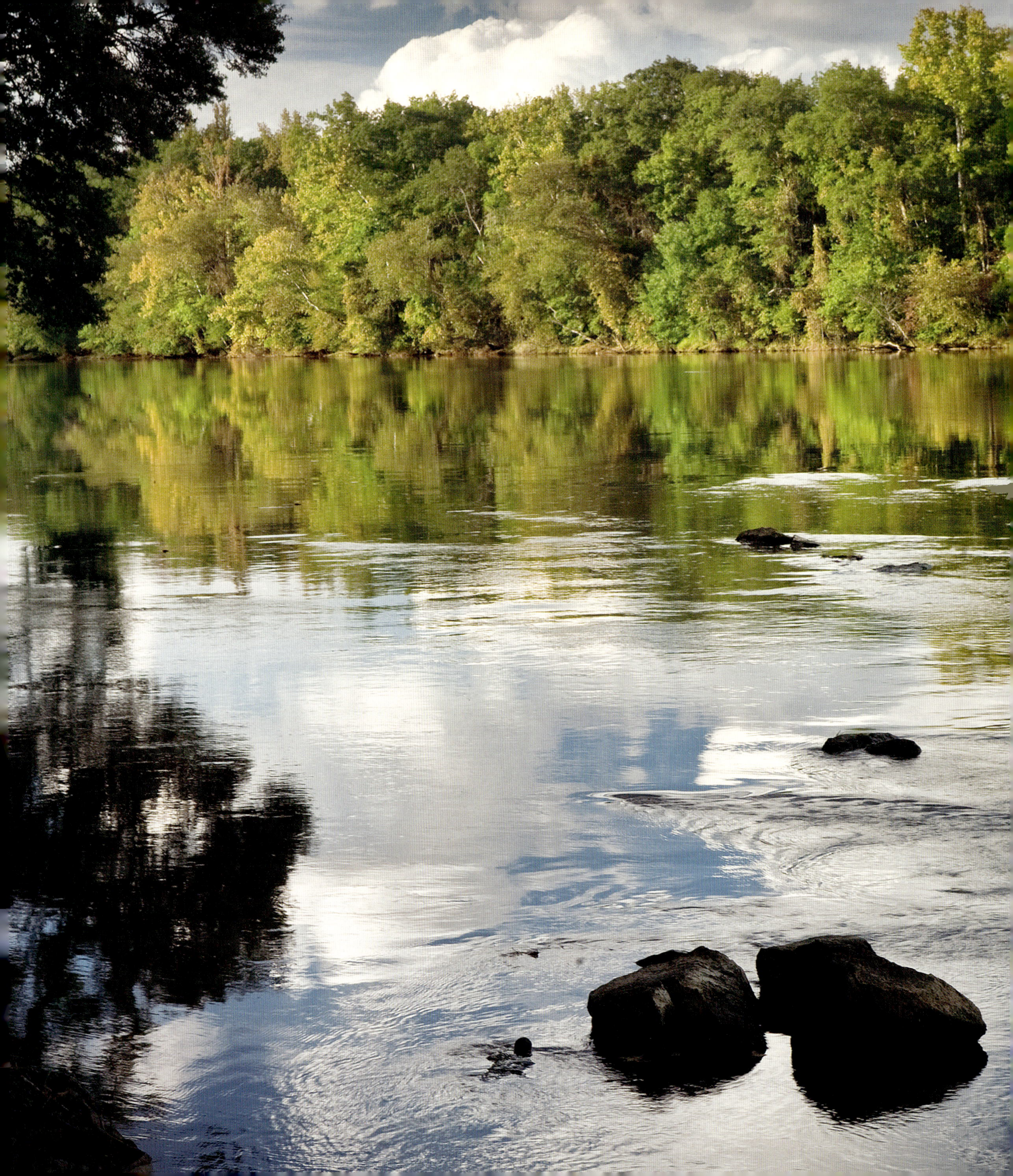

Landsford Canal State Park
National Landmark, National Register of Historic Places

Ruins of a canal system that made the Catawba River commercially navigable from 1820 to 1835 exist here. Come May–June kayakers and crowds come to see the world's largest colony of rocky shoals spider lilies.

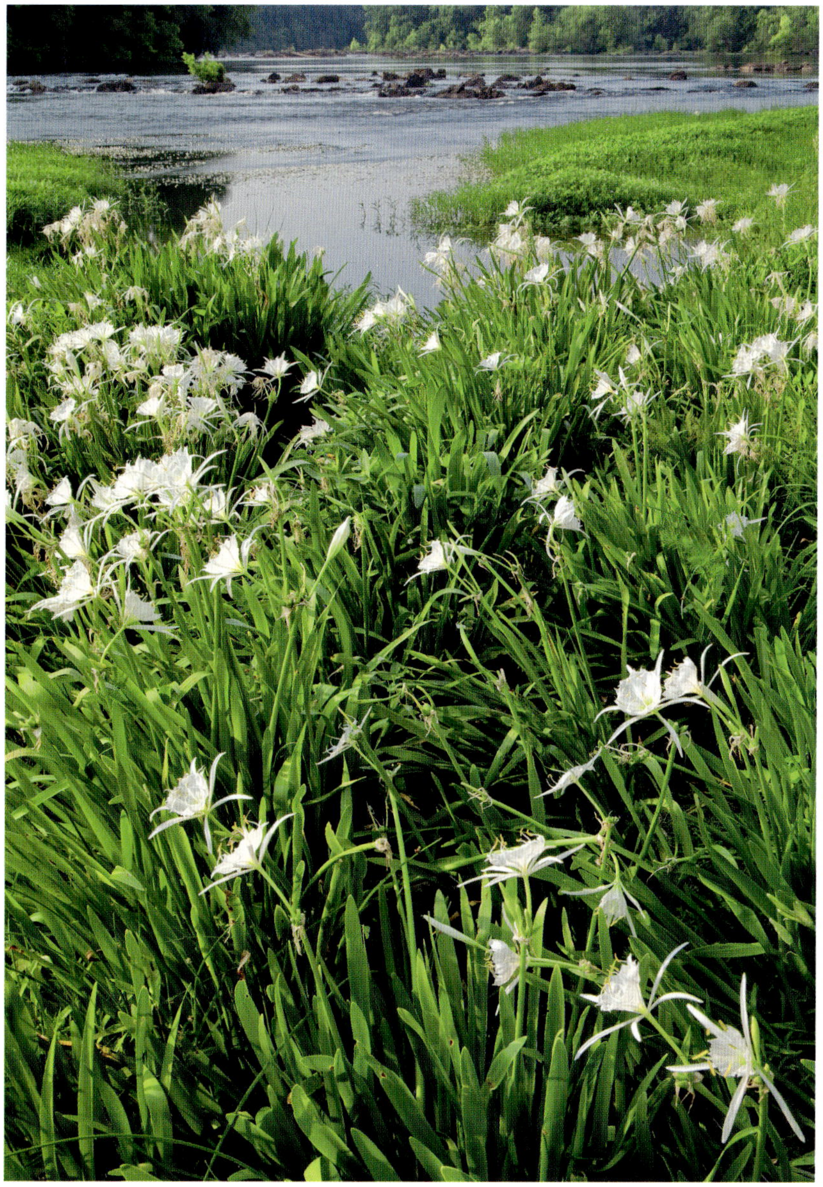

Rocky Shoals Spider Lilies at Landsford Canal

The rocky shoals spider lily (*Hymenocallis coronaria*) requires swift, shallow water, rocks, and sunlight, but damming rivers leave them few places to grow now. On the Catawba River near Chester County's Landsford Canal State Park, you can see the largest known colony of rocky shoals spider lilies. Blooming from early May to mid-June, a white blanket of blossoms covers the river. The lilies exist in just three states, South Carolina, Georgia, and Alabama. Not a true lily, the rocky shoals spider lily belongs to the amaryllis family, which includes jonquils, narcissus, and daffodils.

The Anne Springs Close Greenway

The Anne Springs Close Greenway is a preserve in Fort Mill where 2,100 acres buffer urban development and provide a wide-open space for hiking, biking, horseback riding, picnics, kayaking, and more. The land possesses ties to the Catawba Indians and the Civil War. A membership-driven preserve, the public can access its forests and waters for a fee. The children of Anne Springs Close donated the land in honor of her lifelong commitment to recreation. Here at the Founders Dairy Barn people celebrate a wedding.

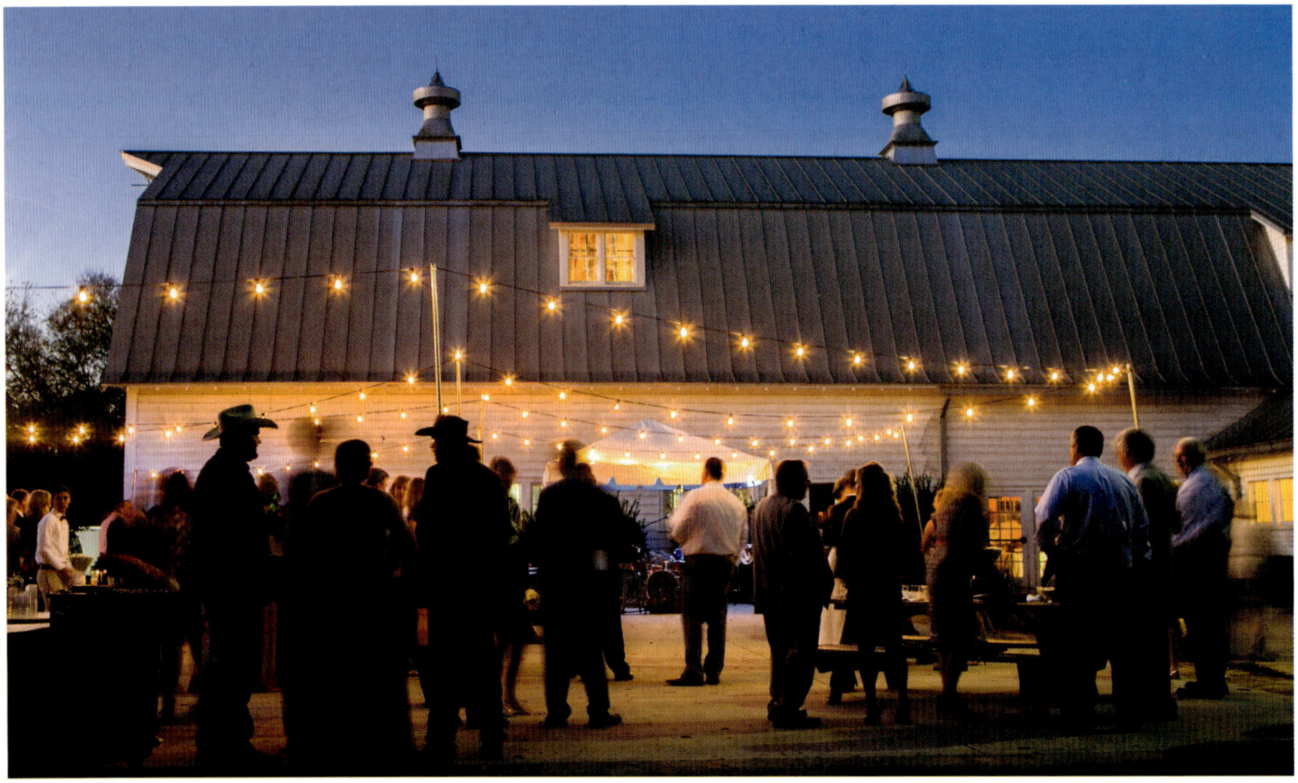

Glencairn Garden

Rock Hill's Glencairn Garden started as David and Hazel Bigger's backyard garden in 1928. It grew into an eleven-acre paradise. A Who's Who of flowering species airbrushes the garden with tints, tones, and hues thanks to azaleas, camellias, dogwoods, other flowering trees, wisteria, and more. Glencairn Garden inspired Rock Hill's annual Come-See-Me Festival. For more than fifty years, Glencairn Garden has showcased nature's finest colors, textures, and shapes. Here you'll find a veteran's garden, tiered fountains, ponds, boardwalks, a stage, and a great place to walk flower-filled alleys.

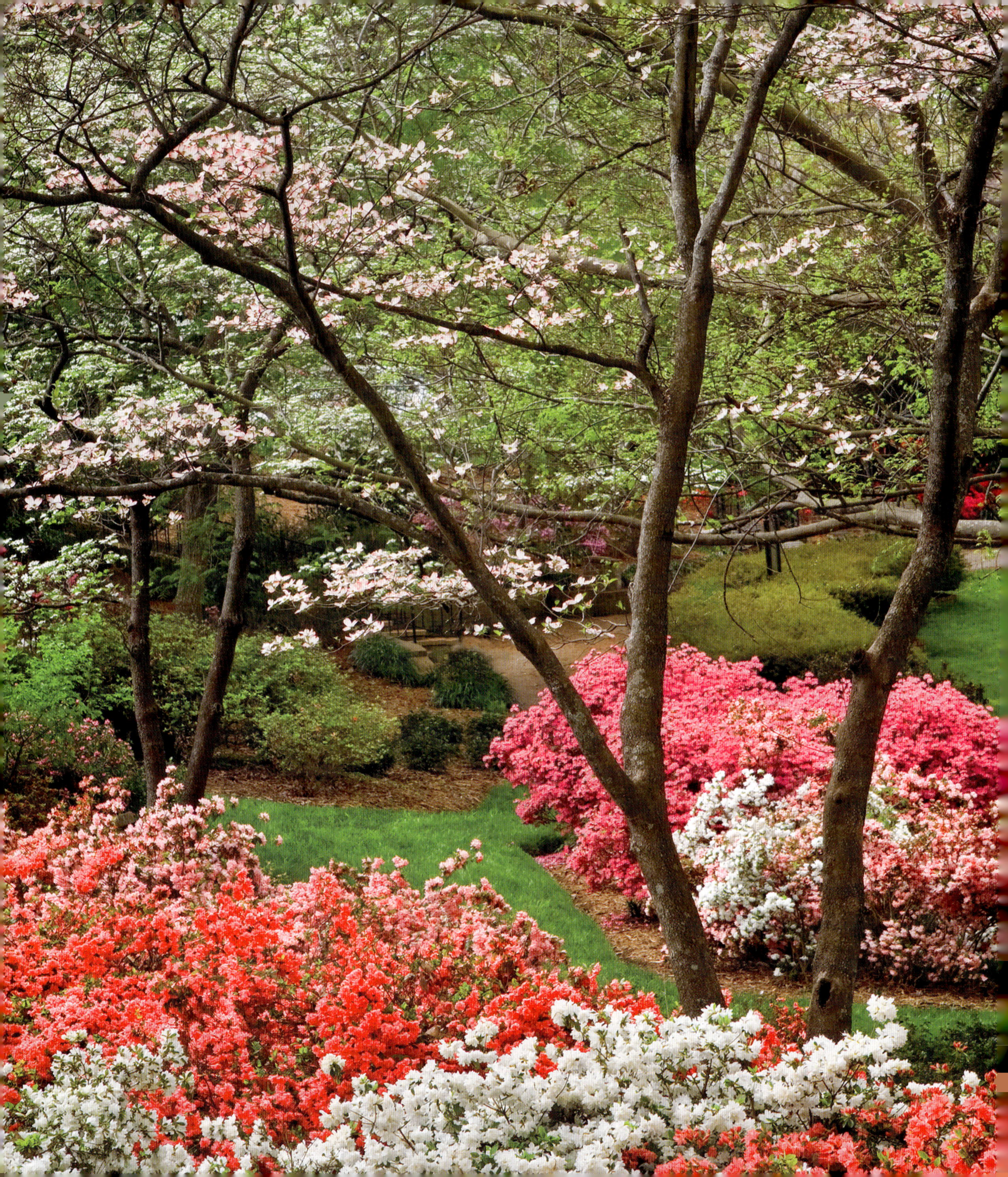

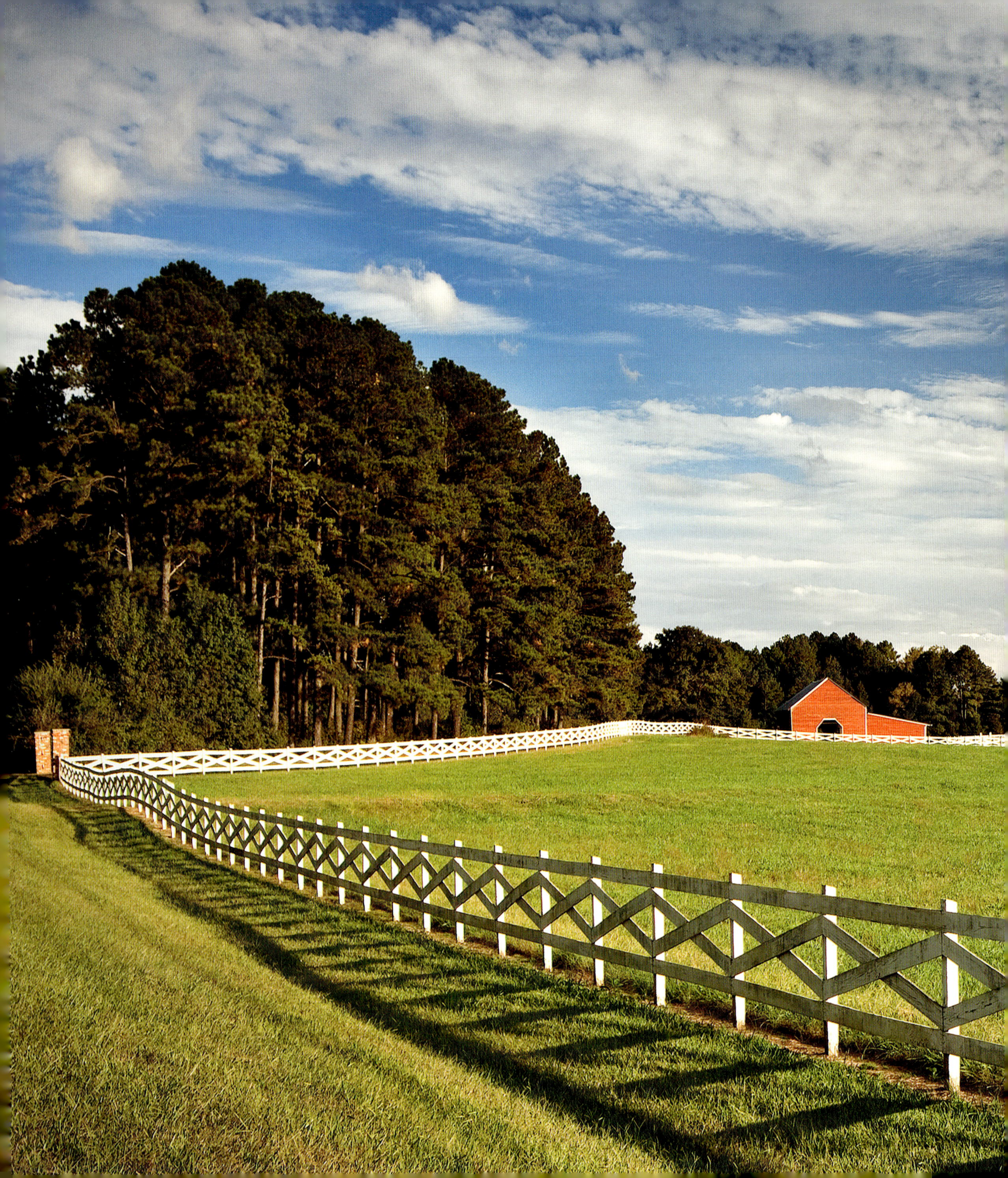

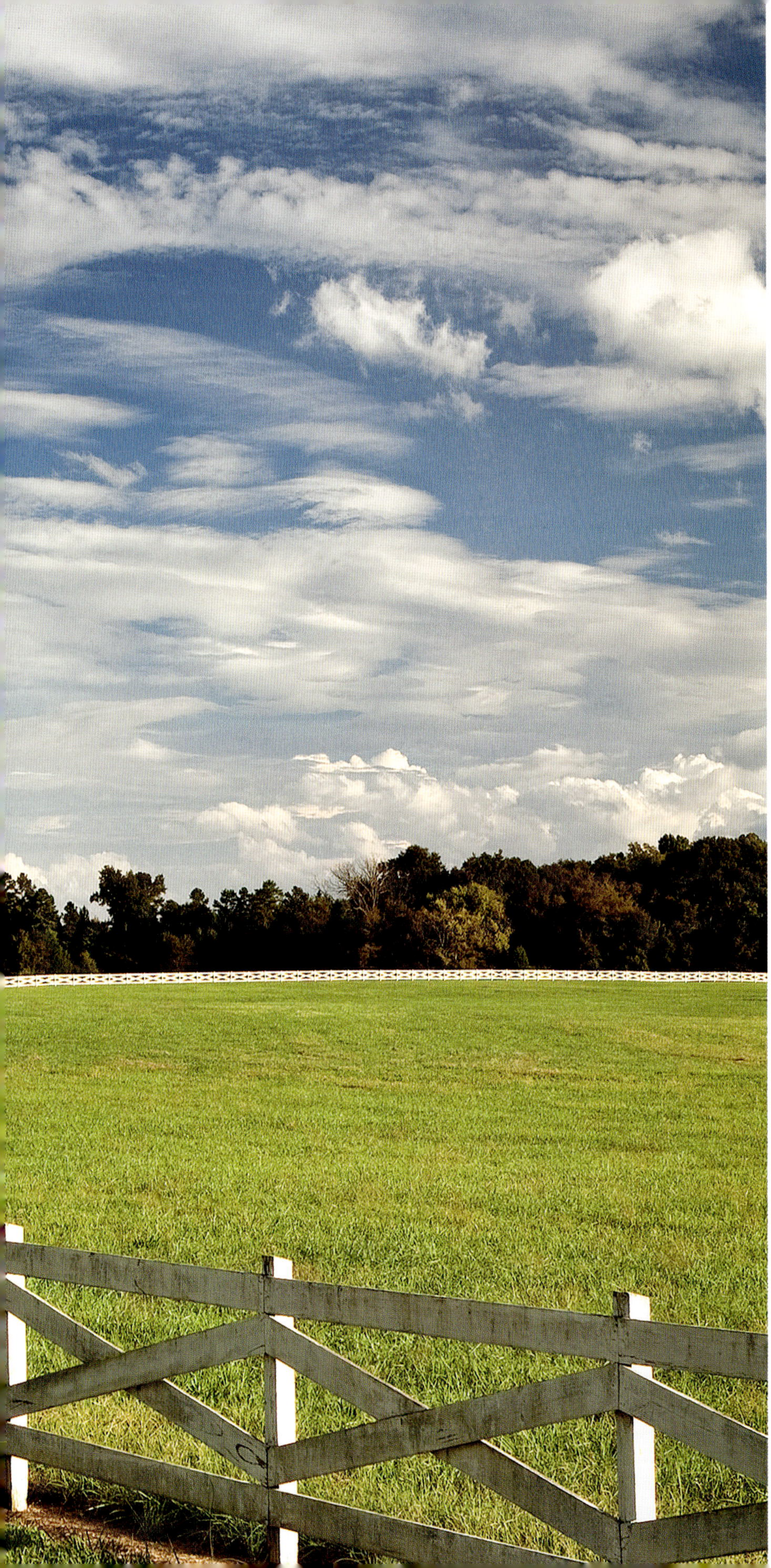

A Classic Farm Setting

Swirling clouds, red barn, green pastureland, and white fence make for a beautiful agrarian setting in Chester County. The barn rises as if it's part of the earth—and it very much is.

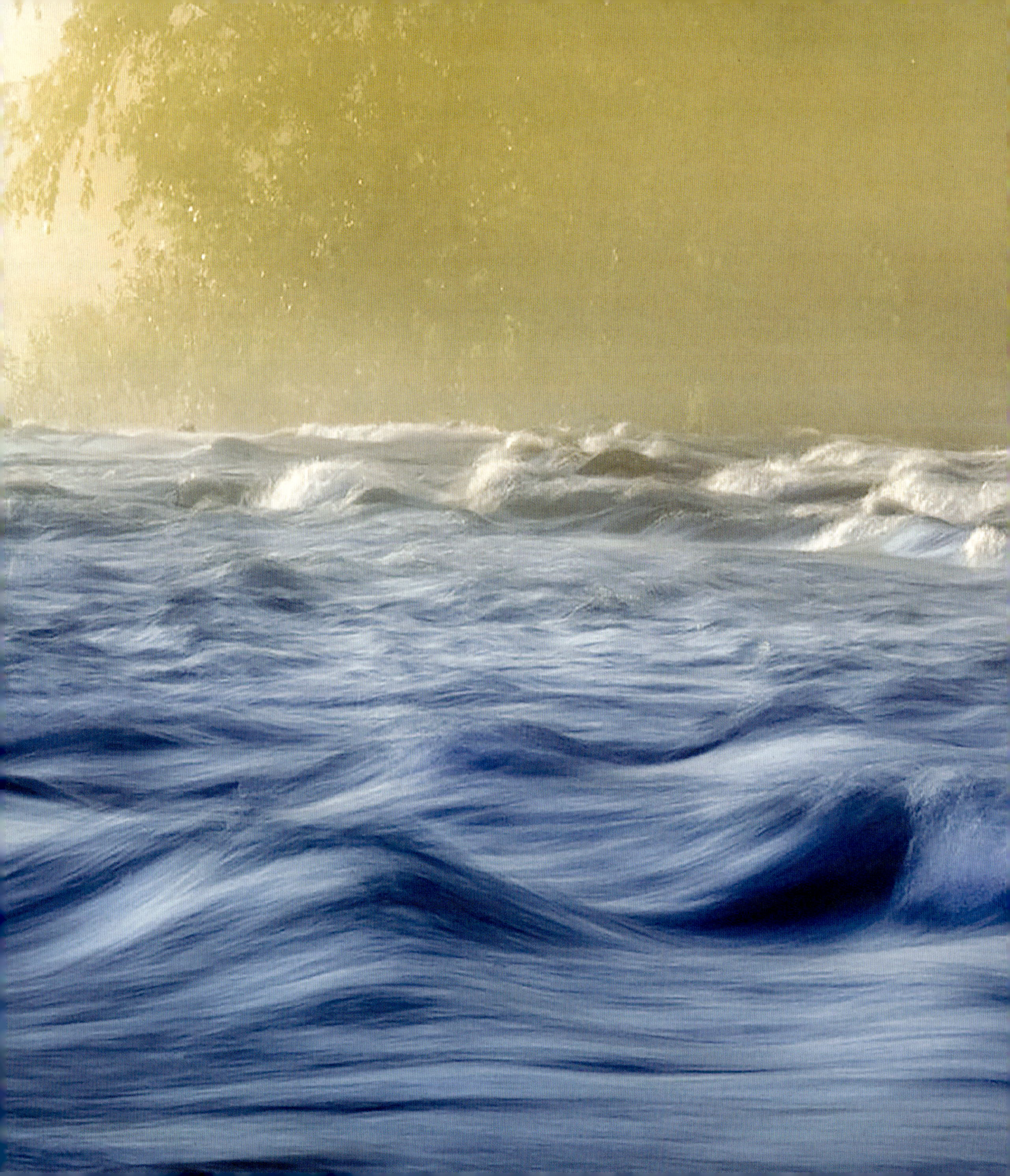

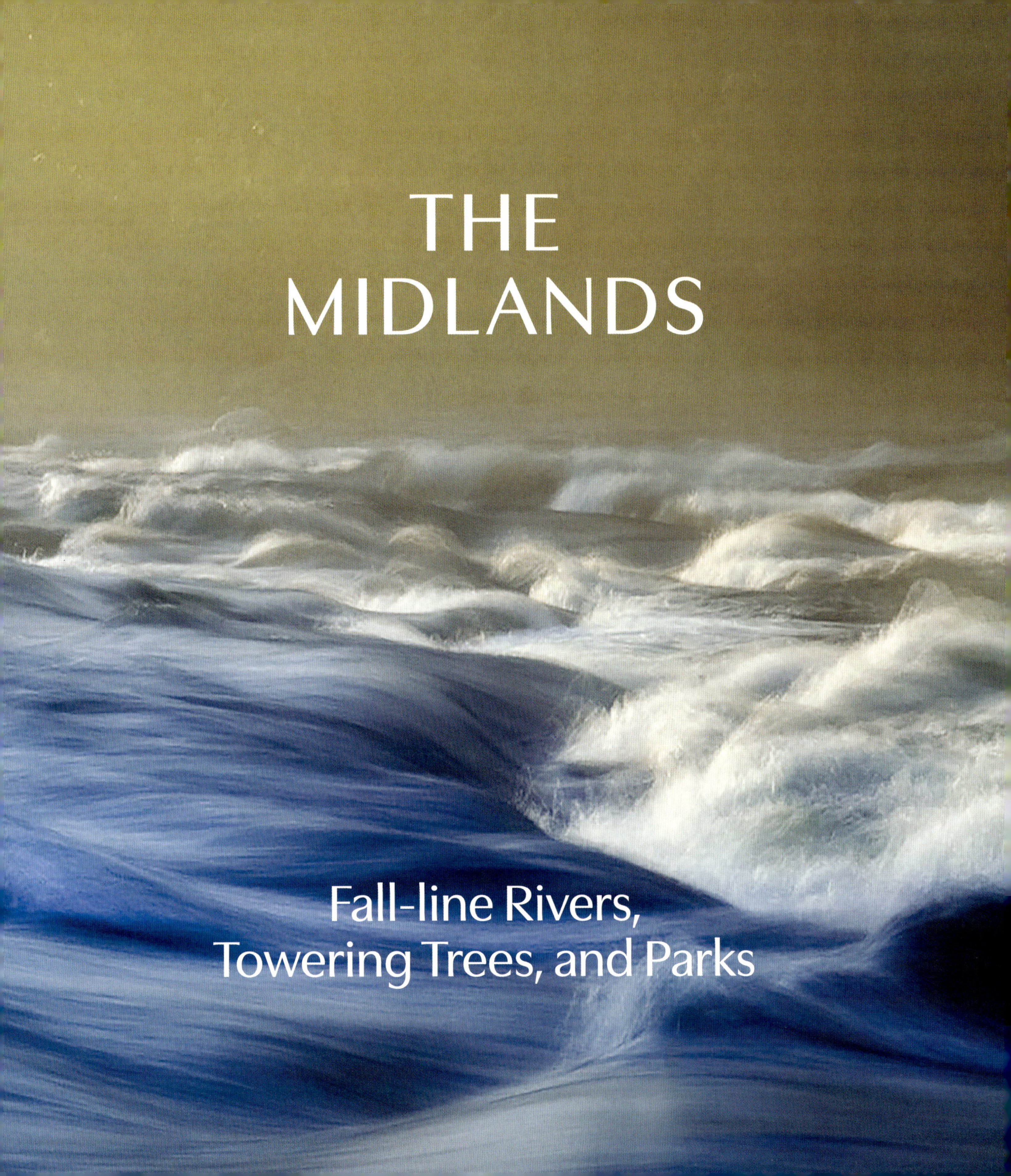

THE MIDLANDS

Fall-line Rivers, Towering Trees, and Parks

OVERLEAF

Saluda River at Daybreak

Just minutes after sunrise, the Lower Saluda River's riffles and rapids reveal the fall line, the end of navigable waters. Many cities sprang up where rivers intersect the Atlantic Seaboard fall line. Here, near downtown Columbia where hard rock meets the sandy alluvial plain, blue water turns white as it crosses into the Inner Coastal Plain.

Gifts aplenty bless the Midlands, gifts like the state's only national park, a crown jewel known as the Congaree National Park. In this region of history, culture, and charm, you'll find a hiking trail, the Cotton Trail, and two rivers that birth a third. You'll see gardens.

One of Sherman's soldiers penned a surprising apology on a Fairfield County church wall.

What's your pleasure? A blazing sunset over one of the state's older lakes. The glow of retro neon lights. A peach orchard in autumn. A relic from the Aermotor Windmill Company. How about the sport of kings, falconry?

Visit a classic tenant home in Saluda County. See historic Edgefield pottery. The secrecy surrounding grilling chickens. Lake City's ArtFields. Strike out and explore a rare snowfall, sculptures, historic churches, and old and new farming practices. That and more wait in the Midlands.

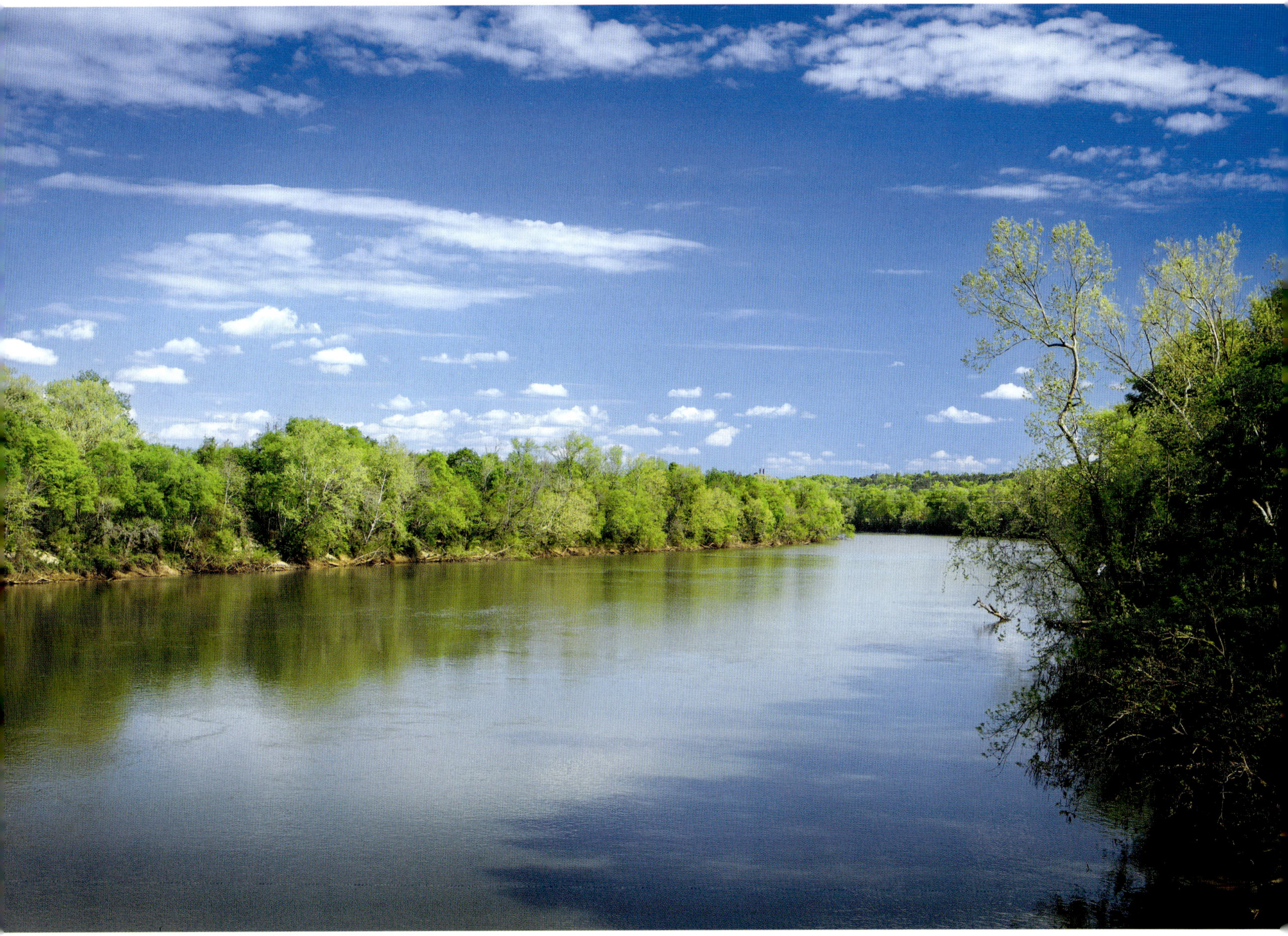

Broad River

Running strong near the Palmetto Trail, the Broad River is one of many rivers named "Broad." Another common name for rivers is "Little," both names from the early days when people identified rivers by their size.

Hopeland Gardens Reflections

Mrs. C. Oliver Iselin bequeathed this fourteen-acre estate to the City of Aiken on her death at the age of 102. Hopeland Gardens opened in 1969 as a public garden, and its reflecting pool, statuary, fountains, and tree-shaded pathways provide tranquility and beauty.

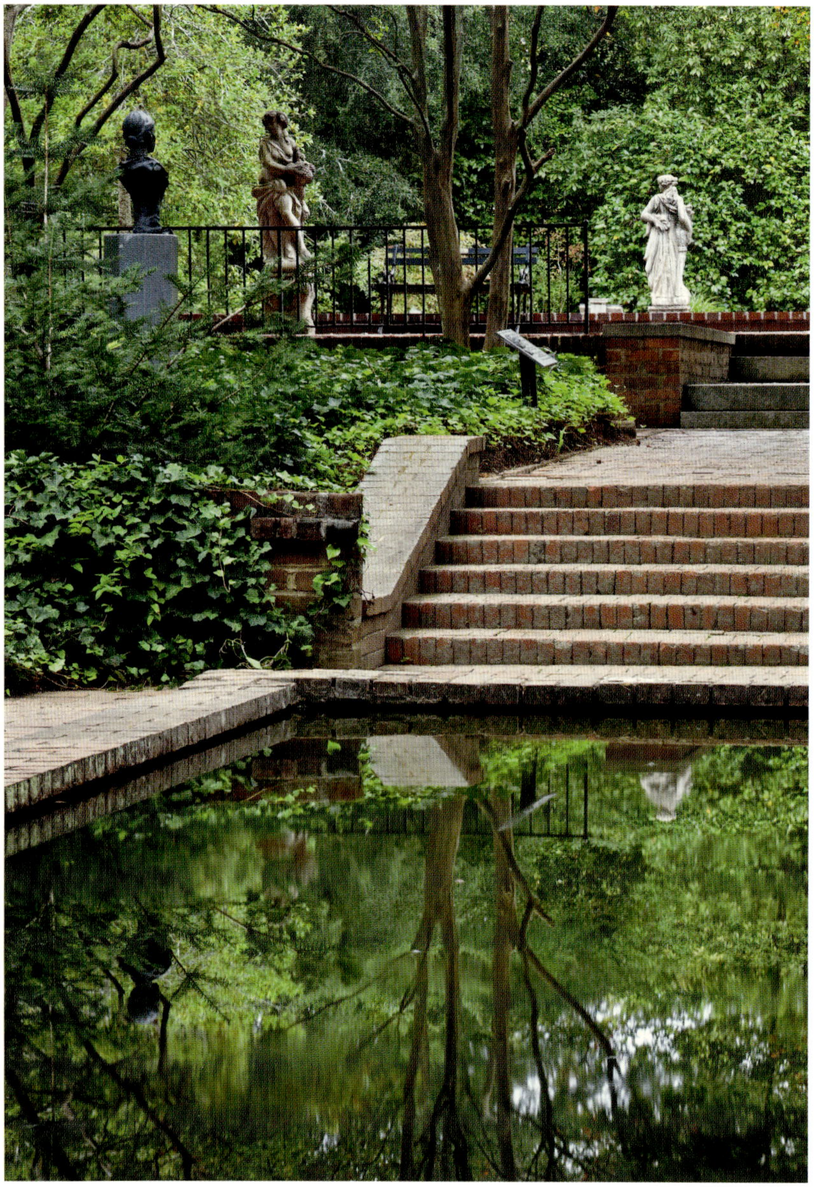

Wateree Sunset

Clouds reflect the sun's aurora-like display over the lake old timers call "the River." Over a seven-year span, folk artist Harold Branham painted Lake Wateree throughout the seasons. His coverage included a full moon over the lake, a lonely fisherman on a bridge, a foraging egret, a white-capping lake, a snow-covered dock, burnt-orange cypress, and other seasonal portraits of one of South Carolina's older manmade lakes.

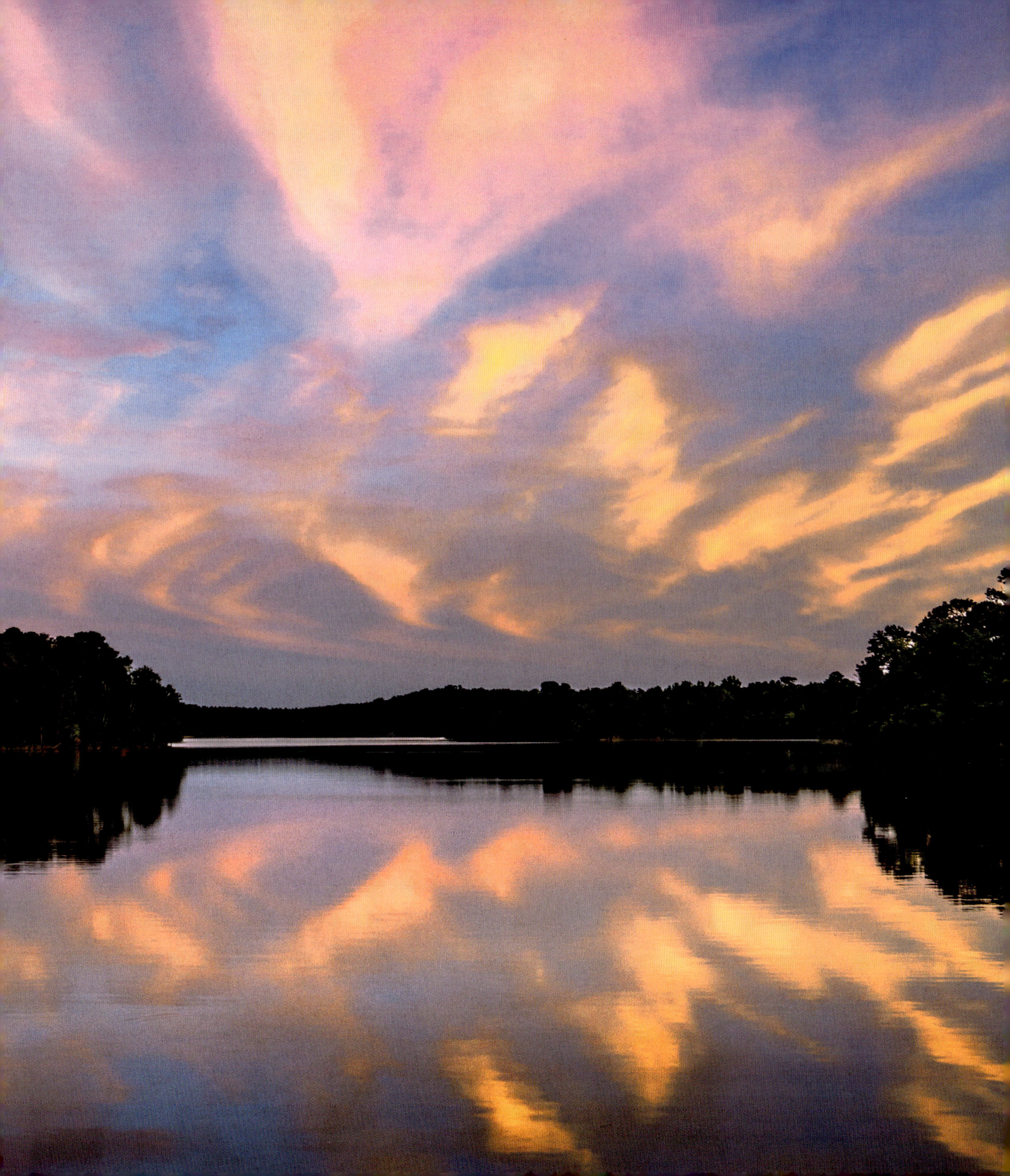

Purcells Goes Retro

Neon's golden age reigned from the 1920s to the '60s. Safety issues, inefficiency, cost, and newer technologies hurt neon's popularity. Purcells's retro look adds a touch of nostalgia for passersby.

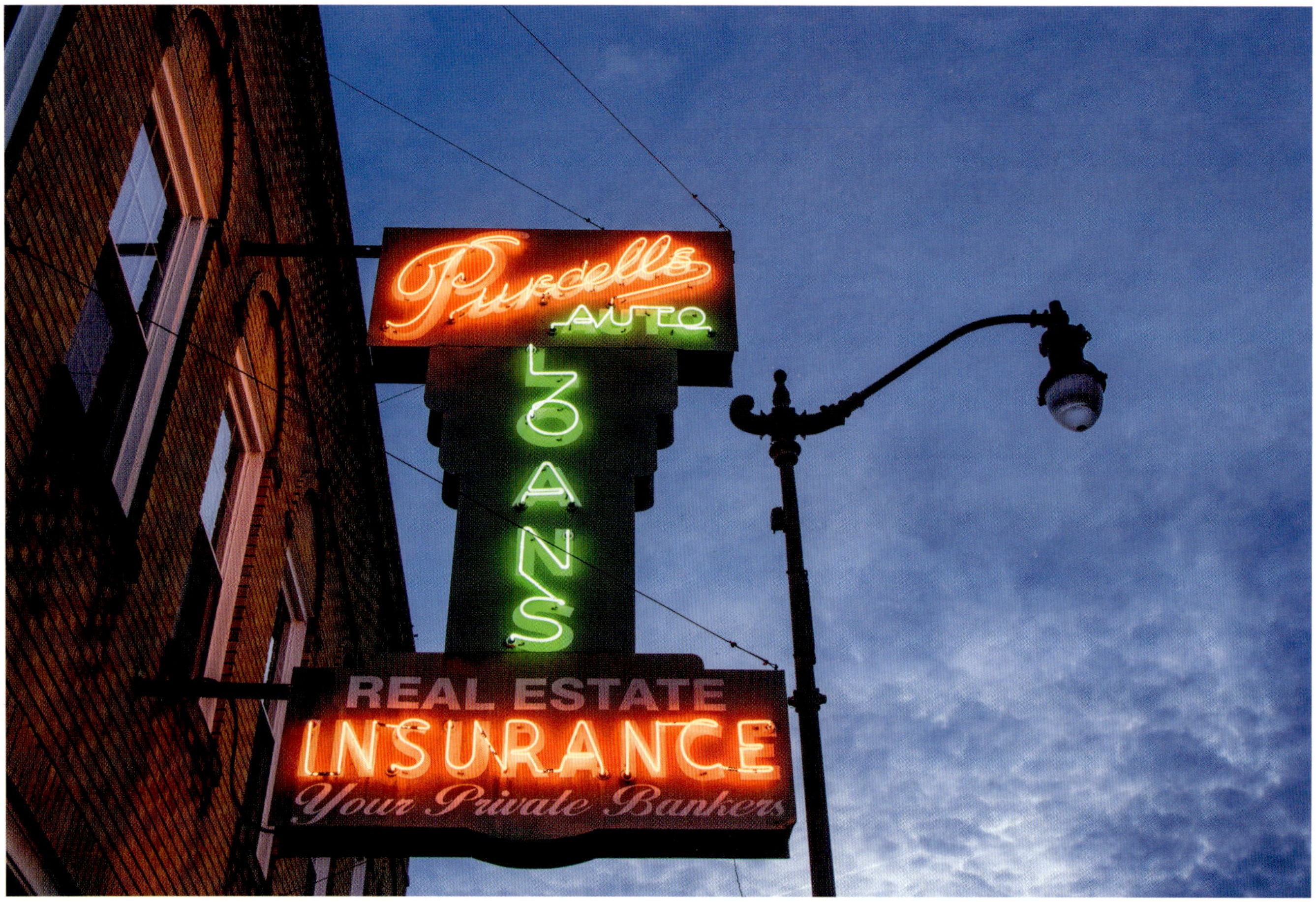

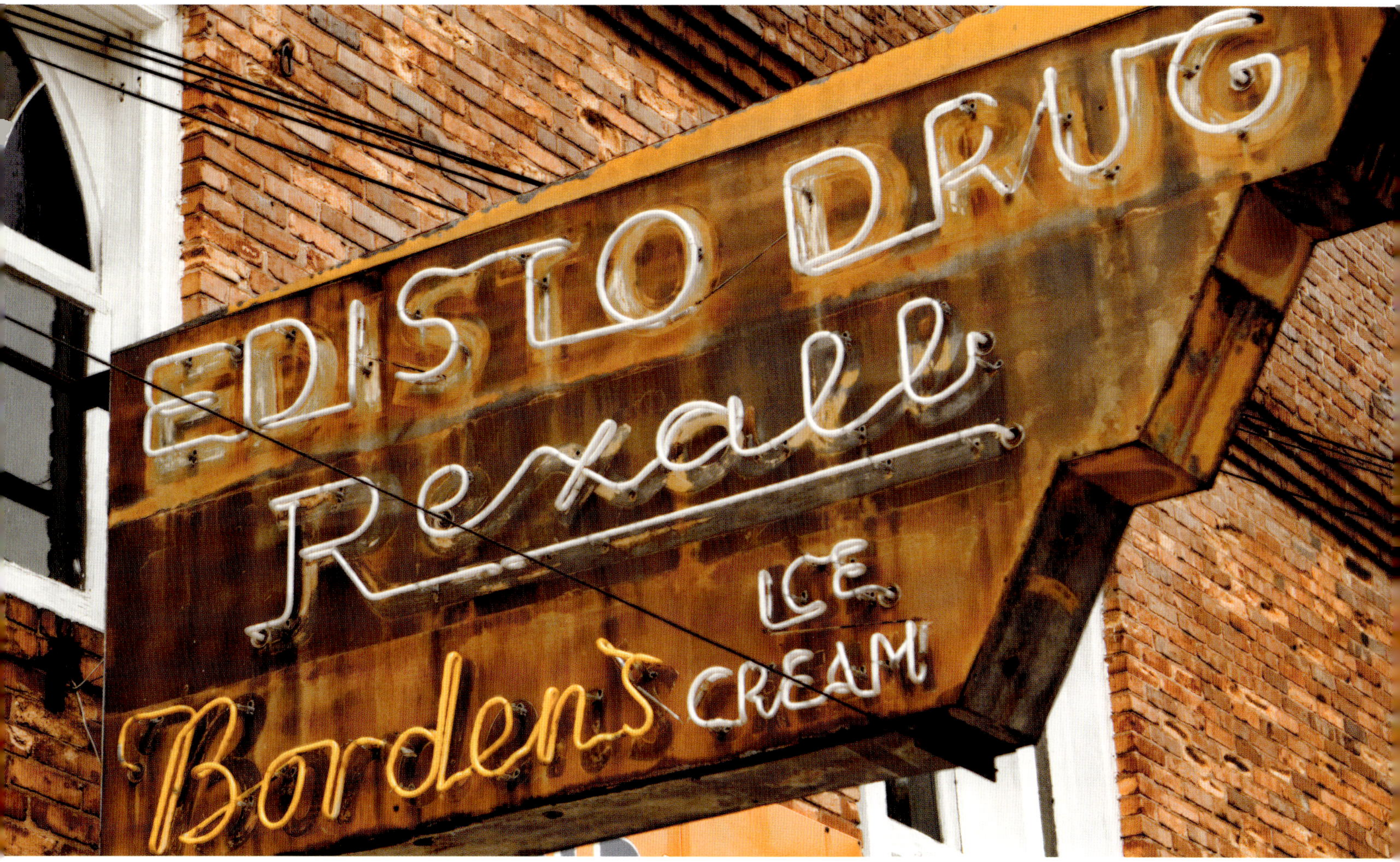

Edisto Drug

This classic drugstore sign in Springfield conjures images of an old marble fountain, soda jerk, and ice-cream sundaes. An honest-to-goodness old-fashioned cash register rings up sales.

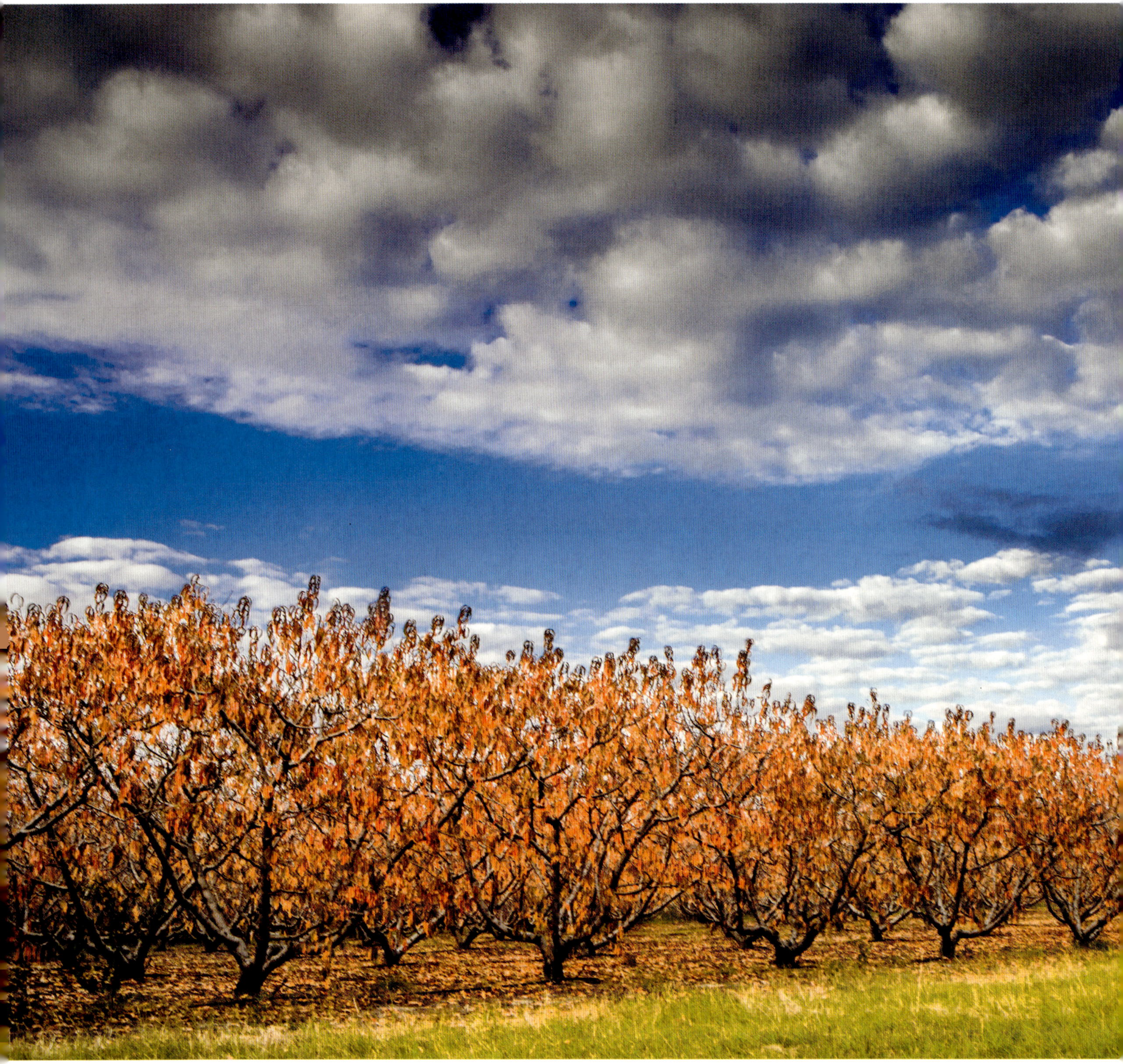

Autumn in the Orchard

An orchard along US 1 near McBee in the fall has its own beauty. Bare trees overwinter and then turn pink in springtime, and the cycle repeats. March orchards burn as if their trees hold thousands of pink candles afire.

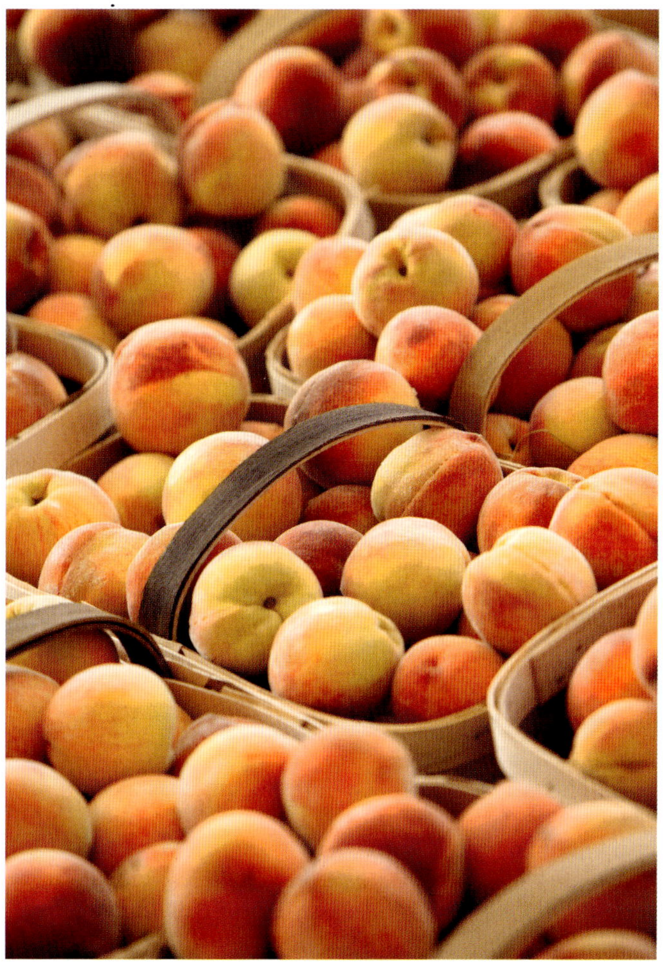

Along the Ridge

Peaches heap up from split-oak baskets along the Ridge, a sixty-mile-long, fifteen-mile-wide region of sandy, loamy soil ideal for growing peaches. Cold air, like water, seeks its lowest point. Damaging cold air flows away from orchards along the Ridge. Note the crease running from one end of the peach to the other: it's called the suture.

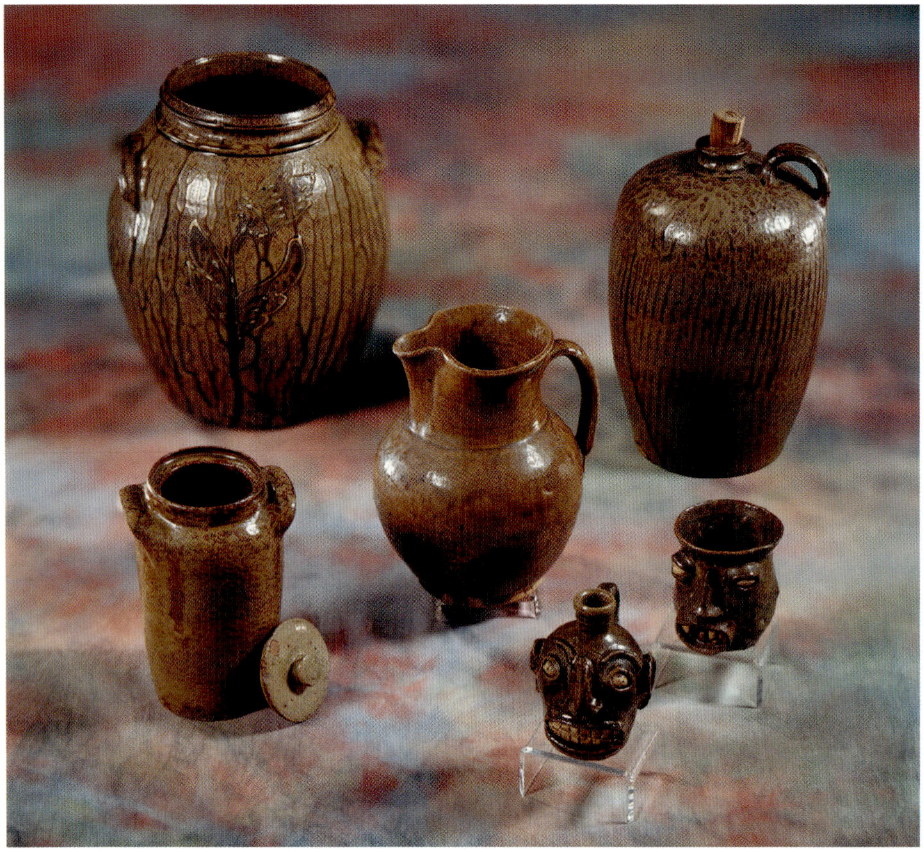

Saluda County Tenant Home

Built as saltbox houses, catslides, and pole cabins, tenant homes long stood with grace and character in pastures and fields. When mules, plows, and hoes gave way to mechanized agriculture, tenants began to abandon them. All that's left of many are chimneys, a pile of bricks, and field stones. Not so, this elegant Saluda home in a field of mown hay.

Edgefield Pottery

Dr. Abner Landrum established the Edgefield Pottery tradition in the early 1800s. Other potteries sprang up across Edgefield District. For over two centuries, Landrum, Chandler, Rhodes, Storke, David Drake, Miles, Baynham, and Hahn made Edgefield pottery. The tradition carries on. These pots are from the collection of the McKissick Museum, University of South Carolina.

Top left: Storage Jar, Collin Rhodes, Collin Rhodes Factory, Shaws Creek, Edgefield District, Alkaline-glazed stoneware, 14⅛ in. Gift to the University through the South Caroliniana Library, 5.105. *Bottom left*: Preserve Jar with Cover, Maker Unknown, Edgefield, South Carolina, ca. 1845, Alkaline-glazed stoneware, 8¾ in. Museum Purchase, 1995.12.00.02. *Center*: Pitcher, Maker Unknown, Edgefield, South Carolina, ca. 1850, Alkaline-glazed stoneware, 10 in. Museum Purchase, 1999.01.00.01. *Top right*: Jug, Maker Unknown, South Carolina, ca. 1890, Alkaline-glazed stoneware, 13¾ in. Gift to the University through the South Caroliniana Library, 6.2035. *Bottom center*: Face Vessel, Maker Unknown, Edgefield, South Carolina, ca. 1860, Alkaline-glazed stoneware, 5¾ in. Gift of Mr. and Mrs. James P. Barrow, 1998.37.120.01. *Bottom right*: Face Cup, Maker Unknown, Edgefield, South Carolina, ca. 1860, Alkaline-glazed stoneware, 5½ in. Gift of Mr. and Mrs. James P. Barrow, 1998.37.120.02.

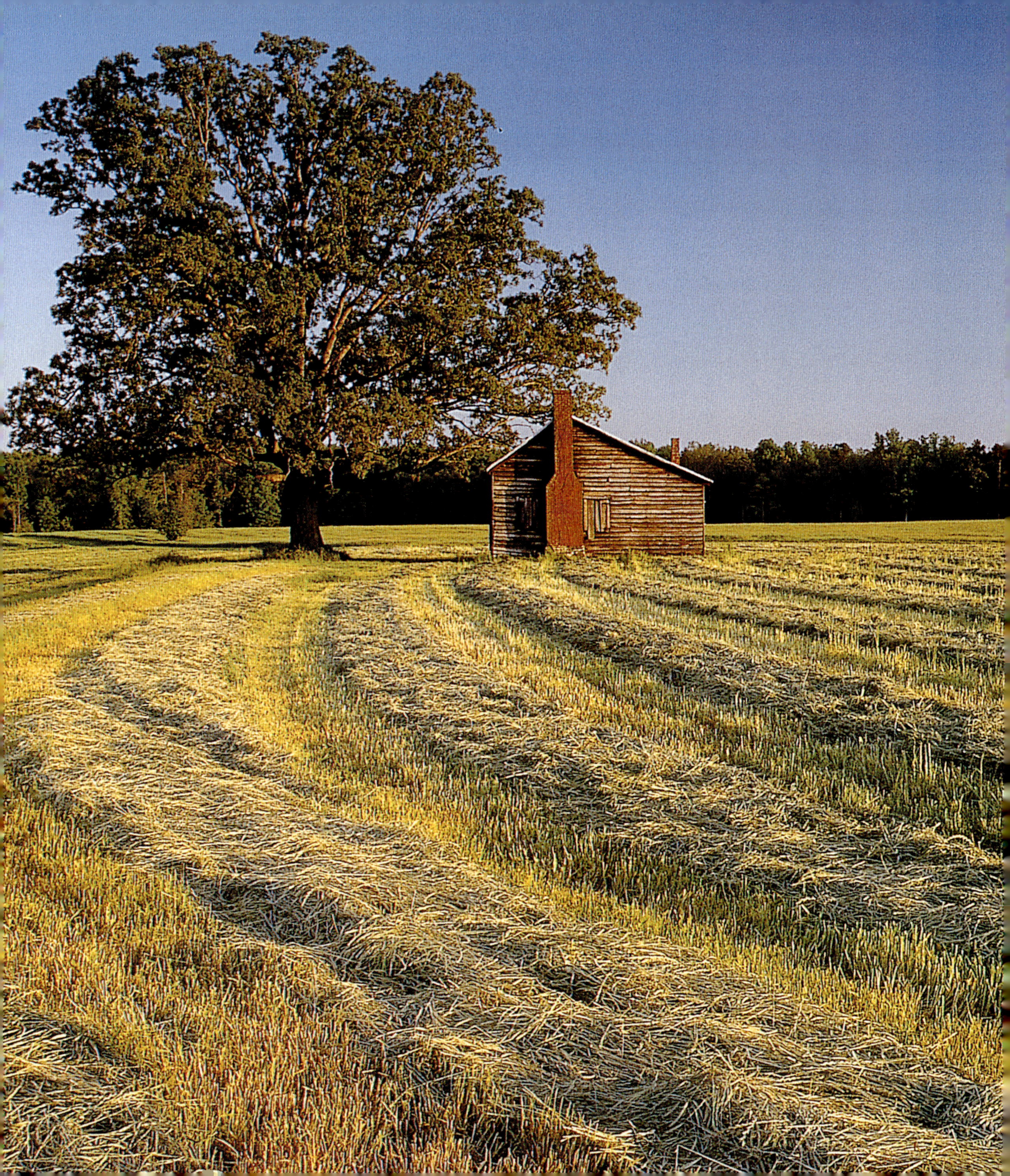

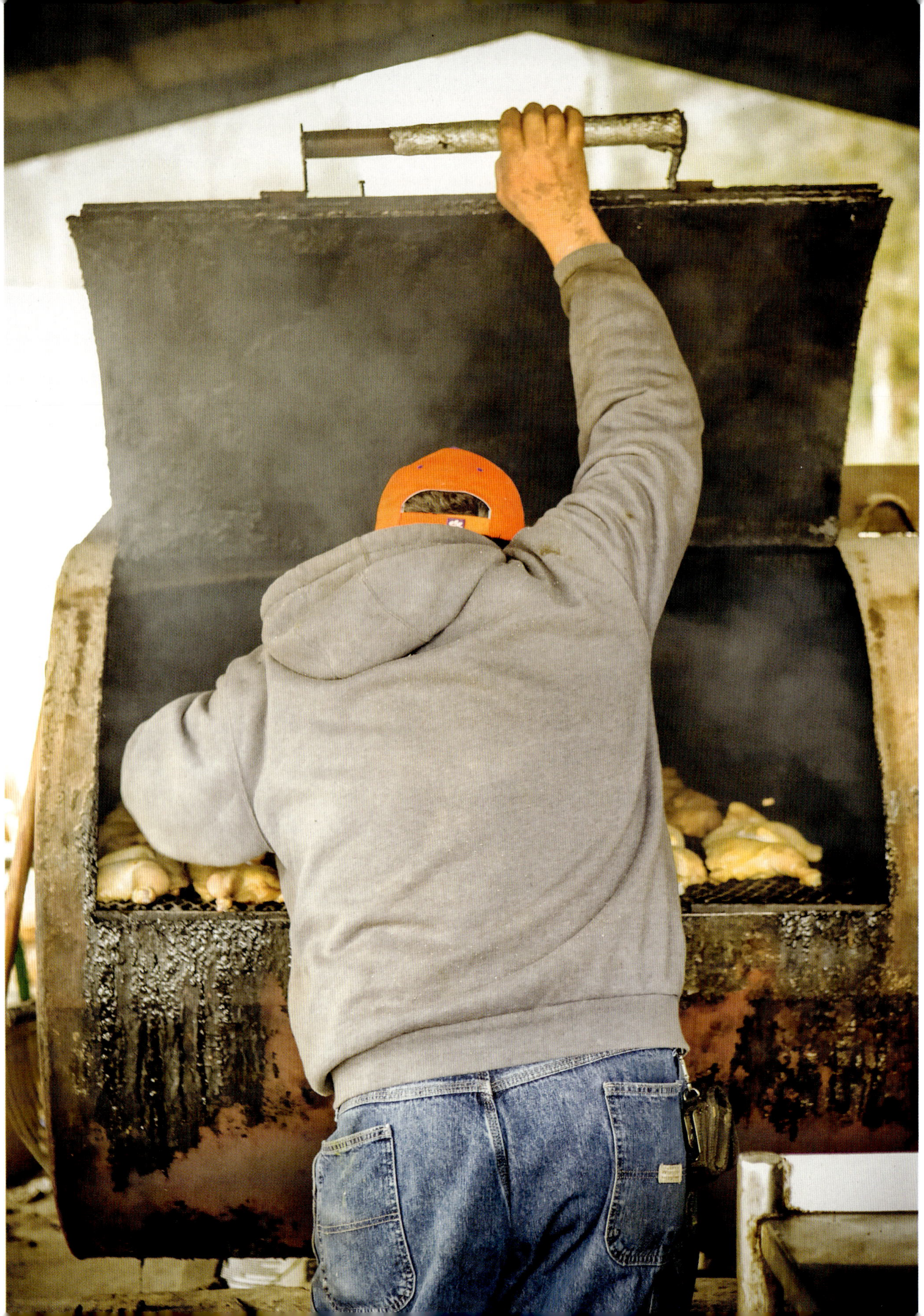

Takin' a Peek

Many a BBQ connoisseur approaches grilling with secrecy. Grilling the chicken over high heat is an elaborate process involving time, temperature, and technique. Don't confuse amateurs with aficionados, and we haven't even mentioned sauces.

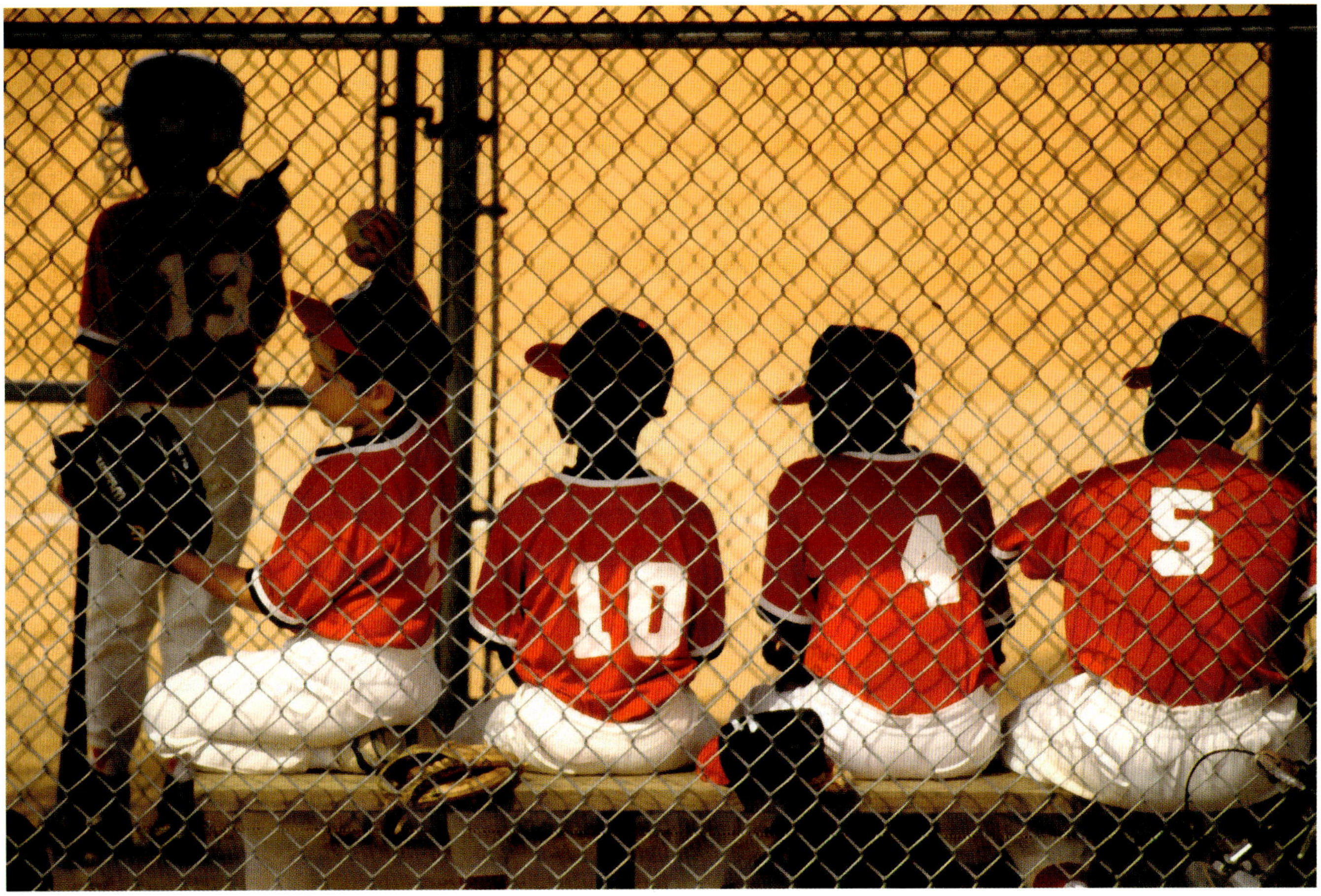

The Boys of Summer

The All-American pastime attracts boys who dream of playing in the big leagues someday. For now, this Lexington County dugout will do quite nicely.

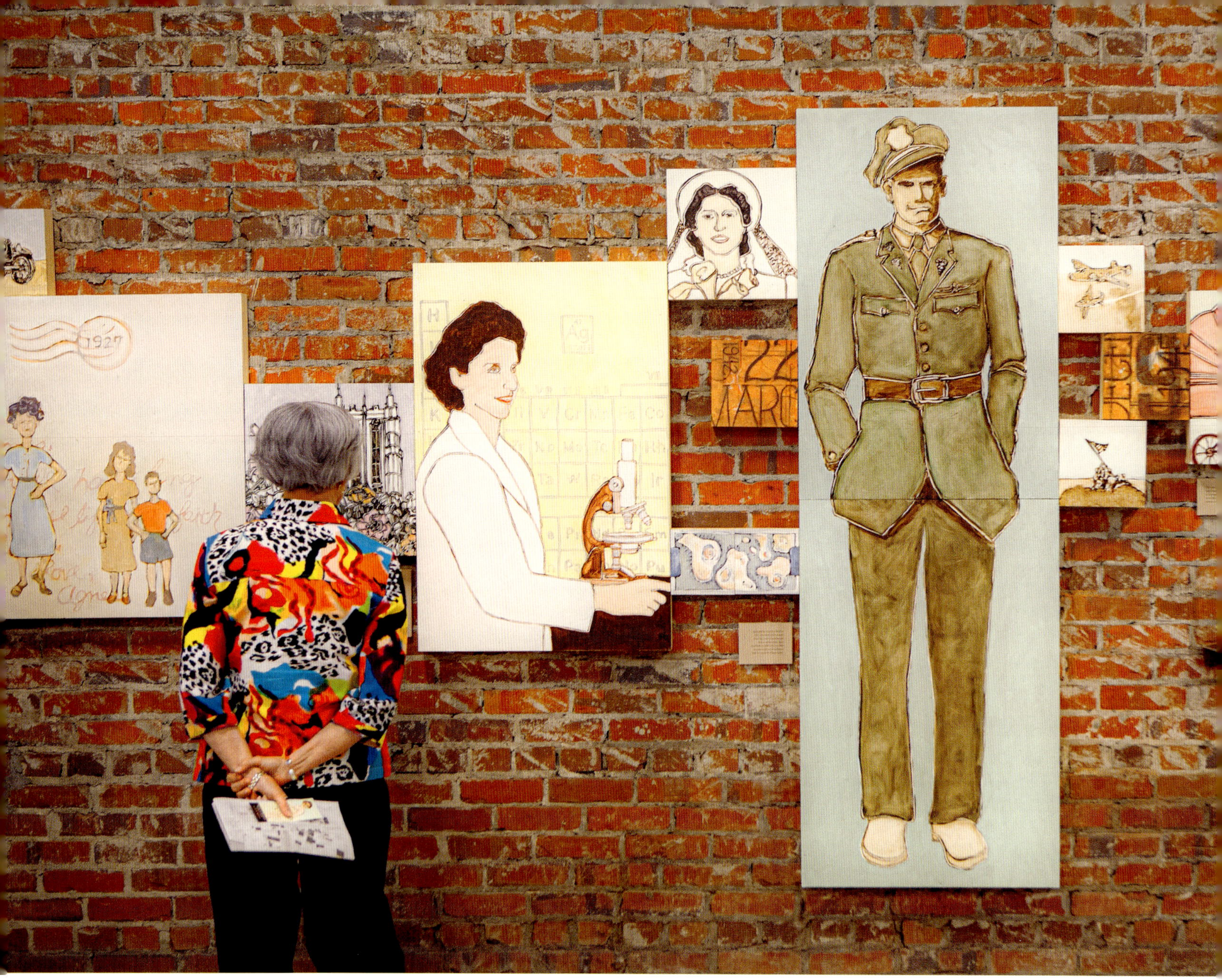

ArtFields

Lake City was once the bean capital of the world. As in Bean Market days, all roads lead to Lake City come April–May. Philanthropist and Lake City native Darla Moore grew up watching farmers employ creativity to sell their crops at market. A creative gardening project on her ancestral farm inspired Moore to support "The South's Most Engaging Art Festival and Competition," known as ArtFields today.

Lake City Community Mural

During ArtFields, Lake City provided wall space and spray paint so visitors and town people could contribute to a community mural.

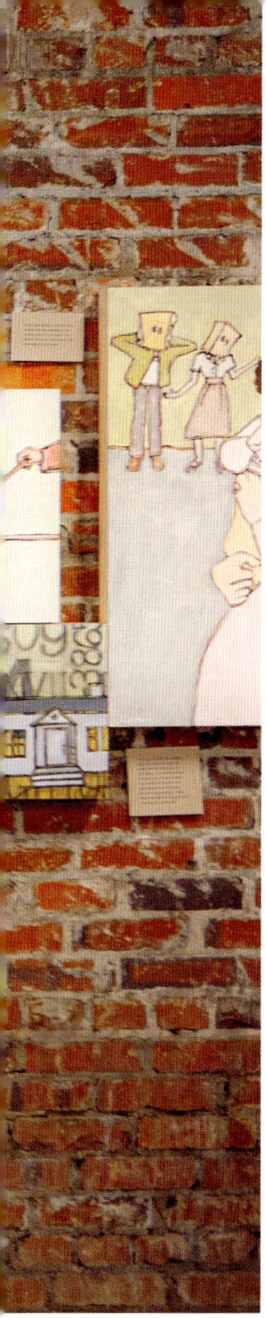

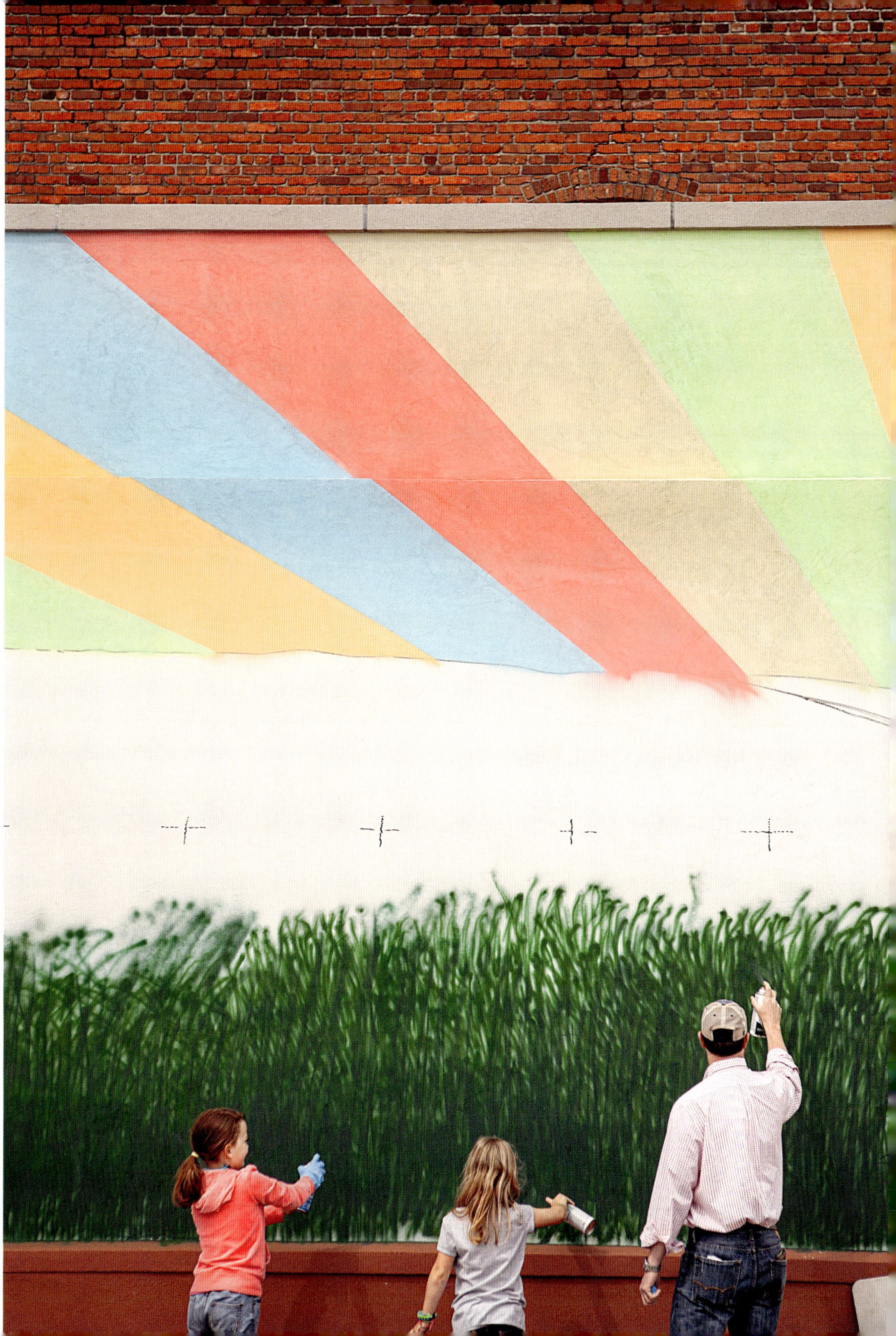

Wind Power

This relic from an old farm harnessed wind to pump water from the ground. The Aermotor Windmill Company still manufactures wind-powered water pumps. A quintessential image of the American West, you'll find windmills throughout South Carolina, one beneath the rainbow in this case.

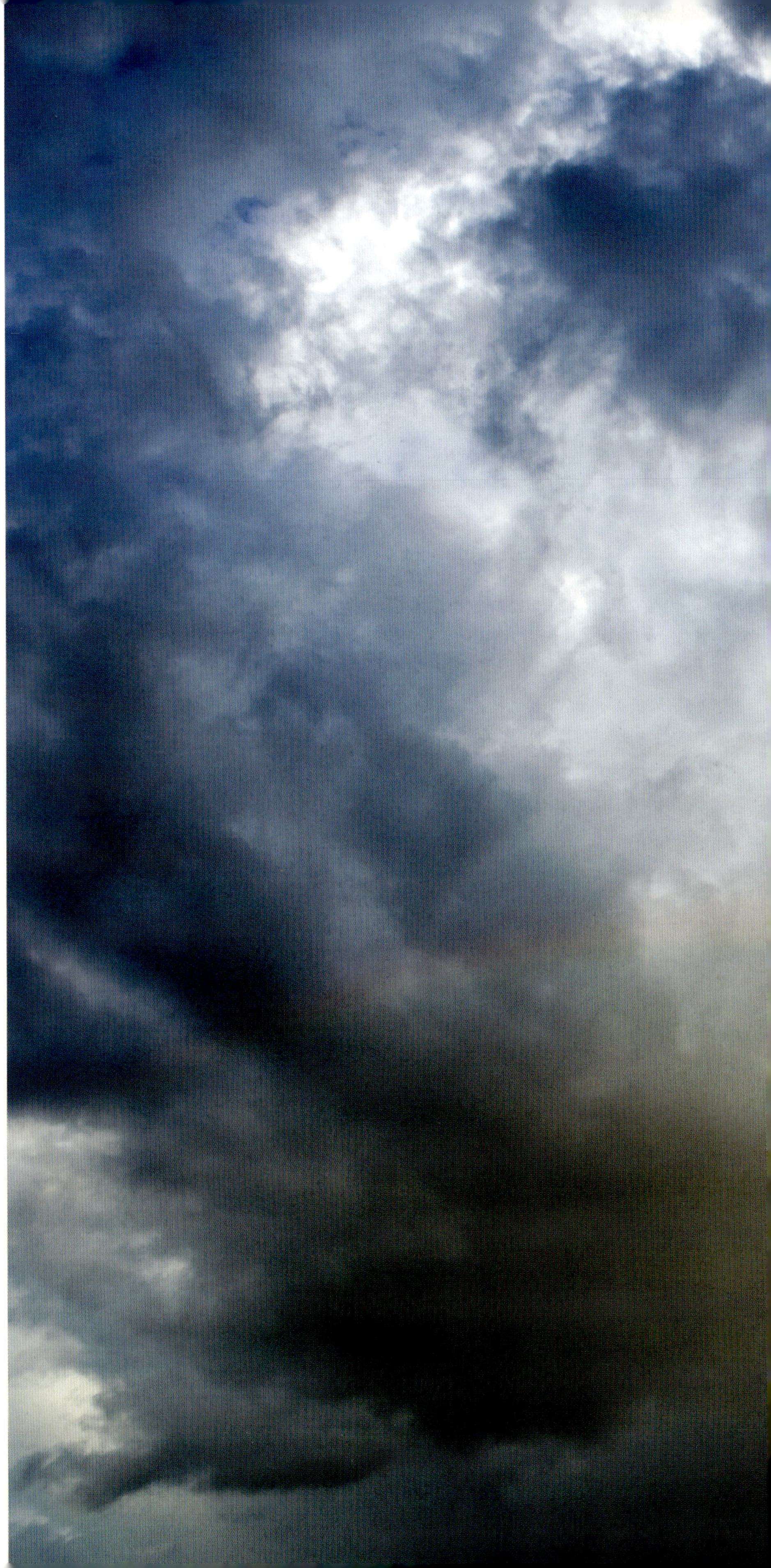

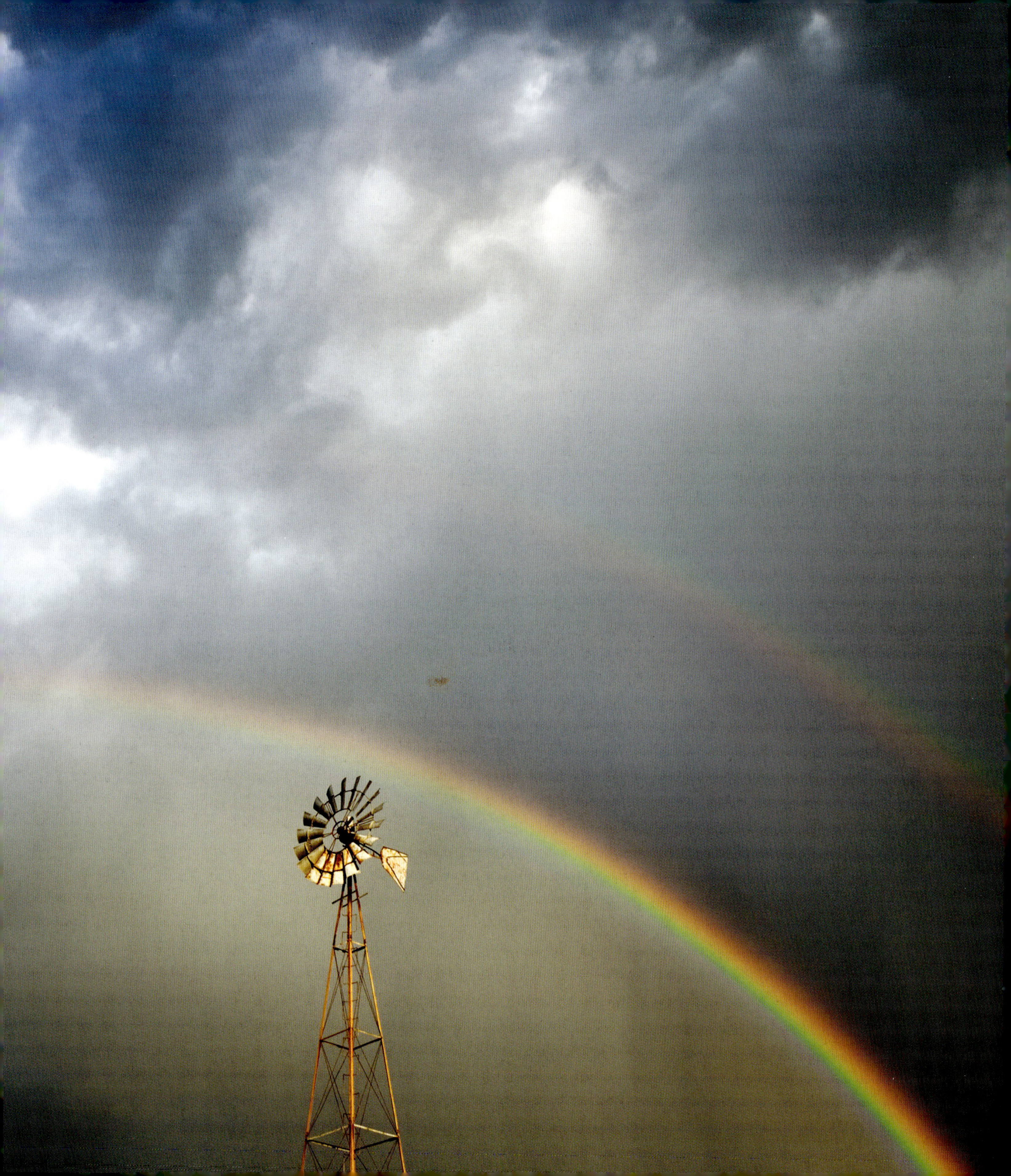

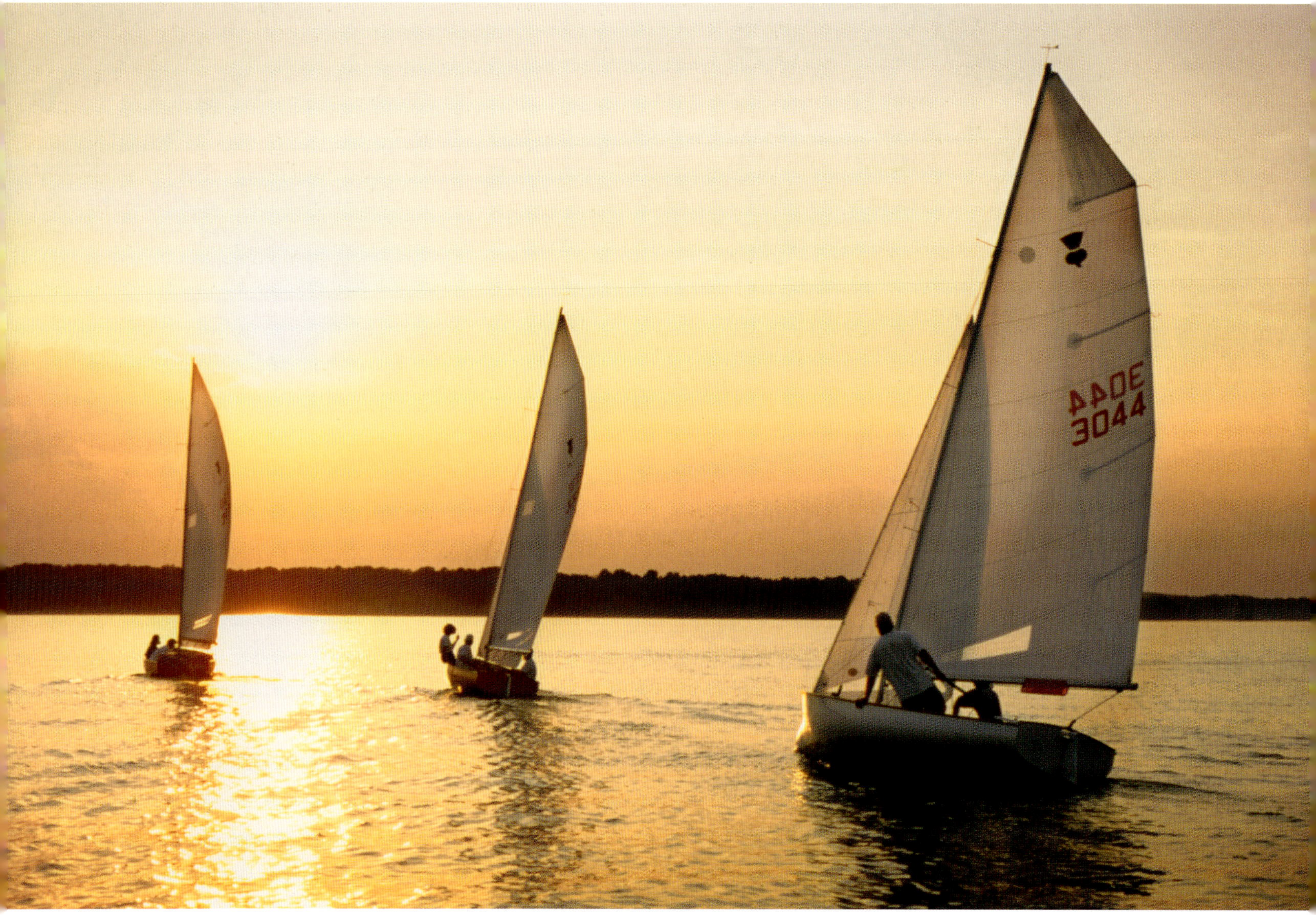

Toward the Light

Clear weather bodes well for these Lake Murray sailors slicing through blazing water.

State Park Sunrise

South Carolina state parks harbor 90,000 acres of protected lands. From the Blue Ridge Mountains to the Atlantic Ocean, state parks protect natural, cultural, and recreational destinations. With forty-seven state-park managed sites throughout the state, a state park, historic site, resort park, or recreational area is close by.

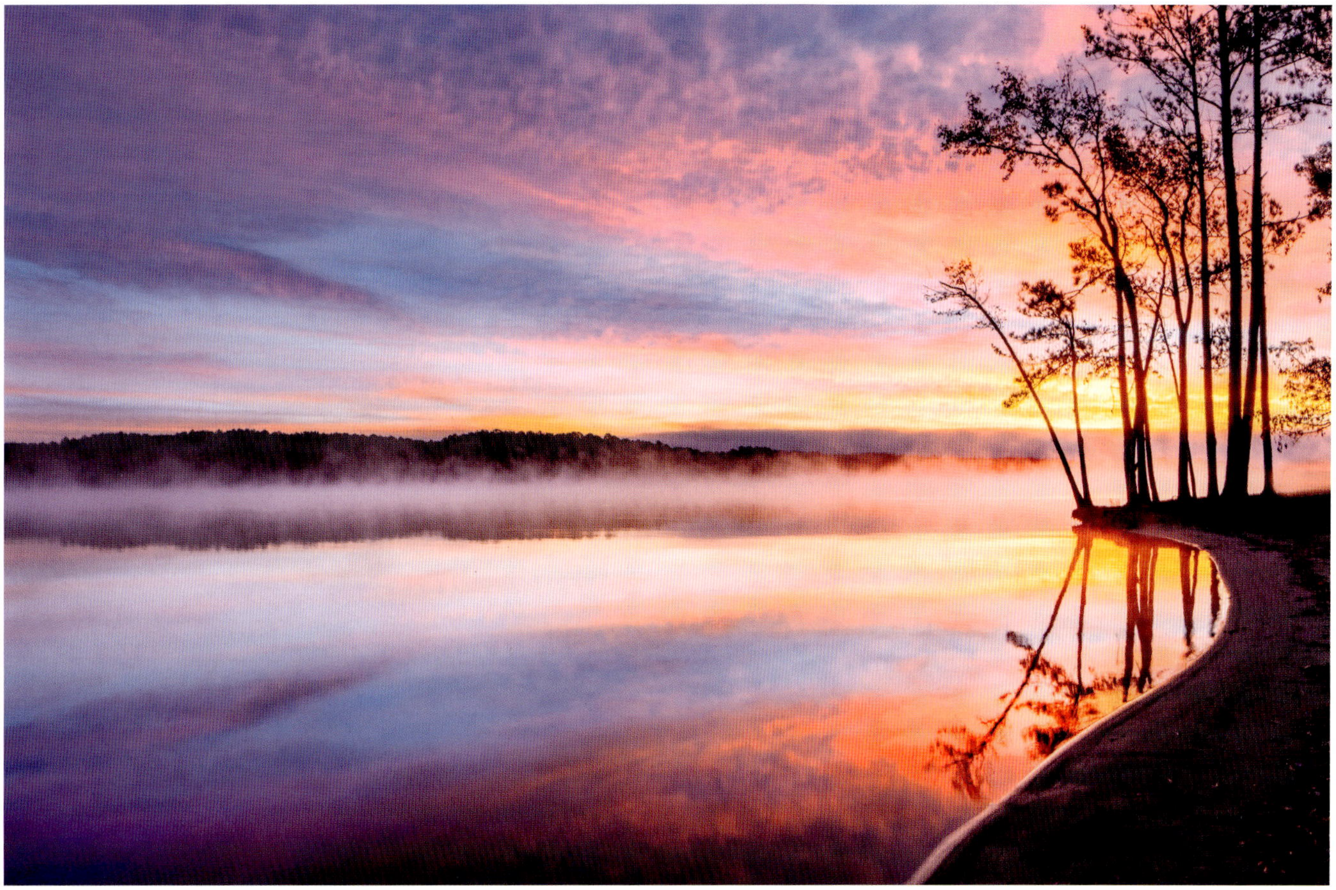

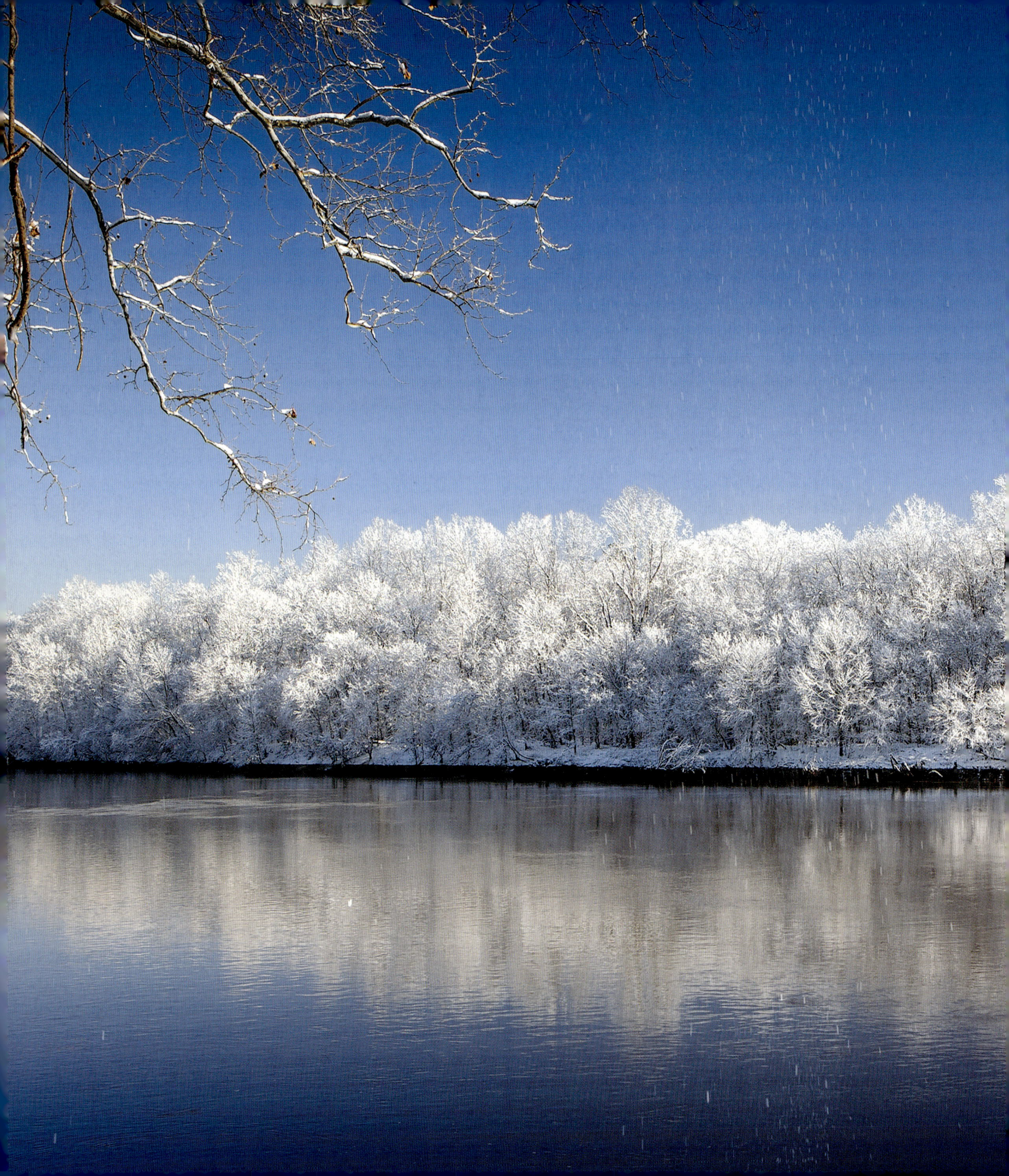

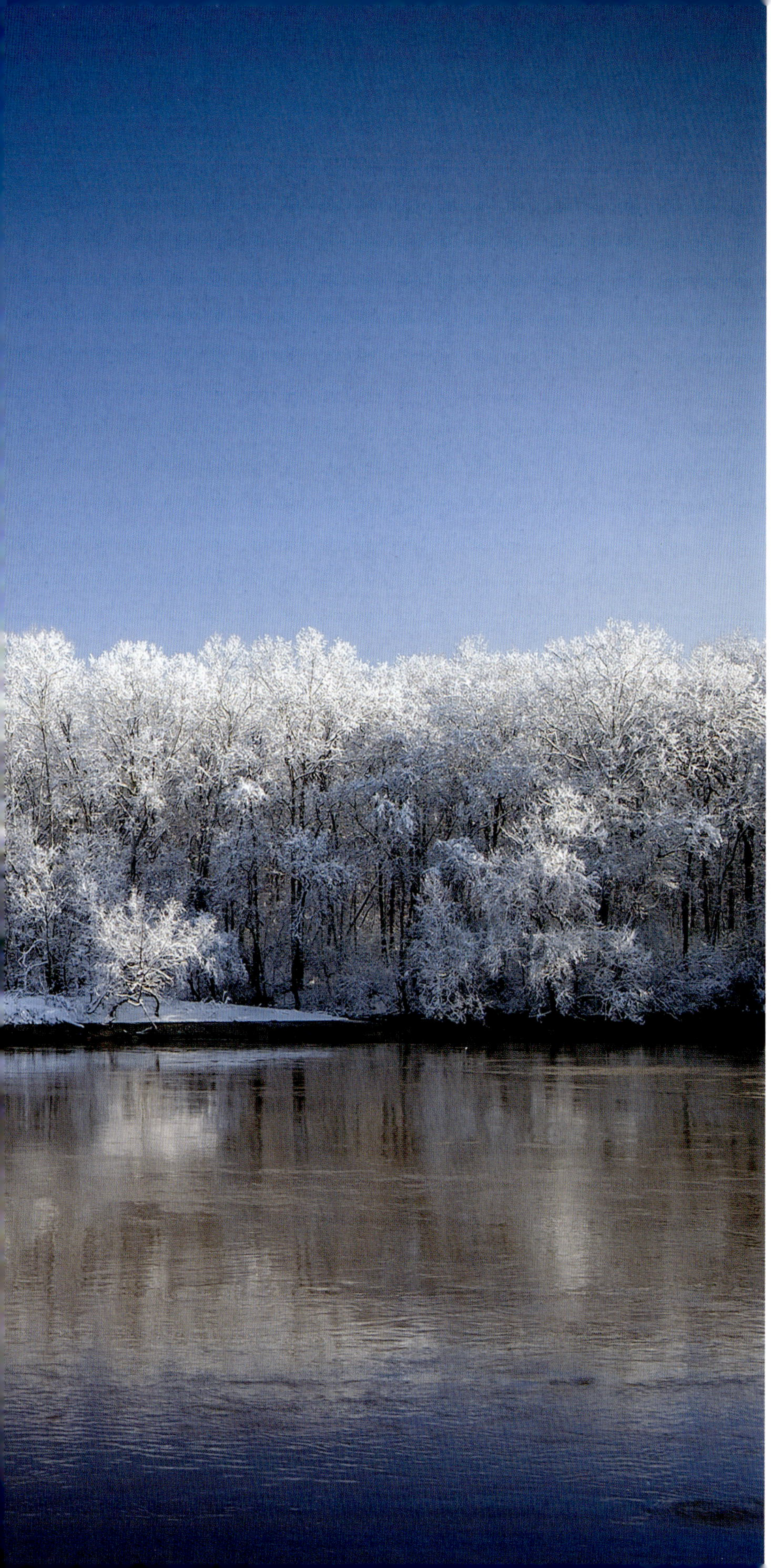

Broad River Snowfall

This early morning dusting of snow vanished by 2:00 p.m. More often than not, such splendor proves fleeting when a South Carolina winter storm passes through. Here today and gone today.

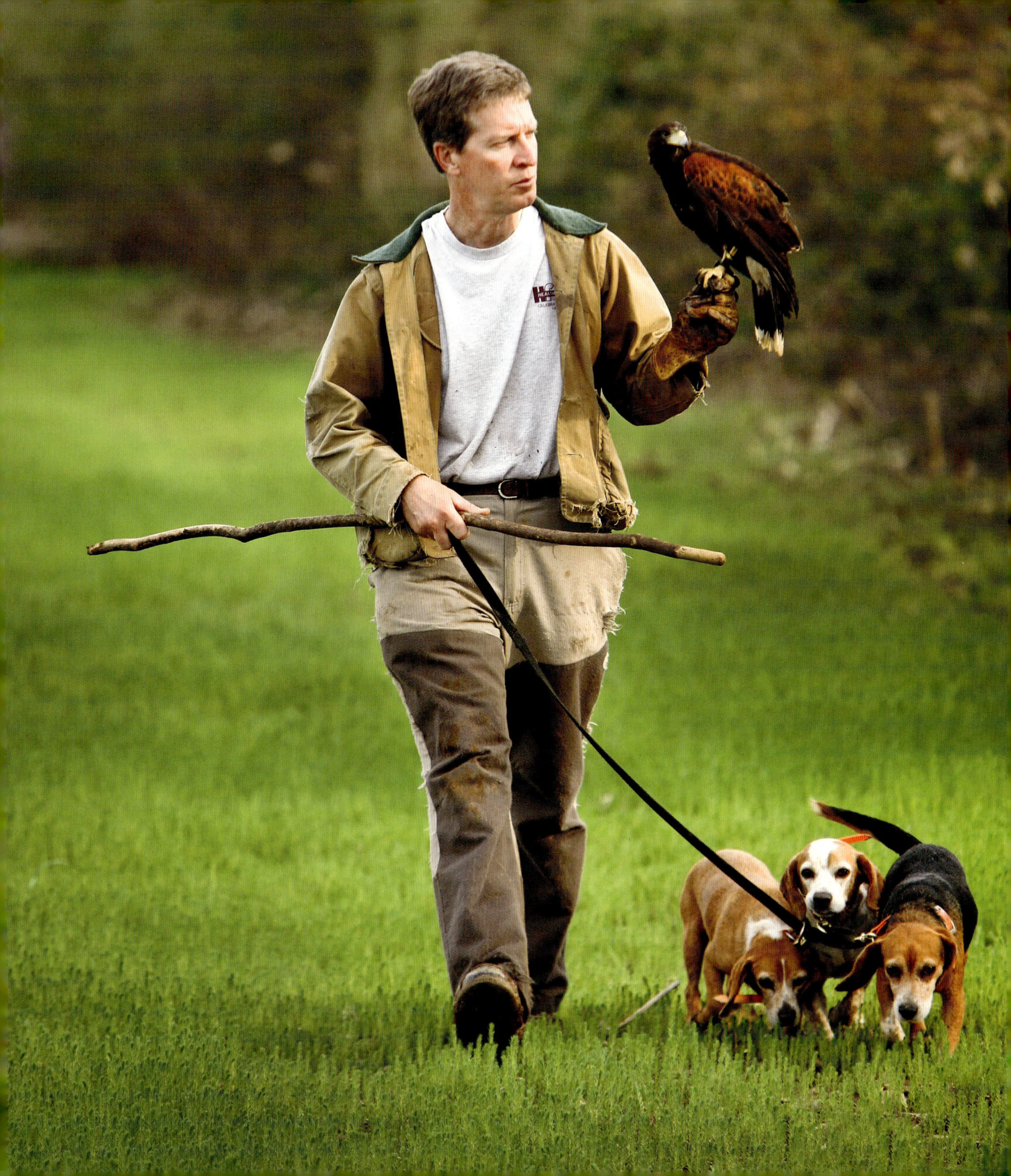

The Sport of Kings

Falconry captures wild quarry in its natural state with a trained raptor. Just minutes earlier Hansel Hart's Harris Hawk, Rocky, caught a cottontail. Hart's beagles Lilly (*left*), Buttercup (*center*), and Bunny (*right*) work well with hawks. Falconers dedicate a lot of time to this ancient sport.

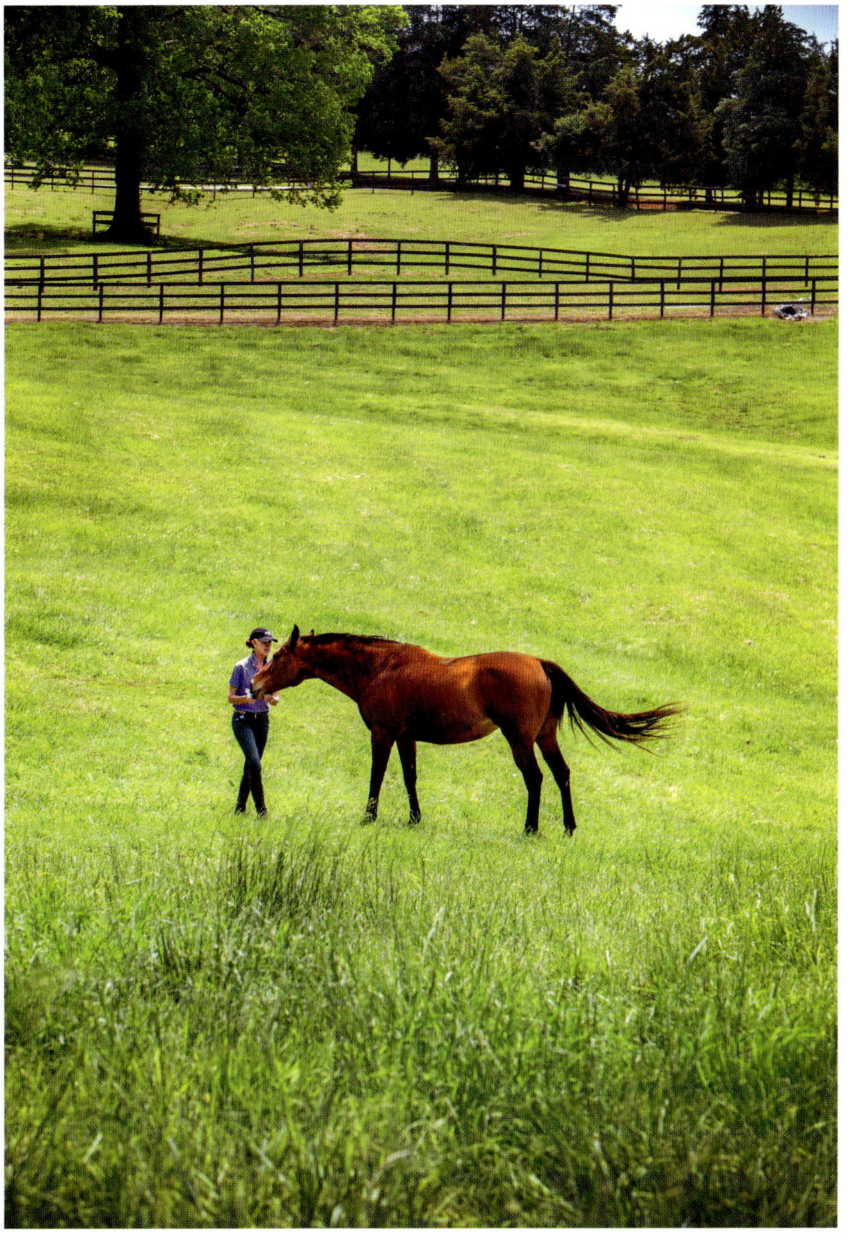

Blythewood Horse Country

Along Highway 21 up Blythewood way rolling hills and hardwoods provide home to horse country. Blythewood possesses a strong equestrian tradition. As well it's home to the University of South Carolina (USC) Equestrian Center where USC's 2015, 2007, and 2005 national champions and 2014 and 2013 Southeastern Conference champions trained.

Buttressed Cypress

Receding black water mirrors cypresses and cypress knees. The knees' purpose remains a mystery.

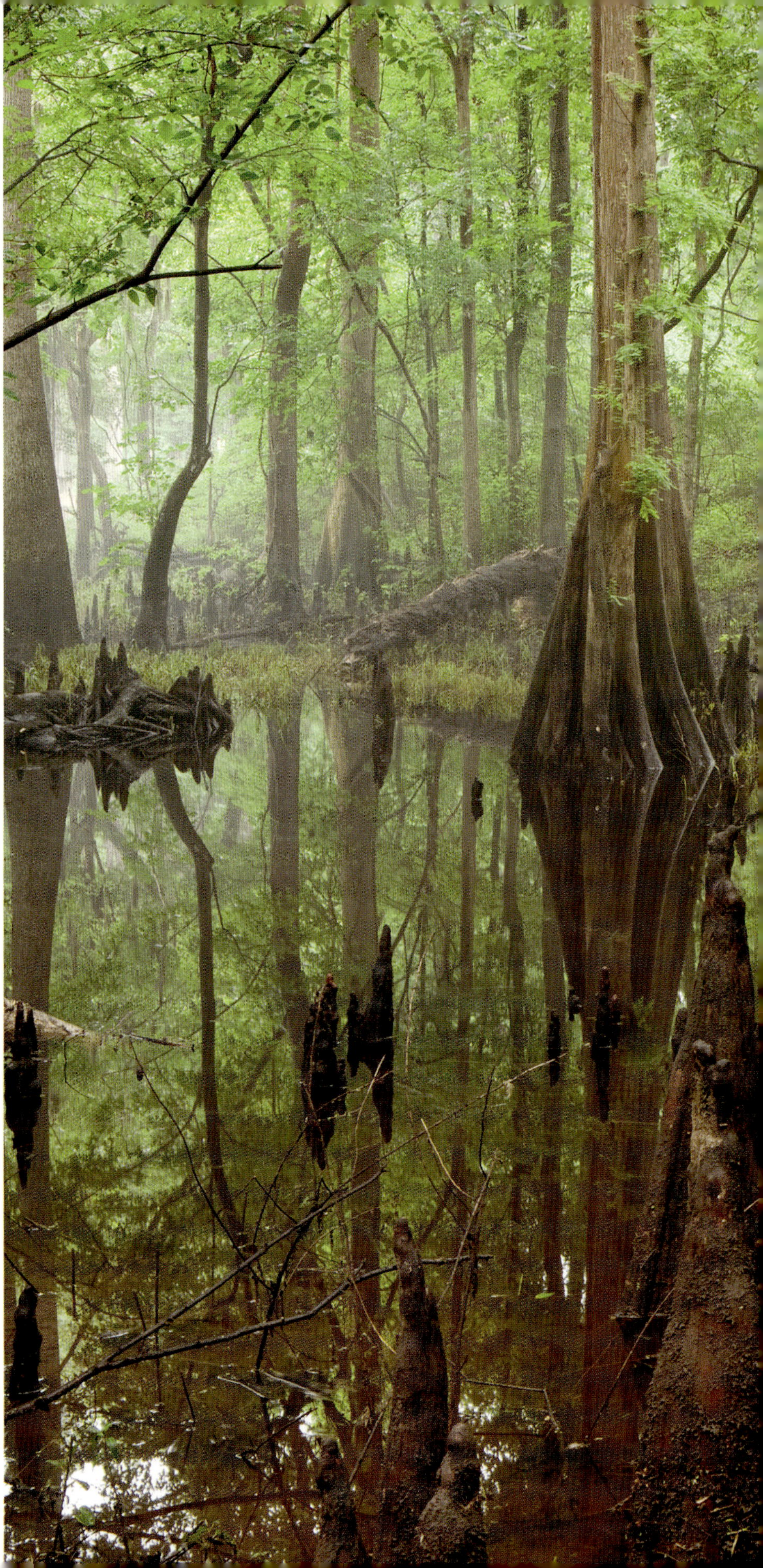

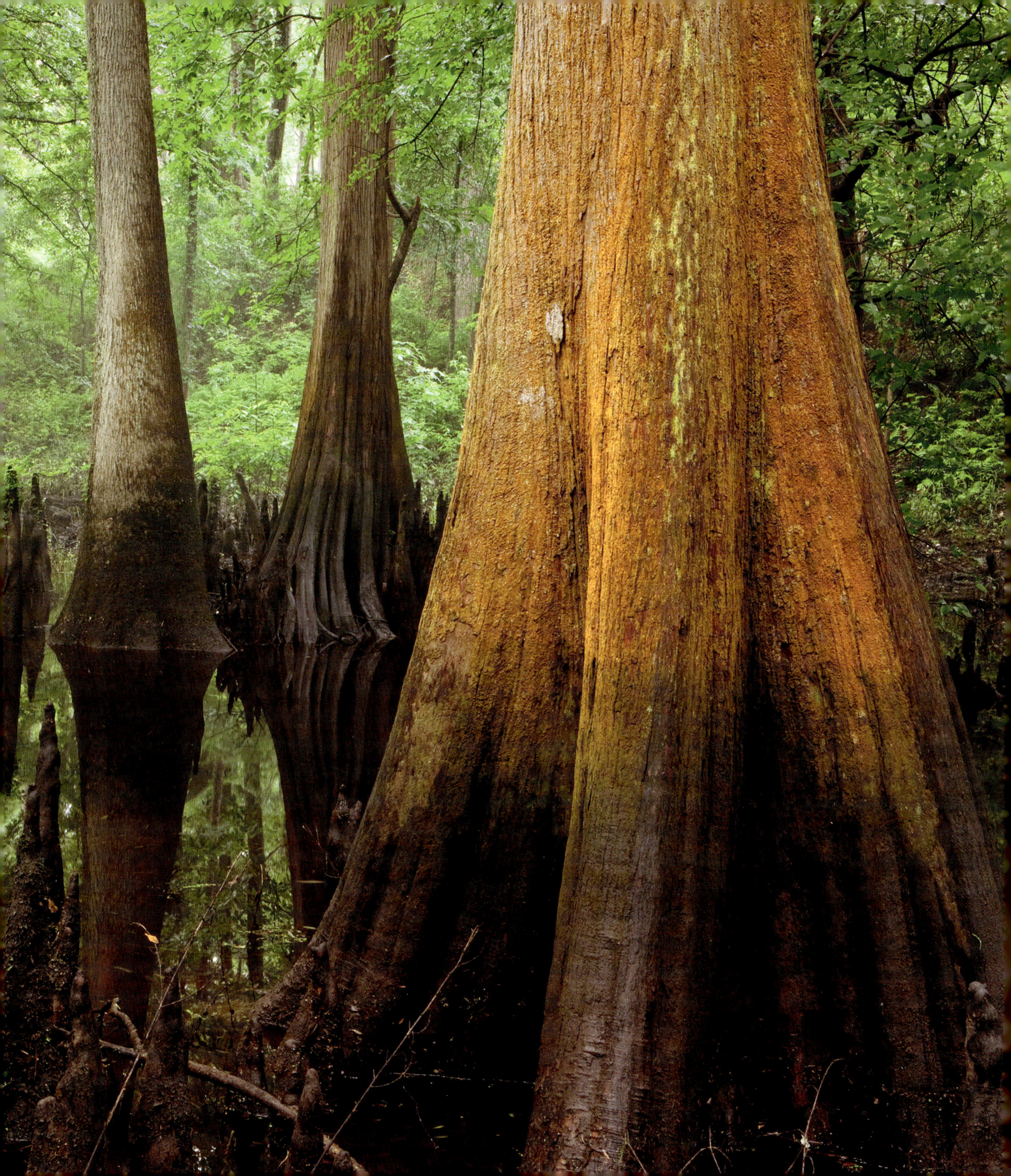

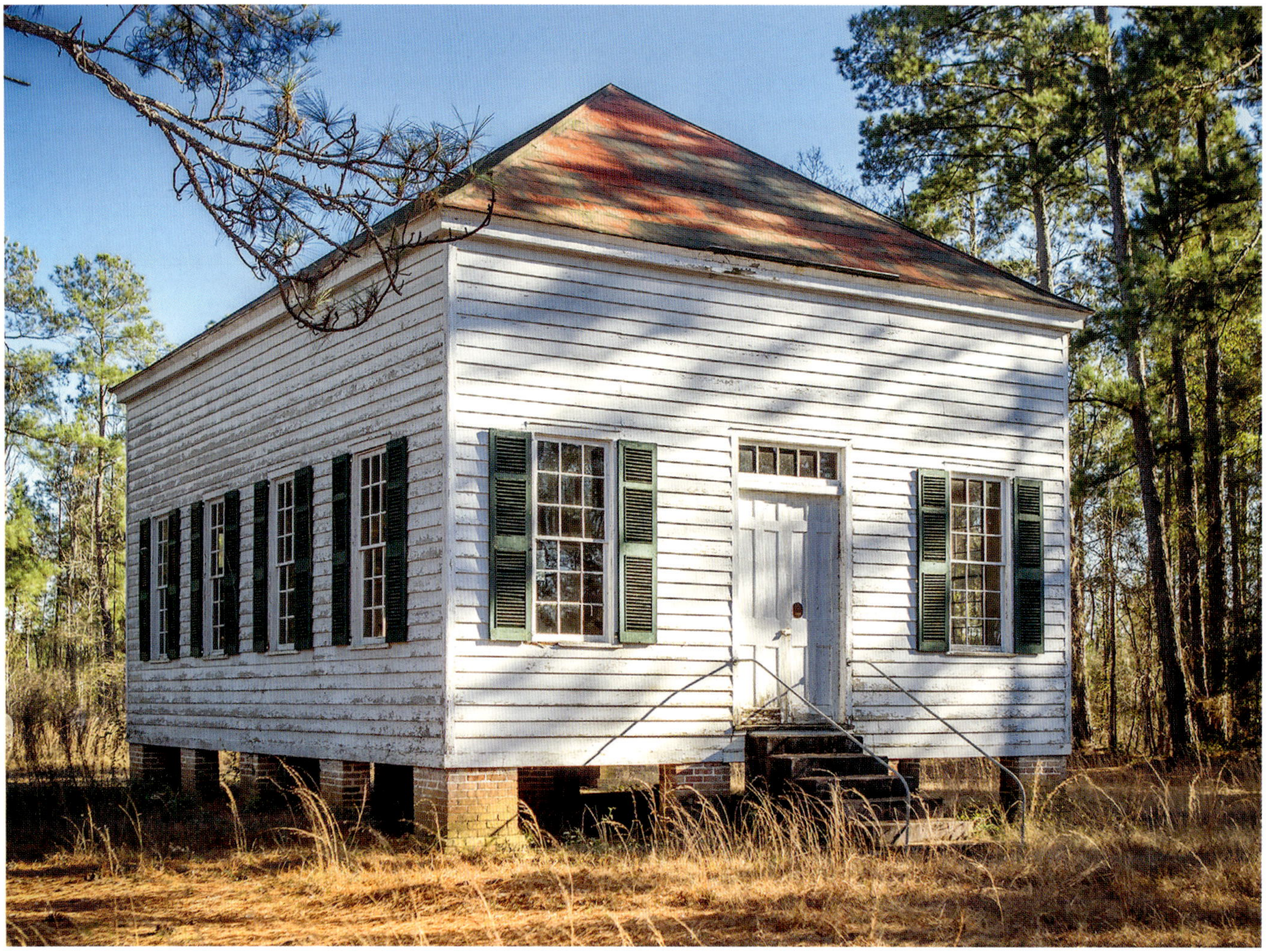

Antioch Christian Church
National Register of Historic Places

Antioch Christian Church, ca. 1835, in Allendale County, was the second Disciples of Christ Church in South Carolina. According to the South Carolina Disciples, it's the faith's oldest standing structure in South Carolina. The "Mother Church" is a one-story, meetinghouse style clapboard structure with a hipped roof. Renovated in 1976.

Old Brick Church, Fairfield County

The Little River Church, known now as the Old Brick Church, was built just north of Jenkinsville in 1788. The Ebenezer Associate Reformed Presbyterian Church was constructed in the meetinghouse style typical of early churches with a key difference. It is brick, unlike the common wood-frame buildings. Union troops commandeered part of the church's floor to rebuild a bridge over the Little River. A Union soldier penciled an apology on a wall: "Citizens of this community: Please excuse us for defacing your house of worship, so much. It was absolutely necessary to effect a crossing over the creek, the Rebs had destroyed the bridge. A Yankee."

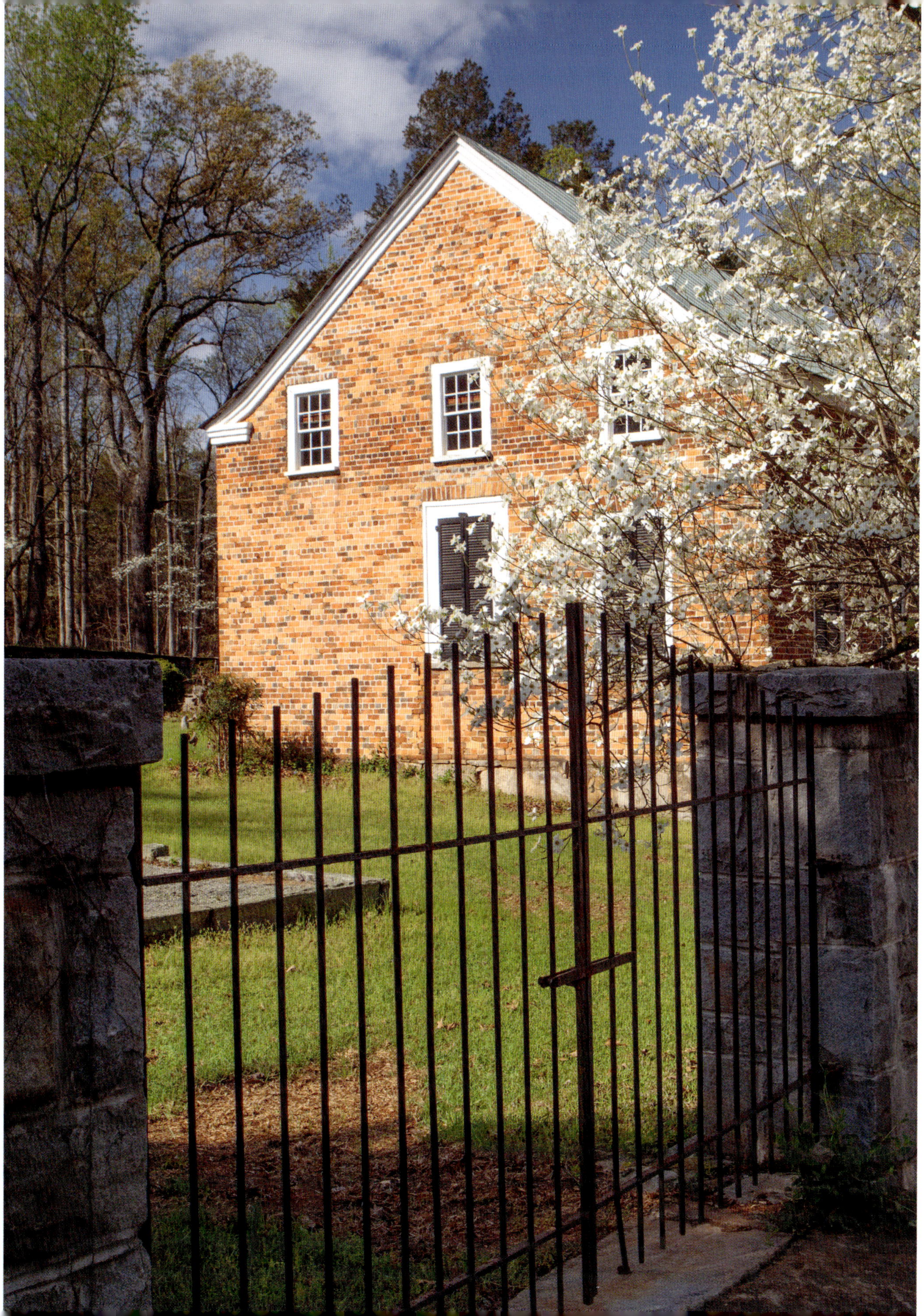

Palmetto Power

Stavros Alexander Chrysostomides sculpted this wrought-iron gate for the governor's mansion. The palmetto achieved state emblem status thanks to the fortress Colonel William Moultrie built on Sullivan's Island. The Battle of Sullivan's Island delivered the first decisive Patriot victory over the British Royal Navy. Sabal palmetto trunks embedded in deep sand absorbed cannon balls like a sponge, minimizing damage.

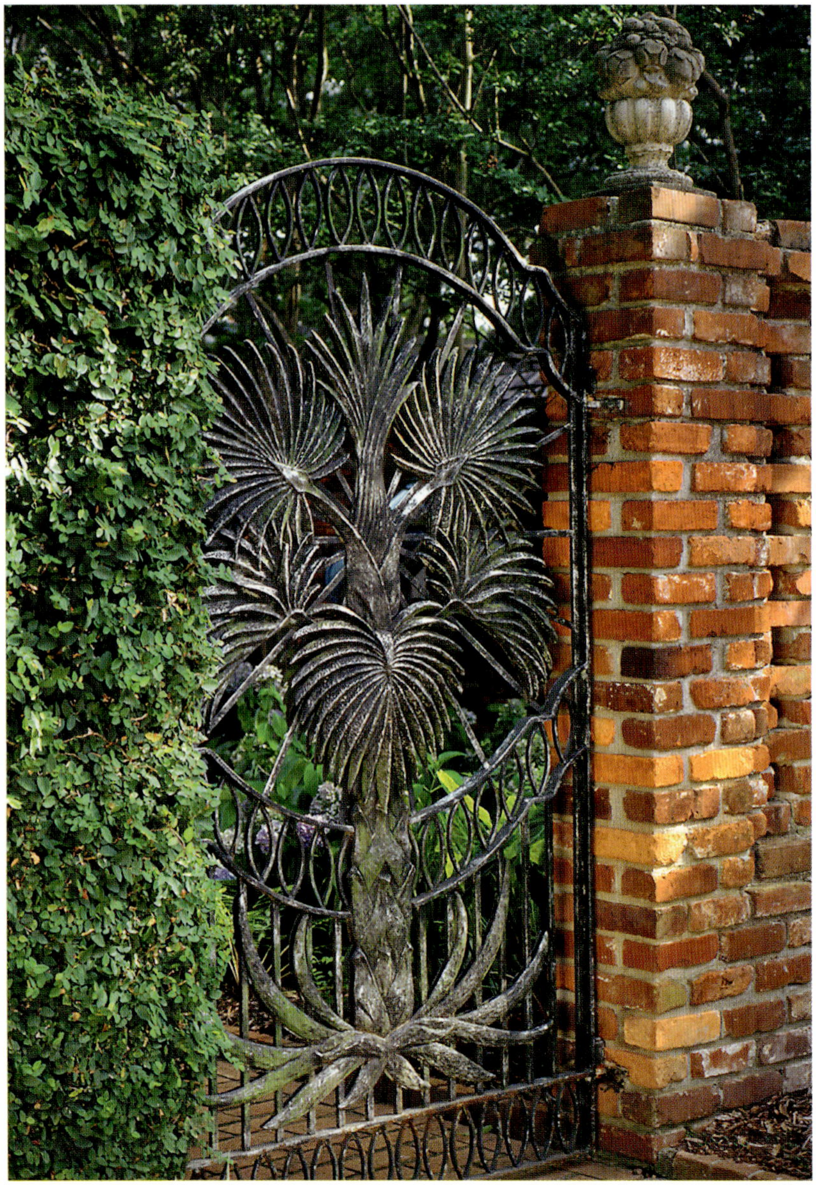

Blowing Glass

Columbia's One-Eared Cow studio began in 1991 when three graduates of the University of South Carolina's School of Visual Art and Design furthered their study of molten glass as an artistic medium.

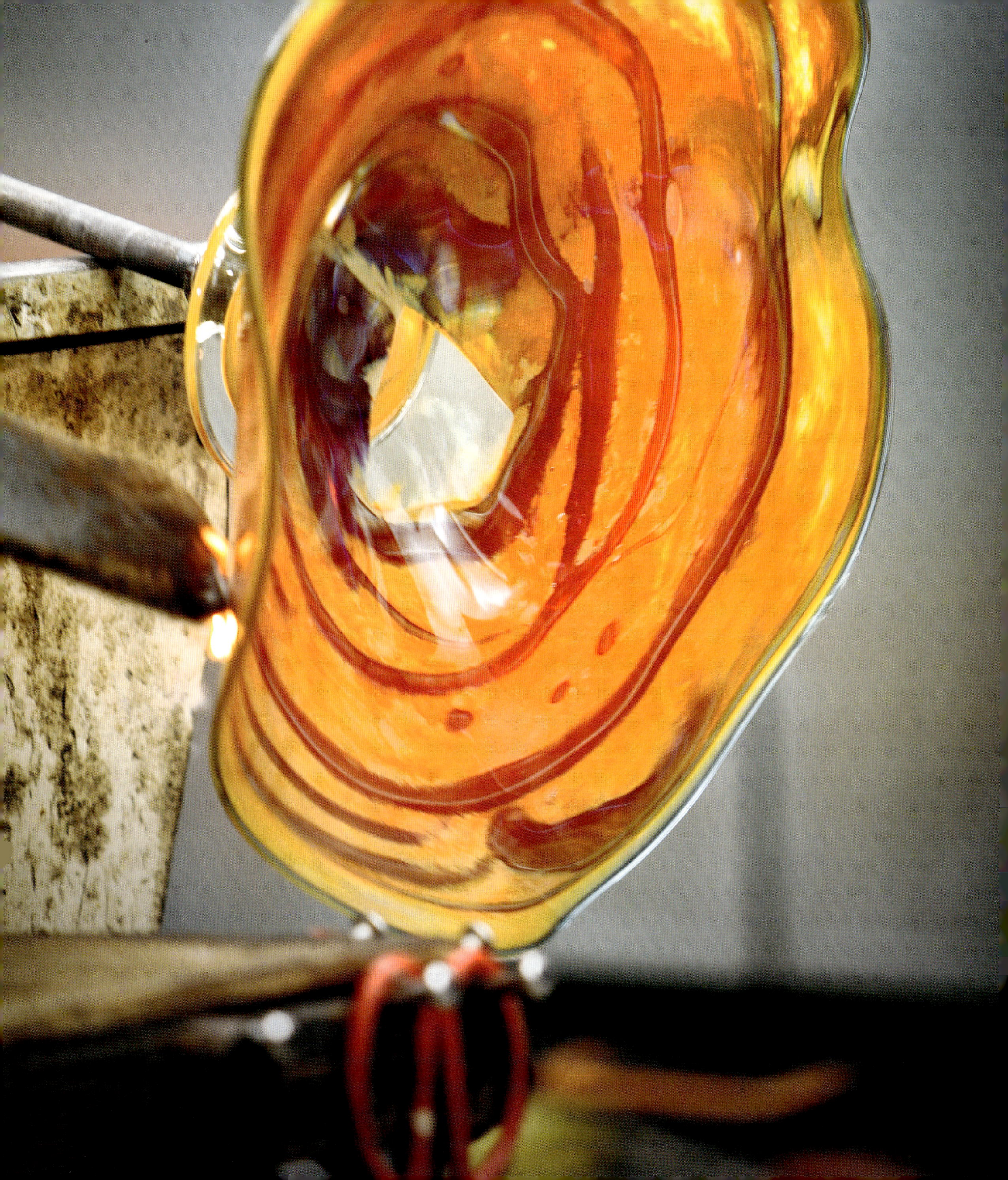

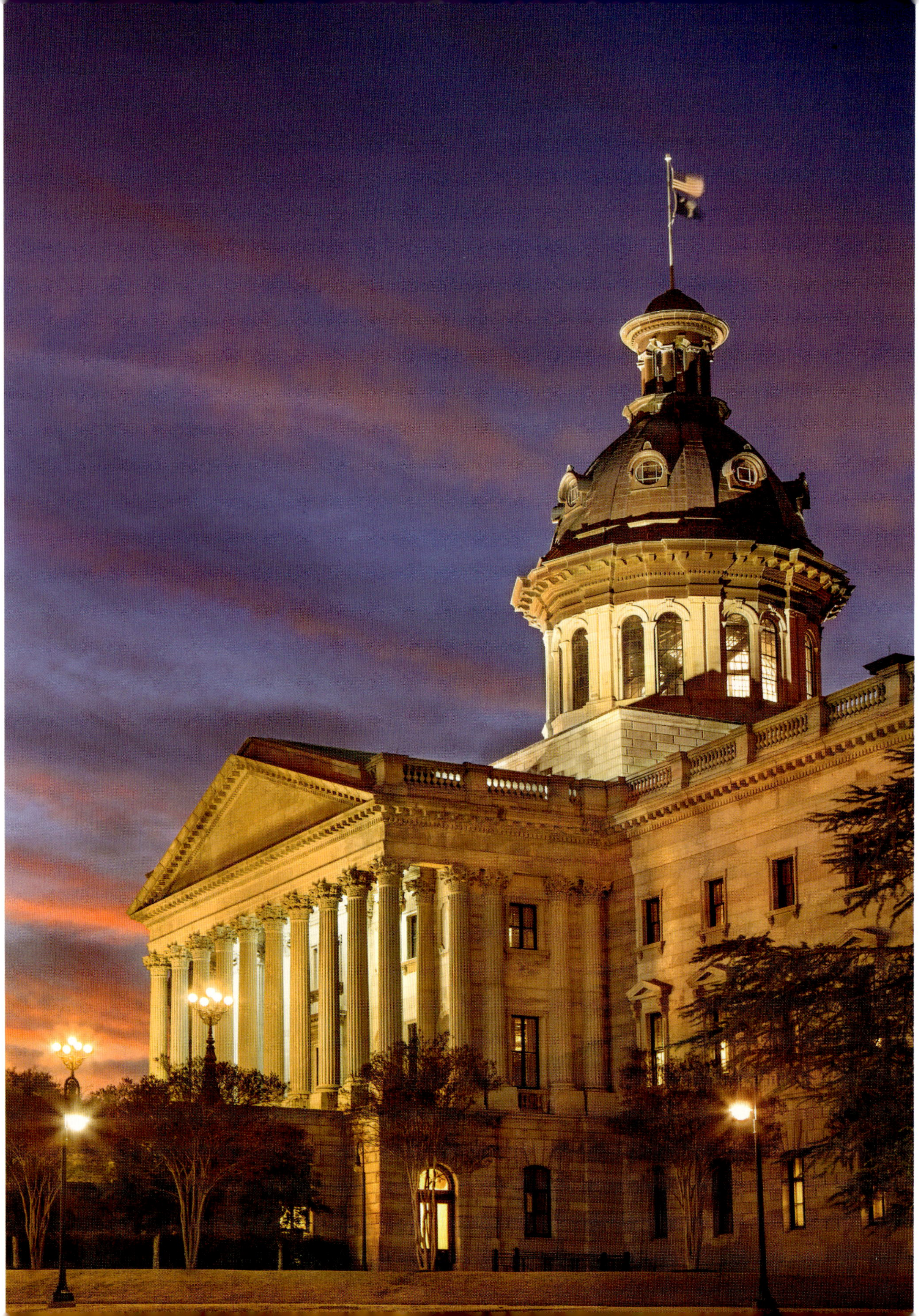

Twilight at the Statehouse

Dusk settles over the Statehouse. Its columns were carved from a single piece of stone. It is believed they are the largest monolithic columns in a public building in the United States.

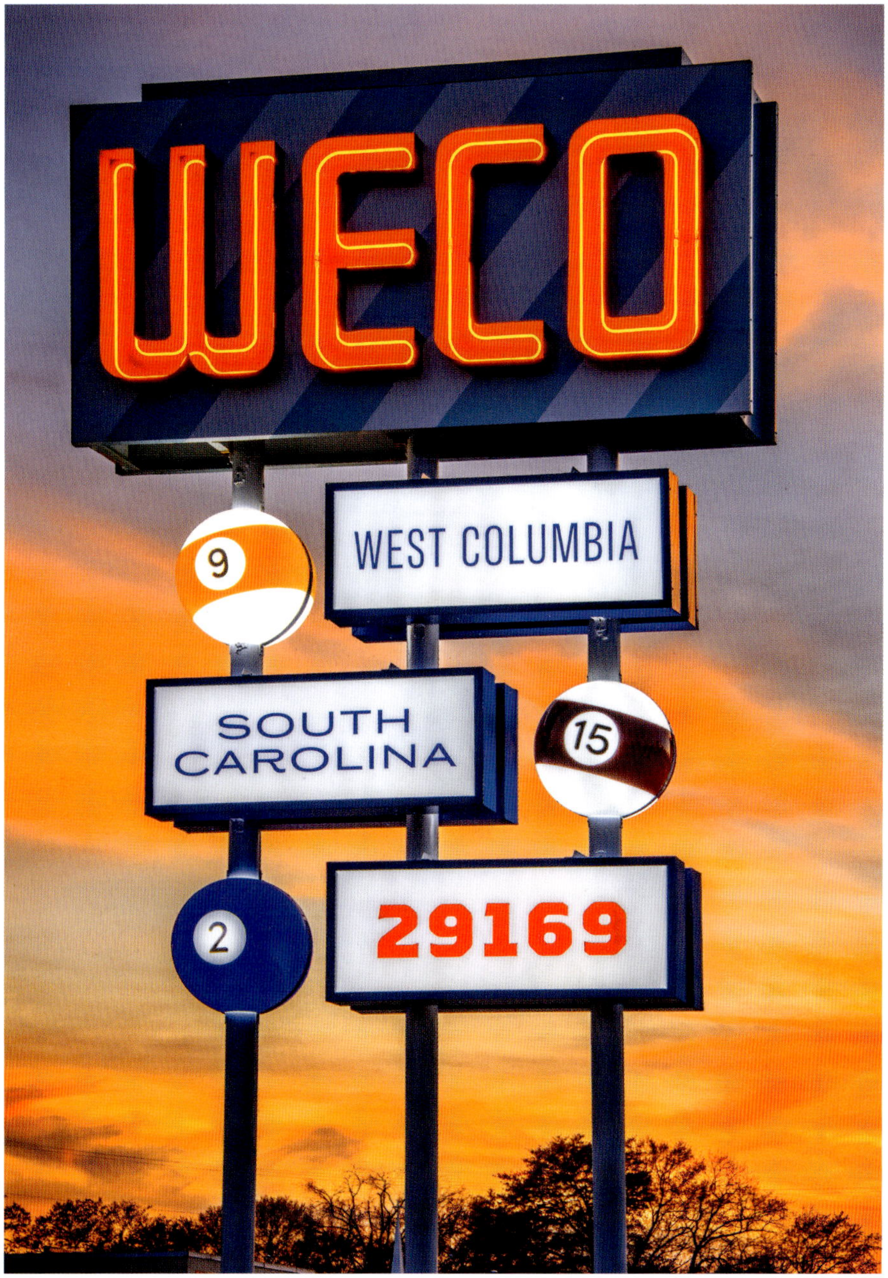

WECO

Built in the late 1940s, West Columbia's WECO began as the Lower Main Market before becoming a Dixie Home Store in 1951 and later a Winn-Dixie. A furniture company, a carpet and tile store, then came 750 Meeting's most notorious era: WECO Billiards. The pool hall racked 'em up from the 1970s to 2001 before trading in the cues and chalk for Charity Thrift in 2002. The WECO sign stayed, but the owner painted the pool balls white. Thanks to a public–private partnership with the City of West Columbia, WECO is back and better than ever. Information courtesy of Riggs Partners, who call 750 Meeting Street home.

State Fair

Twelve October days and nights in Columbia usher in rides, vendors, elephant ears, pizza, cotton candy, the curious, patrons, and competitors. At the South Carolina State Fair, judges review competitions, ranging from wine, beef cattle, fine art, and flowers to home and craft. Lose a friend in the crowd? Meet 'em at the rocket.

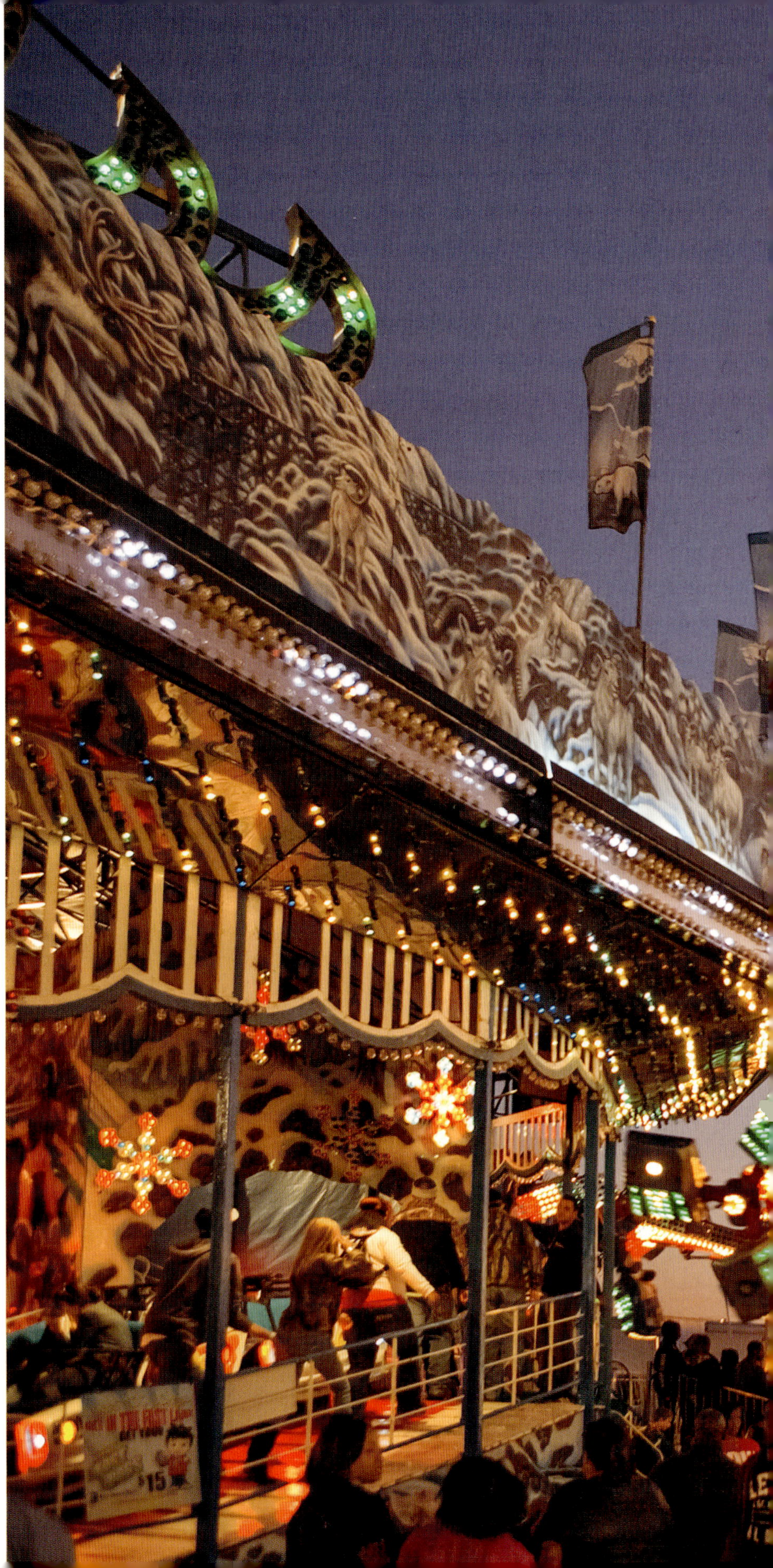

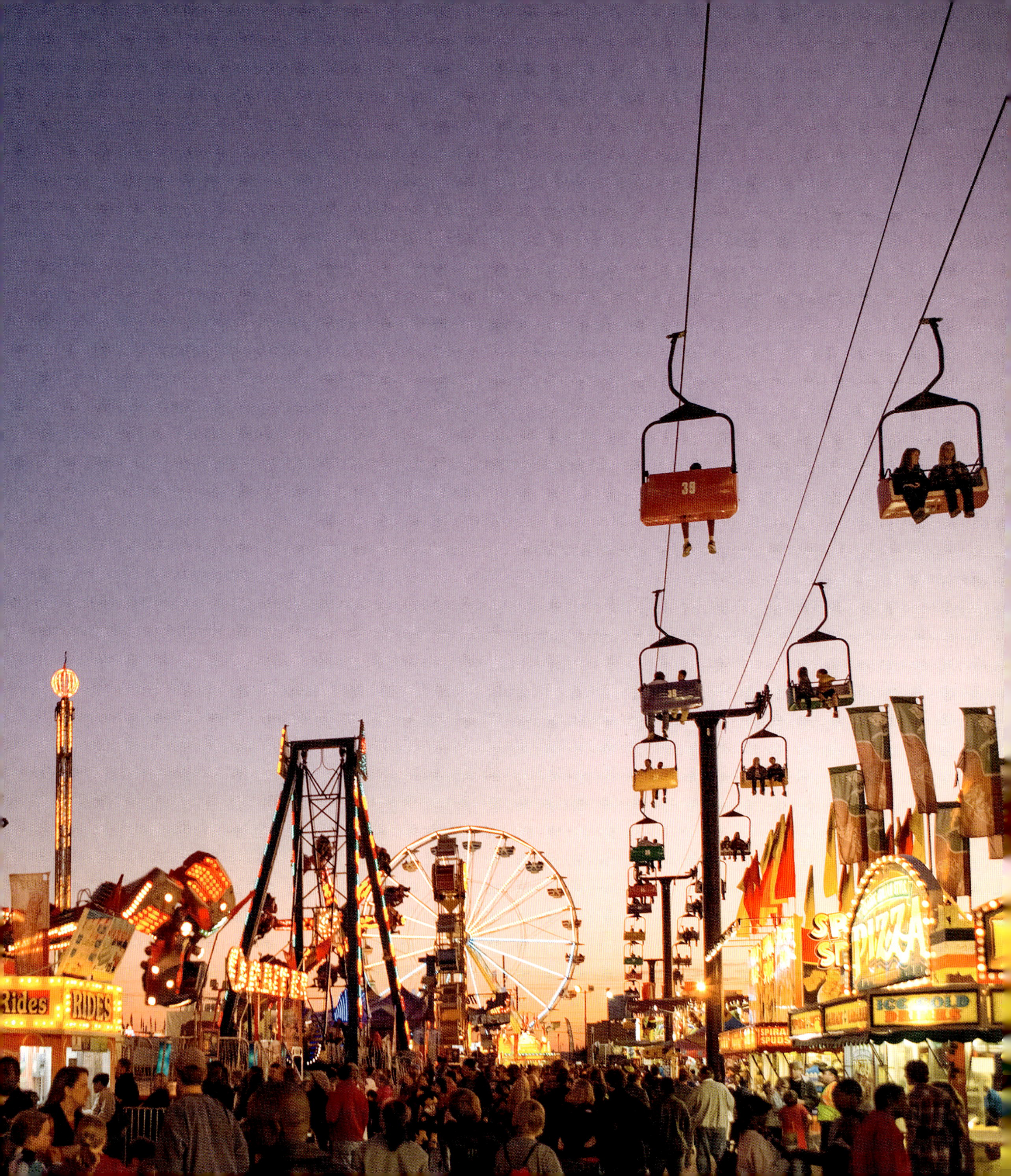
39
Rides
RIDES
PIZZA
SPUDS

Camden Opera House Clock Tower
National Register of Historic Places

Philadelphia's Isaiah Lukens made Camden's clock and brought it to Camden in 1825. Eminent bell maker John Wilbank cast the clock's bell. (He also cast the cracked Liberty Bell's replacement.) The town market building first held the clock, which was moved in 1859 to the new market building. It moved again ca. 1885 to the opera house tower. The original clockworks, which had been replaced, were restored by 1985. Only three Lukens tower clocks still operate in the United States. Camden's is one of them.

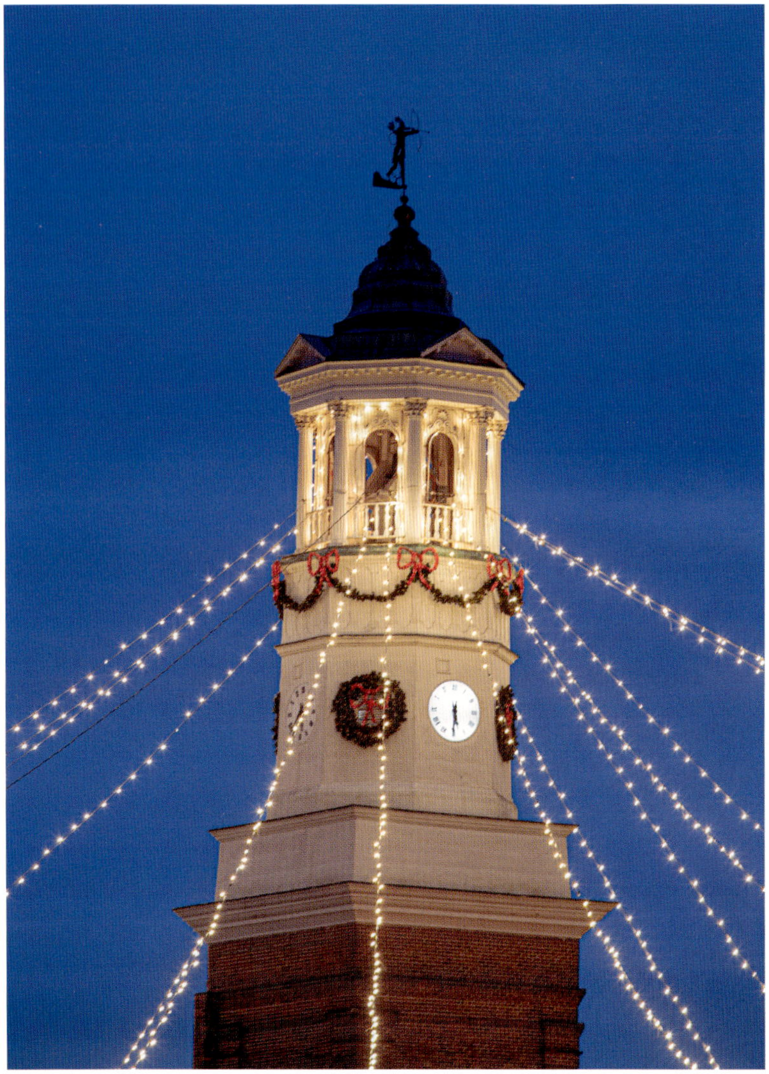

Joseph Kershaw Mansion
National Register of Historic Places

Built from 1775 to 1780 in Camden, Kershaw House, of Georgian architecture, served as the headquarters for Lord Cornwallis and the occupying British army from 1780 to 1781. Burned in 1865 during the Civil War, it was rebuilt from 1974 to 1977. You'll find it in the historic Camden Revolutionary War Site.

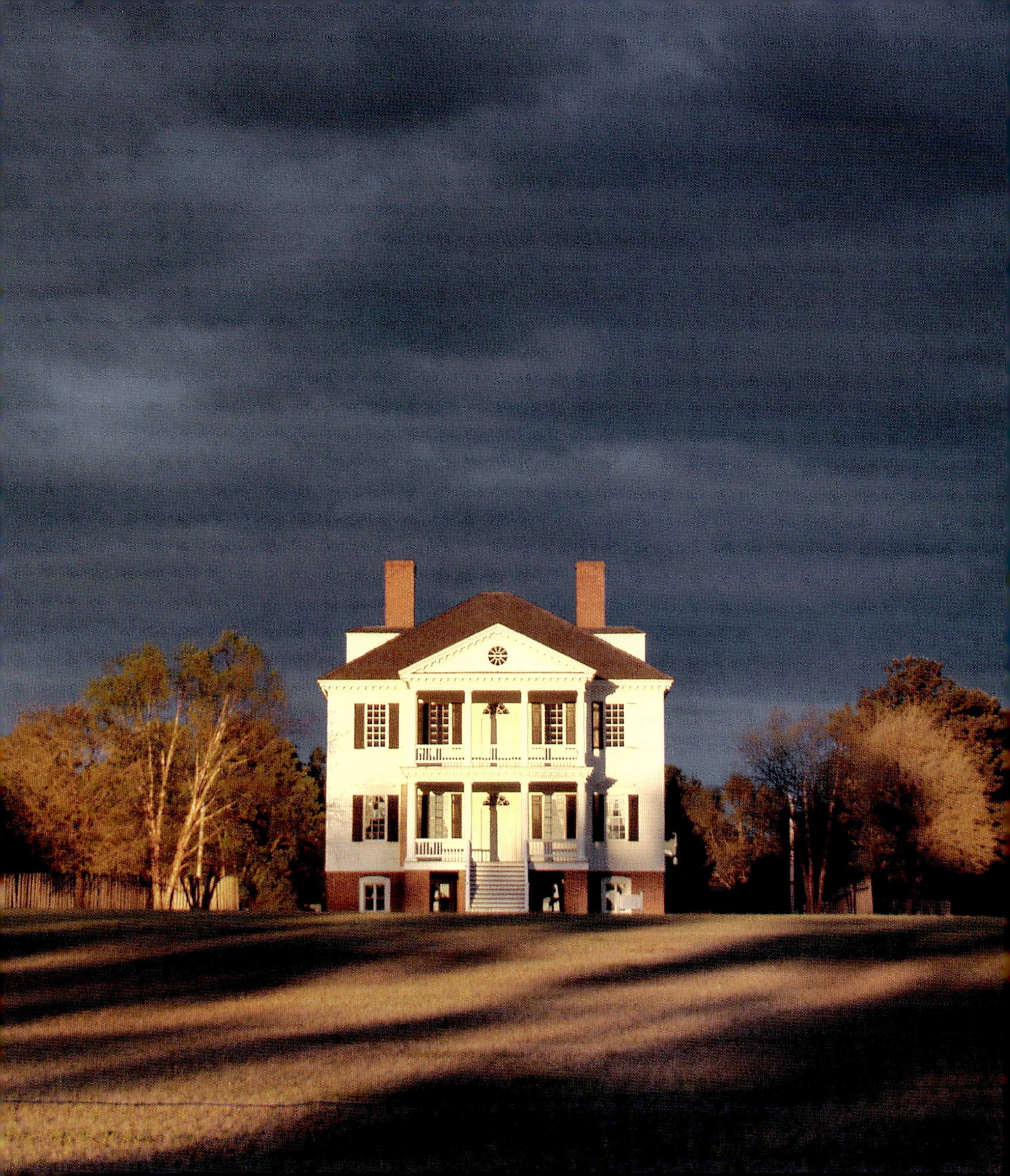

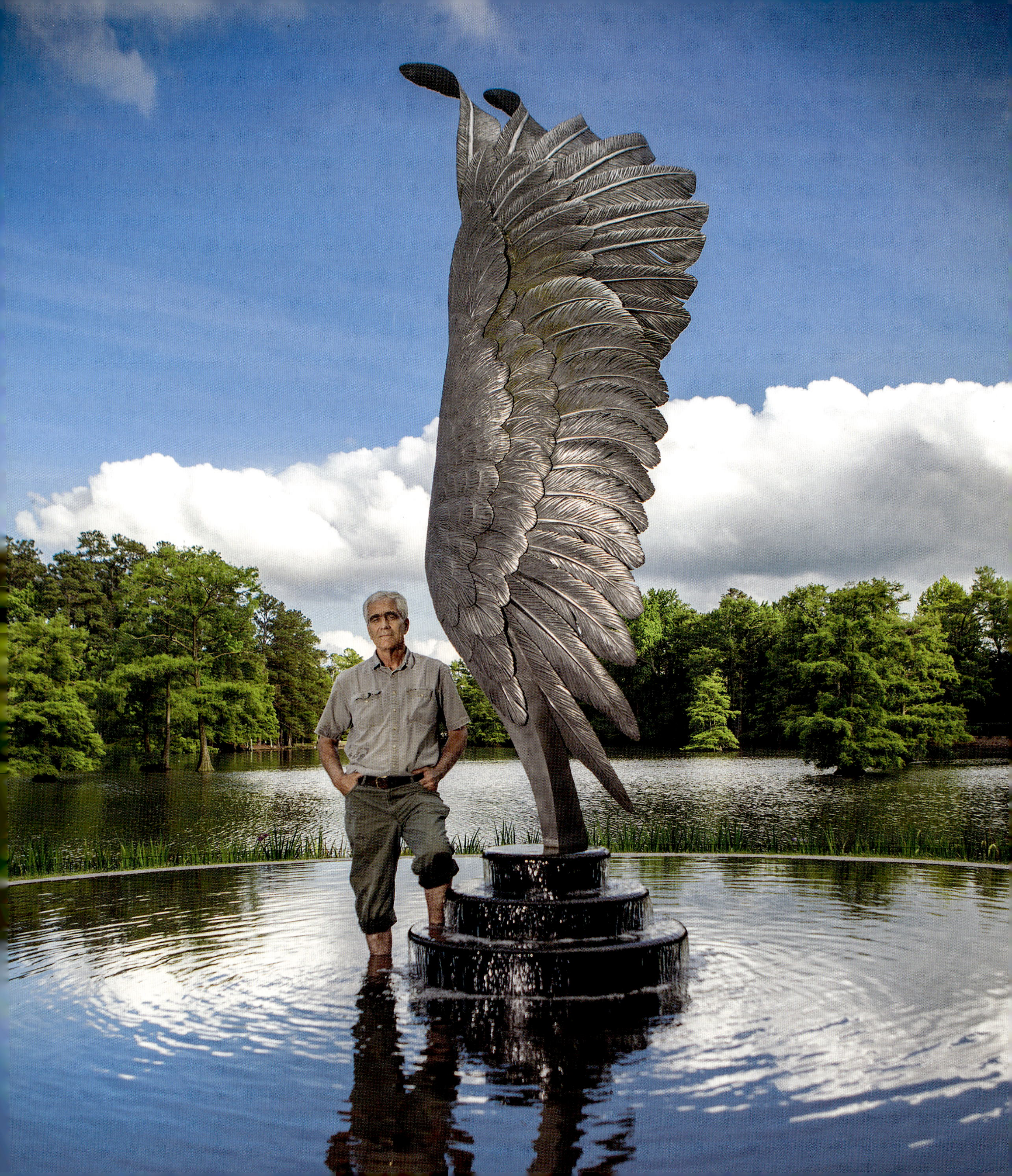

Recovery Stroke

A bird's recovery stroke produces neither lift nor forward momentum, and yet it's essential. The Hollings Cancer Center commissioned Sumter native Grainger McKoy to visualize its mission of treatment and recovery. "Recovery Stroke" resulted. Sumter's Swan Lake Iris Gardens is home to his eighteen-foot sculpture, which represents the wing of a pintail duck in flight. Said McKoy, "This wing position is considered the weakest in bird flight, yet in the artist's eye is the position with the most beauty and grace. All of us are in recovery somewhere in our lives, as is our environment, of which Swan Lake is a unique part." The stainless-steel wing measures fourteen feet in height and weighs approximately 1,500 pounds.

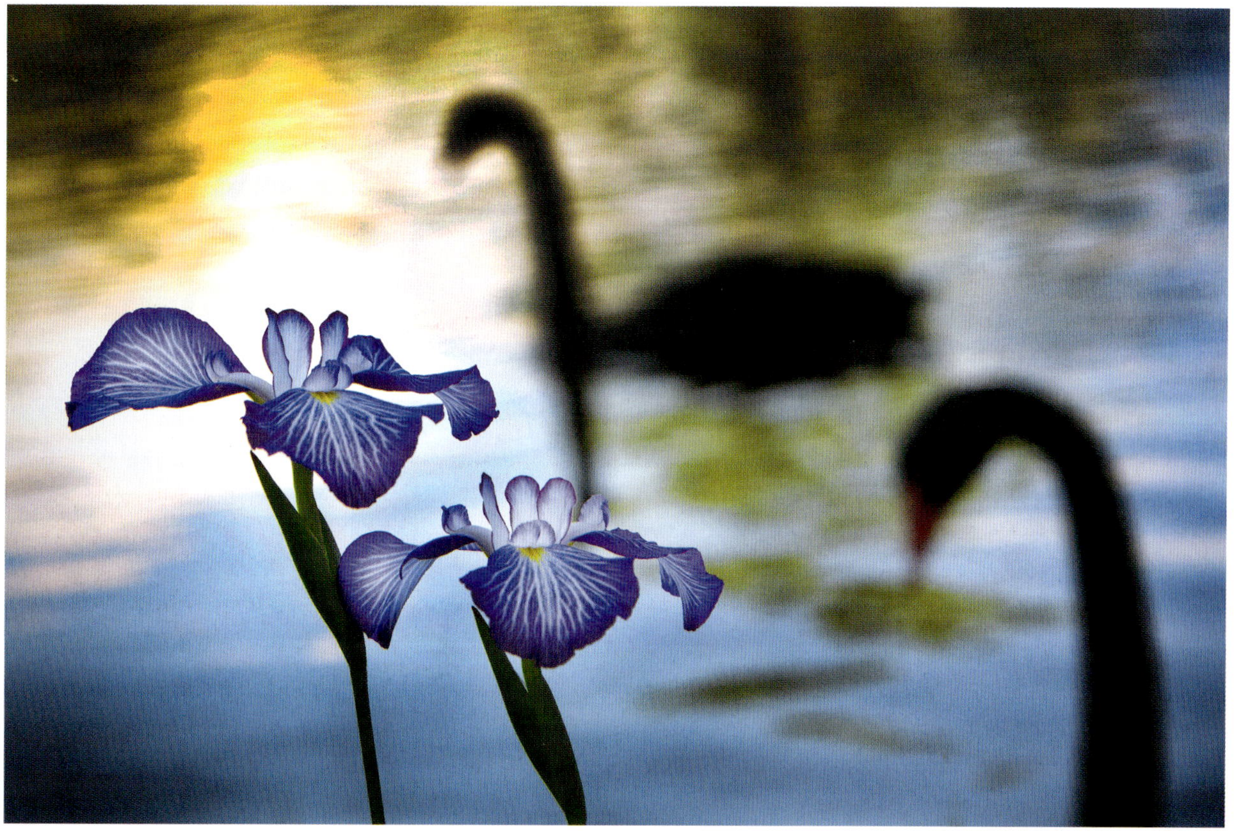

Sumter's Swan Lake Iris Gardens

Here you'll find the country's only public park that features all eight swan species and concentrated plantings of Japanese iris. A Sensory Trail lets the sight-impaired take in the scents and sensations of the gardens; a talking-tree trail tells stories; and a rose garden, azalea garden, butterfly garden, and chocolate garden of edible plants and plants with "chocolatey" fragrance and appearance delight visitors of all ages.

The McColl Block
National Register of Historic Sites

An elaborate cast-iron facade distinguishes the McCall Block, ca. 1889, one of Bennettsville's finest architectural treasures. General John McQueen, who served as a US congressman from 1849 to 1860, established his law offices here in 1828. McQueen was a member of the First Confederate Congress.

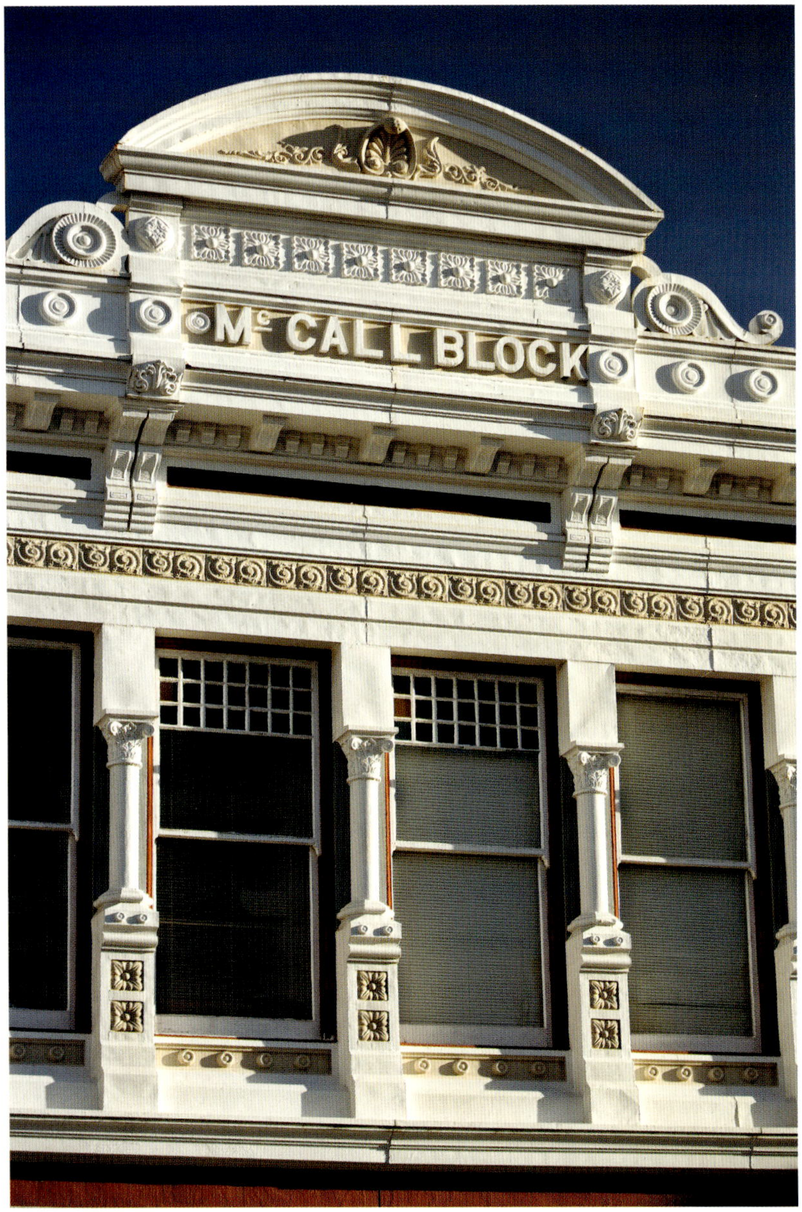

Old St. David's

Established in 1768 in Cheraw, with construction finalized in 1774, Old St. David's Church possesses a deep and humanitarian history. It was South Carolina's last Anglican parish established under British rule, but then war came, during which St. David's served as a hospital for Patriots and the British. Members of the British Highlanders regiment who died from chicken pox sleep in one grave in front of the church.

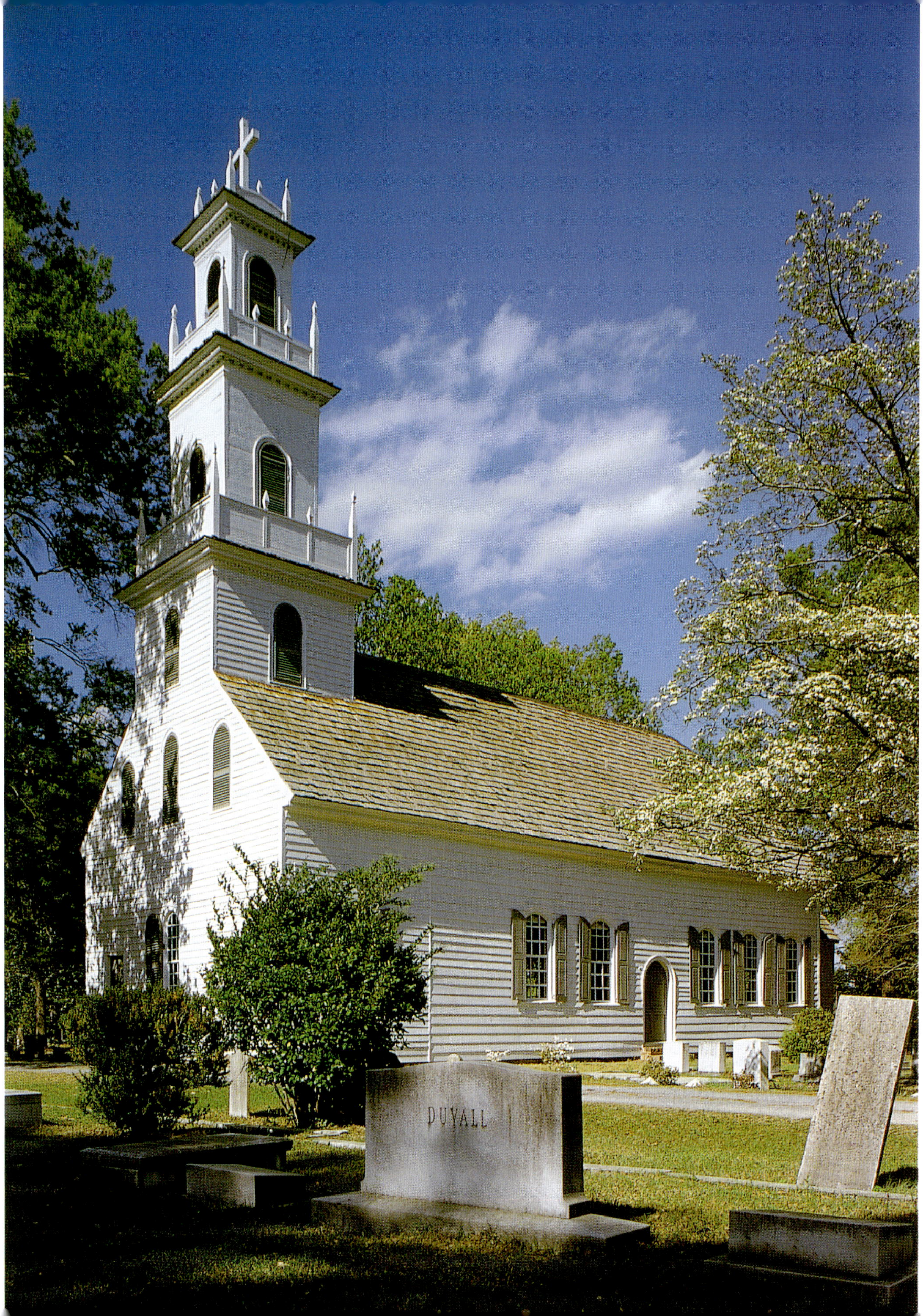
DUVALL

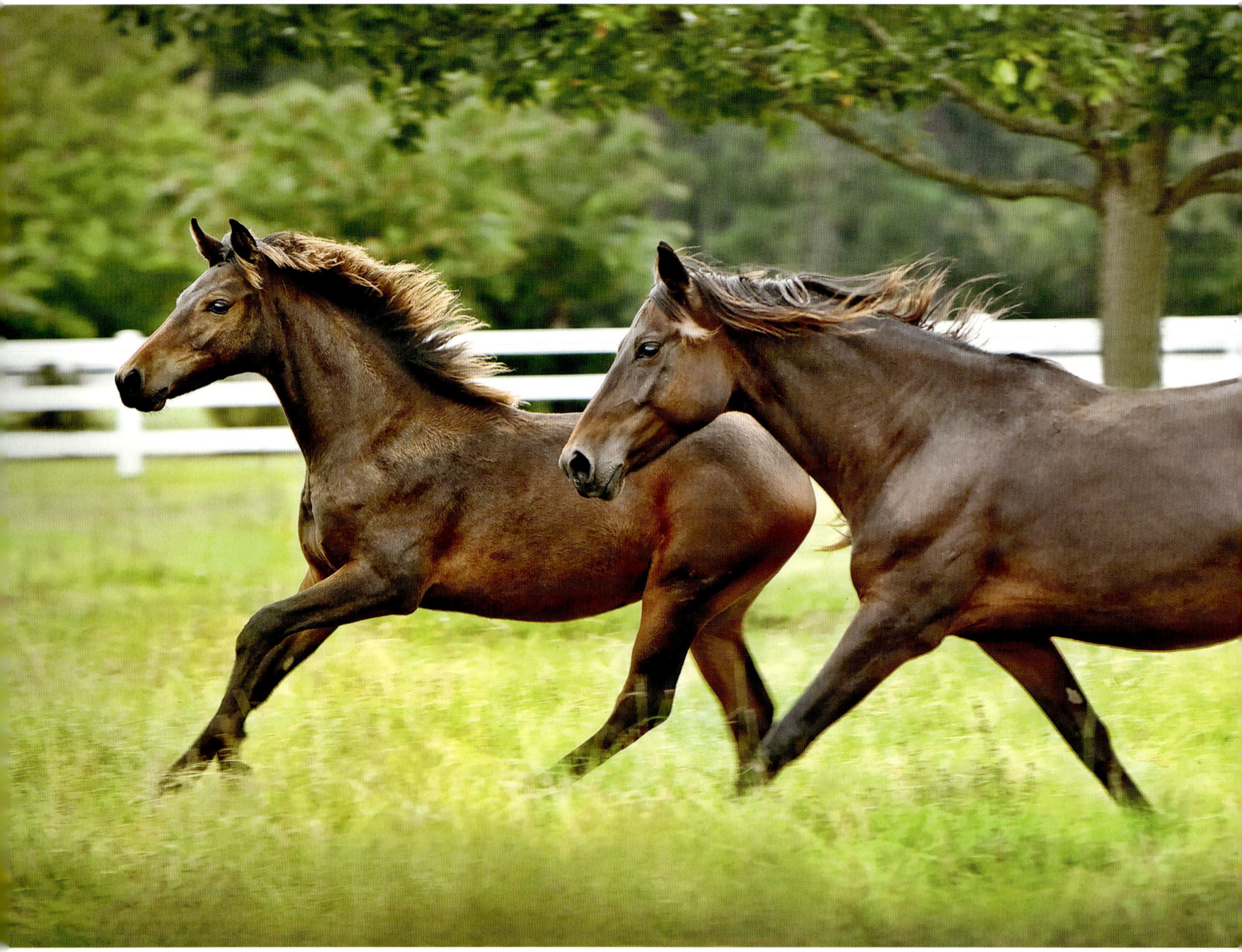

Marsh Tackies

A colonial Spanish horse, Marsh Tackies once roamed South Carolina's Sea Islands and Lowcountry. Then tractors and trucks replaced genuine horsepower, and coastal development extracted its toll. Just over 400 Marsh Tackies remain. The Carolina Marsh Tacky Association works to preserve the breed. ("Tacky," an English word meaning "common" or "cheap," is a misnomer.) Geographic isolation helped it develop into a genetically unique breed. It was designated as the South Carolina State Heritage Horse in 2010.

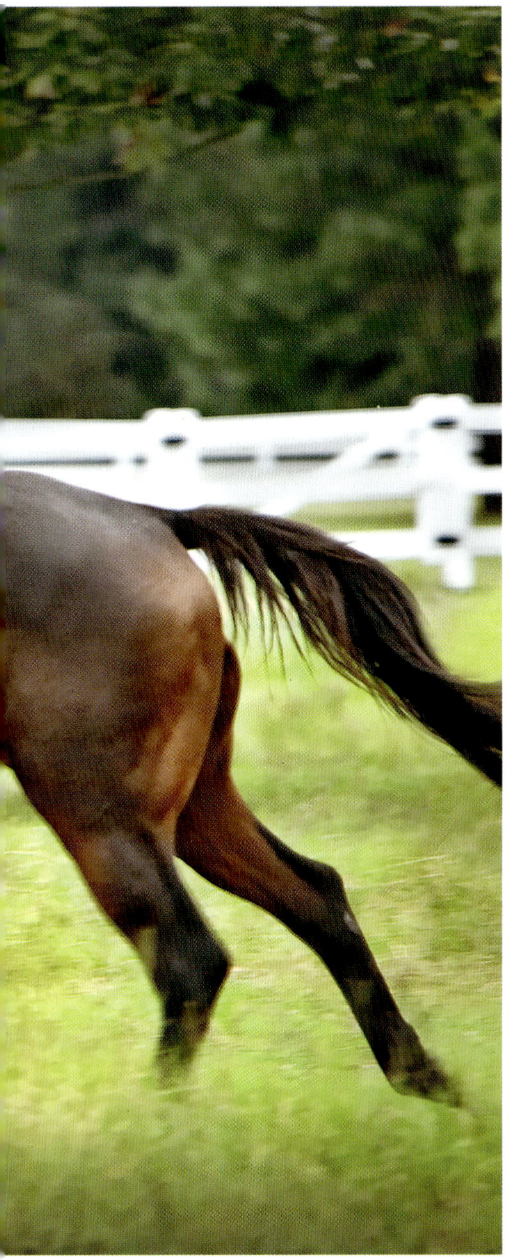

Summer Wheat

No crop covers more of the earth than wheat. The harvest of this summer wheat off US 601, near St. Matthews, gave the farmer the chance to enjoy the fruits of his labor.

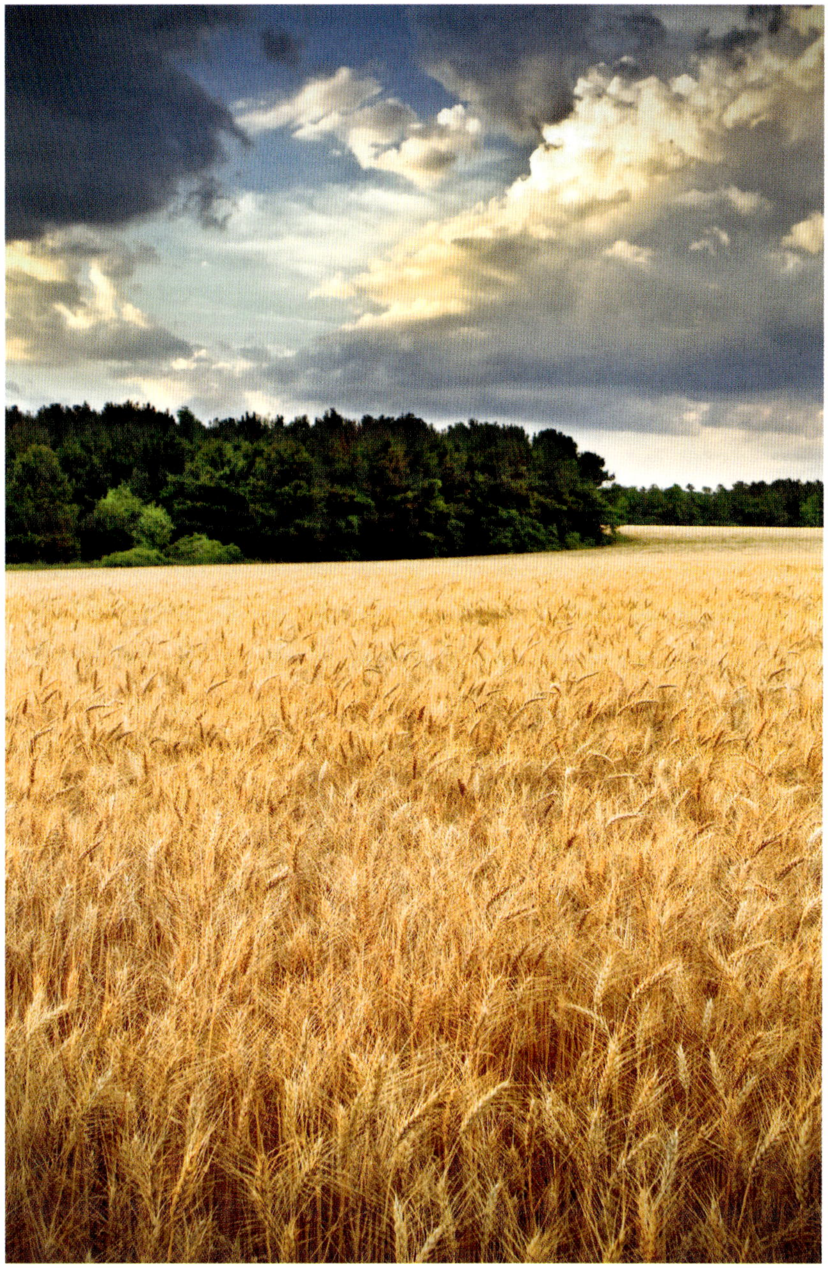

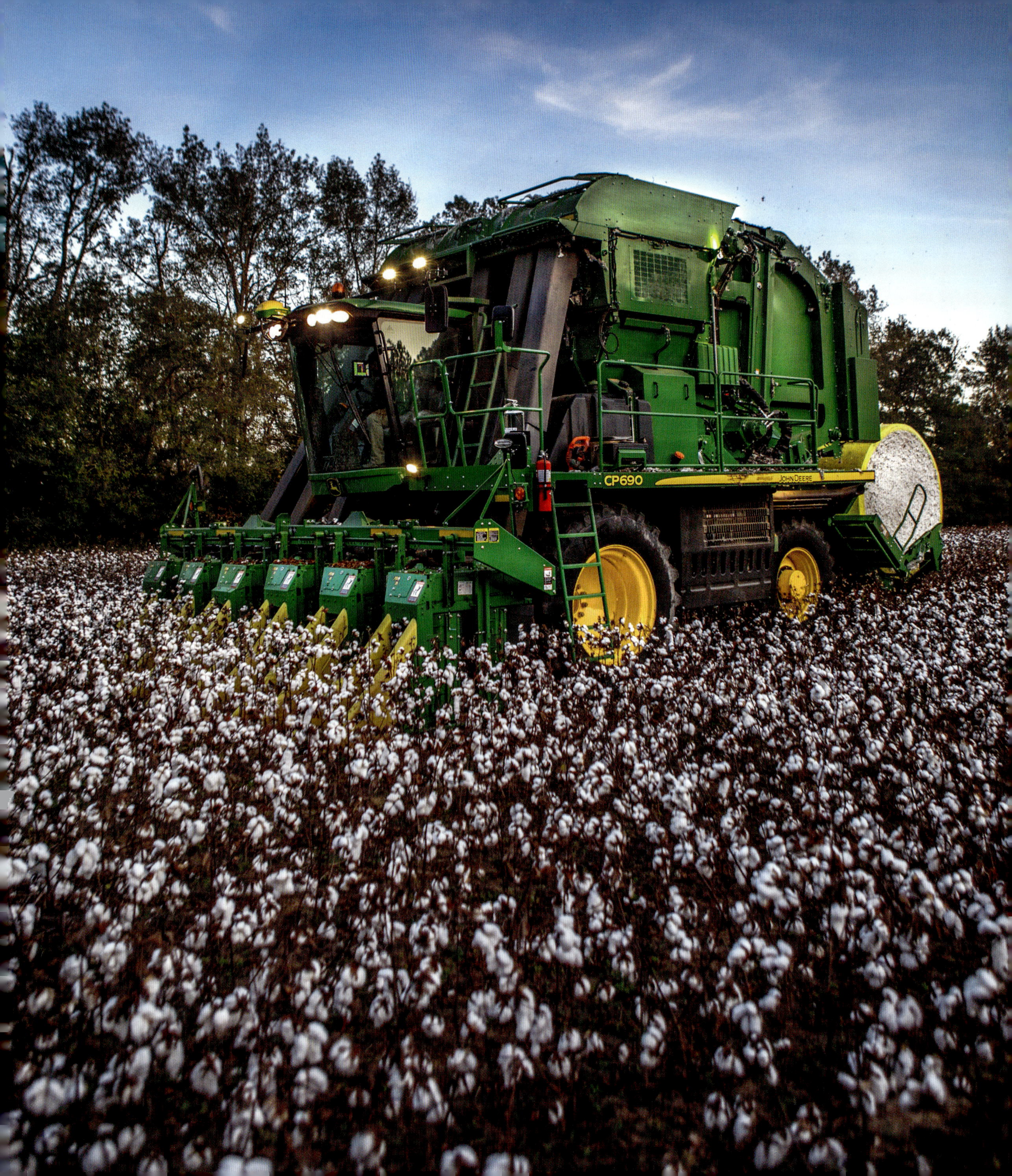
CP690
JOHN DEERE

John Deere CP690

CP stands for cotton picker, and this one weighs 66,000 pounds. It helps turn a field of snowy cotton into textile gold. High-tech cotton harvesters give the farmer a nonstop means of harvesting cotton and makes farming more productive. Today's farmers embrace precision farming and use GPS, drones, smartphones, tablets, and big data to improve the accuracy of planting seeds, applying fertilizer and pesticides.

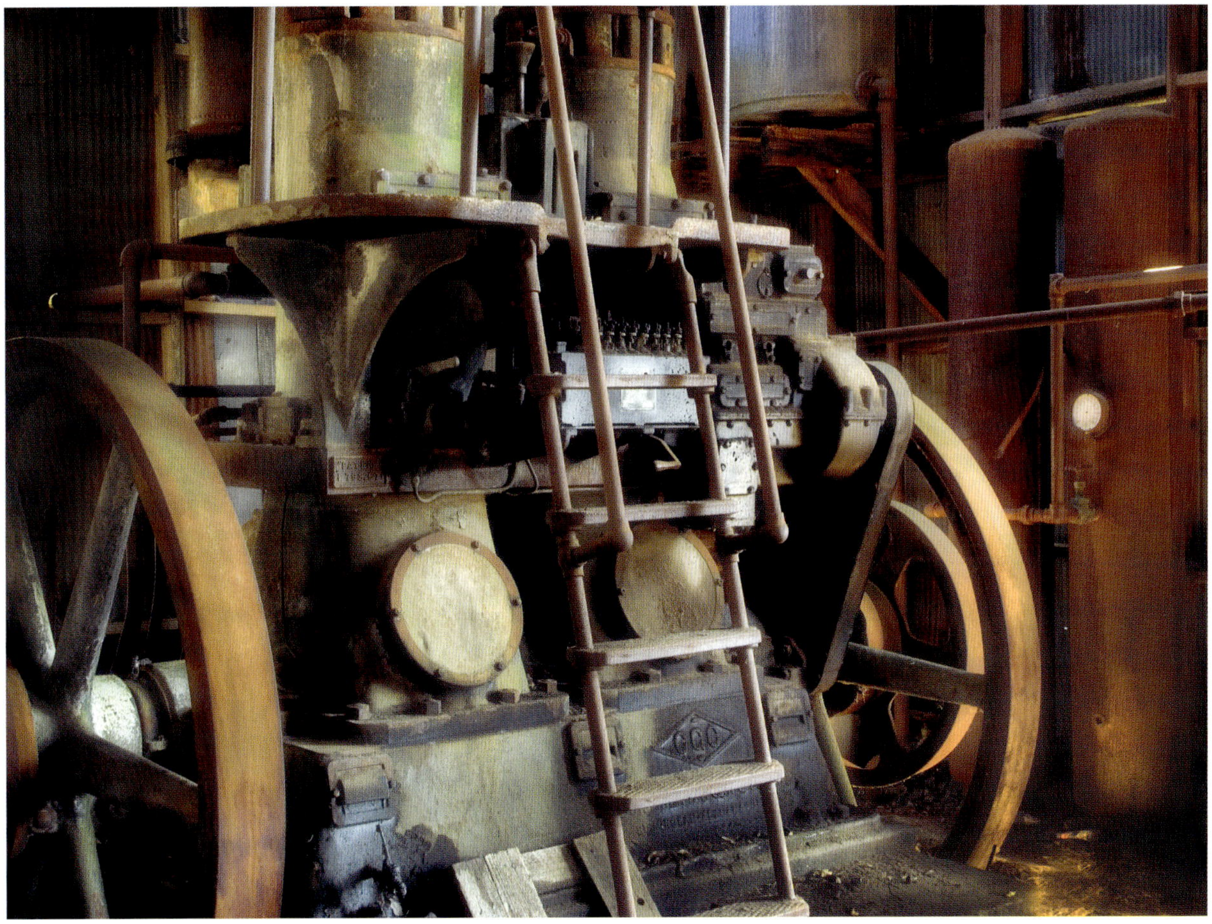

Cotton Gin Engine

With a rhythmic beat, this cotton gin near Cope separated cotton fibers from seeds. The ancestor of this motorized gin, Eli Whitney's 1793 "saw" prototype made the planting of cotton profitable. The gin caused cotton's production to soar from 750,000 bales in 1830 to 2.85 million bales in 1850. By the time of the Civil War, the South was producing two-thirds of the world's supply of cotton.

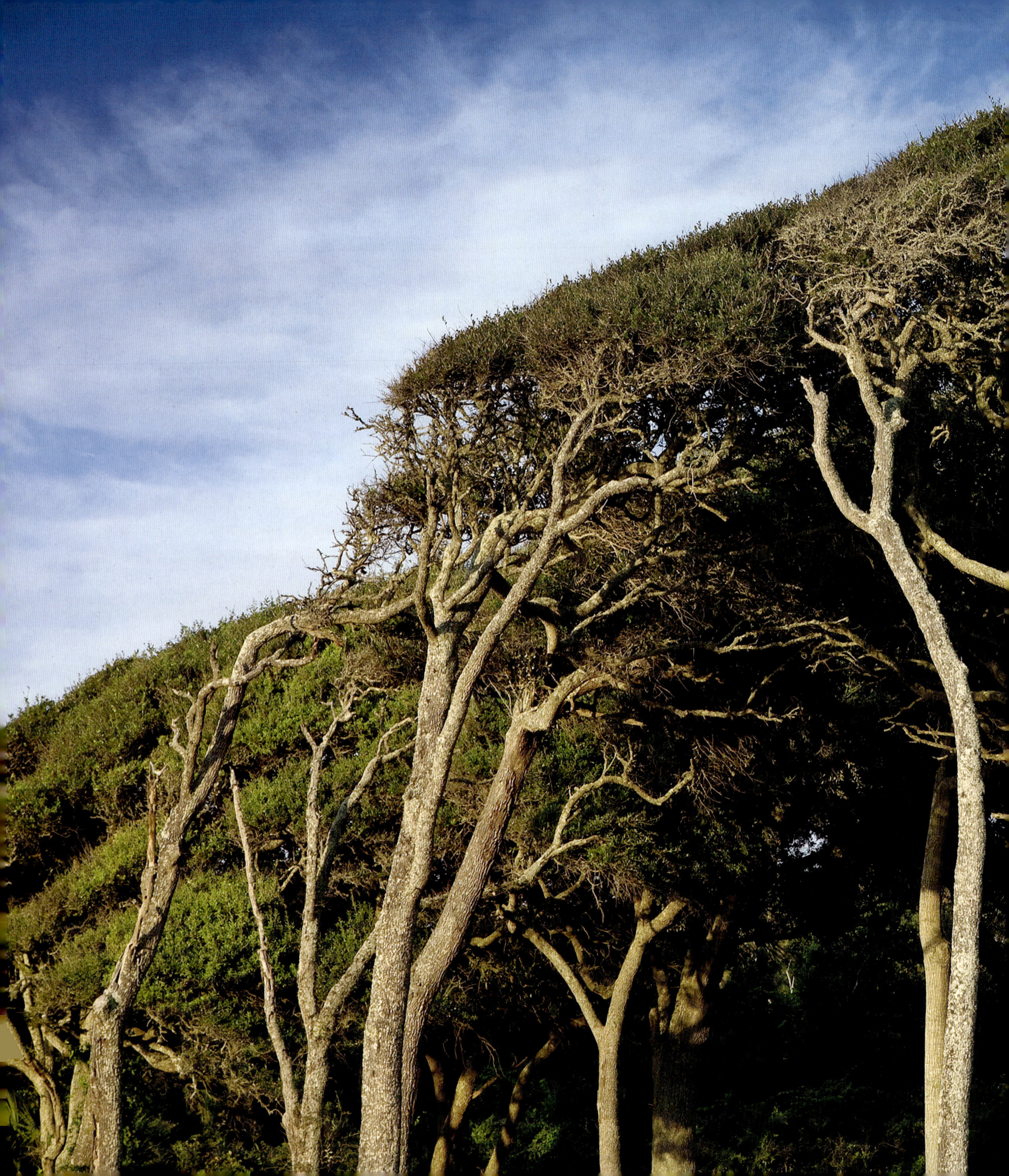

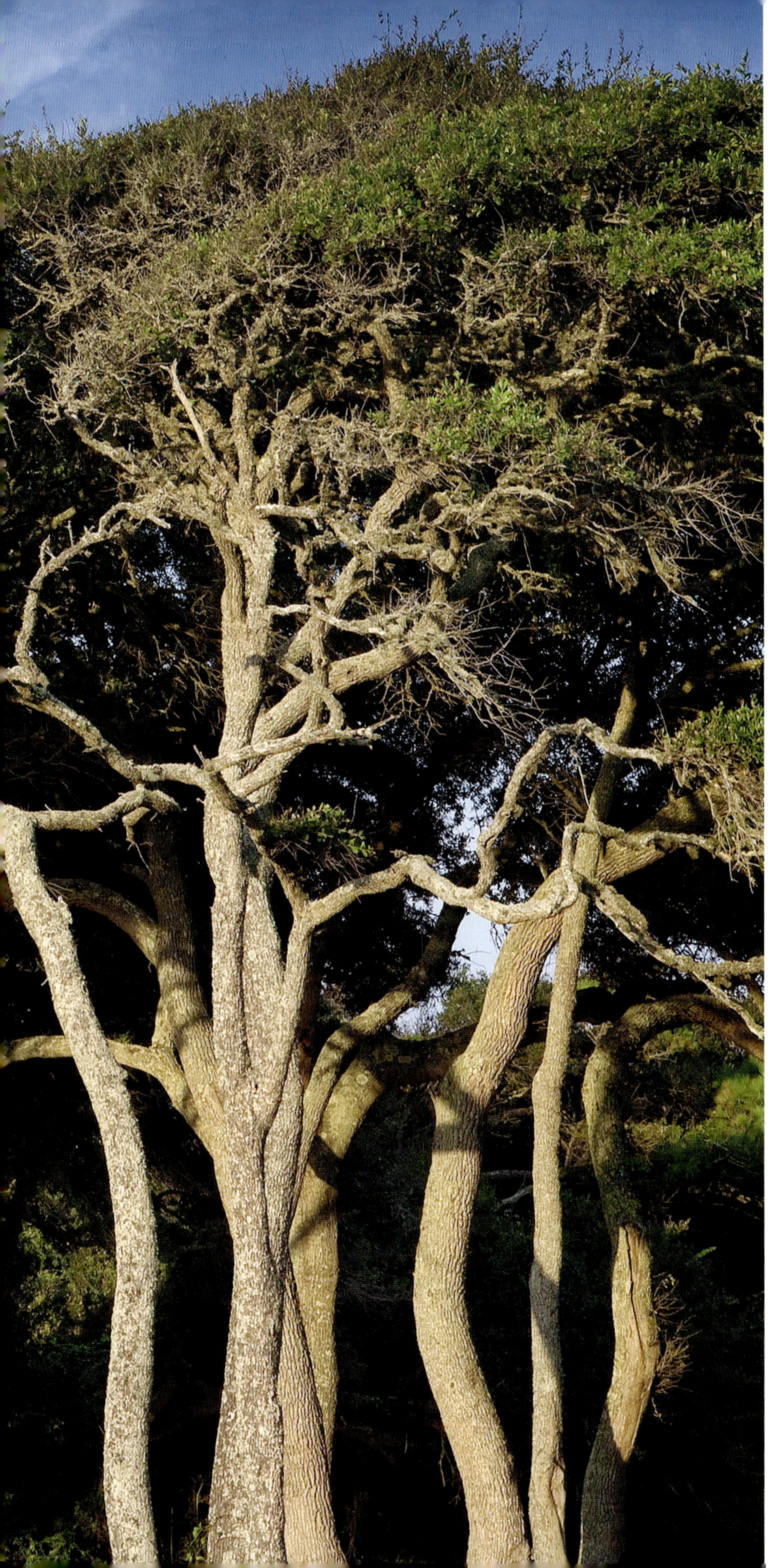

Wind-Sculpted Maritime Forest

Salt spray, winds, and the adverse effects of windblown sand sculpt maritime forests. Airborne salt, deposited on sea-facing branches and leaves, kills them, in effect pruning them. A windswept, sculpted effect results.

Spanish Galleon

Housed in the ocean Drive Beach and Golf Resort, the Spanish Galleon is a club popular with shaggers. The shag, a couples' dance, is South Carolina's official state dance. Couples shag to beach music, which evolved from the blues. The Shaggers Hall of Fame is housed in the same complex.

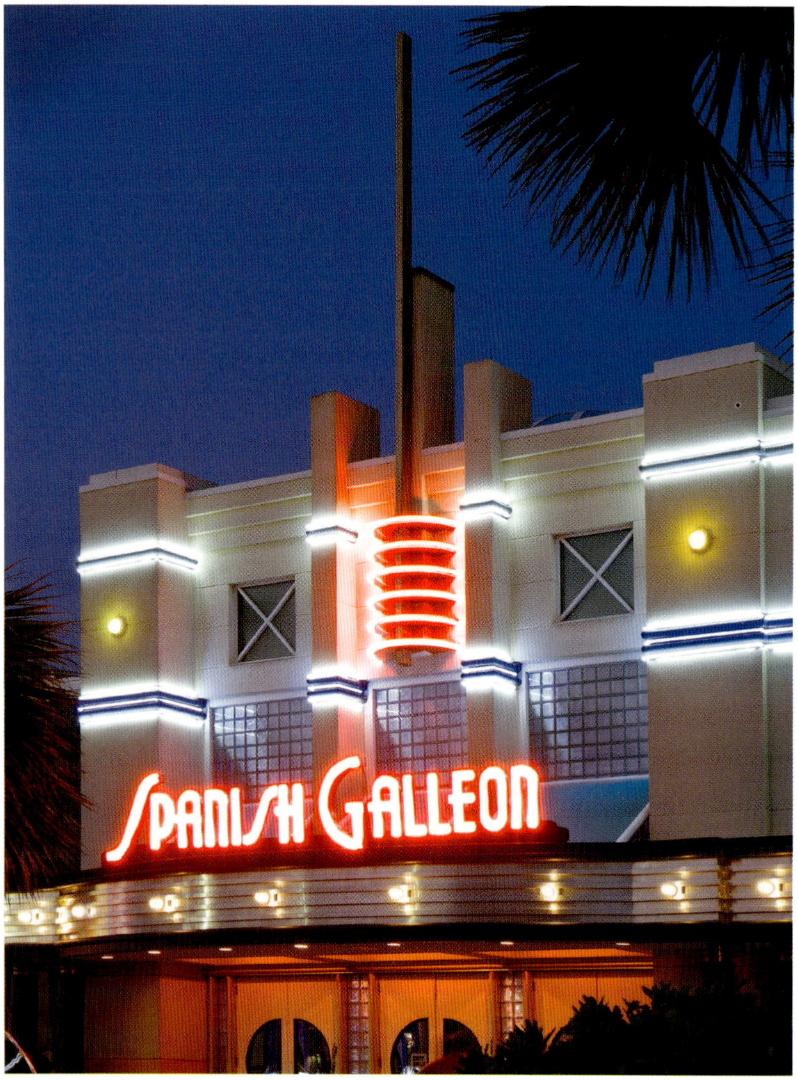

Watching the Wheel in the Sky

At 200 feet the Myrtle Beach Boardwalk SkyWheel is the tallest Ferris wheel in the eastern United States. Complete with a million LED lights and 42 air-conditioned gondolas, a flight, or spin, on the $12 million SkyWheel takes four revolutions and lasts 10 to 15 minutes.

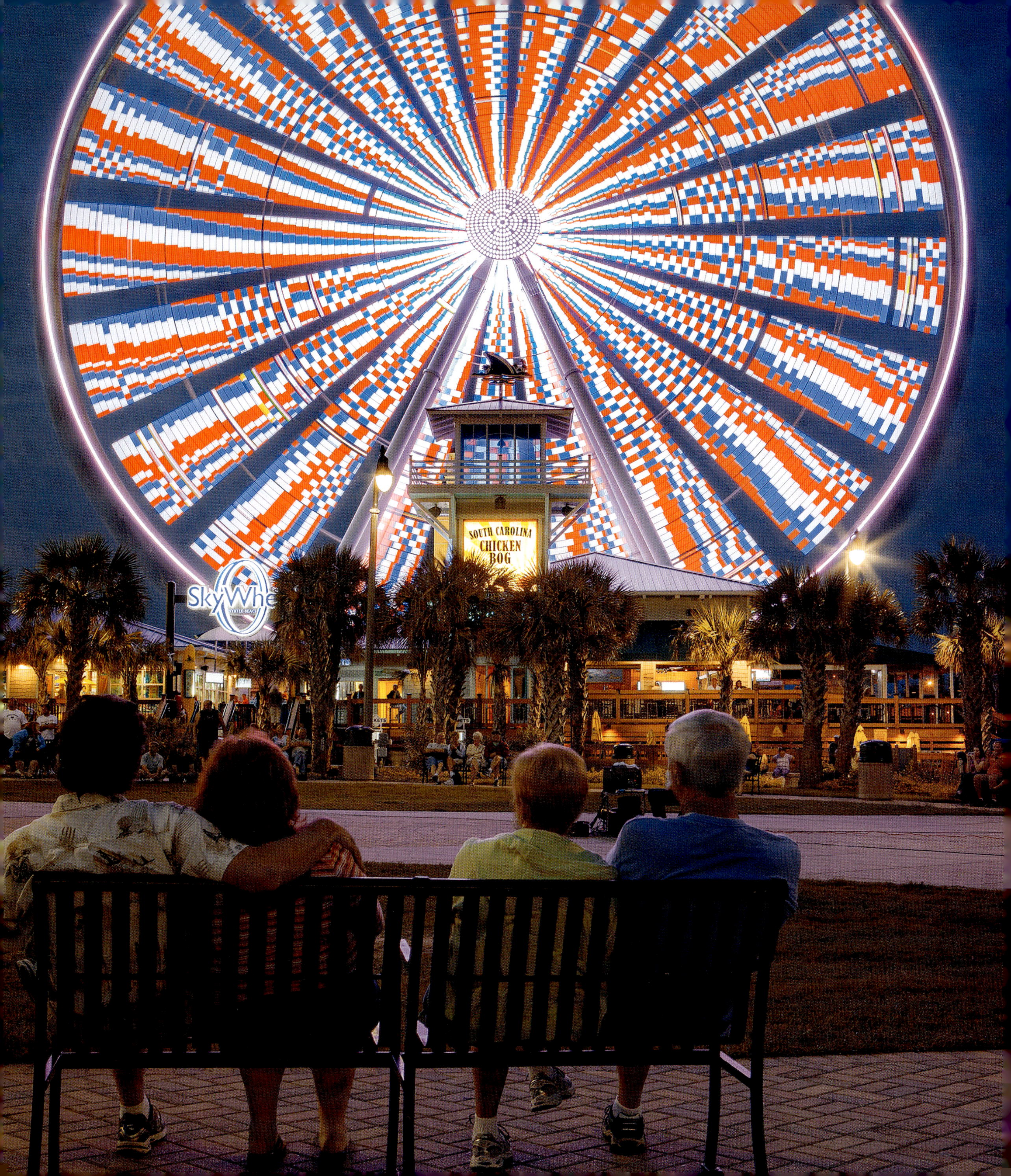
SOUTH CAROLINA
CHICKEN
BOG

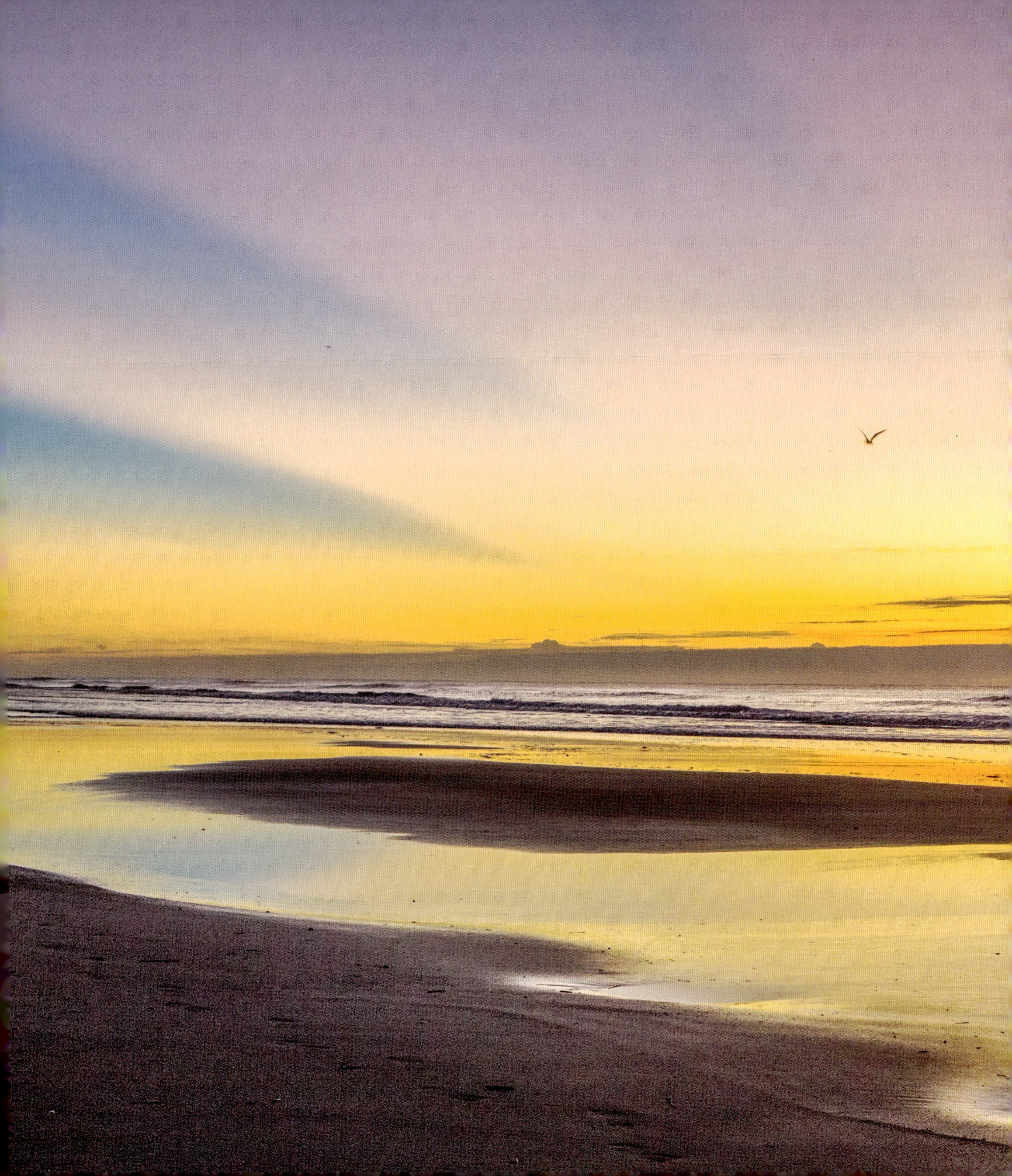

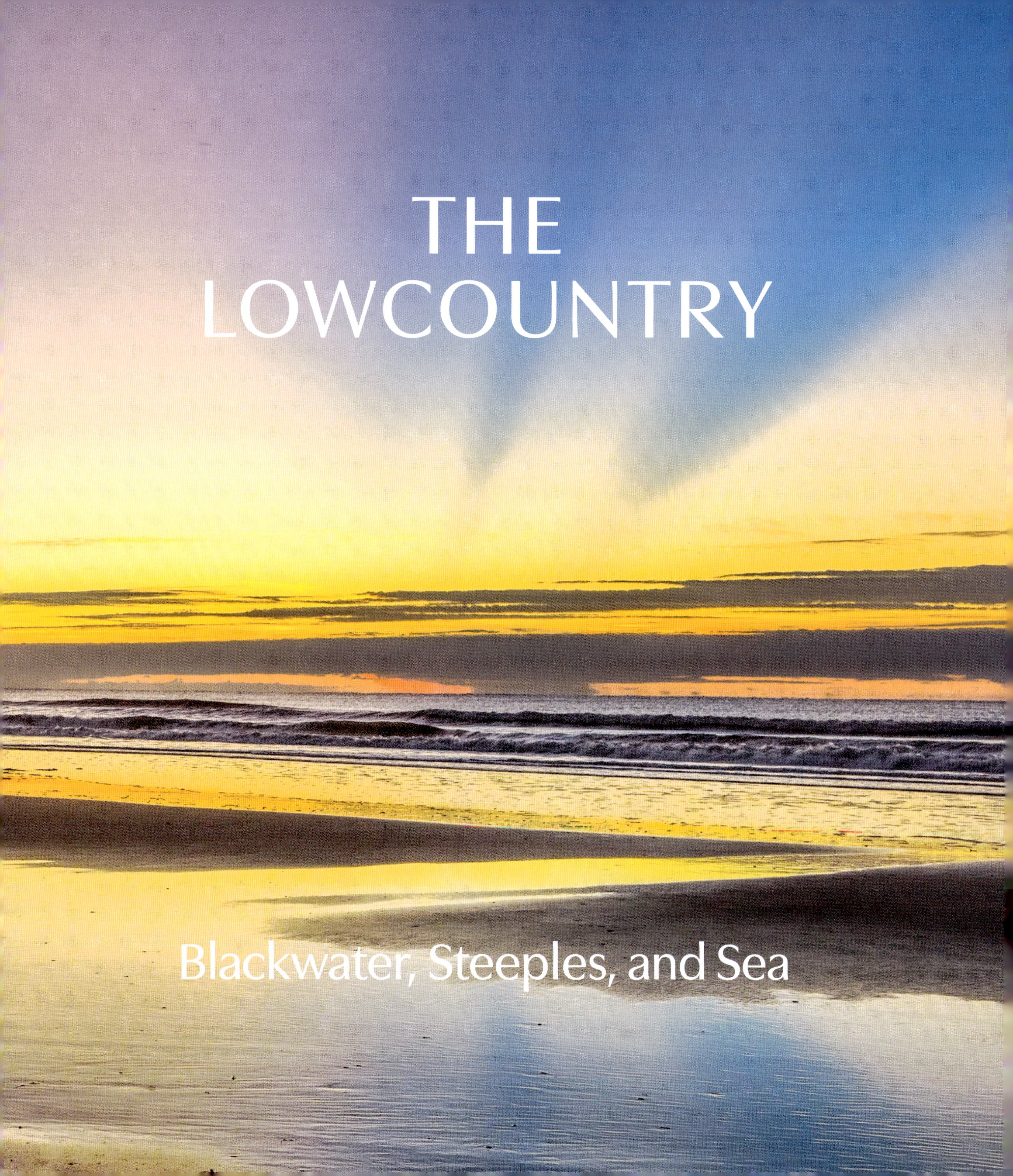

THE LOWCOUNTRY

Blackwater, Steeples, and Sea

OVERLEAF

Storm Aftermath at Sunrise

A storm breaks up near Folly Beach. The rising sun paints the sky and sea neon-like colors.

Atalaya (Spanish for Watchtower) *National Register of Historic Places*

Of Moorish Revival and Mediterranean Revival architecture, Atalaya Castle provided a summer retreat for Archer M. Huntington and Anna Hyatt Huntington. The location near Murrells Inlet afforded a temperate refuge for Anna, who suffered tuberculosis from the mid-1920s to the mid-1930s. A noted sculptor, Anna devoted hours of extensive study to animals in zoos and circuses. She and her husband founded Brookgreen Gardens, a Society for Southeastern Flora and Fauna. Today the Huntington's retreat hosts the best of American sculpture from the nineteenth century to the present. The square tower at Atalaya housed a 3,000-gallon cypress water tank.

The line "a dream within a dream" comes from the tortured genius of Edgar Allan Poe who spent a year on Sullivan's Island. A couplet goes . . . *All that we see or seem, Is but a dream within a dream*. Poe was not writing about the Lowcountry, which seems dreamlike with its gray clouds raining Spanish moss from oaks. No, he was writing about despair and regret.

There's no despair or regret when it comes to the Lowcountry's magnificence. It's as real as weathered workboats tethered to a marsh dock. As real as the delectable architecture we call tabby and as dreamy as magnolia blossoms, azaleas, camellias, and sea oats. It's dreamlike to see the lonely crabber navigate a fog-shrouded estuary at daybreak. And dreamlike to see ibises feathering the air white but concerning as they rise above the whine of a million mosquitoes.

The Lowcountry is flat as a fritter but rises as a watchtower at Atalaya, as a modern miracle of a bridge, and as legions of hurricane-tolerant trees that aren't really trees. You would not be dreaming if you believed a thin long desert edged our coastline because it does.

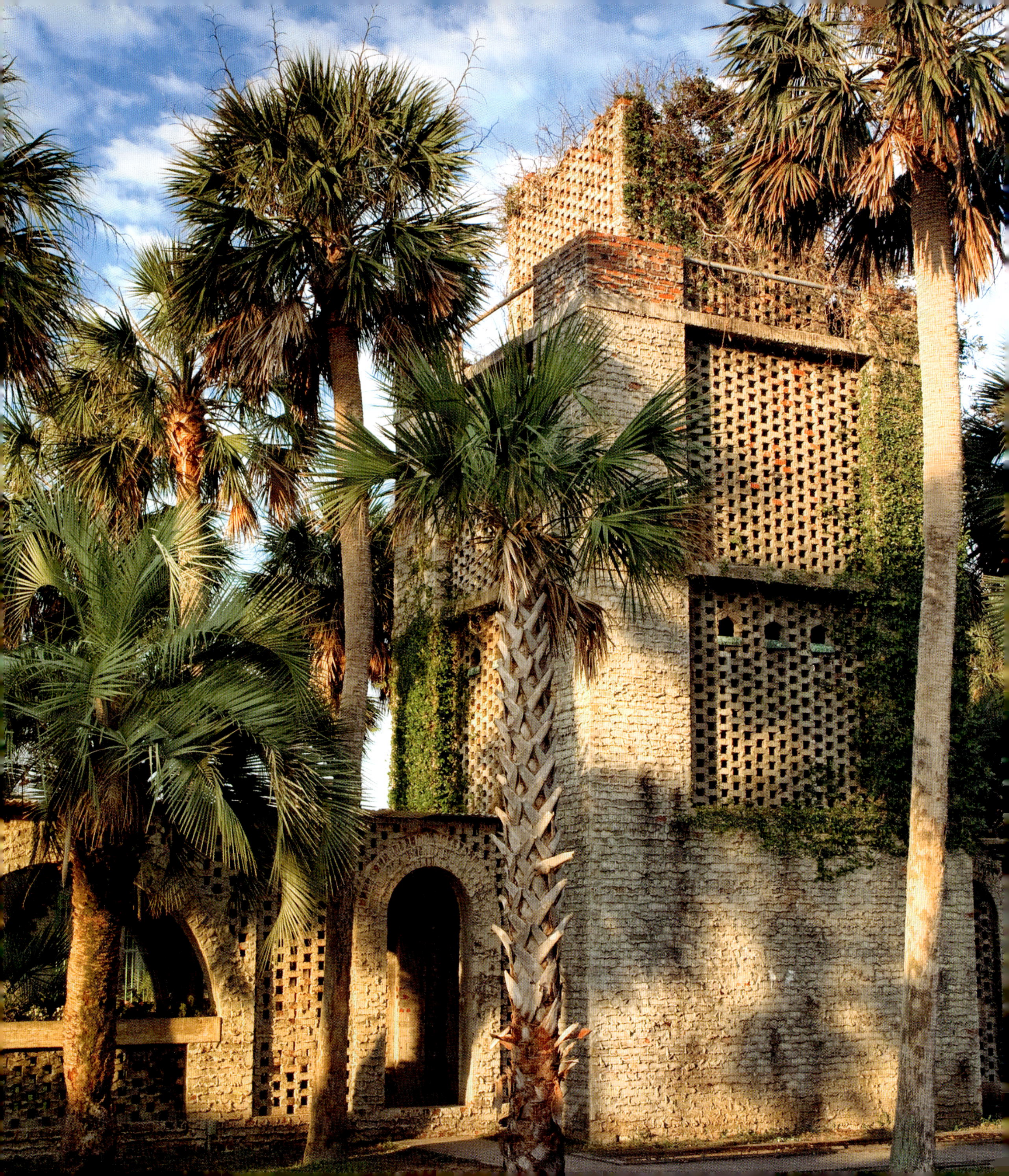

Would you believe we have flying rainbows and ruins as majestic as Rome's? Well, we do. Sweetgrass, luminous nights, and the country's largest assembly of figurative statuary? We have that too. But we have sadness also. The sight of a shrimp boat at dawn fades as change threatens those rugged captains of delectable harvests. Imported shrimp, loss of dock space, and other issues threaten to rob us of wild, domestic shrimp as well as the stirring images of trawlers working the sea.

The Lowcountry isn't a dream within a dream; its many dreams include tabernacles and old rice plantations, gold autumnal marshes, apparitions known as boneyards, and crustaceans with turquoise claws. Add to that, sandy lanes tunneling through live oaks heavy with moss, carnivorous plants, old churches, crepe myrtles, and cobblestoned streets. We can't overlook artists and sculptors nor buttressed cypress, black water, blue creeks, and ghost crabs' tunnels of sand. And we haven't even scratched the surface.

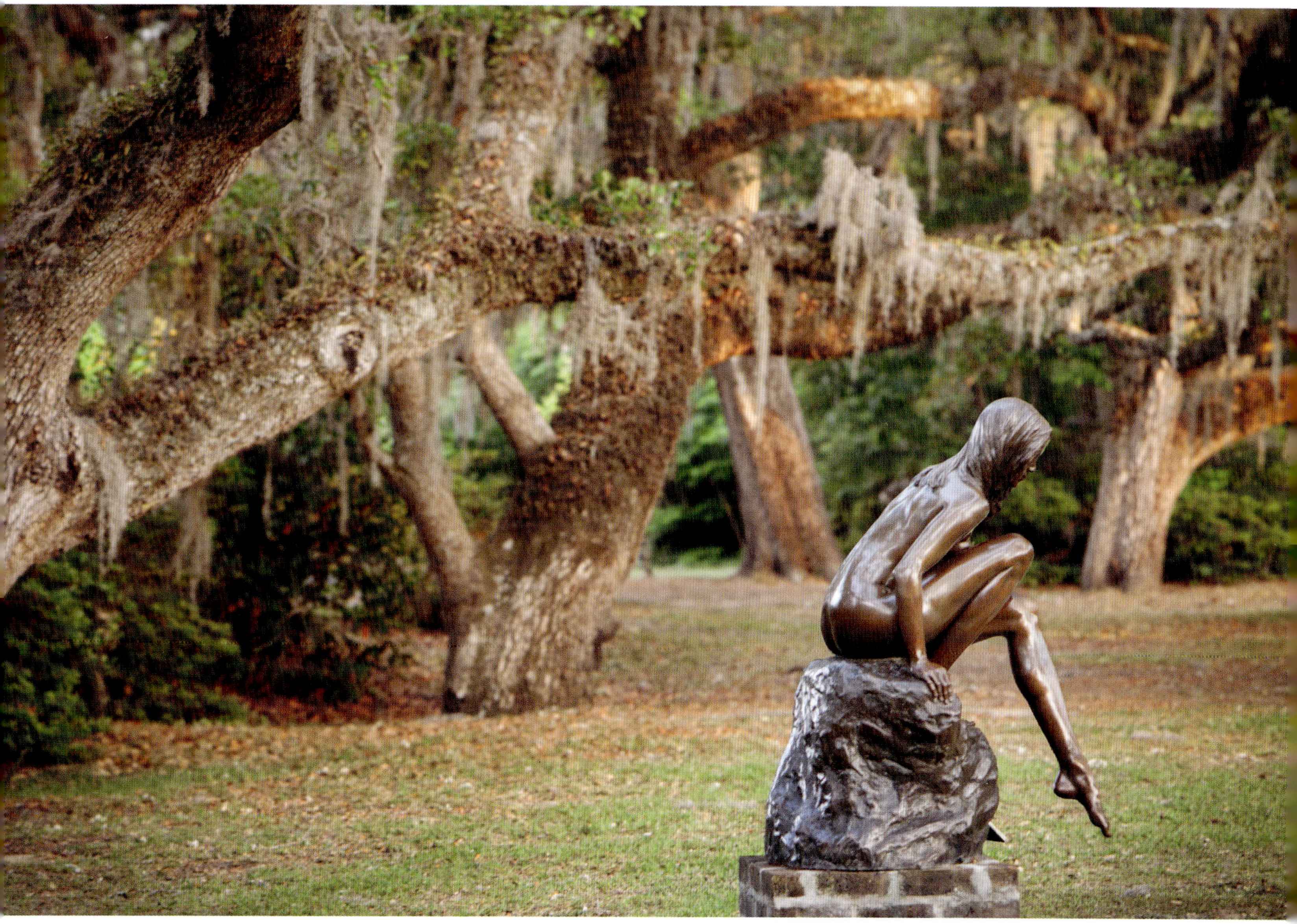

The Bather

Gwen Marcus worked for two years exclusively on her bronze sculpture, *The Bather*, now a permanent installation at Brookgreen Gardens. Of her model, a dancer, Marcus said, "She and her energy are the soul of the sculpture." Patrons visiting the country's largest, most comprehensive collection of American figurative sculpture can experience the energy of Marcus's *The Bather* in a garden setting. Praised for its accuracy and sensitivity toward the human form, Marcus's works exude strength, energy, spirituality, and sensuality.

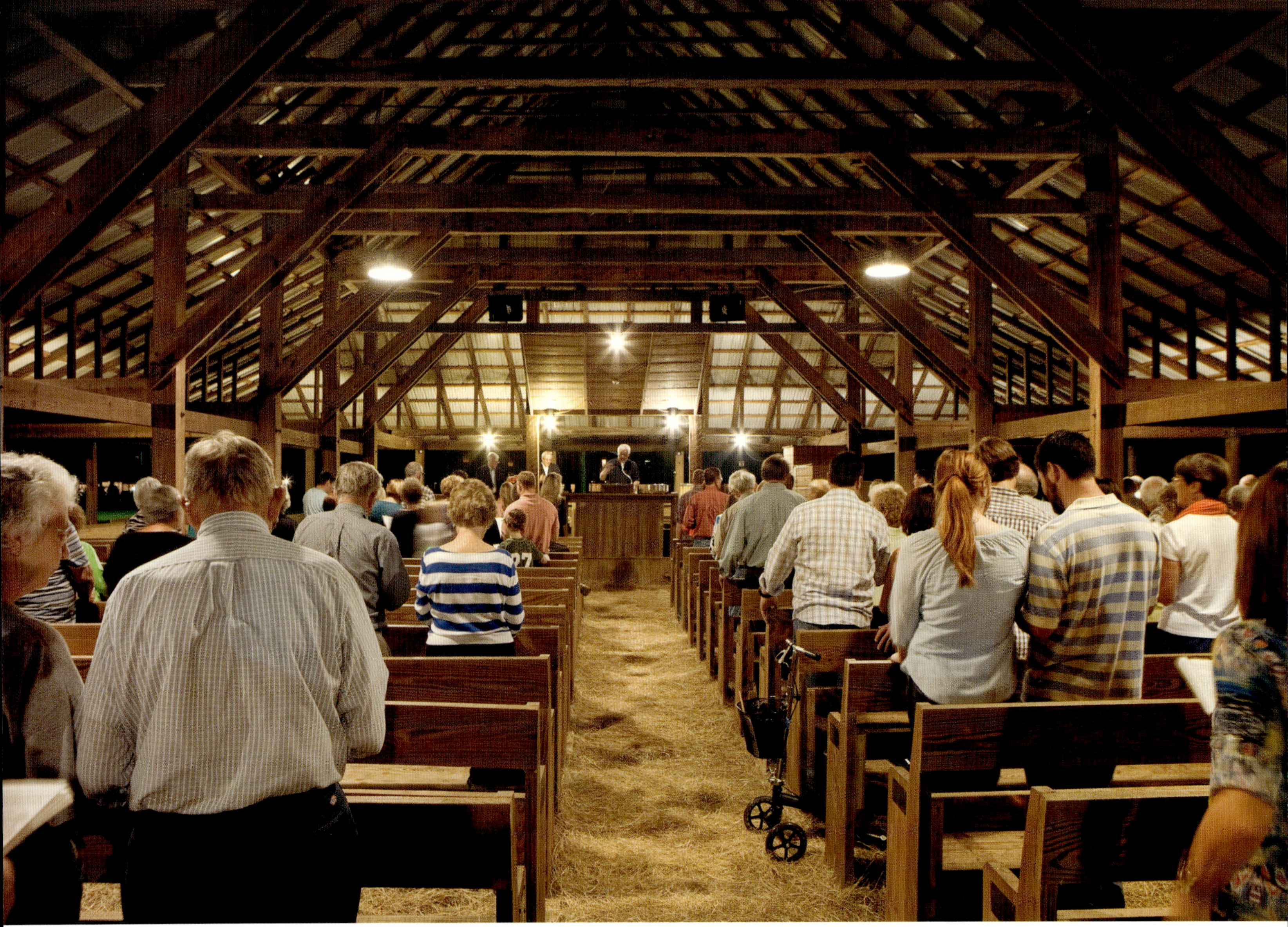

Indian Field Methodist Campground Tabernacle
National Register of Historic Places

The Indian Field Campground Meeting tabernacle stands in the center of ninety-nine tents where people live, pray, and socialize for eight days. Early on, people stayed in covered wagons and makeshift tents. In the 1840s rustic framed cabins called tents appeared. While camp meeting began for religious purposes, today it's a revival and reunion. In simpler times parents pinned a paper tag to children's shirts with their tent number on it. That way stray toddlers could be returned to their tent.

William Bowman

At Indian Field Methodist Campground near St. George, William Bowman blew the horn at key times, calling campers and their guests to worship and quiet time. Bowman's Uncle Shell Johnson blew the horn at Indian Field Methodist Campground for 75 years, last blowing the horn at 103 years of age.

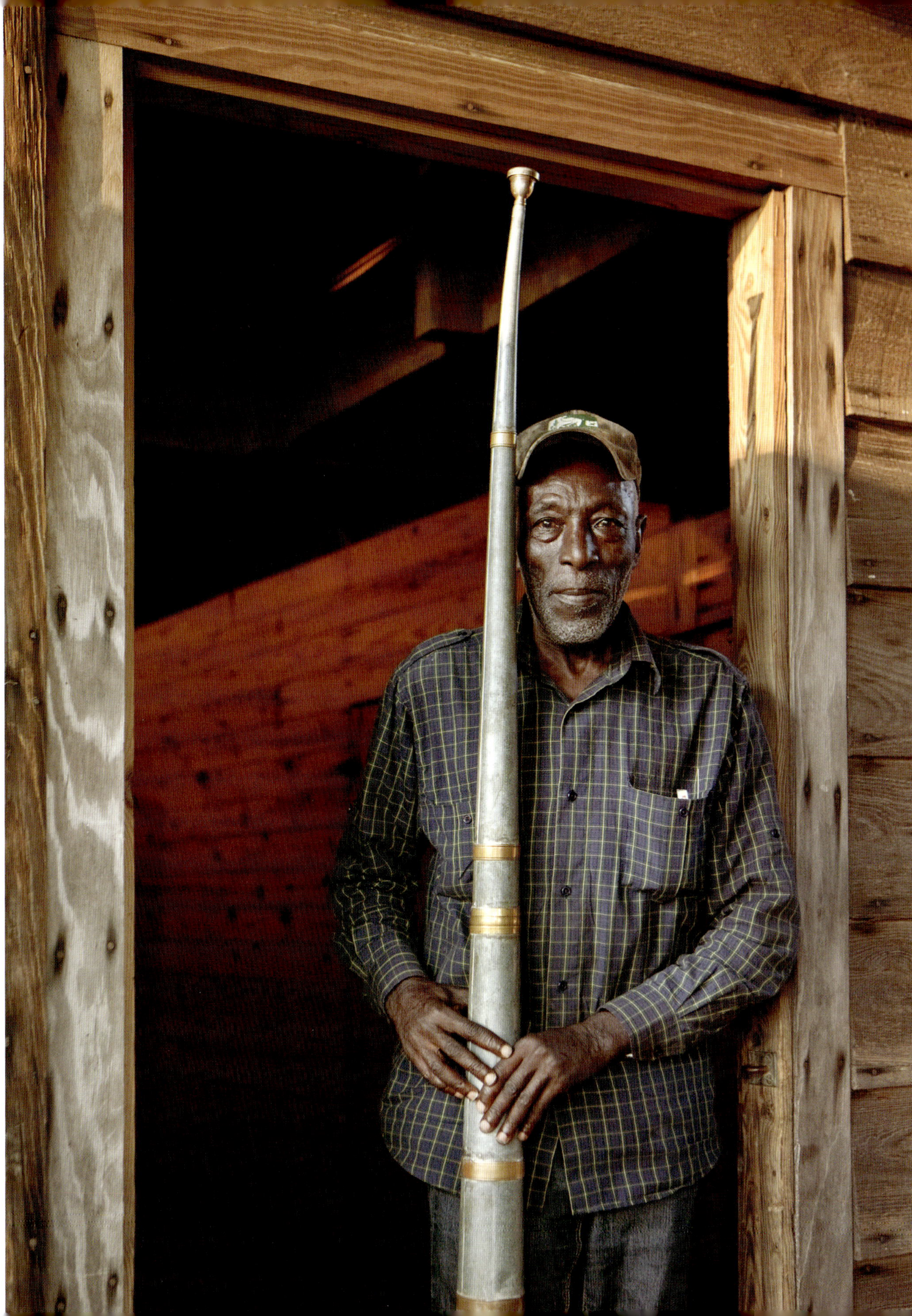

The Winnowing Barn

At Mansfield Plantation, millions of pounds of Carolina Gold passed through this old barn after much labor. Before the rice could make its way to the barn, women pounded the grain. Then the rice went to the winnowing barn, where women shook it loose from the chaff and swept it into chutes in the barn's floor. As the rice tumbled into a muslin tarp attached to the stilts—a giant sack—the chaff blew away.

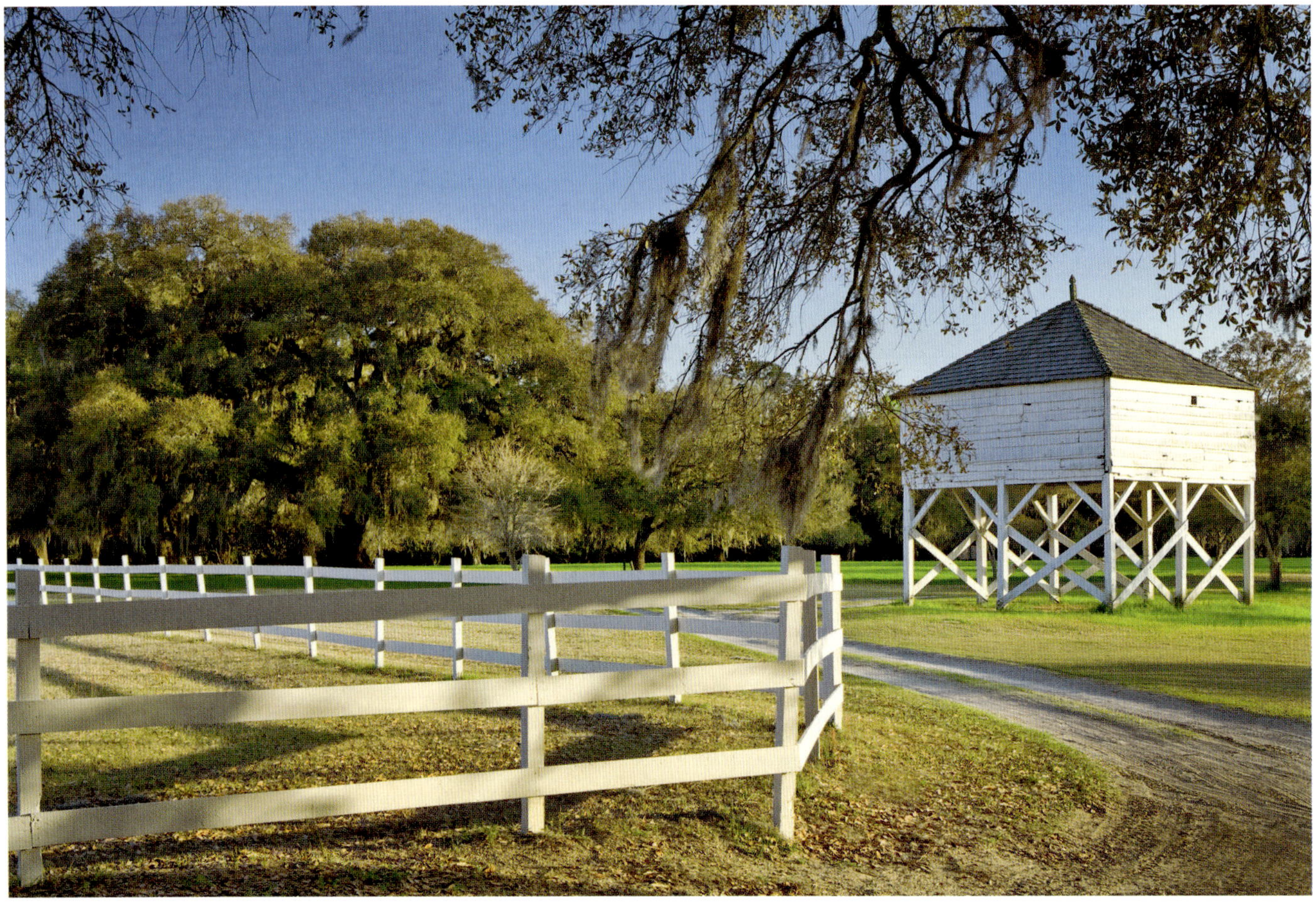

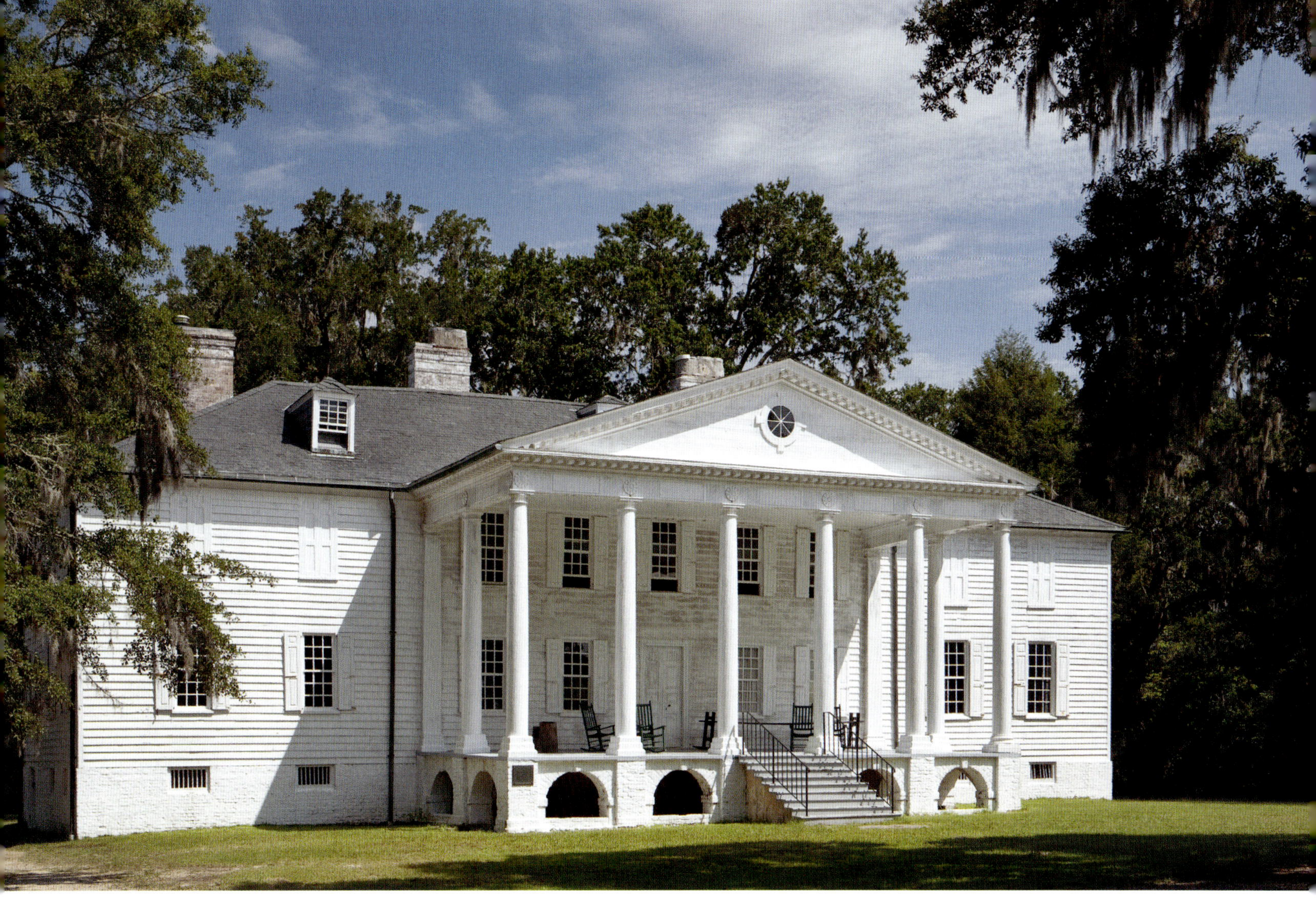

Hampton Plantation
National Landmark, National Register of Historic Places

Built in 1735, Hampton Plantation offers visitors one of the earliest examples of the use of a giant portico in domestic American architecture and South Carolina's finest example of a large two-and-a-half-frame Georgian house. In the twentieth century Archibald Rutledge hunted and explored here, receiving the inspiration and experience that informed many of his poems and books. Rutledge served as South Carolina's poet laureate from 1934 to 1973.

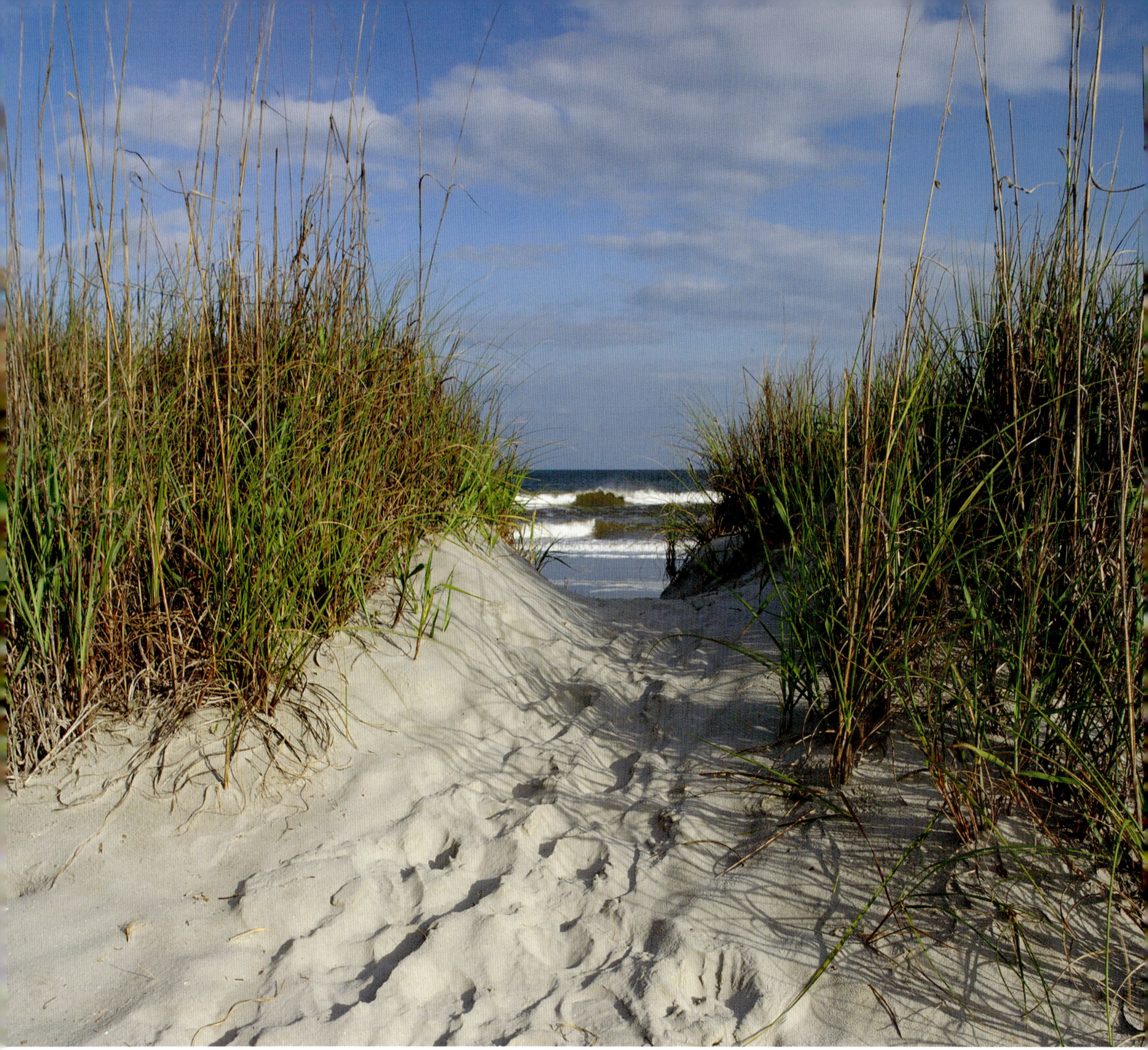

Pawleys Island Portal

A break in the dunes frames Atlantic breakers. Dune traffic is not a good thing.

OUR SEASIDE DESERT

Sand dunes, far more than mounds of sand, provide barriers to the sea and vital habitat to wildlife species. They're an essential, yet harsh, habitat. Beachgoers who make the mistake of walking barefoot over summer beach sands see just how hot dunes get. Many are aware of the sun and its skin cancer danger but don't realize how challenging the heat is to plants or dune's importance.

People don't think of a dune as a desert by the sea, but some of North America's drier areas are the dunes lining the Atlantic Ocean. Beachgoers who walk through dunes cross one of the more unique habitats around; that is, a thin, long desert habitat that's *xeric*, containing little moisture.

Dune's shifting sands, strong winds, salt water, and blazing sun make for a harsh environment. It takes a specially adapted plant to survive on dunes. Plants like sea oats stabilize dunes, which is one reason it's illegal to pick the heads of sea oats. The plants splashing green onto dunes are special. They are salt-tolerant and used to living in sand where water pours right through, if it doesn't evaporate first.

People's desire to be as close as they can to the sea has destroyed massive amounts of dune communities. Many years ago, people considered dunes and dune vegetation nuisances to be flattened before building seaside homes, hotels, and restaurants. Today we know better. Unique vegetation anchors dunes and keeps them from blowing away. Dunes themselves provide crucial barriers against high tides and hurricanes. And dunes add a touch of beauty to the coast that's incomparable.

We don't have dune systems like we once did. If you want to see what the Atlantic coast used to look like, go to Hunting Island State Park where magnificent dune systems tower fifty feet high, much like scenes from desert movies. Crosswalks and wind fences? Use them. They help stabilize dunes.

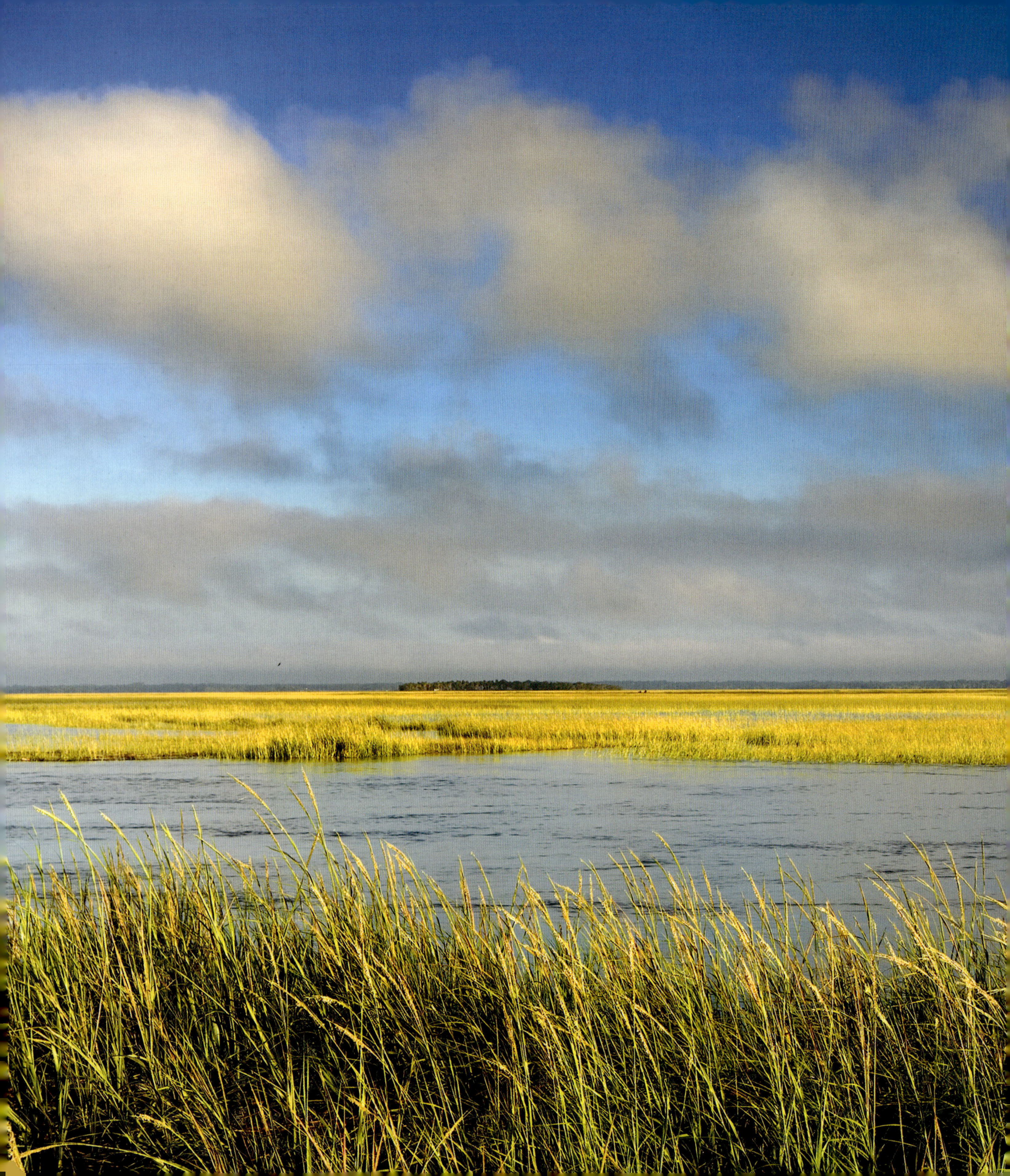

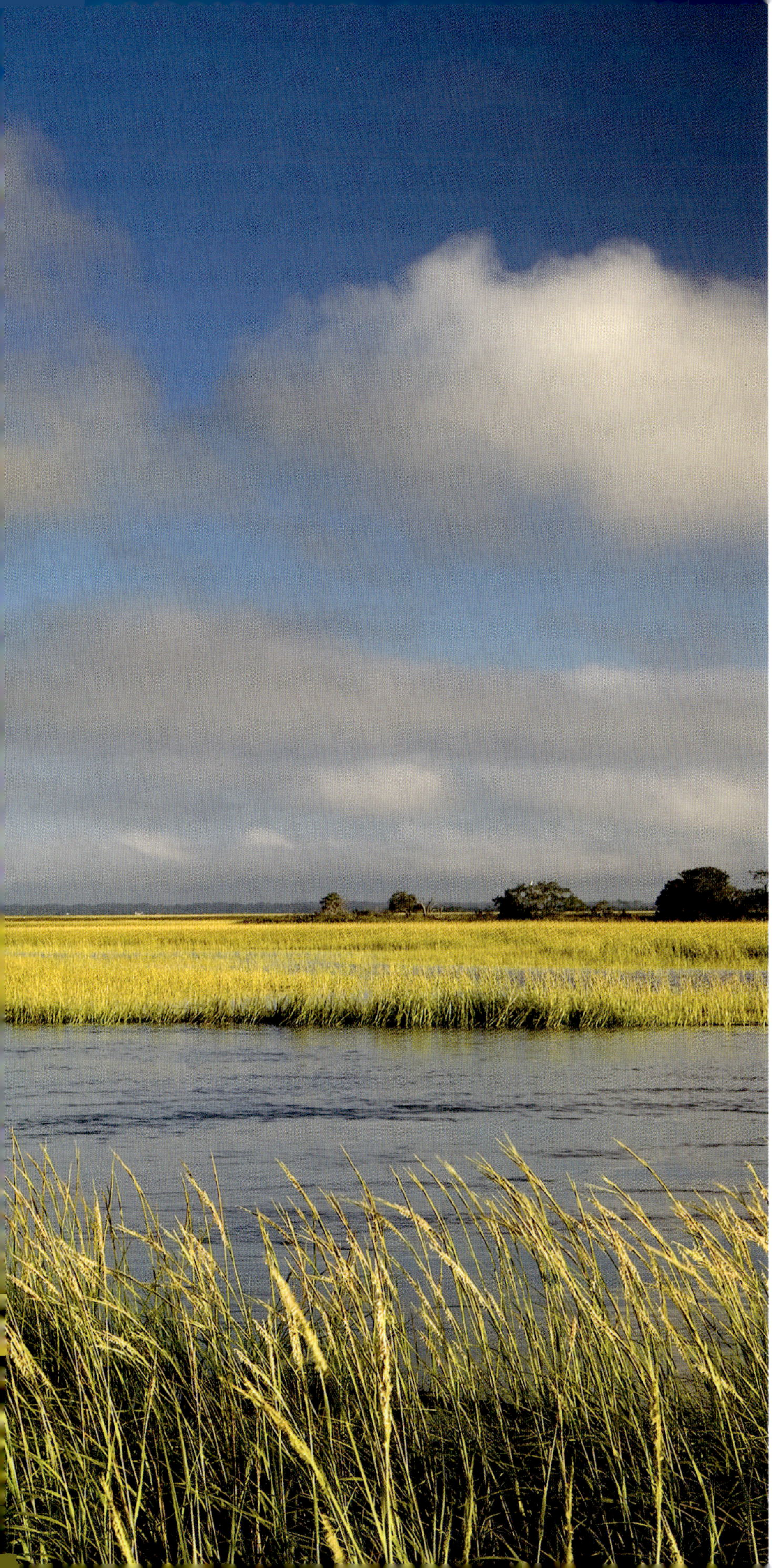

Incoming Tide

This Charleston County coastal wetland in gold autumnal glory provides food, cover, and habitat for fish species, shrimp, blue crab, and many other life forms. When the tide goes out, this creek will carry nutrients out to sea, doing its part to uphold the estuary's role as the nursery for the Atlantic Ocean.

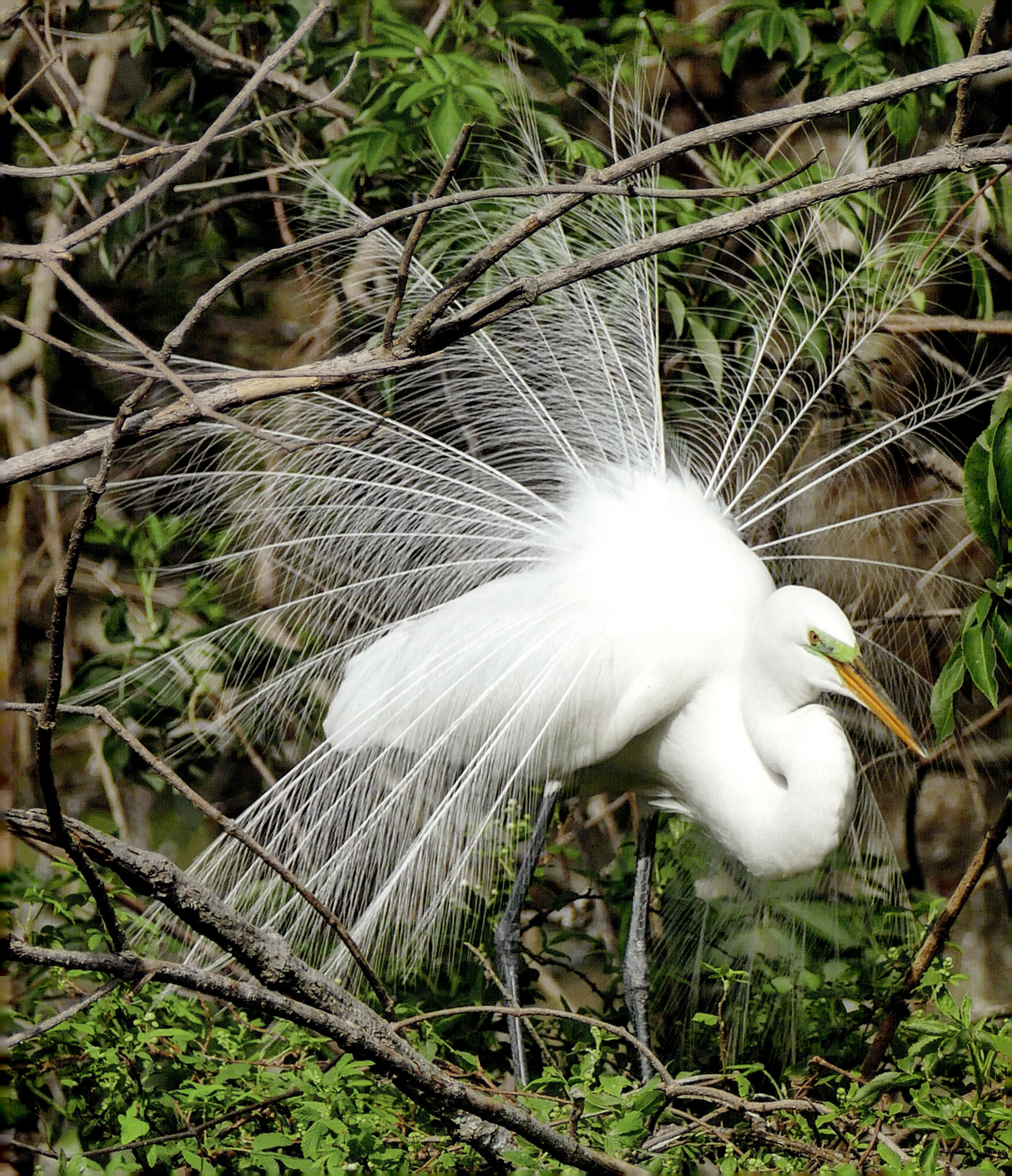

Great Egret

Lost beneath the snow-white plumage is the nest of seemingly haphazard fiddlesticks-like construction. The male begins nest construction but then brings materials to the female, and she finishes nest building. Other names for the great egret (*Ardea alba*) include American egret, common egret, great white egret, and angel bird.

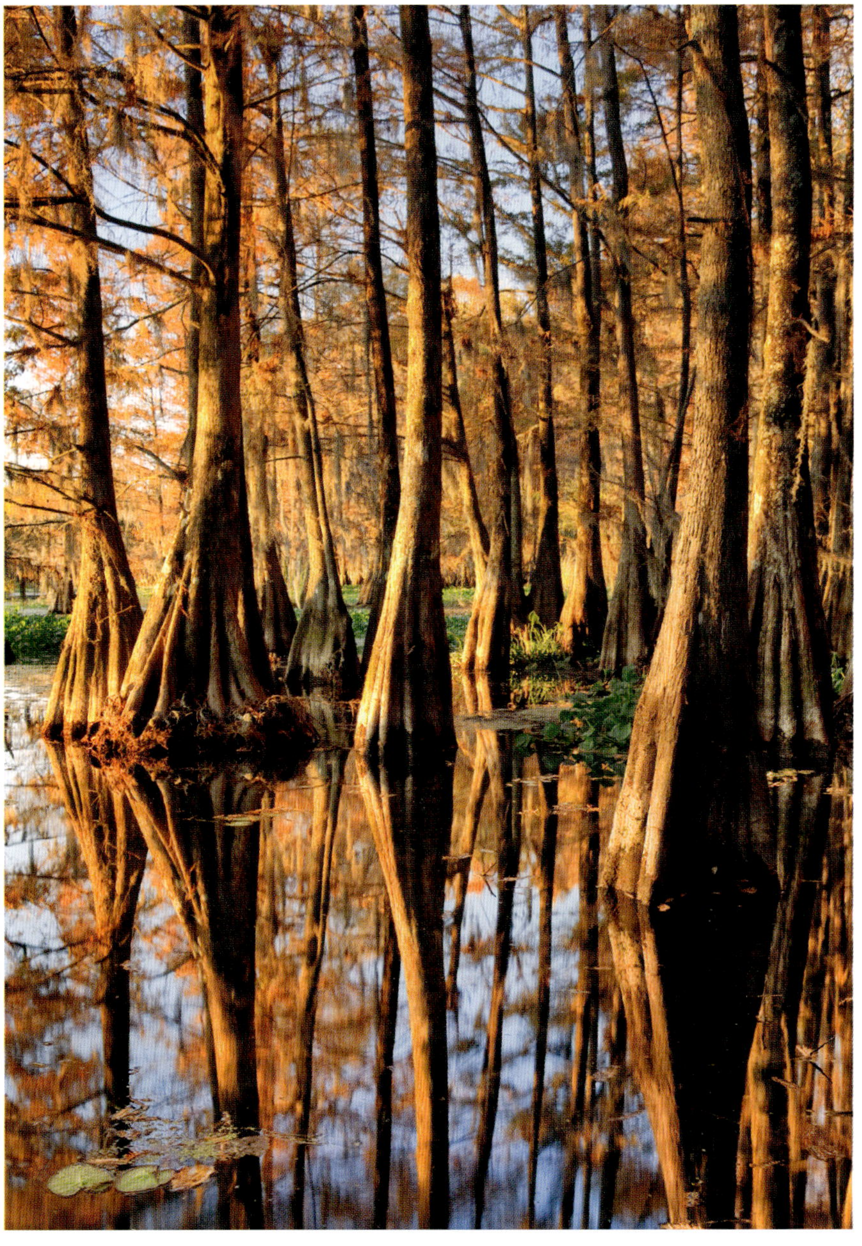

Lake Marion Cypresses

Flooded cypresses, a common scene in the Lowcountry, give the region uncommon beauty and a sense of mystery. Bald cypress and pond cypress are not true cypresses. True cypresses, members of the Cupressus family, are not native to the southeastern United States.

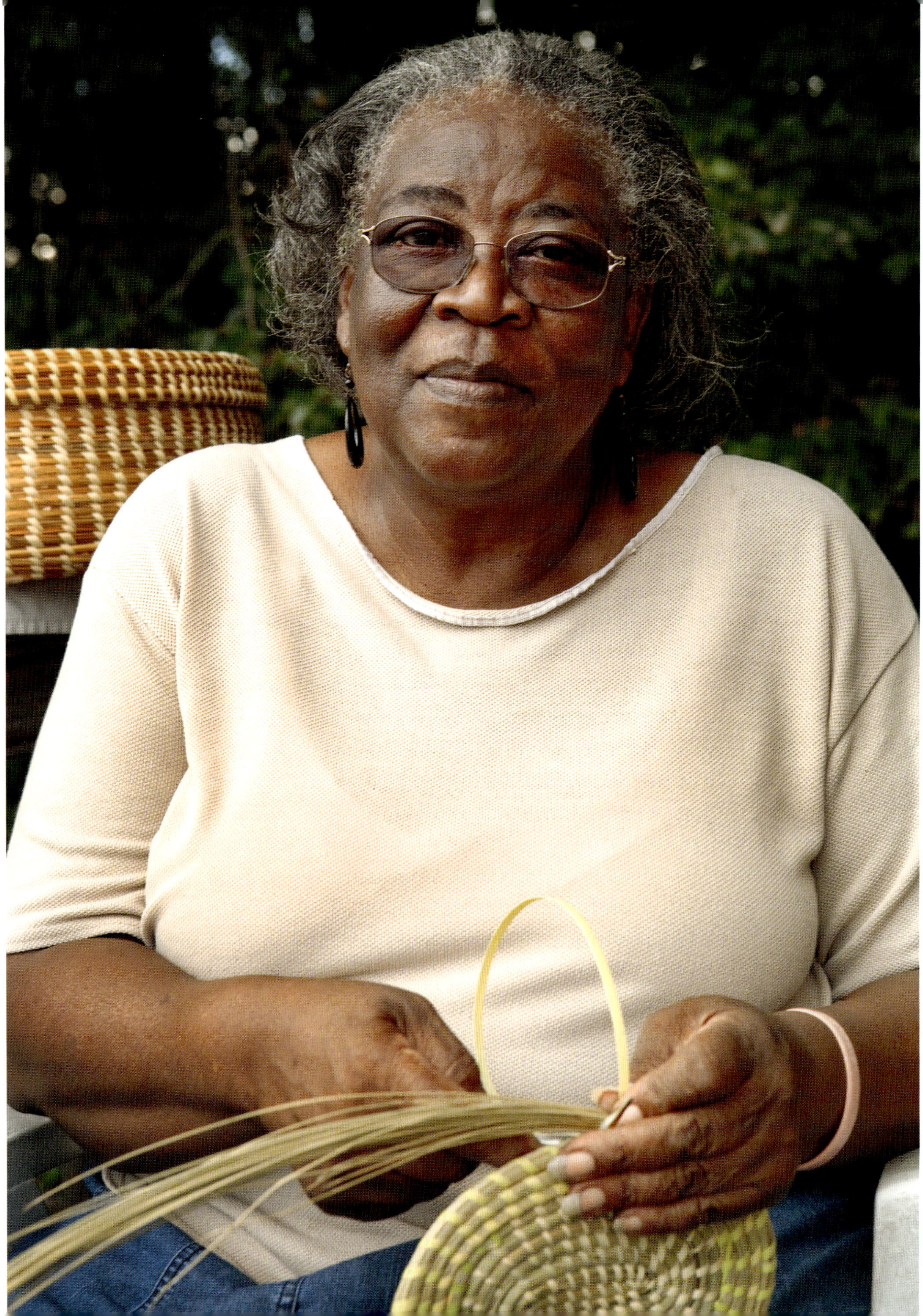

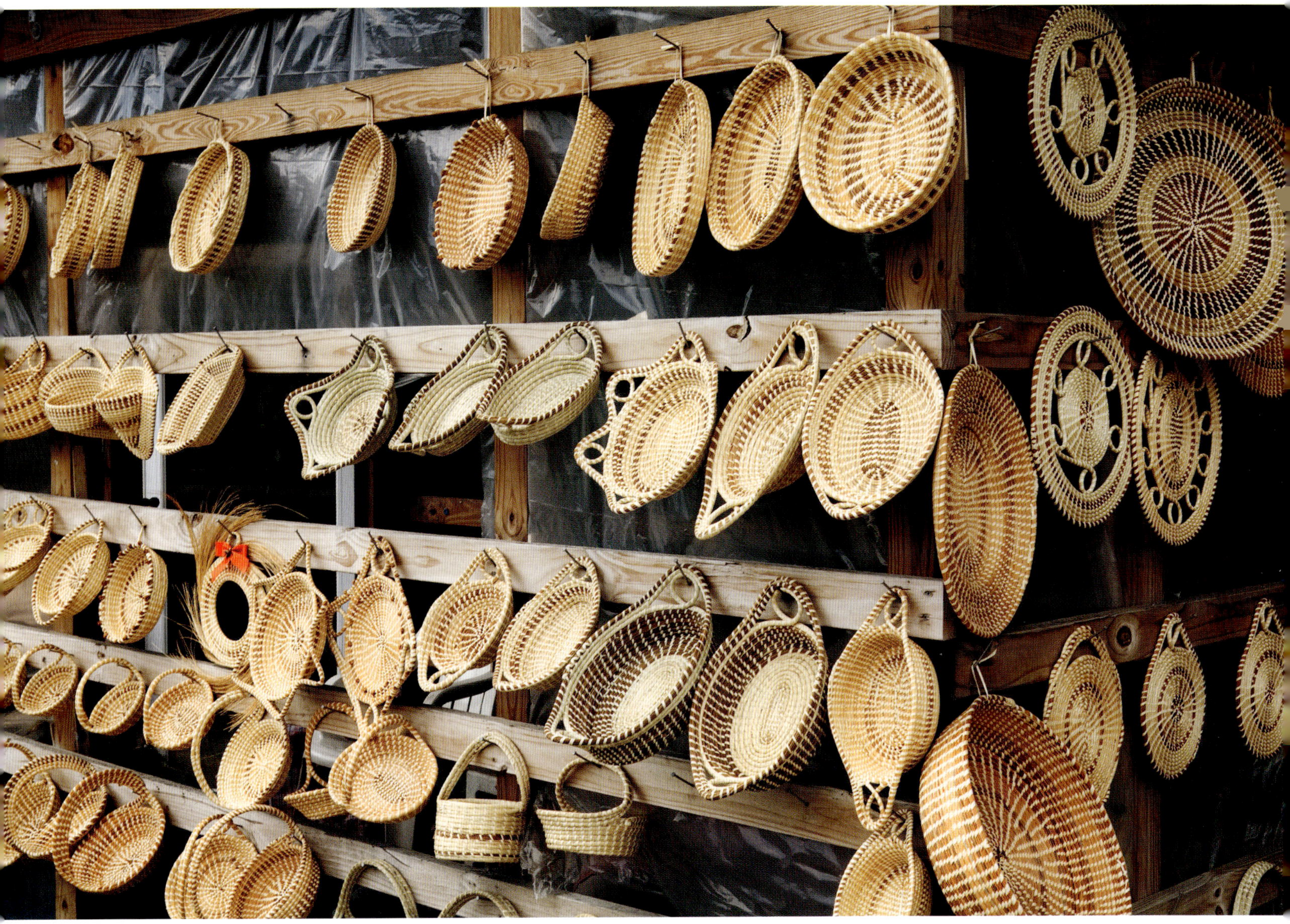

Elizabeth Eady, Mount Pleasant Basket Weaver

Elizabeth Eady wove baskets all her life. "I made my first piece before I went to the first grade." She used forks and spoons just as her predecessors did. "Break those handles off, file 'em down, and start weaving." Elizabeth and her sister, Mabel, would unpack their baskets and hang them with care on their US 17 stand. Elizabeth Eady died June 2022, and Mabel died May 2017, taking a precious heritage with them.

Elizabeth and Mabel's Stand

When they would arrive at their stand, Elizabeth and her sister, Mabel, would unpack their baskets and hang them with care on nails jutting from their stand. Sweetgrass basket weaving, passed from generation to generation, is one of the country's older African diasporic art forms.

Natural Materials

Like other basket makers, the Eady sisters used sweetgrass, needle rush, pine needles, and palmetto leaves in fashioning their baskets and other items. Some materials, like pine needles and needle rush, add color and strength. Sweetgrass, a latecomer that saw use beginning in the early 1900s, provides greater flexibility, allowing more intricate designs.

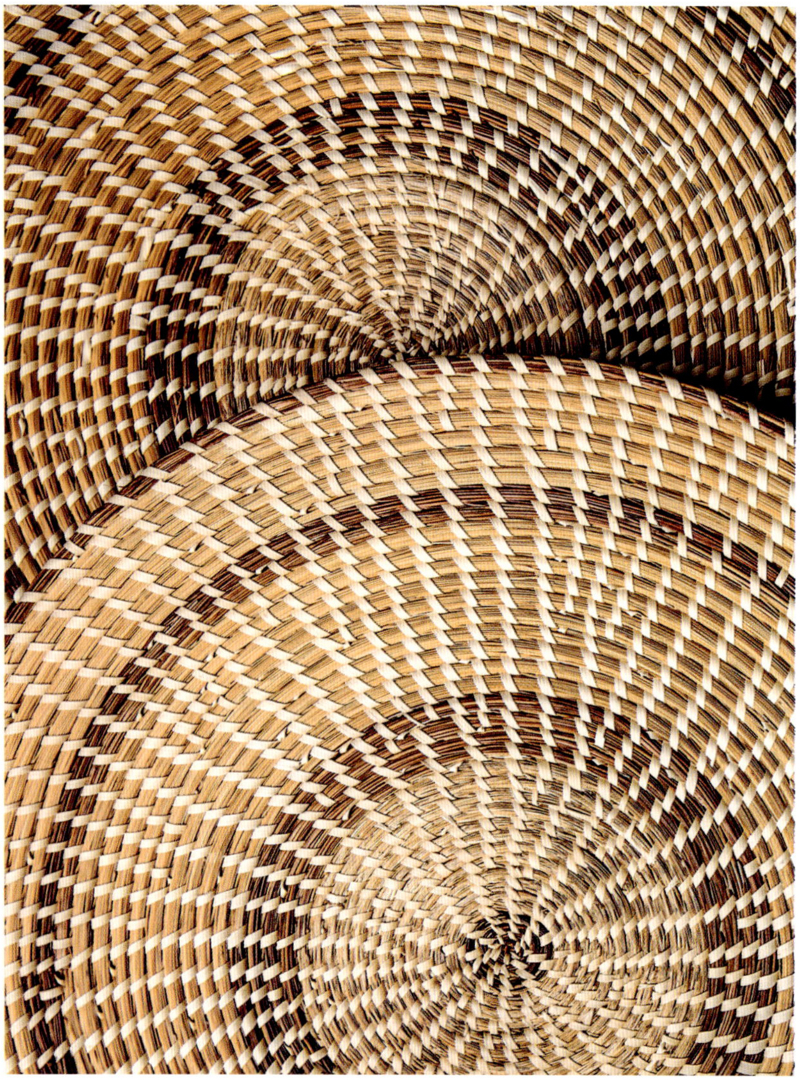

Kiawah Sweetgrass

Pullers slip sweetgrass from its roots, and weavers dry it in the sun before weaving the grass into coils. Travelers along US 17 have long seen basket weavers laying out their Gullah wares made from *Muhlenbergia filipes*, commonly known as purple muhly grass. Sweetgrass grows behind dune lines and along the fringes of marshes and forests. Today's weavers must go farther afield to find sweetgrass; much of it is out of reach behind the walls of gated communities.

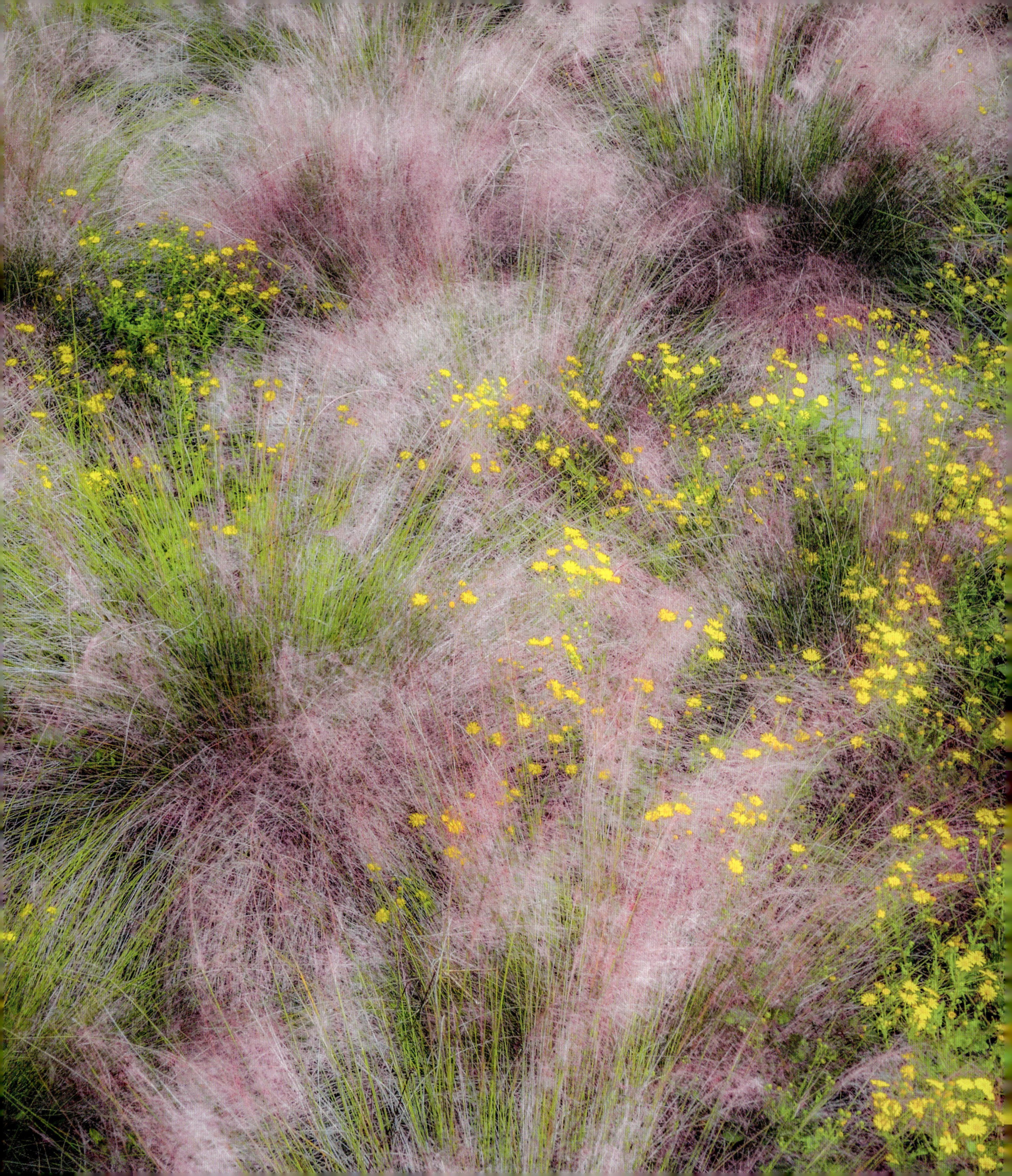

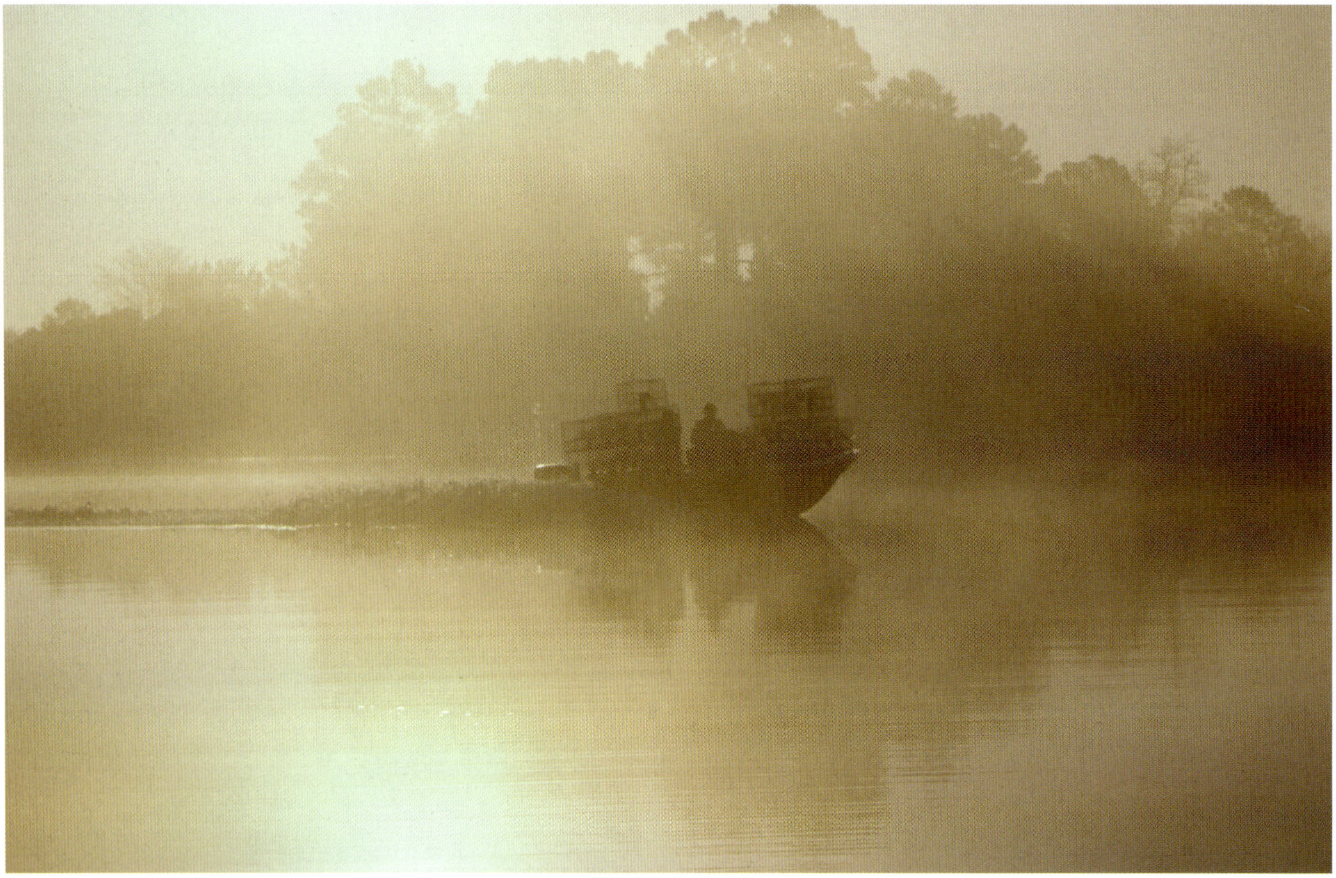

A Crabber's Day Begins

Pots stacked and ready, a commercial crabber begins his quest for *Callinectes sapidus*. The Atlantic blue crab's scientific name means "savory beautiful swimmer." The common name, "blue crab," refers to its sapphire-hued claws. October to December is the preferred time to trap larger crabs. Cool, early morning mists create a romantic image: the crabber who goes it alone.

Blue Crabs

These blue-clawed, olive-carapace predator–scavengers will eat their own kind. Strong swimmers thanks to their paddle-like pair of legs, blue crabs generally live three to four years. Their native range runs along the Atlantic Coast of North and South America from Nova Scotia to Argentina, including the Gulf of Mexico.

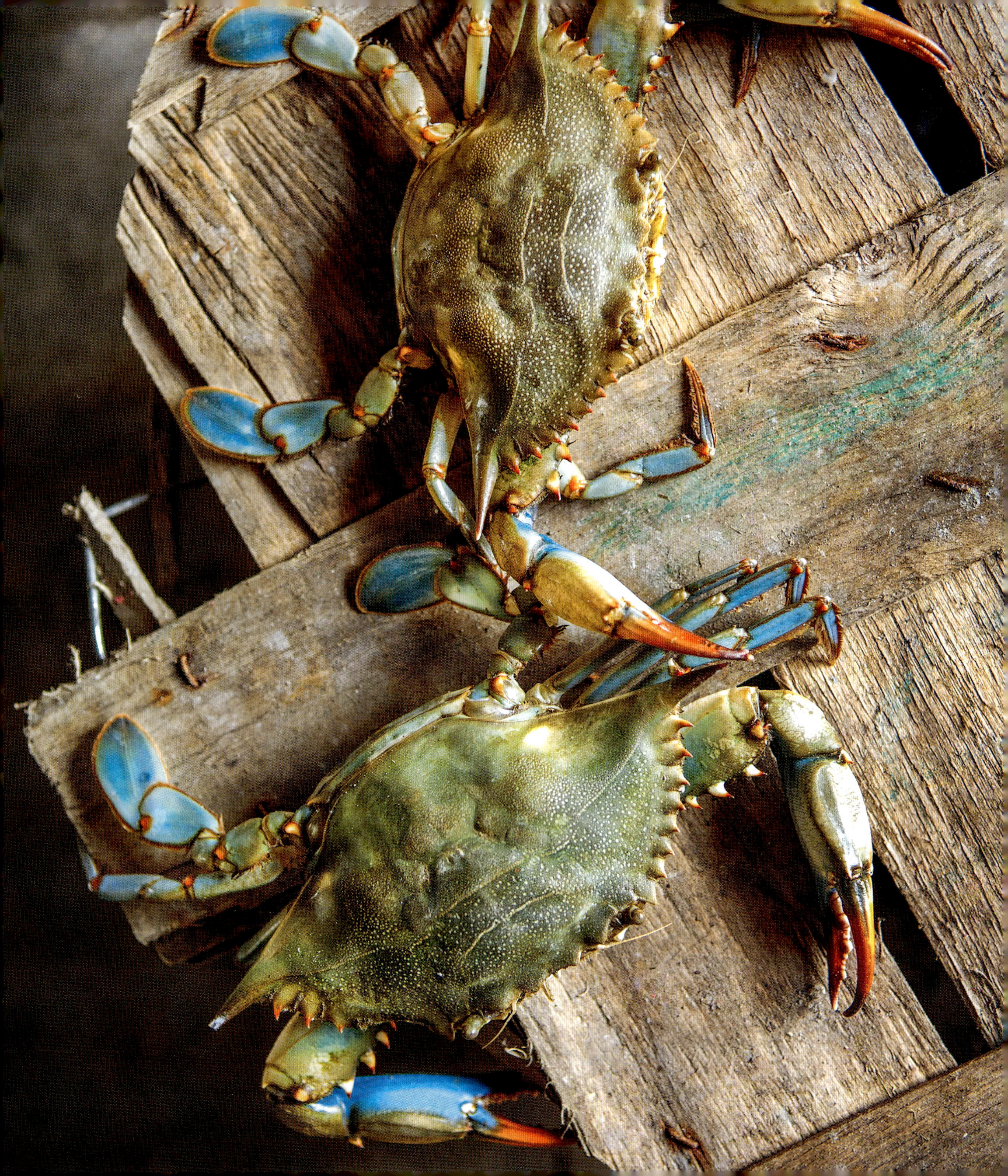

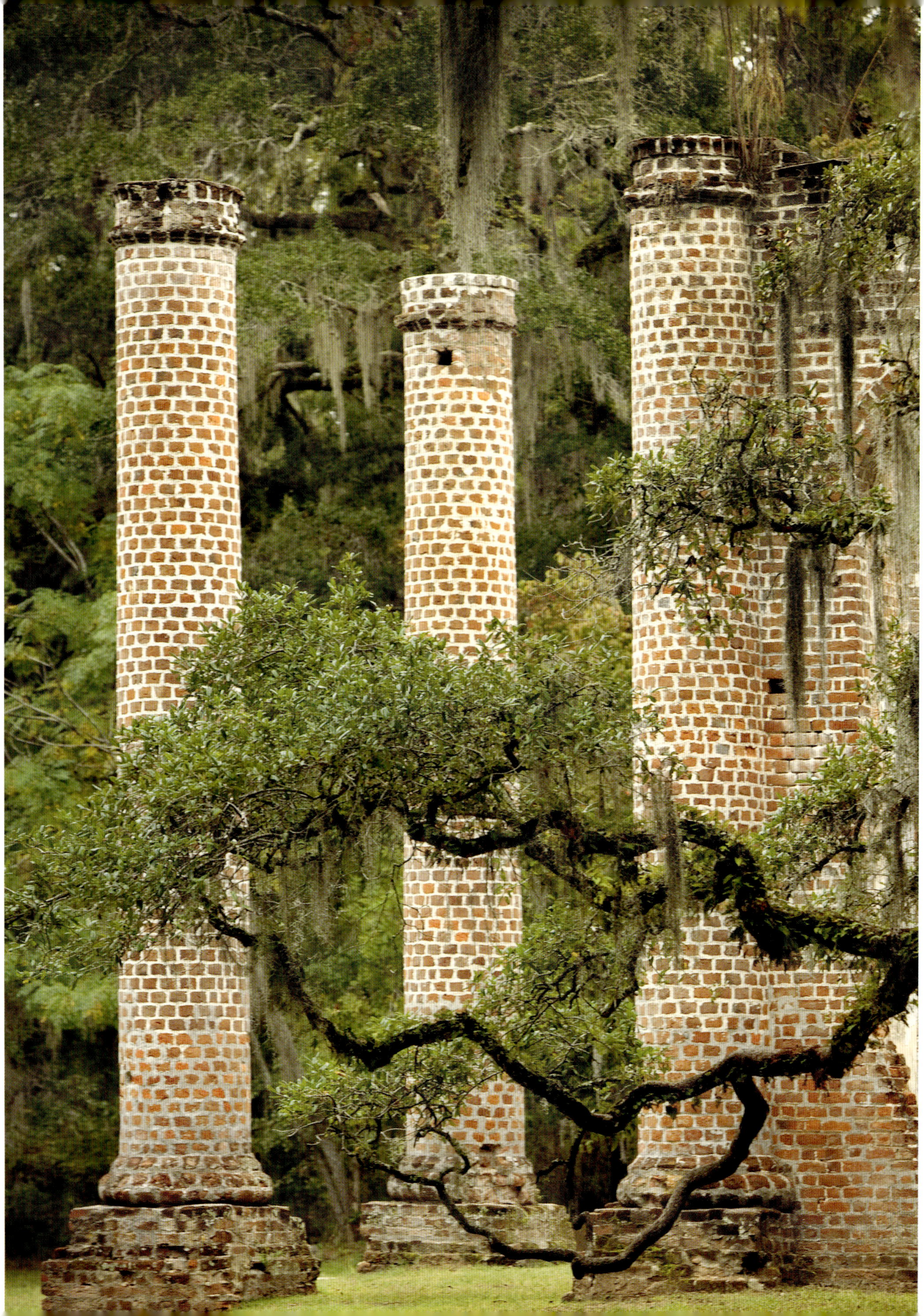

Old Sheldon Church
National Register of Historic Places

Prince William Parish Church, built 1745–55, is among the country's early Greek Revival structures. Known also as Old Sheldon Church, inside the ruins rests Colonel William Bull, who helped General Oglethorpe select Savannah's location and layout. General William T. Sherman's Fifteenth Corps under General John Logan burned the church January 14, 1865, never to be rebuilt.

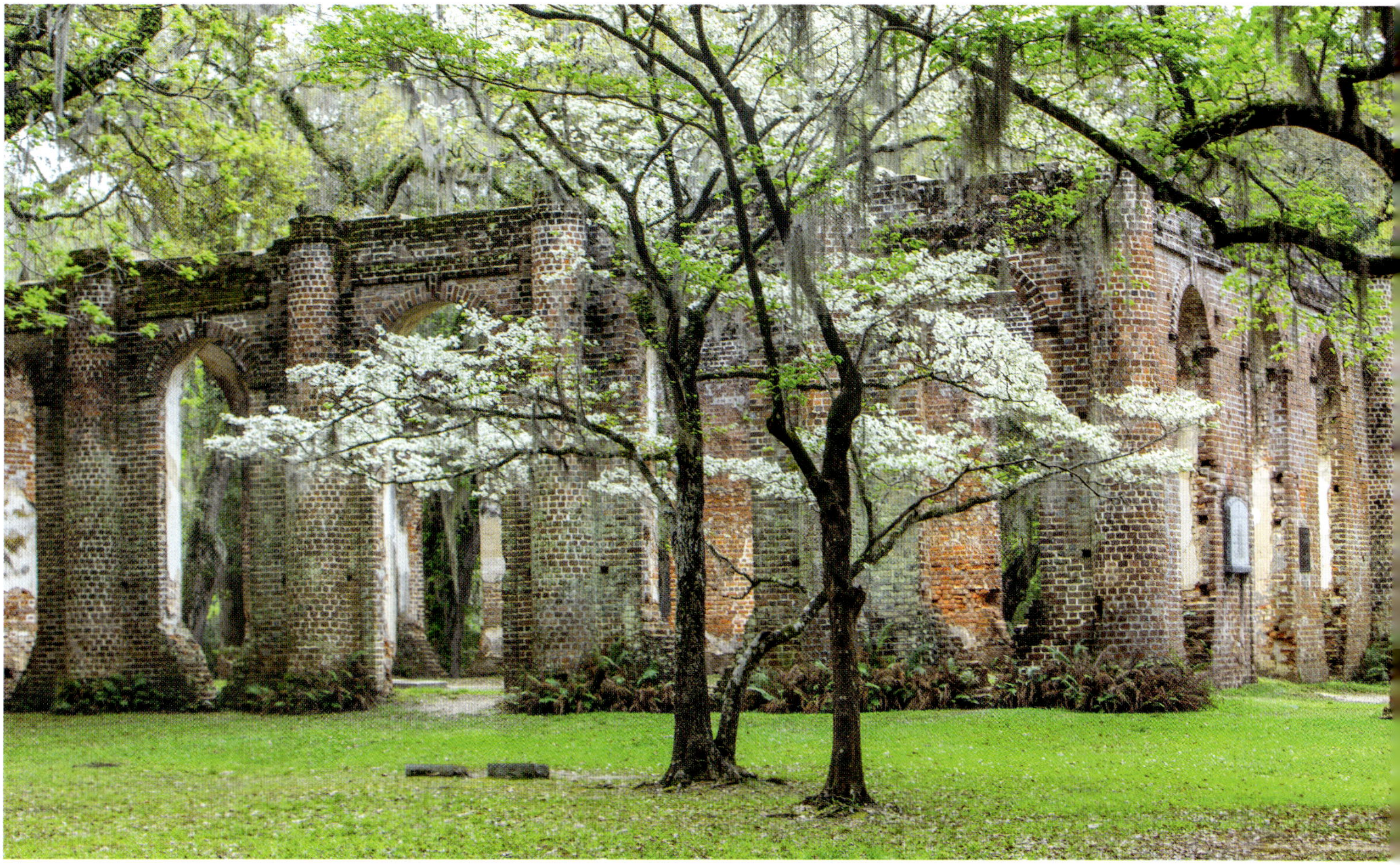

Like A Greek Temple

If the Old Sheldon Church ruins in Beaufort County remind you of a Greek temple, they should. It's said the church was the first purposeful attempt in America to imitate a Greek temple. Walk among the graves and imagine the old church restored. Walk the grounds and find the old handpump. Don't be surprised to see photographers about. This photogenic church honors the Bull family, whose Carolina plantation and ancestral home in England both went by Sheldon Hall.

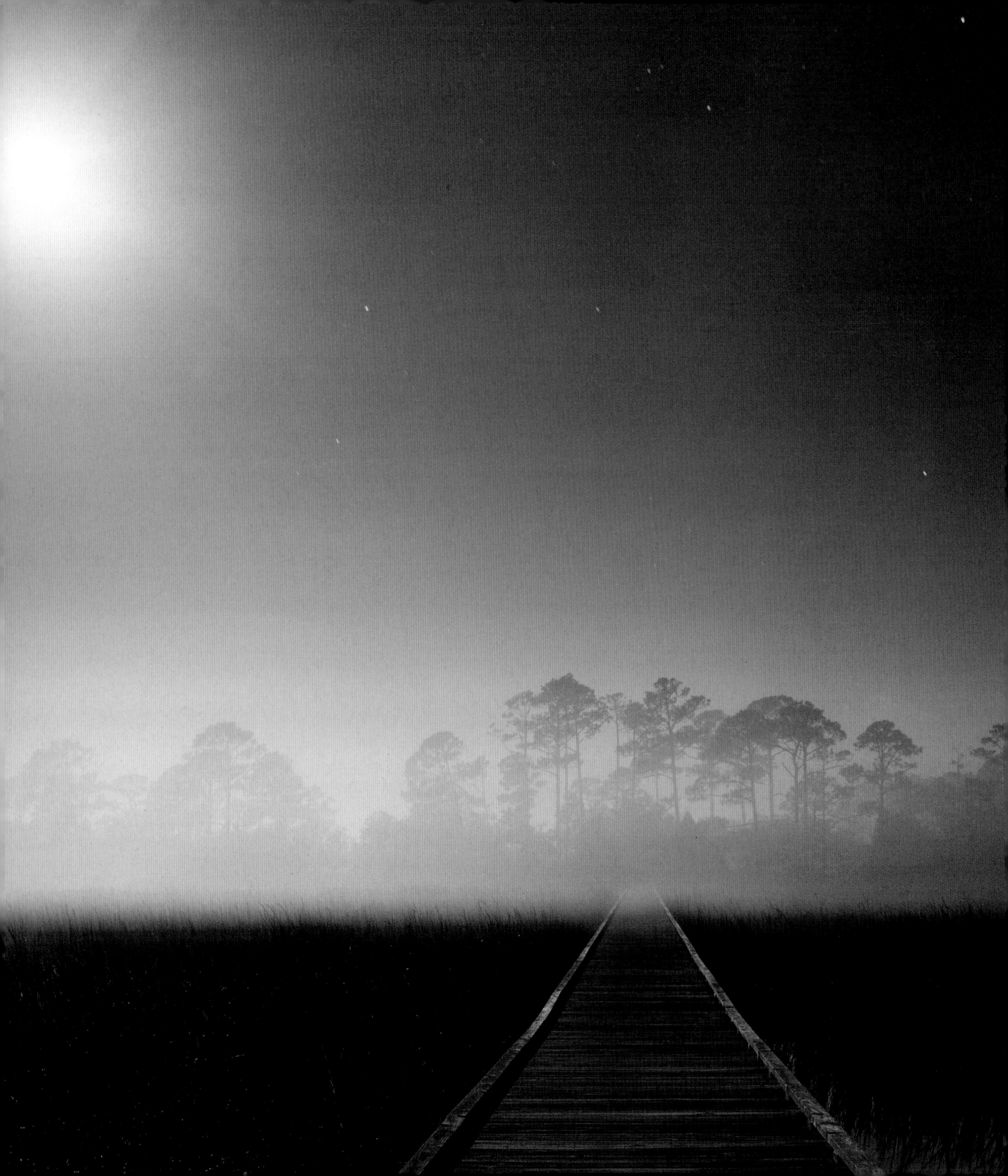

Rising Mists at Nightfall

Moonlight brightens a Hunting Island boardwalk leading to a hammock.

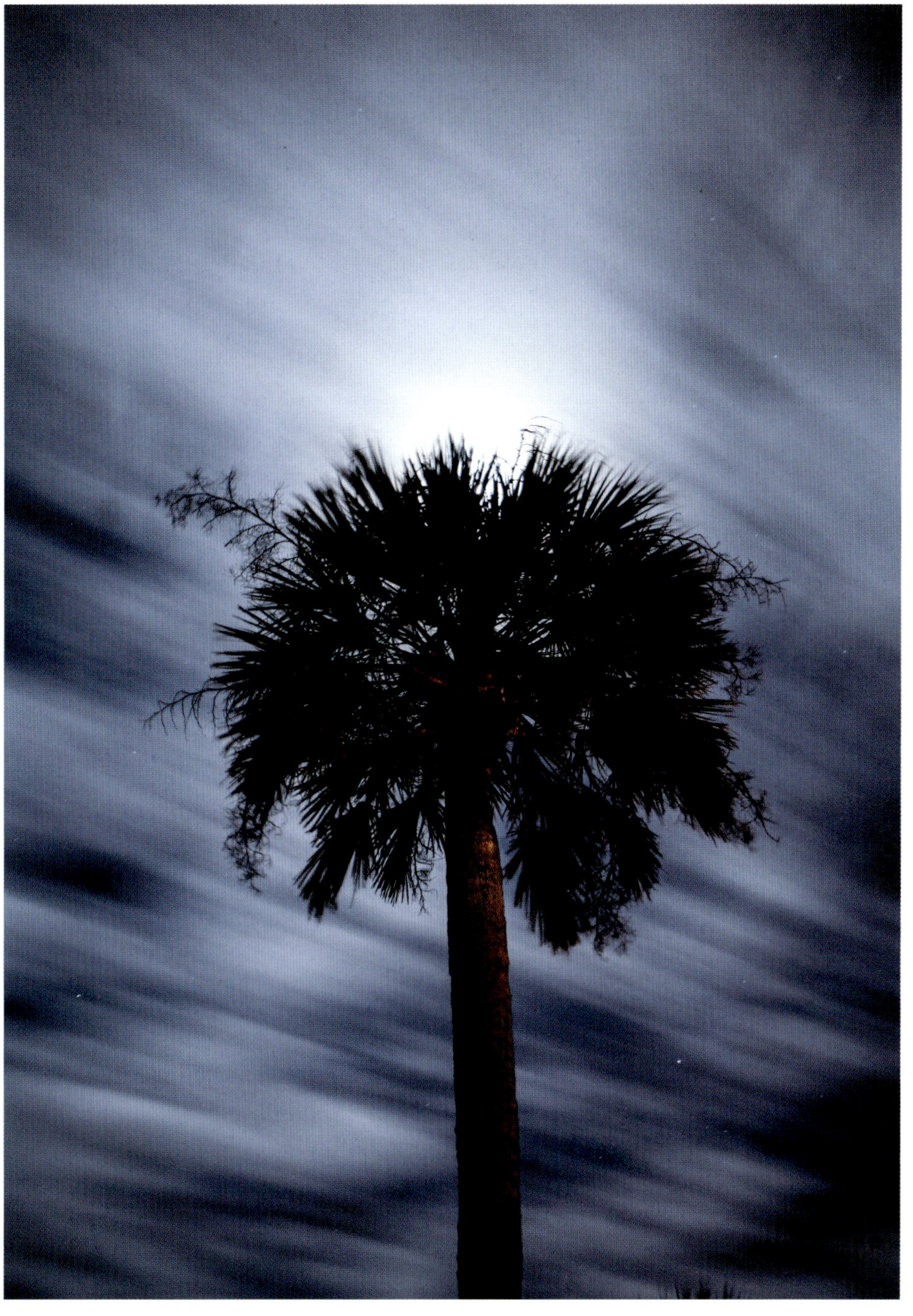

Luminous Night

Stars emerge in a 30-second exposure of a shining cloud sky as the moon crowns a palmetto at Folly Beach.

Monarch of the Lowcountry

Angel Oak, the 2004 South Carolina Heritage Tree, shades John's Island. Although the giant tree and its outspread limbs appear angelic, Angel Oak is named after its owners from long ago, Martha and Justus Angel. Local lore holds that the spirits of the enslaved appear as angels around the tree. This southern live oak (*Quercus virginiana*) is estimated to be 400–500 years old.

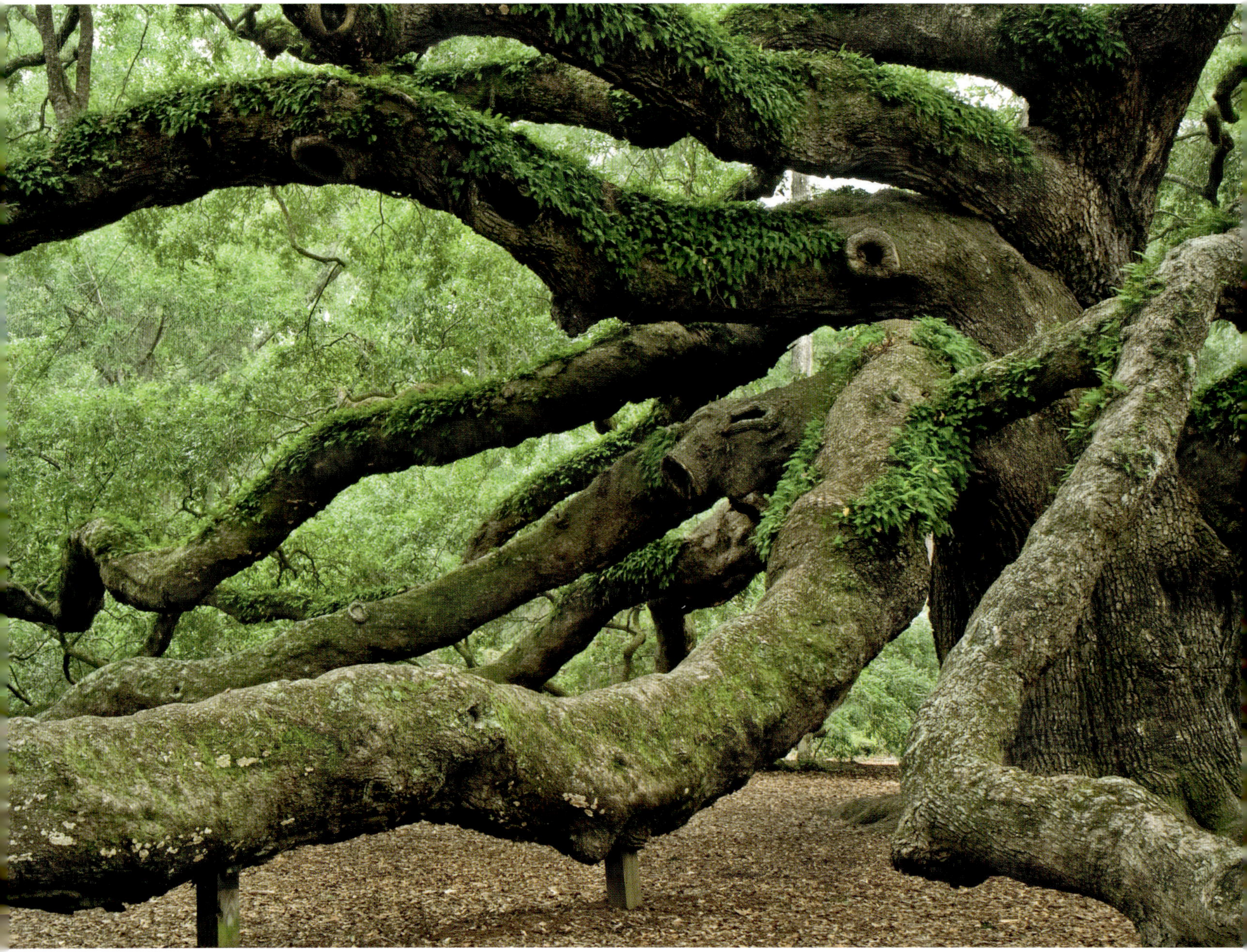

GRAY LADY OF THE LOWCOUNTRY

You cannot think of the Lowcountry's swamps and blackwater rivers without conjuring up Spanish moss (*Tillandsia usneoides*). Spanish moss and the Lowcountry go together like William Faulkner and Mississippi, like Sidney Lanier and the Marshes of Glynn. You won't find a Hollywood movie about antebellum South Carolina that doesn't show live oaks and Spanish moss. The Lowcountry's image is forever framed by moss-draped oaks and cypress.

Along with afternoon thunderstorms, sweet iced tea, the song of frogs after rain, and choruses of crickets and katydids, South Carolina would not be South Carolina without the gray lady of the Lowcountry.

A Cherokee legend accounts for how Spanish moss came to be. A traveler and his long-flowing raven-haired bride-to-be wanted to start a plantation near Charleston. As the couple surveyed the plantation site, a band of Cherokee attacked. As a warning to stay away from Cherokee land, they cut the woman's long dark hair and threw it into an old live oak. The hair shriveled, turned gray, and spread from tree to tree.

We call it Spanish moss. Of course the plant is neither Spanish nor moss. Someone should have named it "Weeping Widow," for when the wind picks up, the oak and cypress seem to weep. Given the South's romantic image and loss of the Civil War, that's a figure of speech that seems not just right but just.

Gothic, beautiful, and feminine, Spanish moss is the gray lady of the Lowcountry.

Painted Bunting

Mating season. "It sounded like hundreds were there," said Robert Clark of all the painted buntings at Eddings Point, St. Helena Island. Audubon South Carolina refers to this dazzler as a "flying rainbow." The bird seems to be faring better than once believed, for now. Species in the cardinal family, *Cardinalidae*.

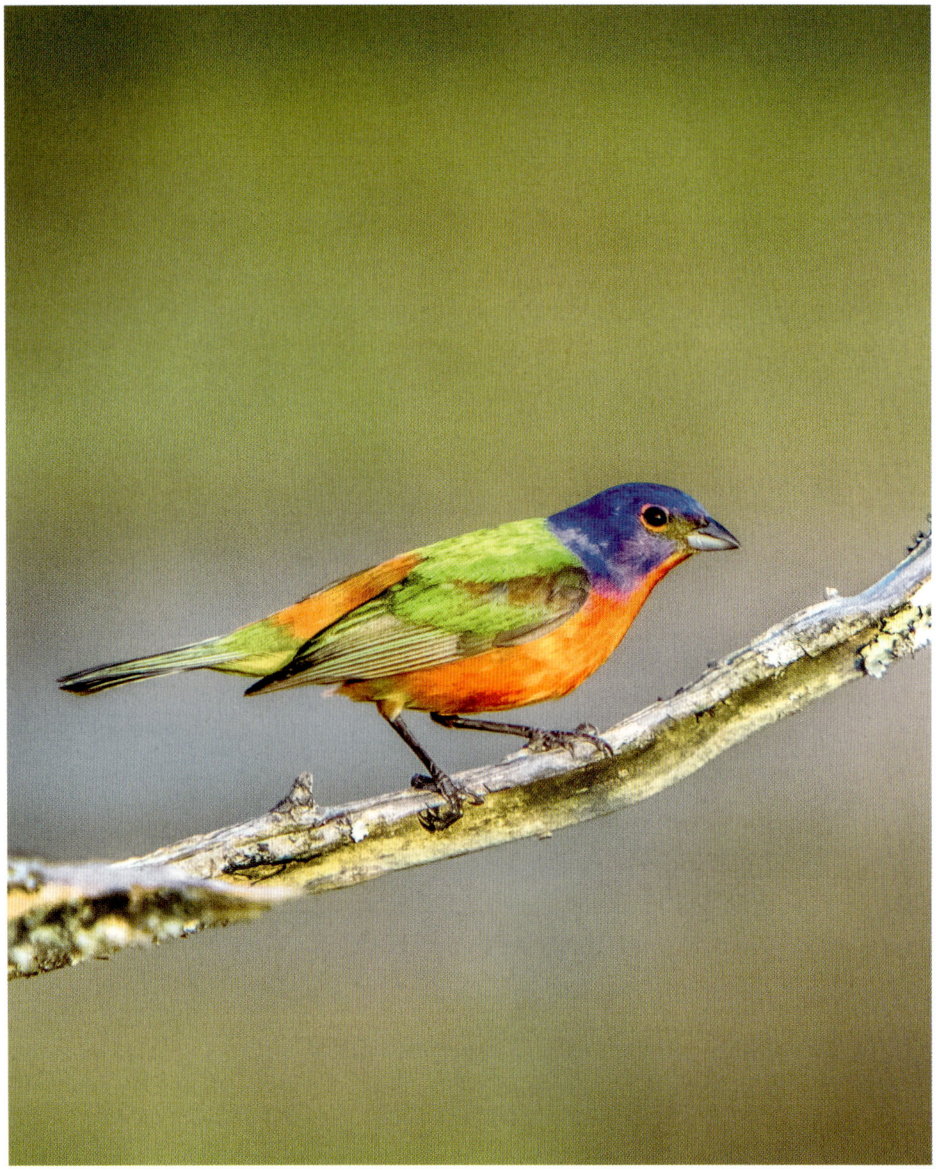

Eddings Point

Mists add an air of mystery to a classic Lowcountry setting at Eddings Point, St. Helena Island.

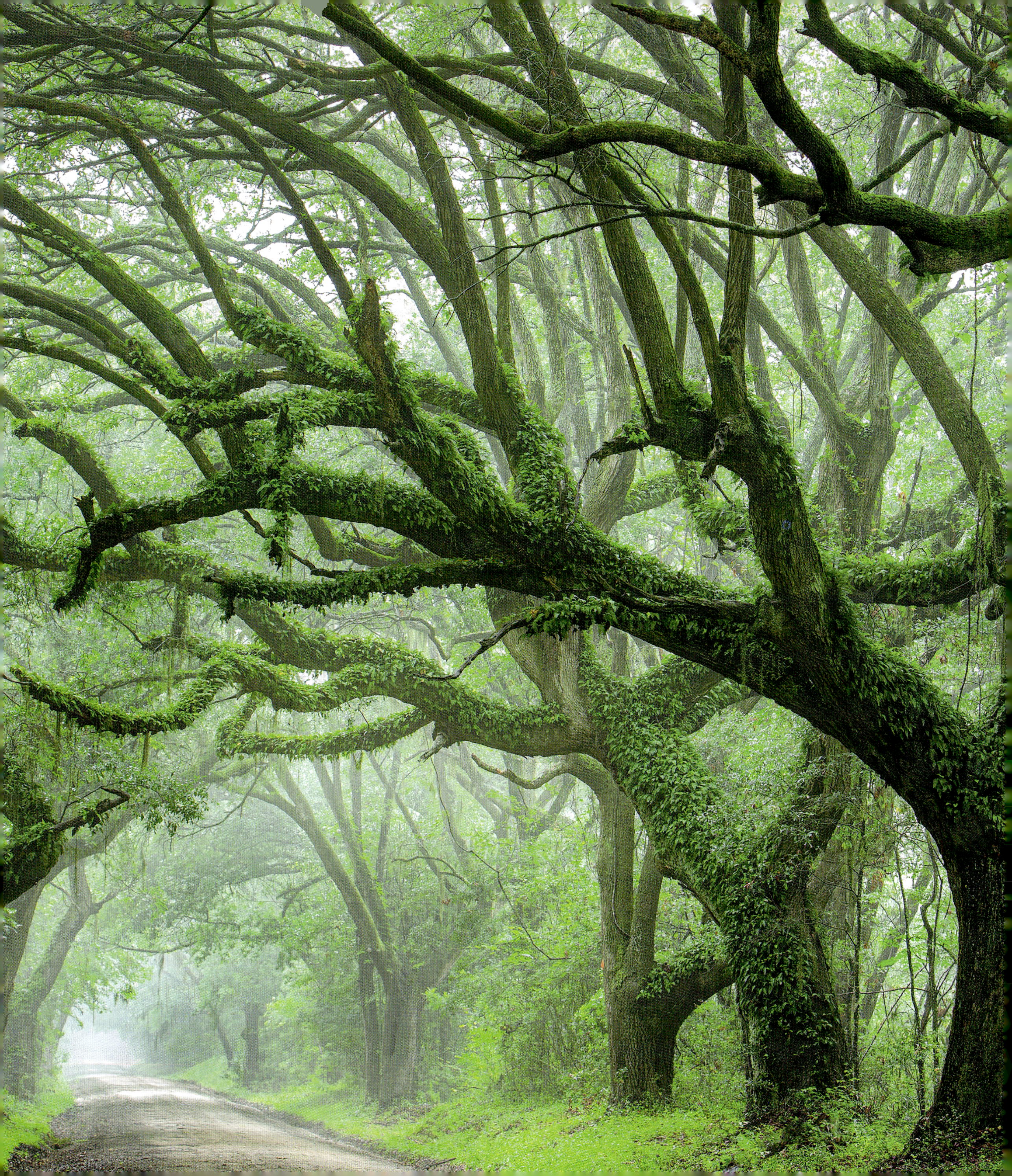

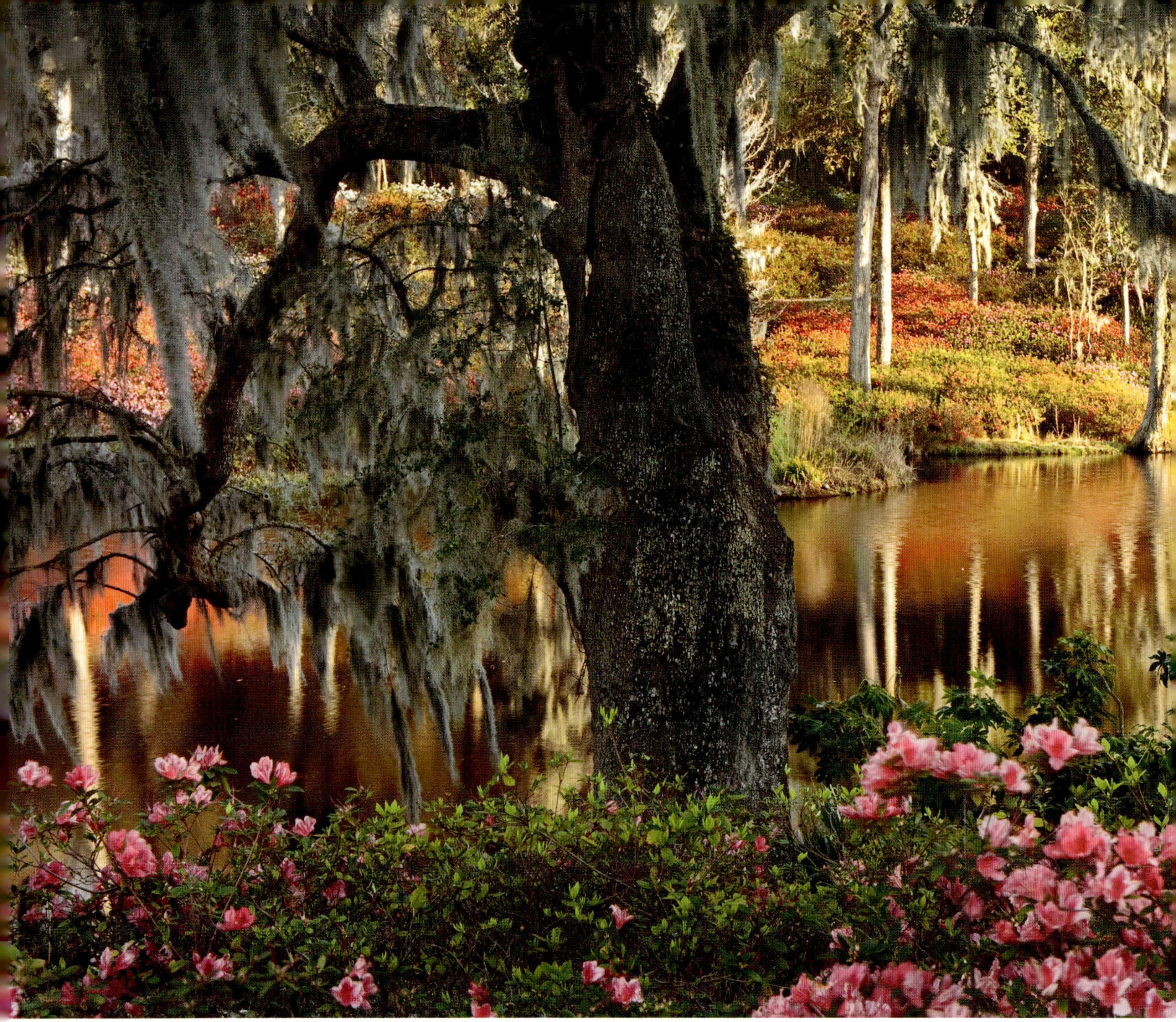

Middleton Place Azalea Pool

In 1741 Henry Middleton set out to create gardens in the grand classic style popular in Europe. Geometry and balance, rational order, vistas, focal points, and the unexpected guided the creation of his gardens. The Reflection Pool and Azalea Pool once shared similar shapes, but over the years the elements gave the Azalea Pool less-formal contours.

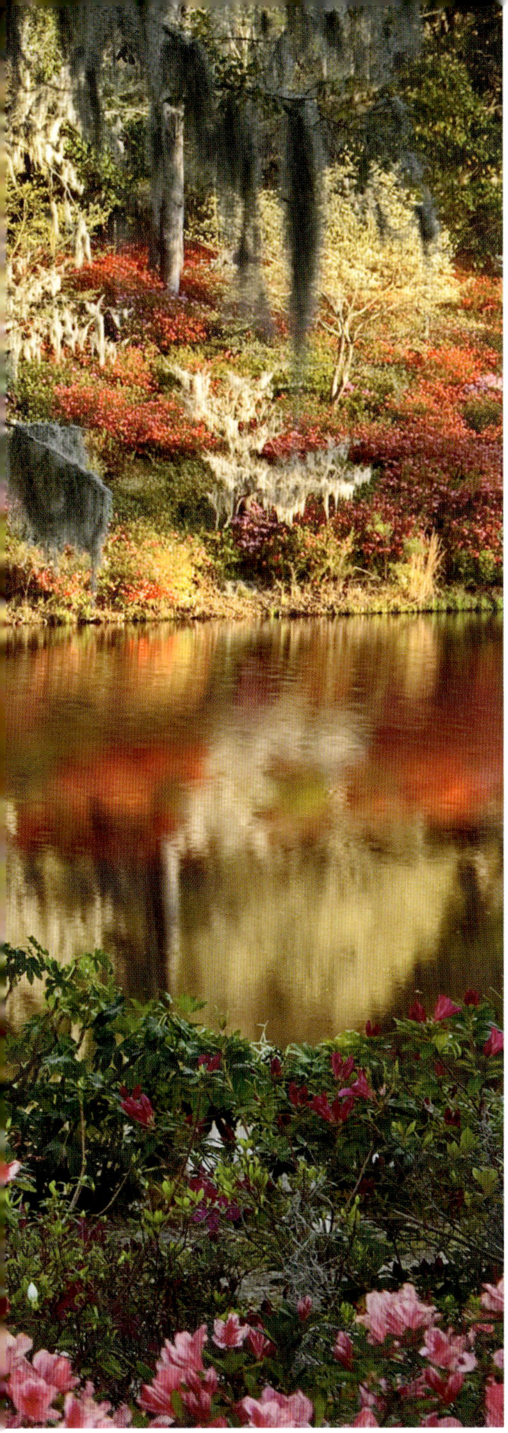

Middleton Place

Built ca. 1738, the house you see is the south dependency, one of two smaller buildings on each side and apart from the three-story mansion Henry Middleton completed. Civil War action destroyed the main house and its north dependency, and the 1886 earthquake finished off the ruins.

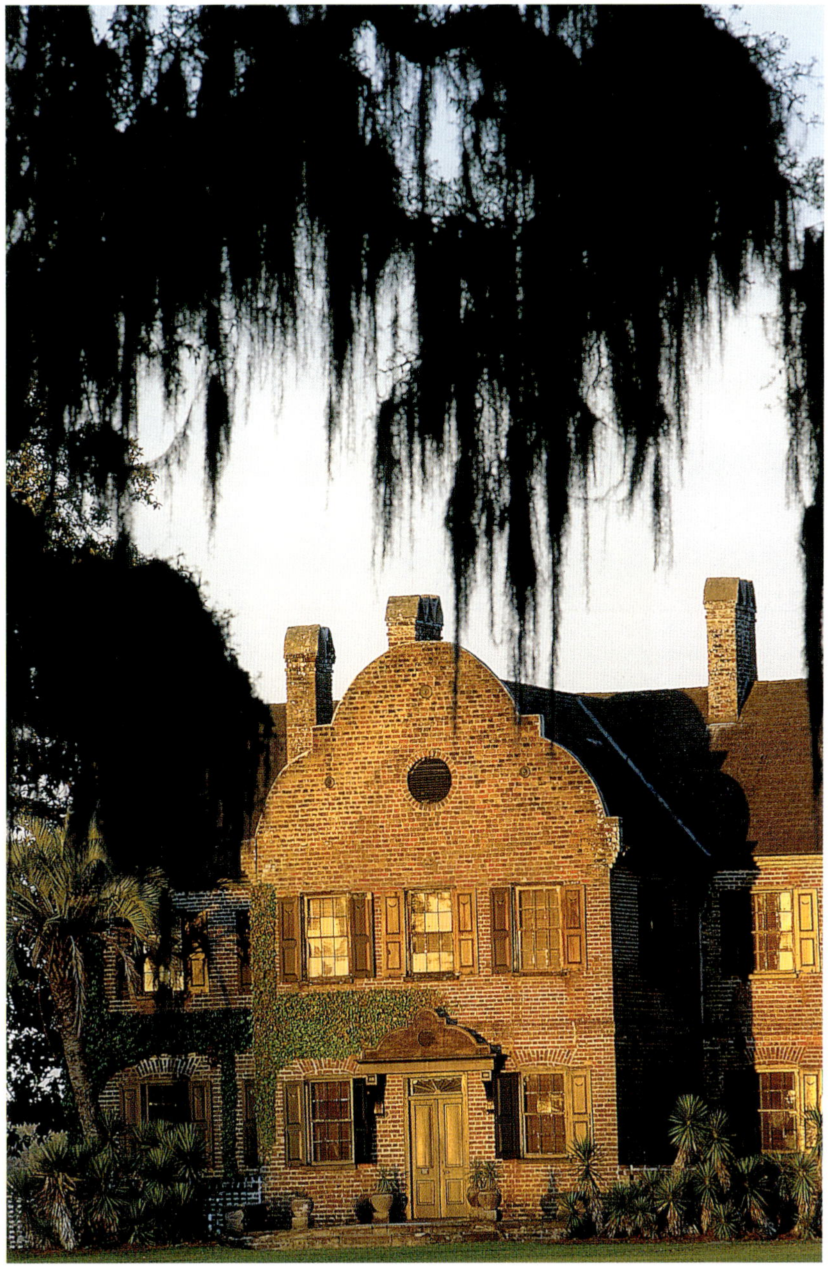

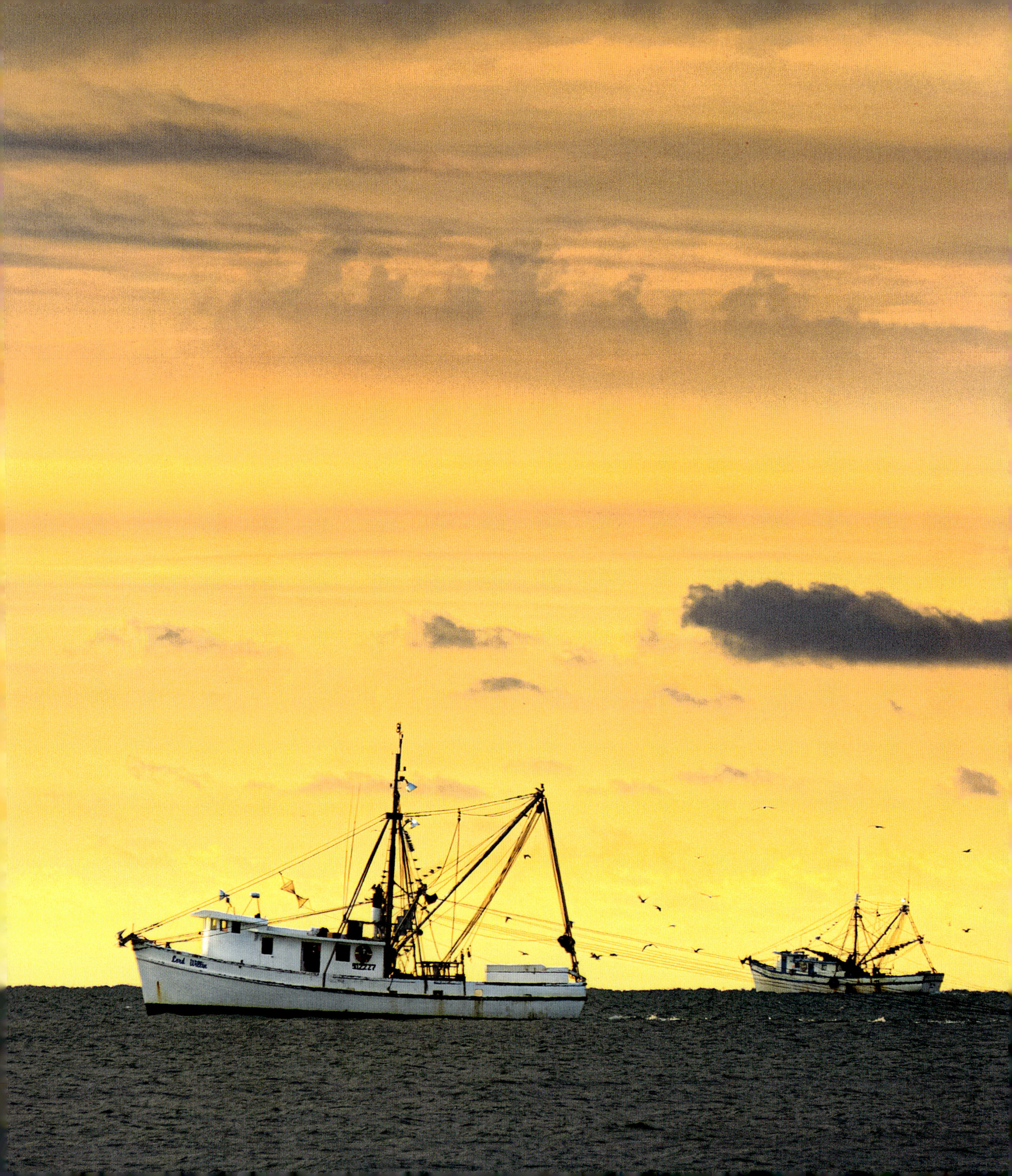

Shrimpers' Plight

Across the Southeast hardworking independent shrimpers face the loss of dock space where they can offload catches and take on fuel and ice. South Carolina is not immune to this problem. Other issues such as high fuel and insurance costs and waterfront property's potential for development make shrimp trawlers a vanishing sight. Those who enjoy shrimpers' delectable harvest will surely miss them, just as photographers and artists will miss the photogenic trawlers.

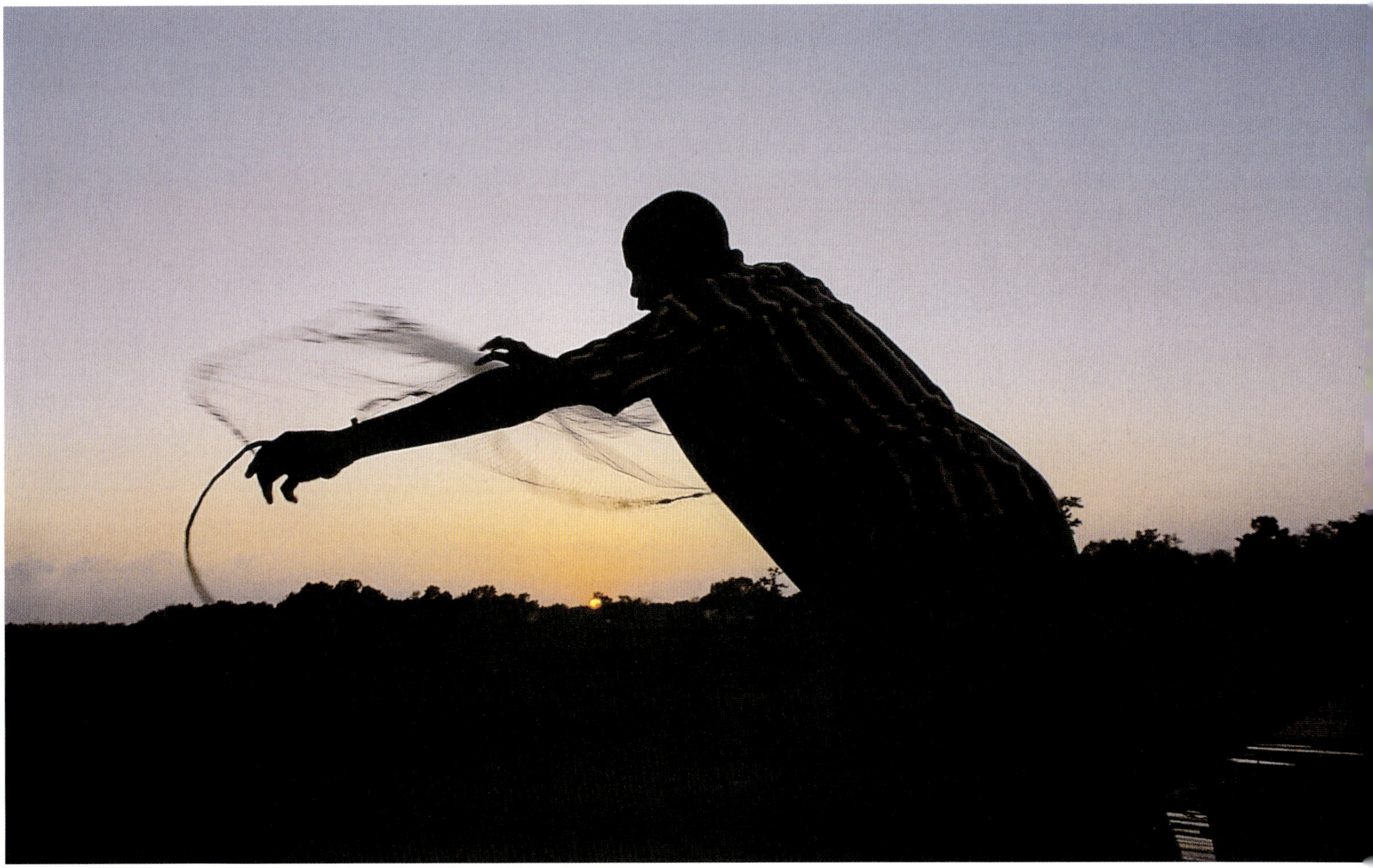

The Harvest

A fisherman sends the net flying in a shimmering circle. Sinking rapidly, the net ensnares shrimp and small fish at this tidal creek at Huntington Beach State Park, Murrells Inlet, Georgetown County.

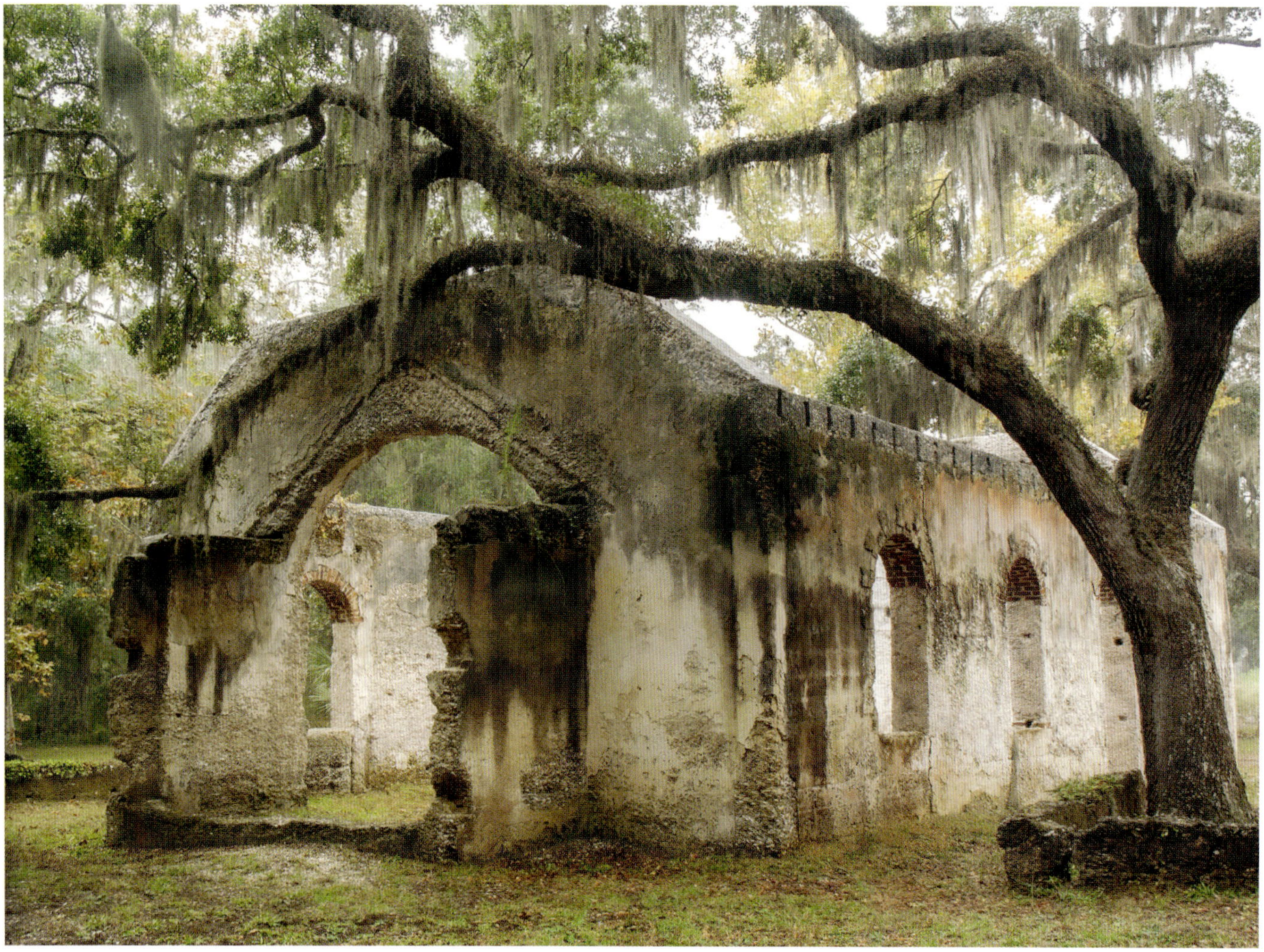

Chapel of Ease

With Beaufort's main parish church a bit far, St. Helena's Chapel of Ease made it more convenient for area planters and their families to worship. Built in the mid-1700s, but destroyed by an 1886 forest fire, the Chapel of Ease is now a shell of tabby walls and old bricks.

Delectable Architecture

Long ago oysters gave men sustenance and building materials. They built tabby structures that time would turn into ruins. Cotton magnate George Edwards built structures of tabby on Spring Island. So, what was the recipe for making that delectable building concoction? Builders burnt crushed oyster shells. That yielded lime, which they mixed with whole shells, sand, and water in equal measures and poured into forms, which Lowcountry air and sunlight dried. Today, picturesque tabby ruins remind us of oyster shells' use as a building material.

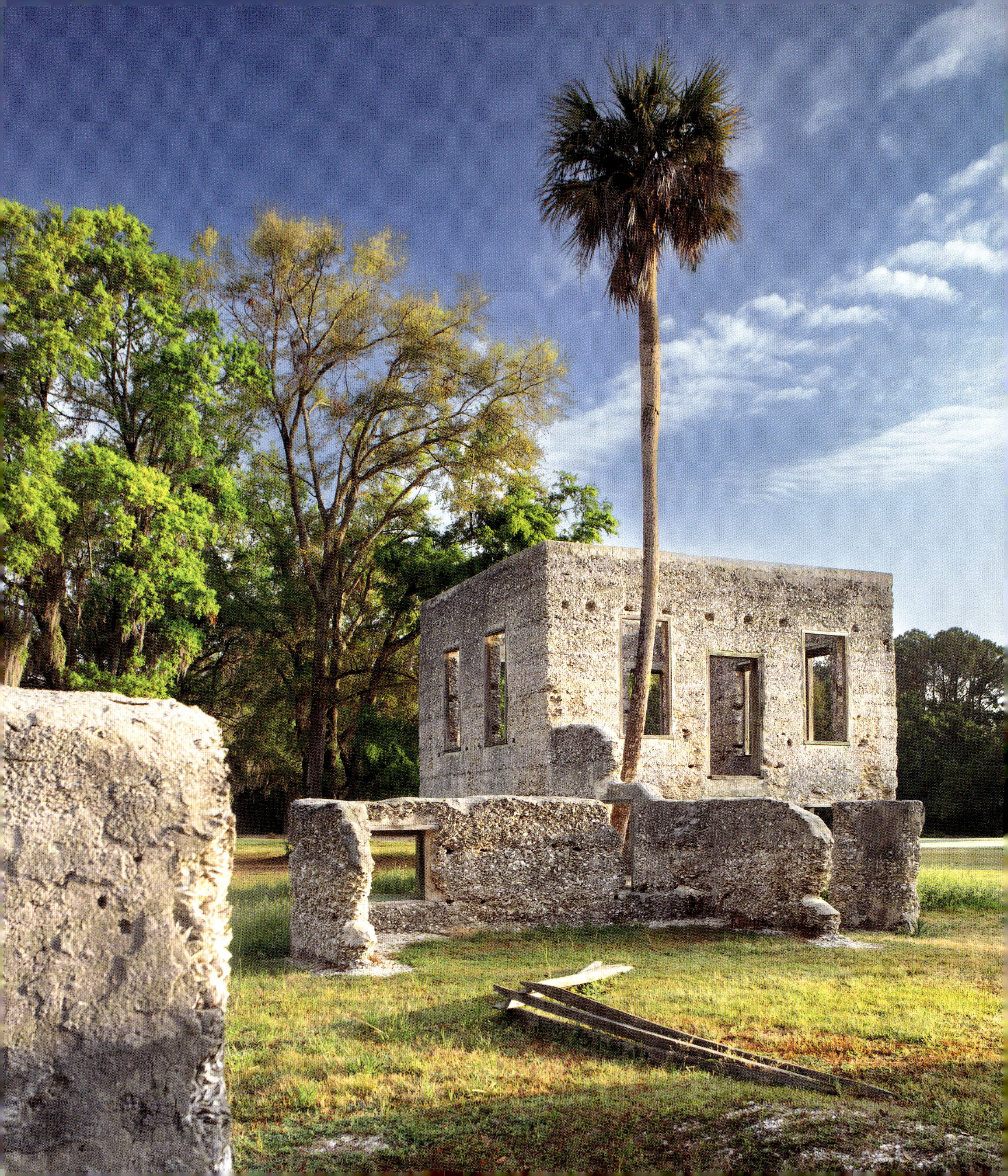

Hunting Island Boneyard at Moonrise

Vivid colors, a crescent moon, and white bone-like trees gave rise to "boneyard," a term locals apply to the resting places of maritime forests conquered by the sea.

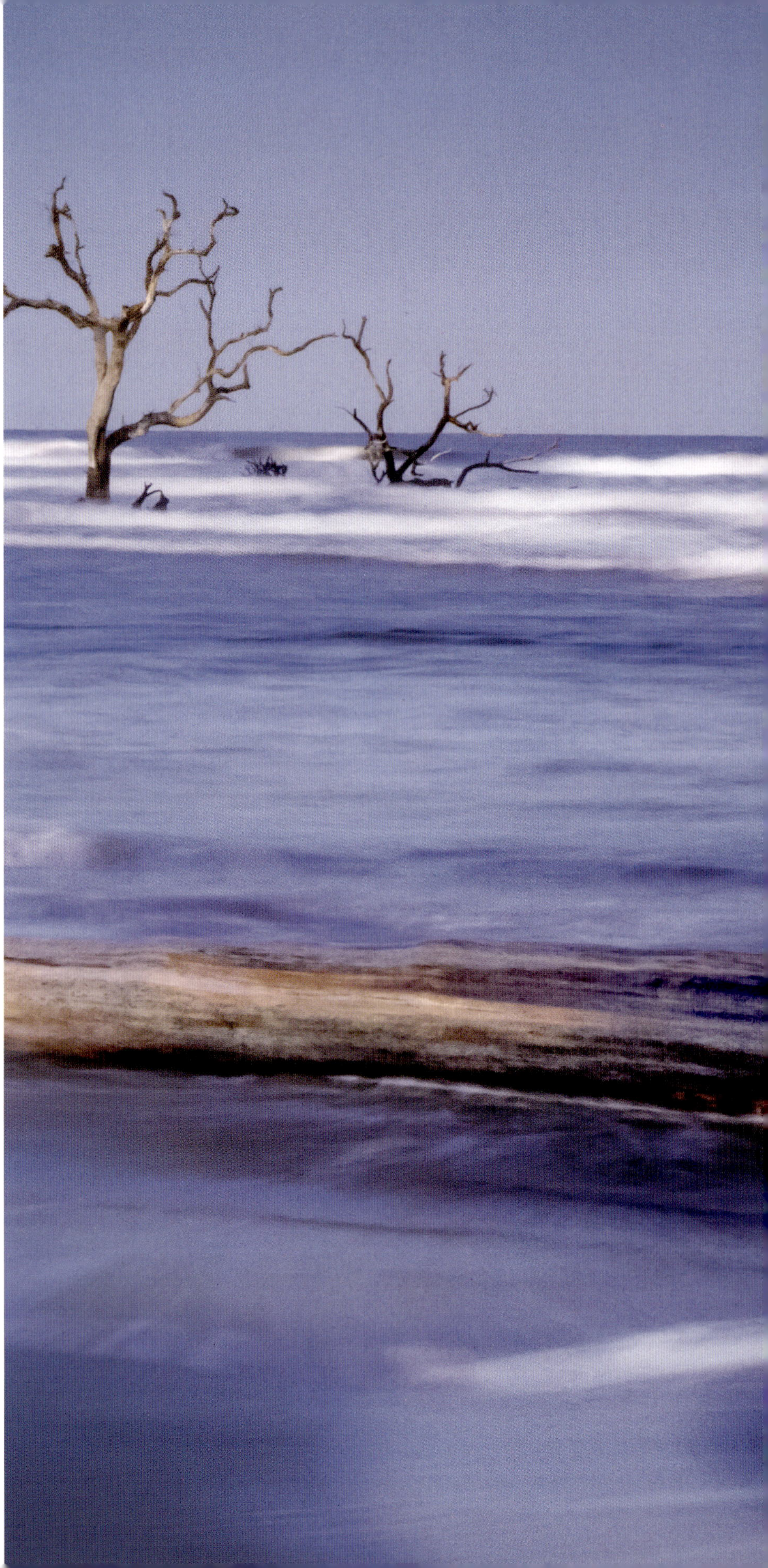

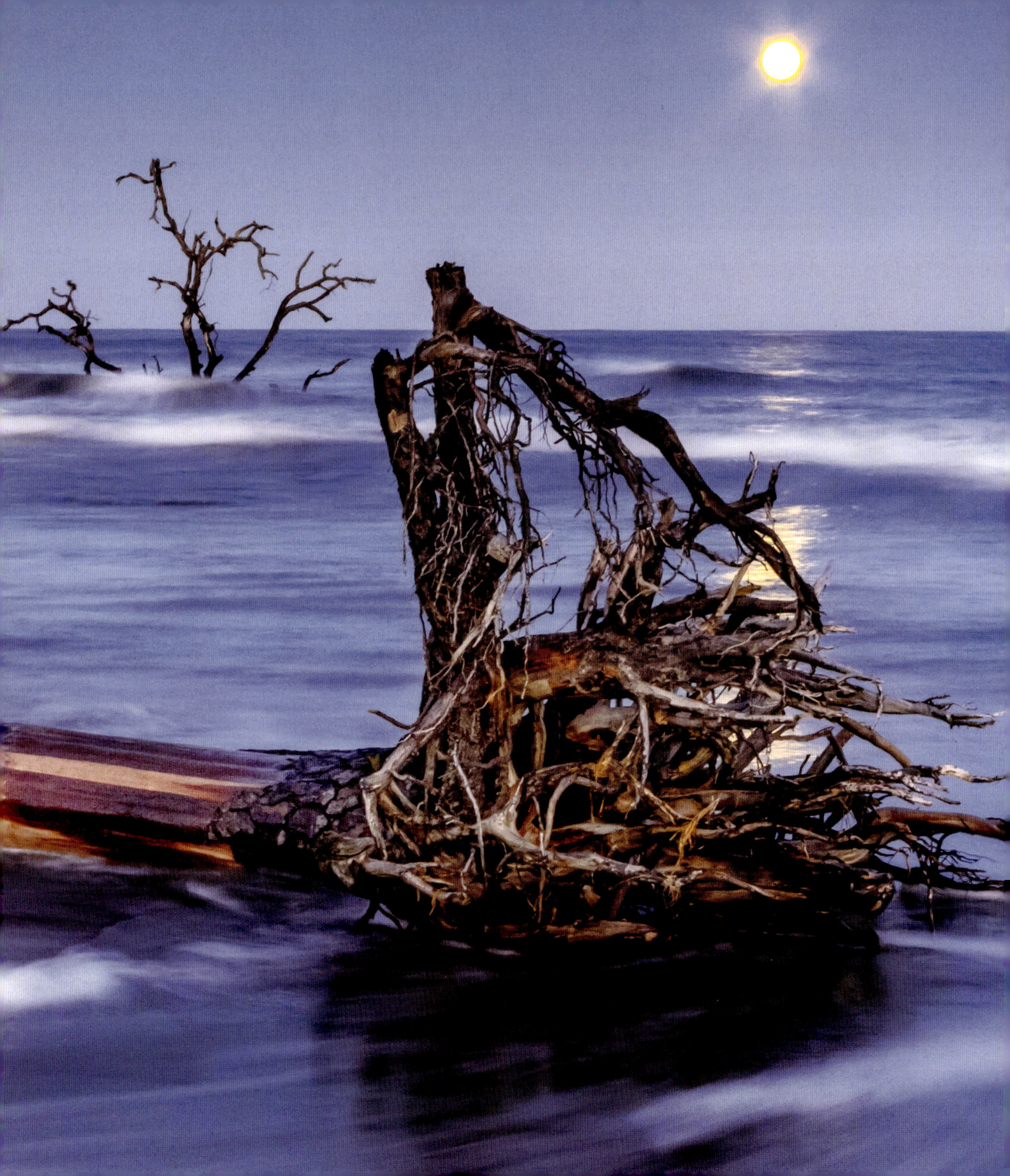

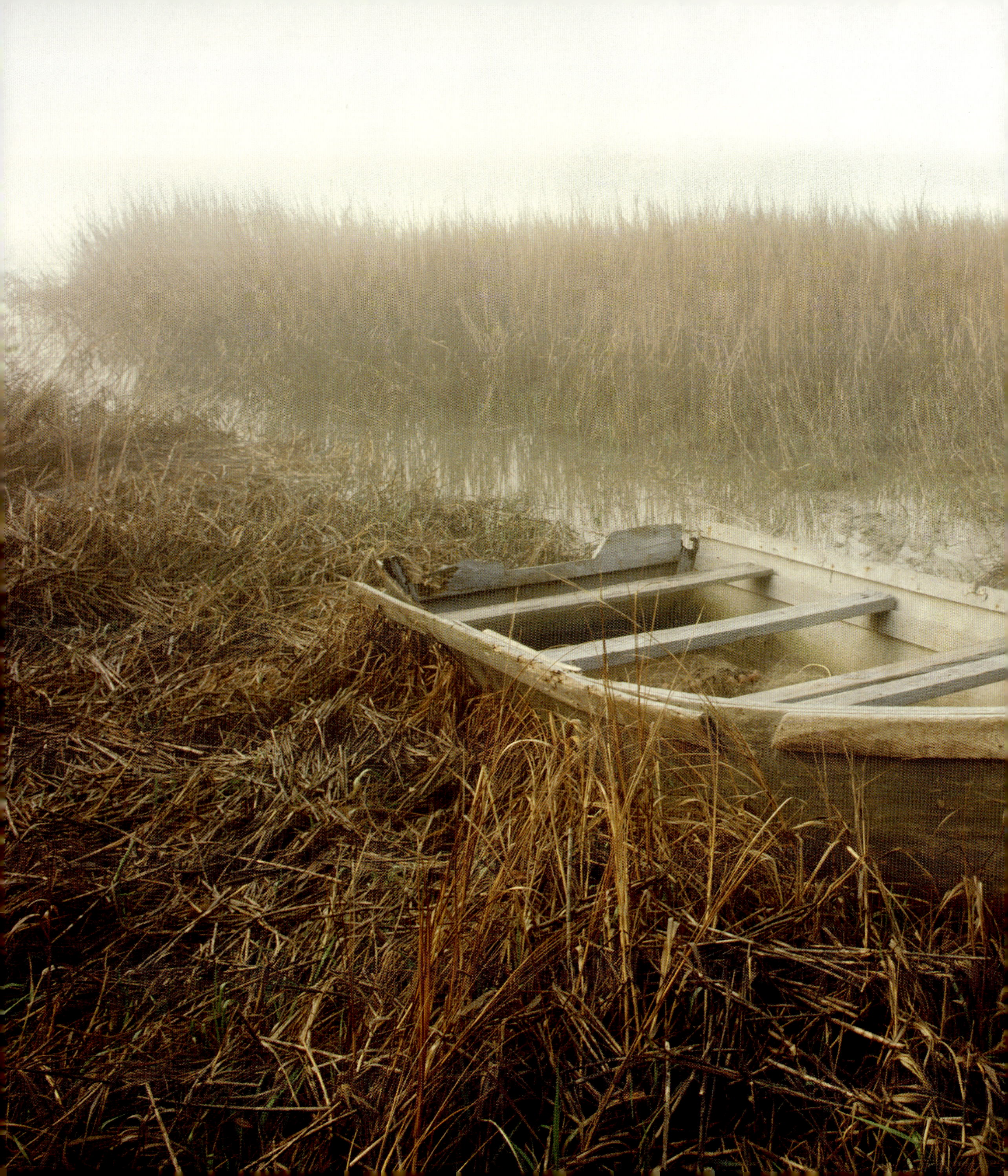

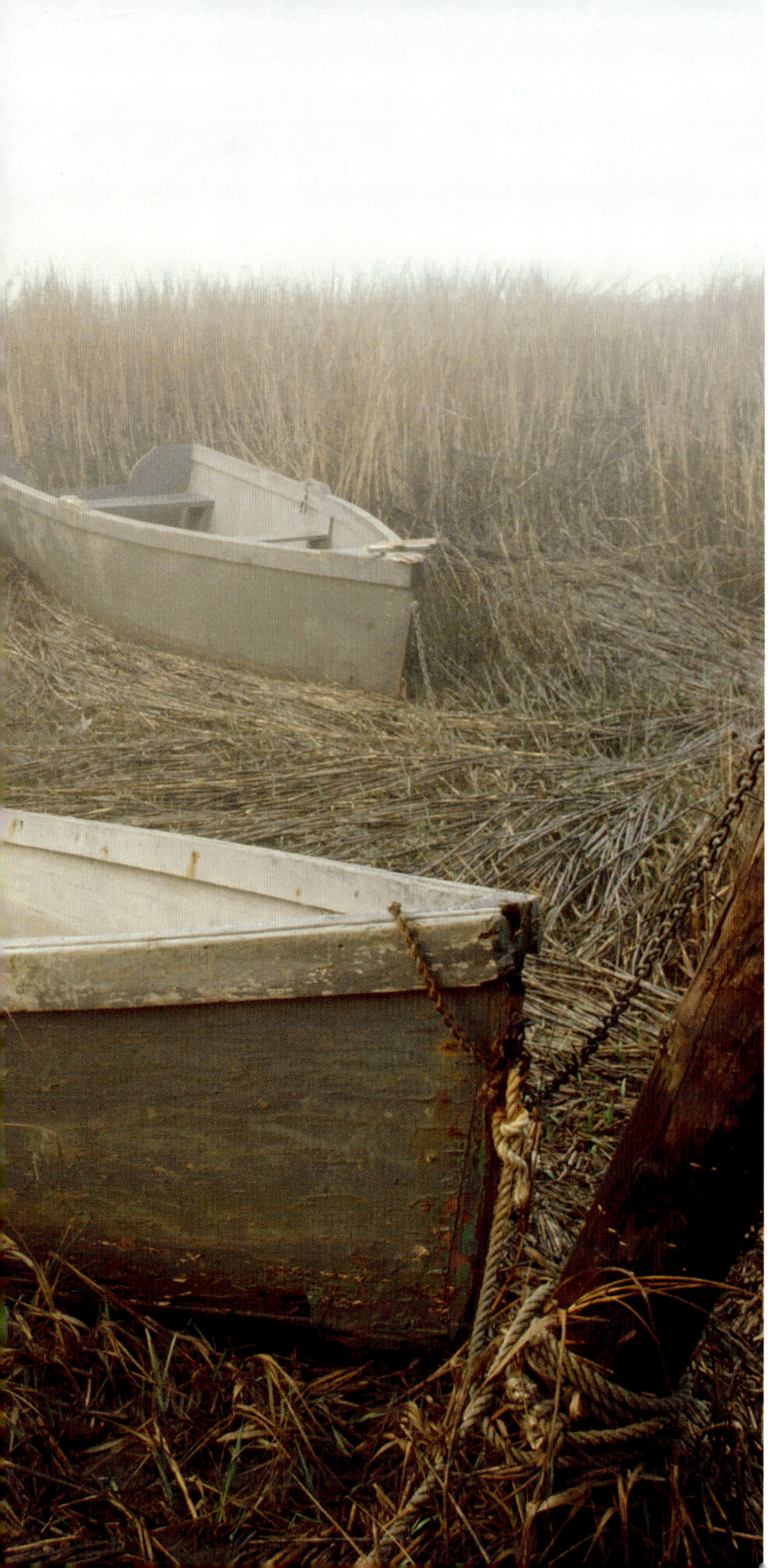

Workboats

Weathered wood, worn ropes, and rusting chains rest in a Beaufort County marsh. It's tempting to call them bateaux, but boats such as those more properly are riverboats. These aged craft are workboats, and they've fed many a soul.

Roastin' & Steamin'

Coals, a sheet of tin, steam, a salty fragrance, oyster knives, saltines, buckets, cocktail sauce—few things celebrate the sea's bounty like an oyster roast with friends and family. Always have your own oyster knife and keep it close by from January to March.

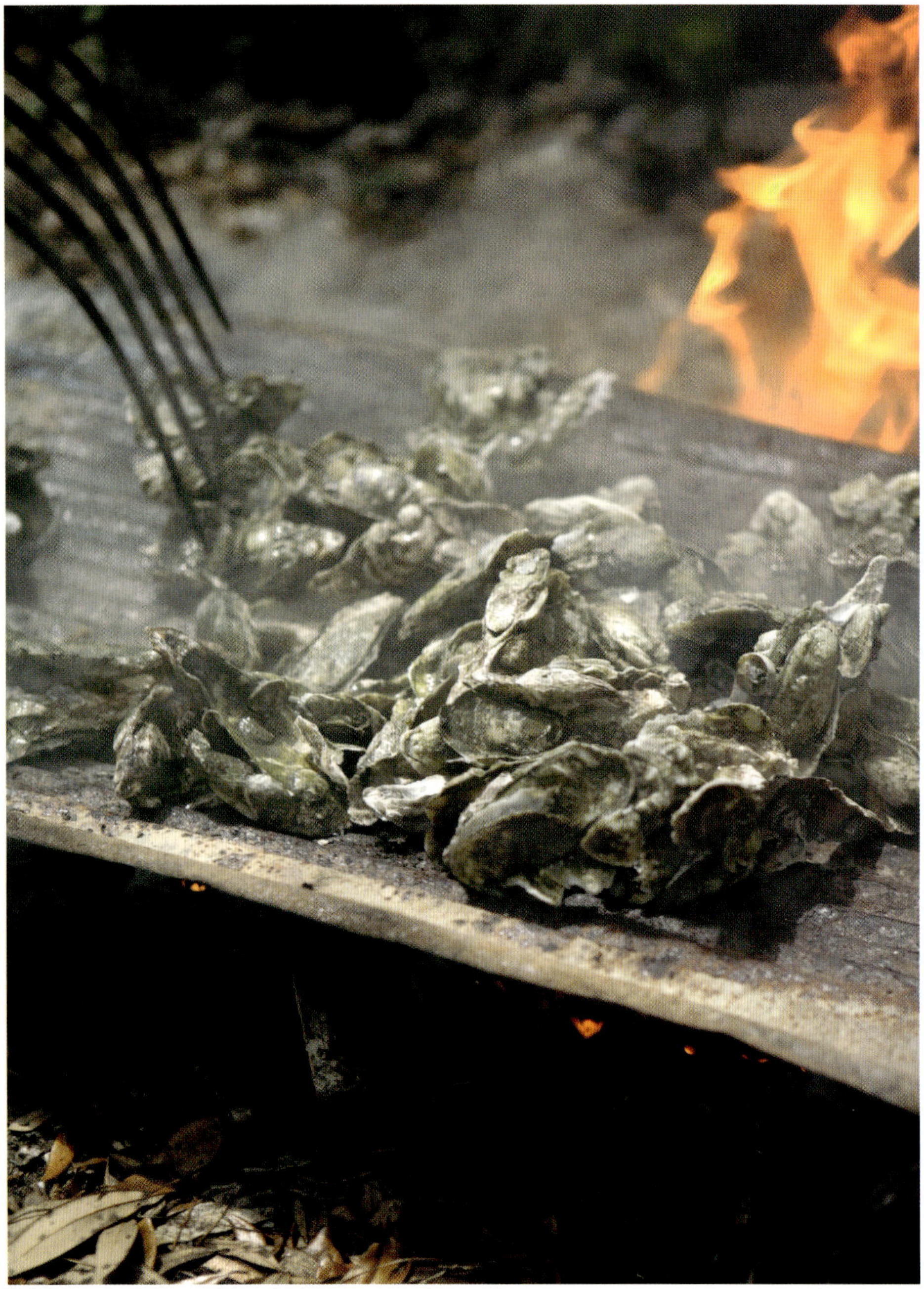

The *Everett Gene*

Up well before daybreak. Negotiating wind and tides. Finding the hot spots. Staying afloat days at a time? A normal lifestyle is out of the question. The challenges keep mounting. Unless something changes the tides, the postcard-like images of trawlers like the *Everett Gene* backed by the rising sun may well be a vanishing sight.

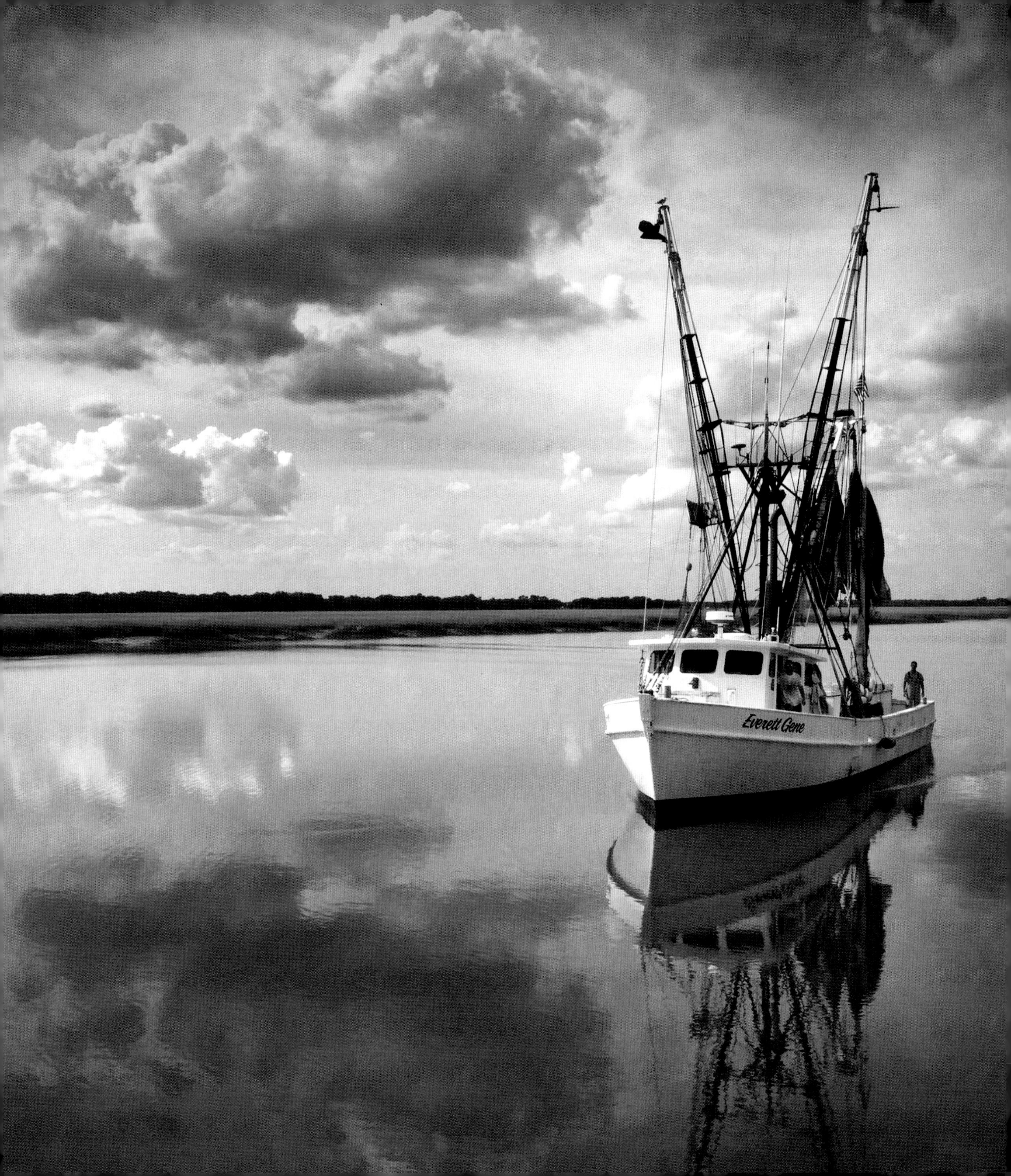
Everett Gene

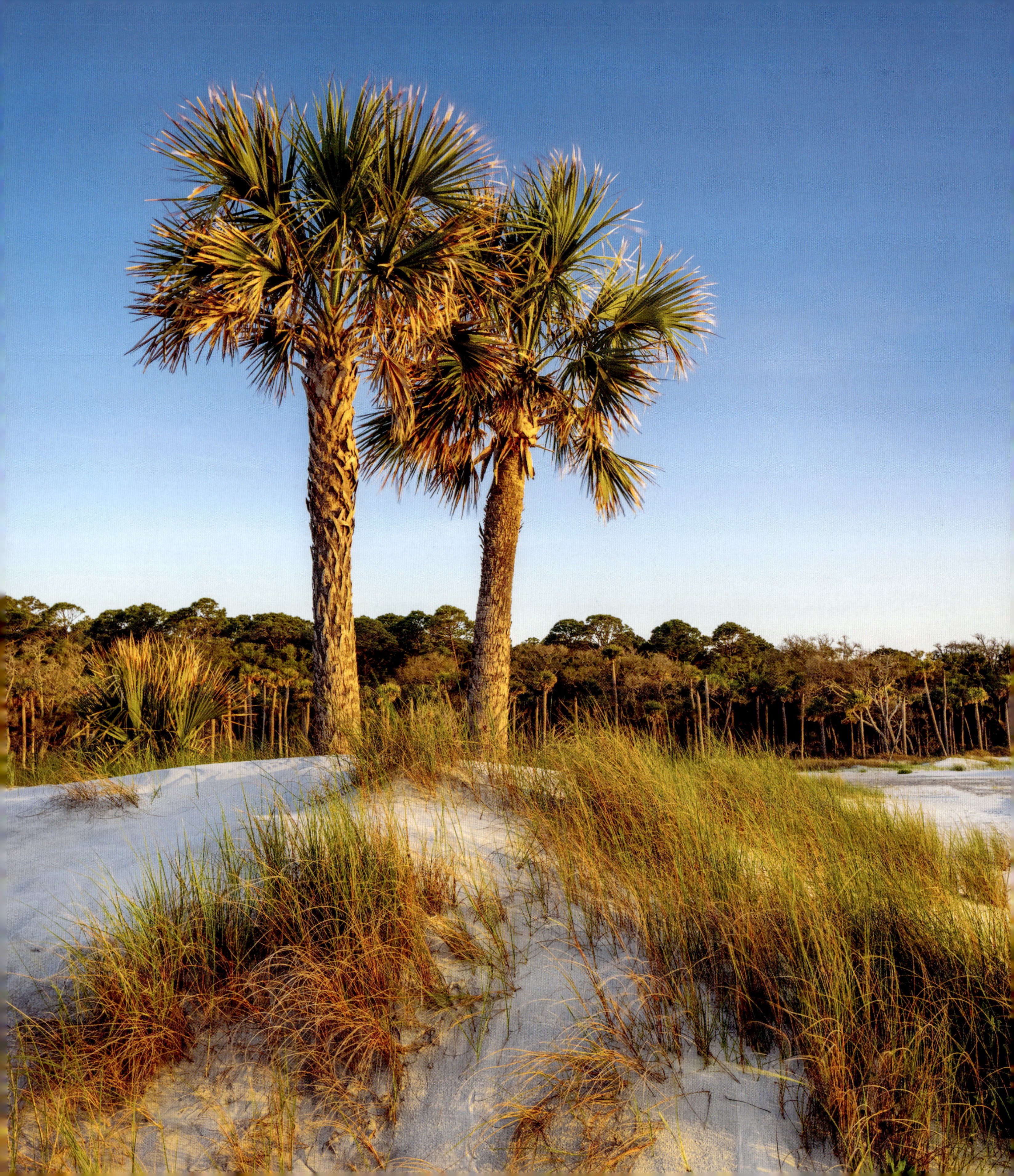

Overlooking the Dunes

Sand dunes, a desert by the sea. Shifting sands, salt water, and brutal sun mean it takes a special plant to live here, and South Carolina's state tree, the sabal palmetto, is a survivor. A soft trunk and strong root system enable it to withstand hurricanes. Botanists don't view it as a tree because it doesn't have a solid wood trunk.

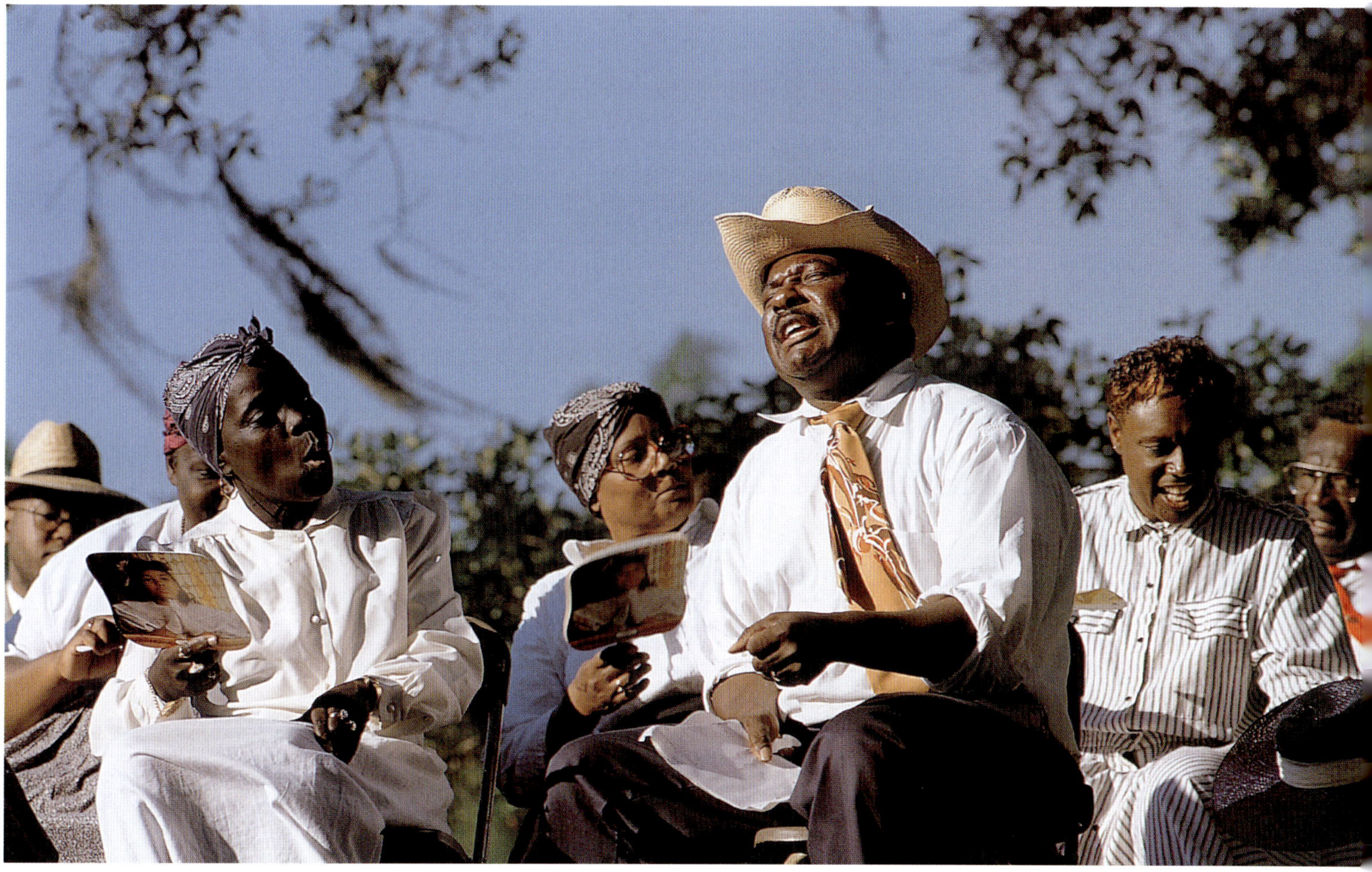

Deep-rooted Southern Music

The Mount Zion African Methodist Episcopal Church Gospel Singers performed at Middleton Place during the Spoleto Festival. Complex harmonies and a lively stage presence kept the crowd wanting more.

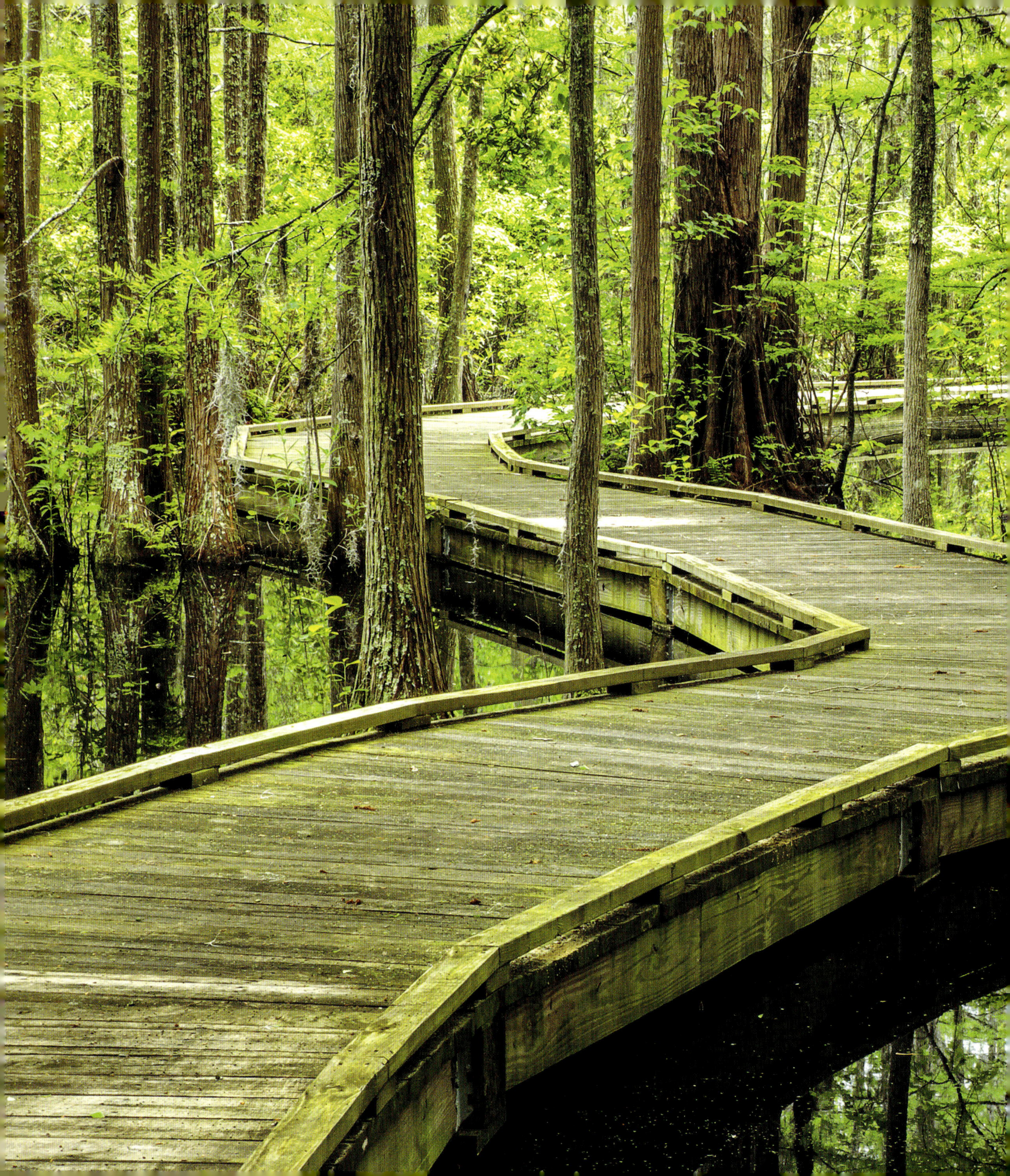

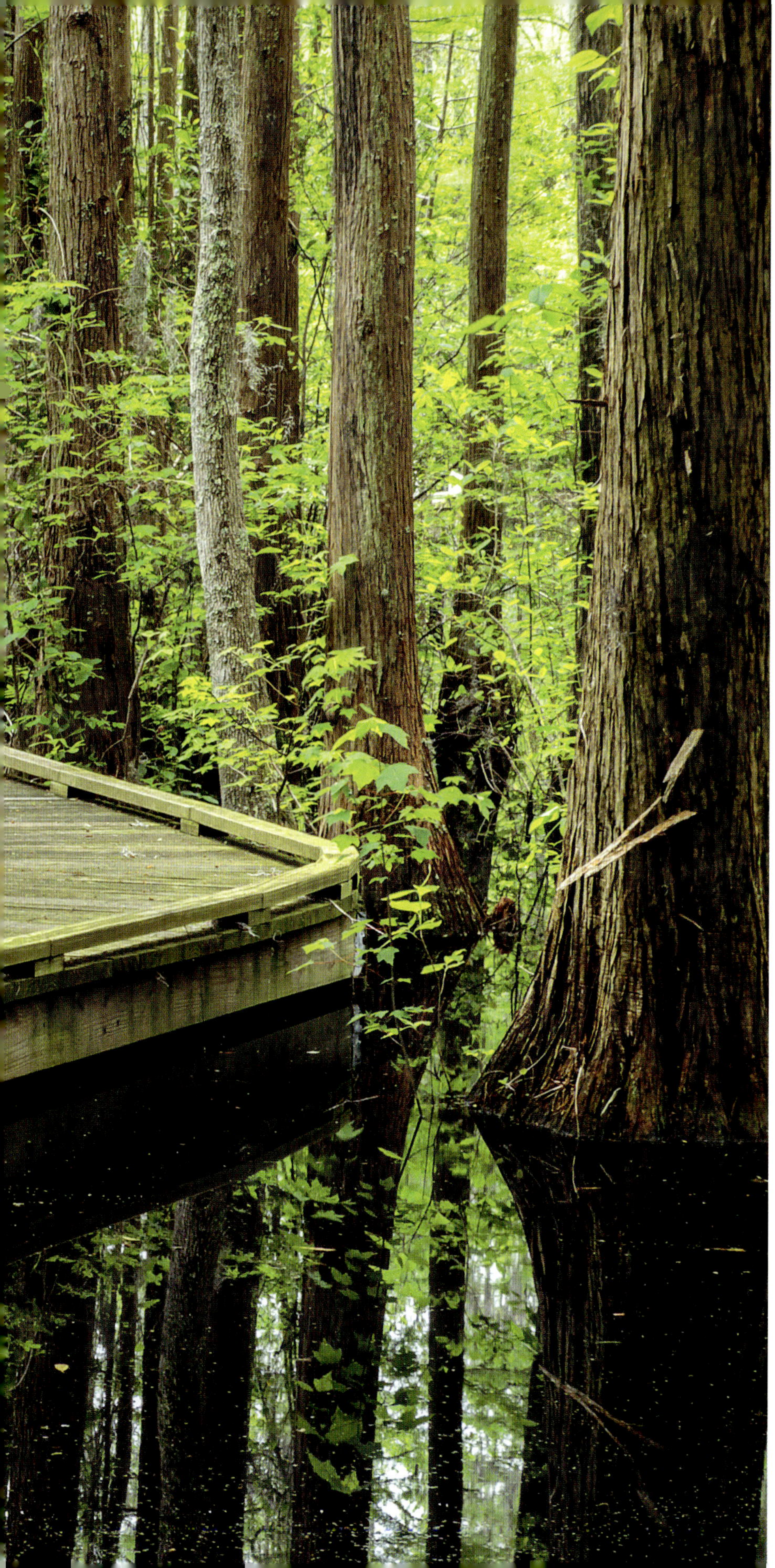

Woods Bay's Spring Finery

Woods Bay is one of the Mid-Atlantic Coastal Plain's few large, intact Carolina bays. In spring its fresh green leaves and cypress needles seem to tint the boardwalk snaking through its interior. Spilling into Florence, Clarendon, and Sumter counties, Woods Bay includes marsh, sandhills, oak-hickory forest, and shrub bog. You'll find swamps, savanna areas, and a pine barren along with its sand rim. A cypress-tupelo community dominates its interior.

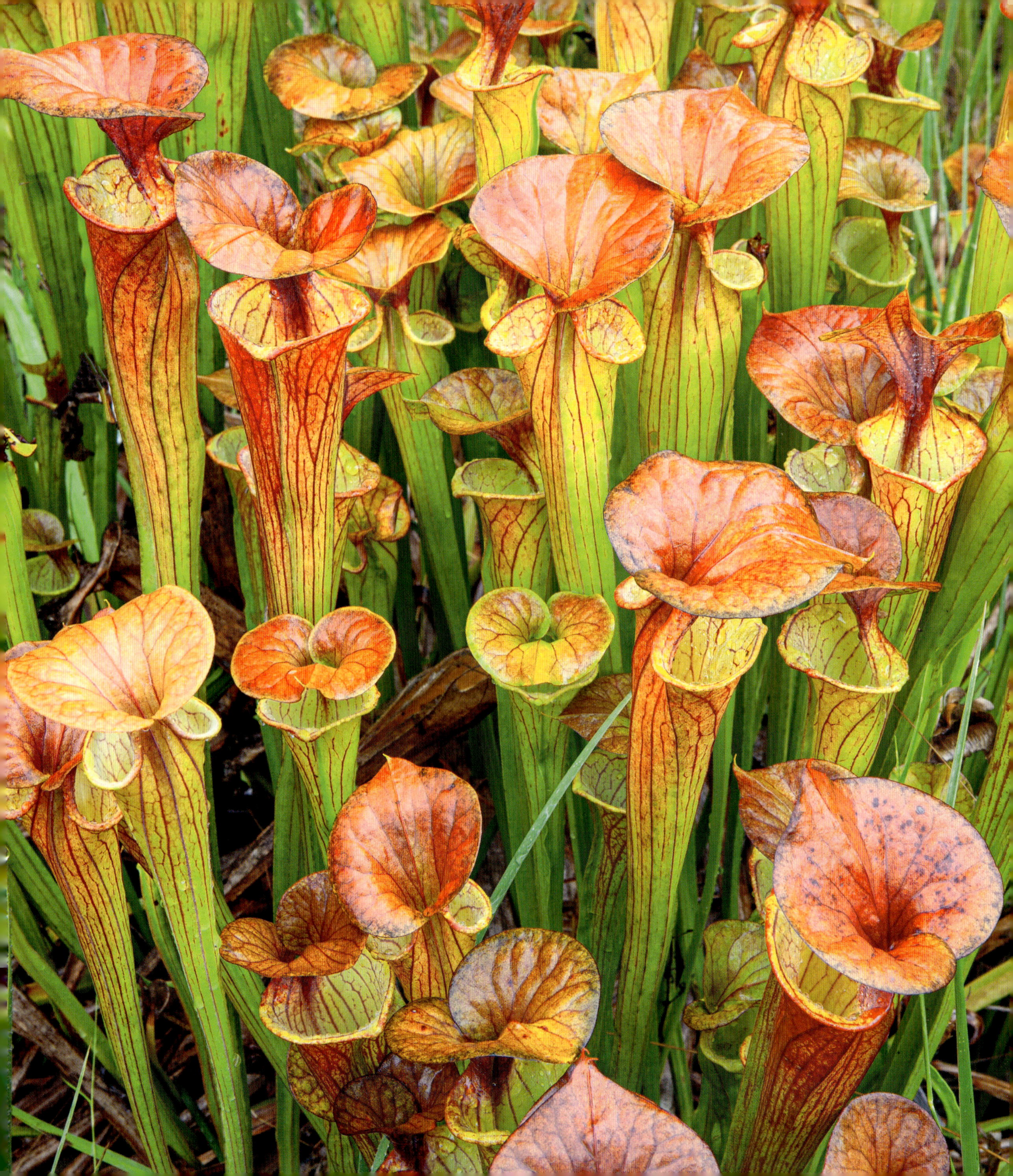

Beautiful but Deadly

The carnivorous pitcher plant is death made beautiful. In certain Carolina bays, colonies of pitcher plants shoot up like alien cities. Their throats are like long, lean pitchers. Insects catch the fragrance of their "nectar" and fly or crawl into and down the long throat. Escape is nearly impossible, and the insect ends up in a broth of juices, similar to stomach acid, where it turns into food for the plant.

CAROLINA BAYS

Carolina bays, shallow, elliptical depressions in the Atlantic Coastal Plain, occur in flat landscapes made of sand, sandstone, limestone, and other sedimentary materials. Their long axes run northwest to southeast, giving them a parallel appearance. Larger bays possess rims of white sand on their southeastern end. Some rims stand fifteen feet high; widths can extend several hundred feet. Often the sand is as white as snow. Thick layers of soil and peat deposits characterize many bays.

Most hold seasonal rains, making them periodic wetlands important to migrating waterfowl. Herons, egrets, and wood storks frequent them as do dragonflies, Carolina anoles, salamanders, leopard frogs, and green tree frogs. Isolated wetlands, they sometimes overlap or occur as a smaller bay inside a larger one.

From the ground they look like swamps. That perception changed in 1930, when the city of Myrtle Beach contracted Fairchild Surveys to take aerial photographs of the area. Later, when Roosevelt's Department of Agriculture studied East Coast aerial photography, the astounding discovery that the Carolina bays were oriented in a parallel manner surfaced. Carolina bays are so named because the bigger and better bays exist in the Carolinas and because of the preponderance of bay trees in them.

These elliptical depressions may well be the world's most mystifying landform. People once believed meteor swarms created these strange swamplands. No meteorite evidence, however, has been found. Experts say the bays are too shallow to be impact craters. Other theories border on the bizarre. Some "experts" claimed dinosaur footprints created the bays. Others claimed ancient volcanic activity formed them.

As to how many exist, estimates run from 500,000 to as many as a million thanks to new detection technologies such as Light Detection and Ranging (LiDAR), a remote sensing method that illuminates a target with laser light. Bays of various sizes dimple South Carolina's coastal plain.

Two major questions need answers. What formed the bays, and when did they form? A credible though nonexciting theory explains the bays' shape. Over geological time prevailing winds and wave action shaped the bays and piled sand at their southeastern end. That, however, takes nothing from these hauntingly beautiful swamps and their temporary waters so important to amphibians and other species.

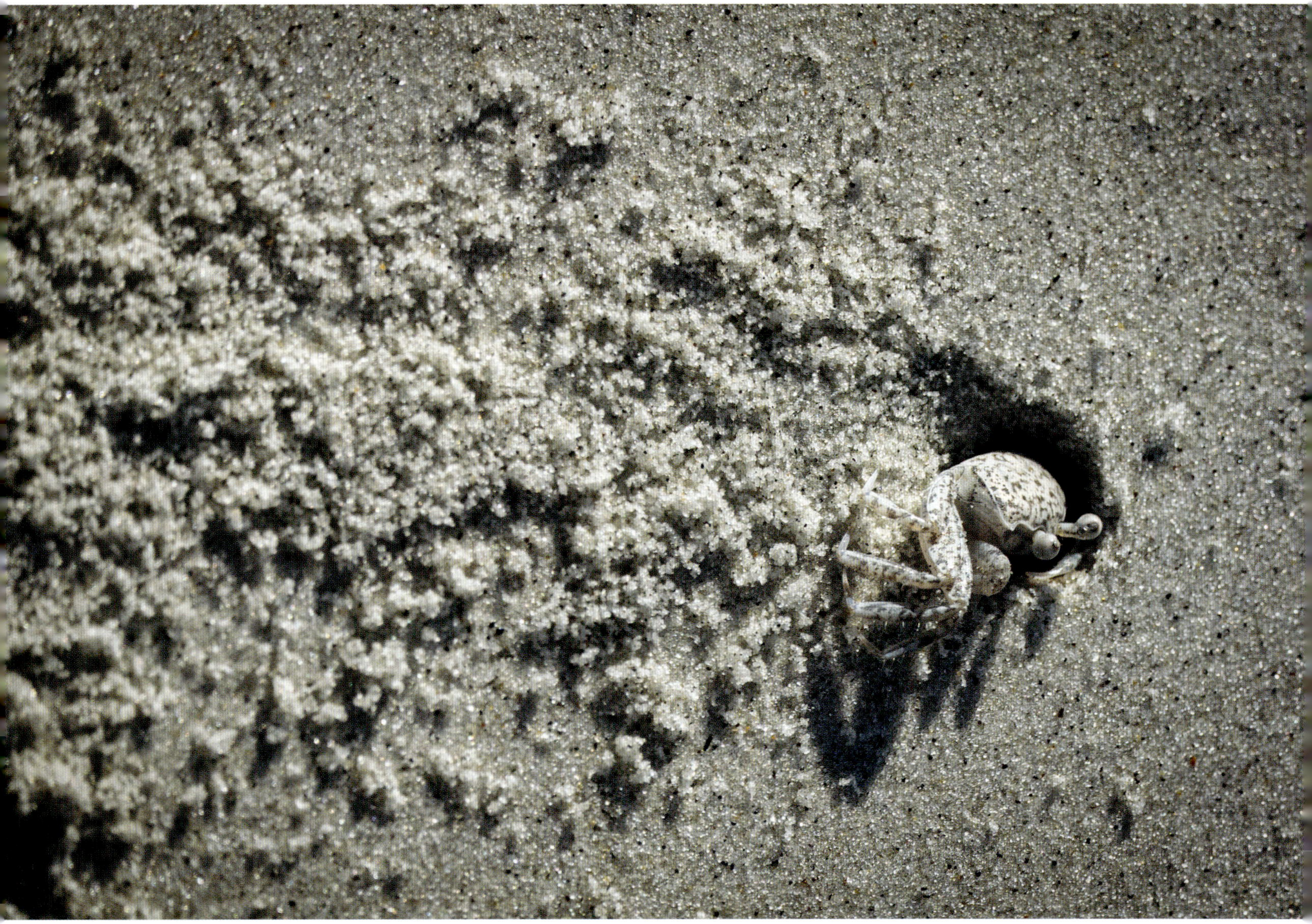

Excavating a Home

The Atlantic ghost crab (*Ocypode quadrata*), what many call a sand crab, makes trip after trip digging its burrow, retreating with a load of sand to be tossed aside. The excavated fan of sand is testimony to this sand crab's hard work. Somewhat able to match their surroundings, they're grayish white, sometimes straw colored. Night scavengers, they're extremely quick, especially when their bulbous eyes spot danger. With the eyes' ability to rotate 360 degrees, little escapes their notice.

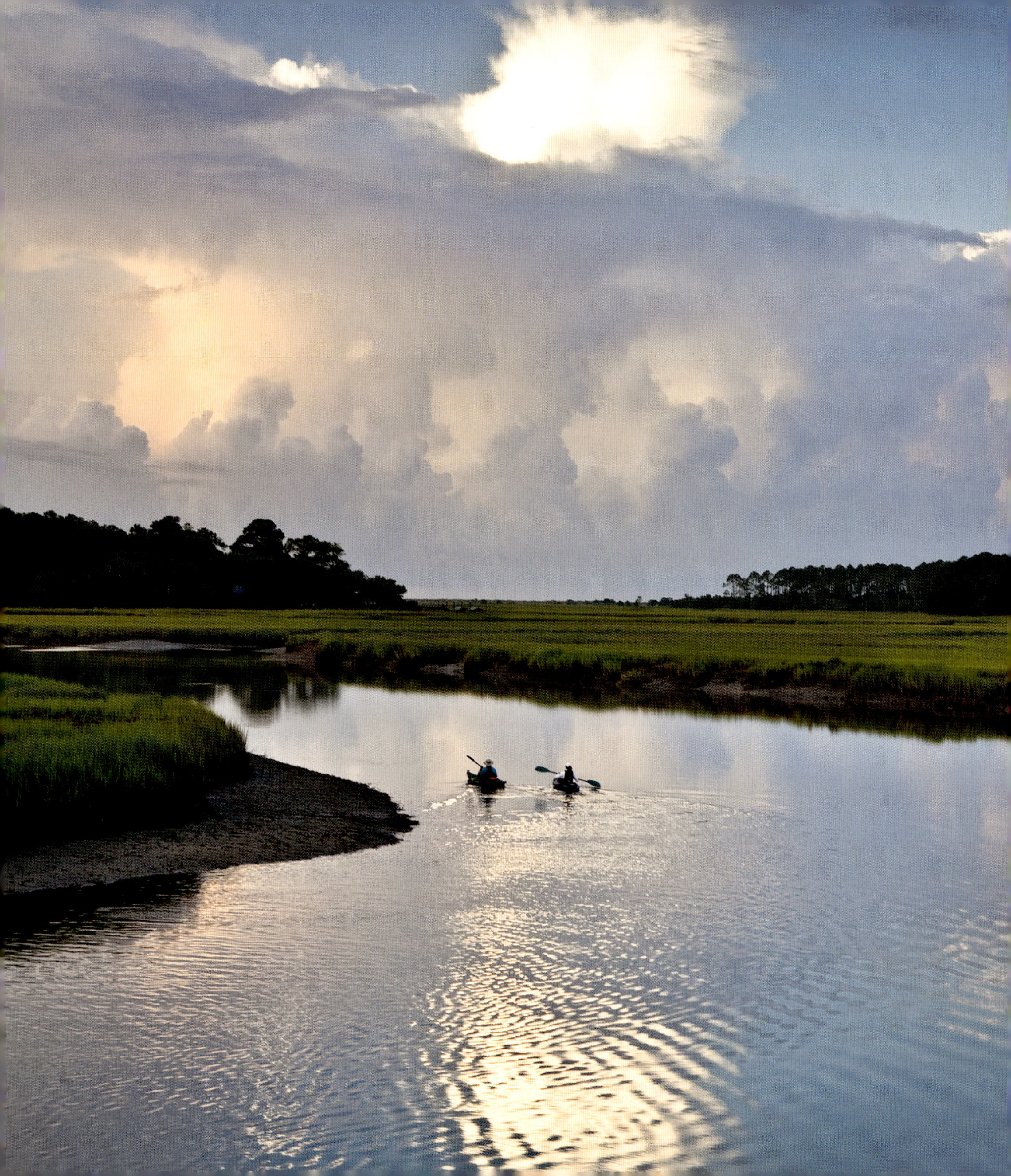

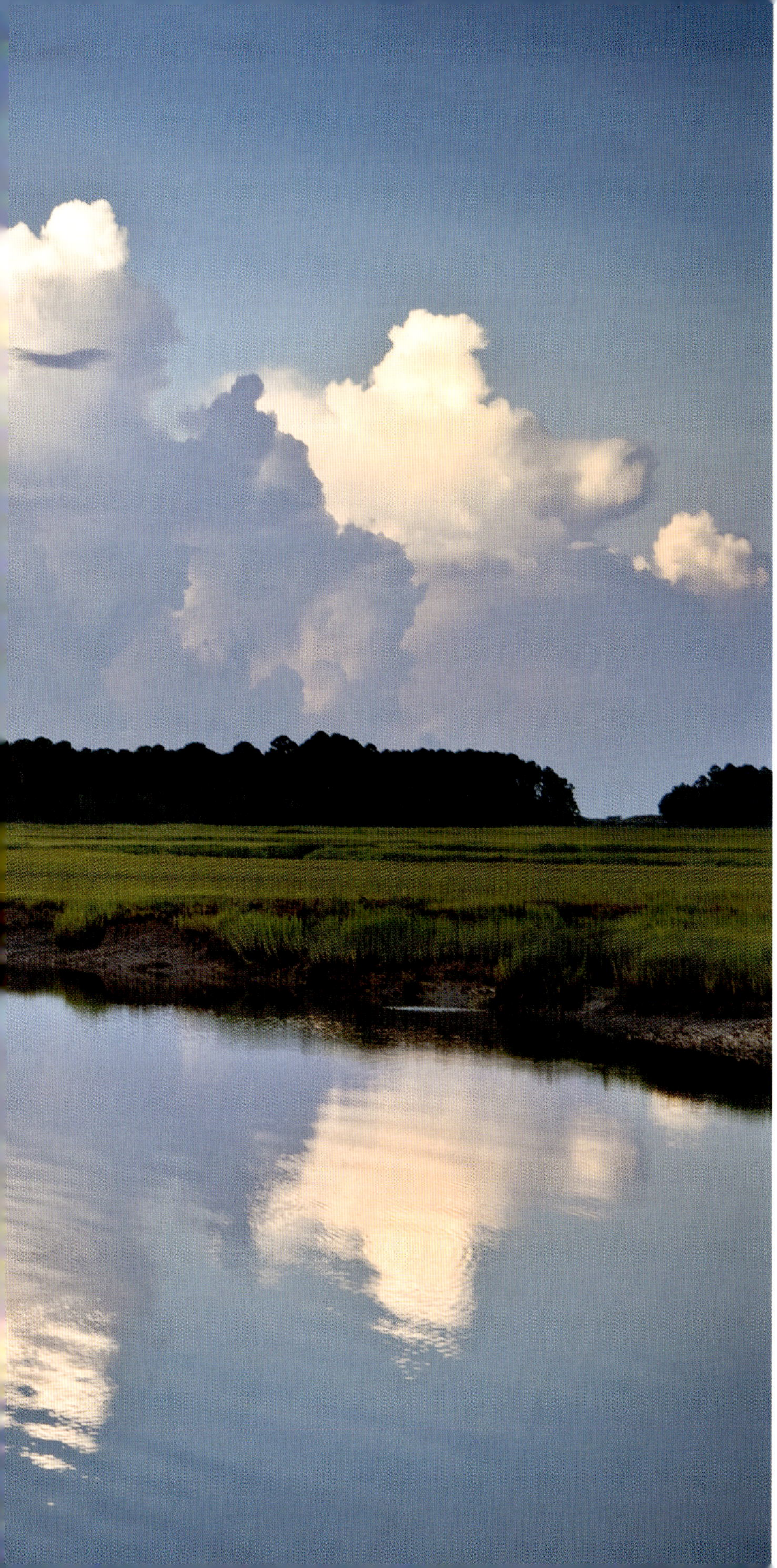

High Tide

Kayakers navigate the Kiawah River, a waterscape rich with beauty and wildlife. While it's common to spot wading birds, other possibilities include dolphins, manatees, and sea turtles. Silent and low in the water, kayakers possess stealth, and that makes nature watching one of the joys of kayaking.

Iron Heart

Behind St. John's Reformed Episcopal Church, 91 Anson Street, Charleston, you'll find Philip Simmons's "Heart Gate." Simmons's design reveals his tender touch, faithfully crafted in his shop by his nephew, Carlton Simmons, and cousin, Joseph Pringle. A single-heart and double-heart gate grace church grounds. Pictured is the right half of the double-heart gate as you approach it from Menotti Street.

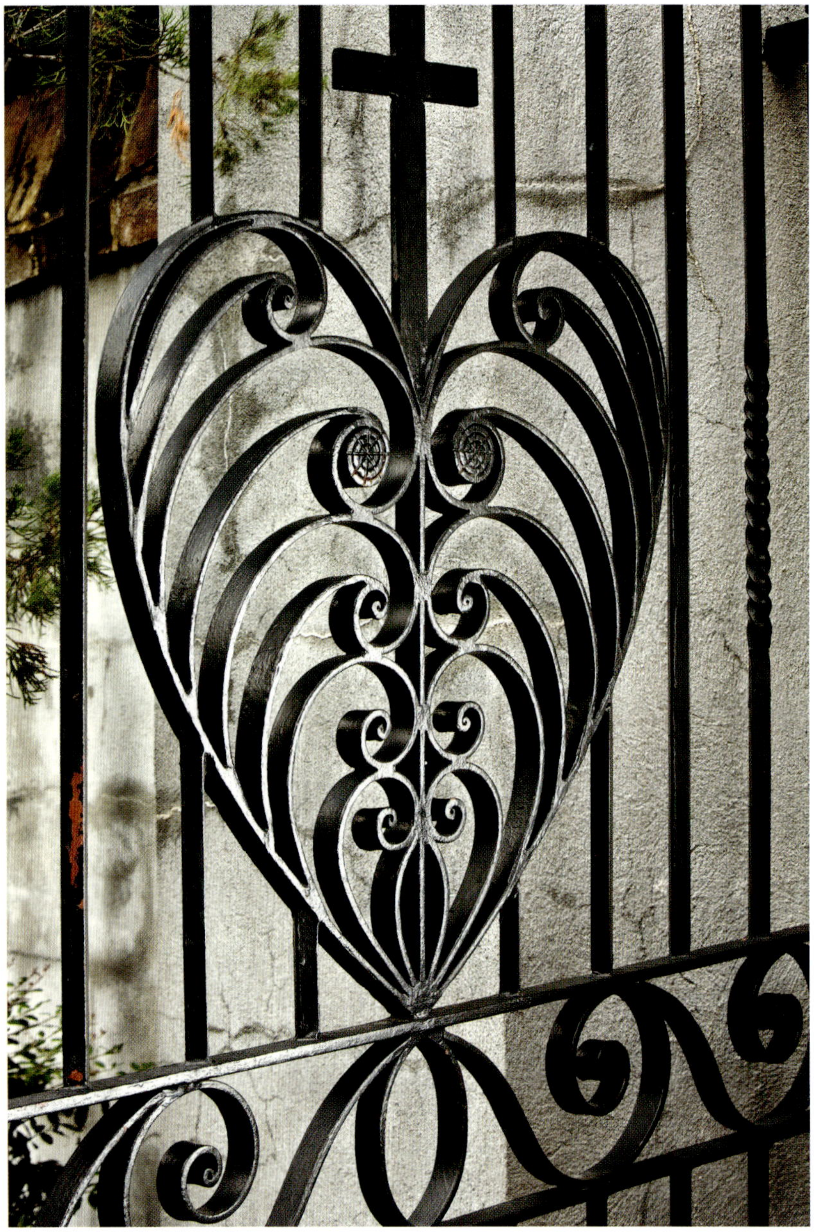

St. Michael's Anglican Church

Though the architect of this church is unknown, it follows the tradition of Sir Christopher Wren, whose style was prevalent during the colonial period and up to the Gothic revival of 1841. The steeple stood 186 feet high before the 1886 earthquake dropped it eight inches. Once known as St. Philip's Church, the name changed when the General Assembly of the Province authorized a larger church be built onsite called St. Michael's. In 1993 Smith of Derby in London restored the Ainsworth-Thwaites clock, thought to be the country's oldest functioning colonial tower clock.

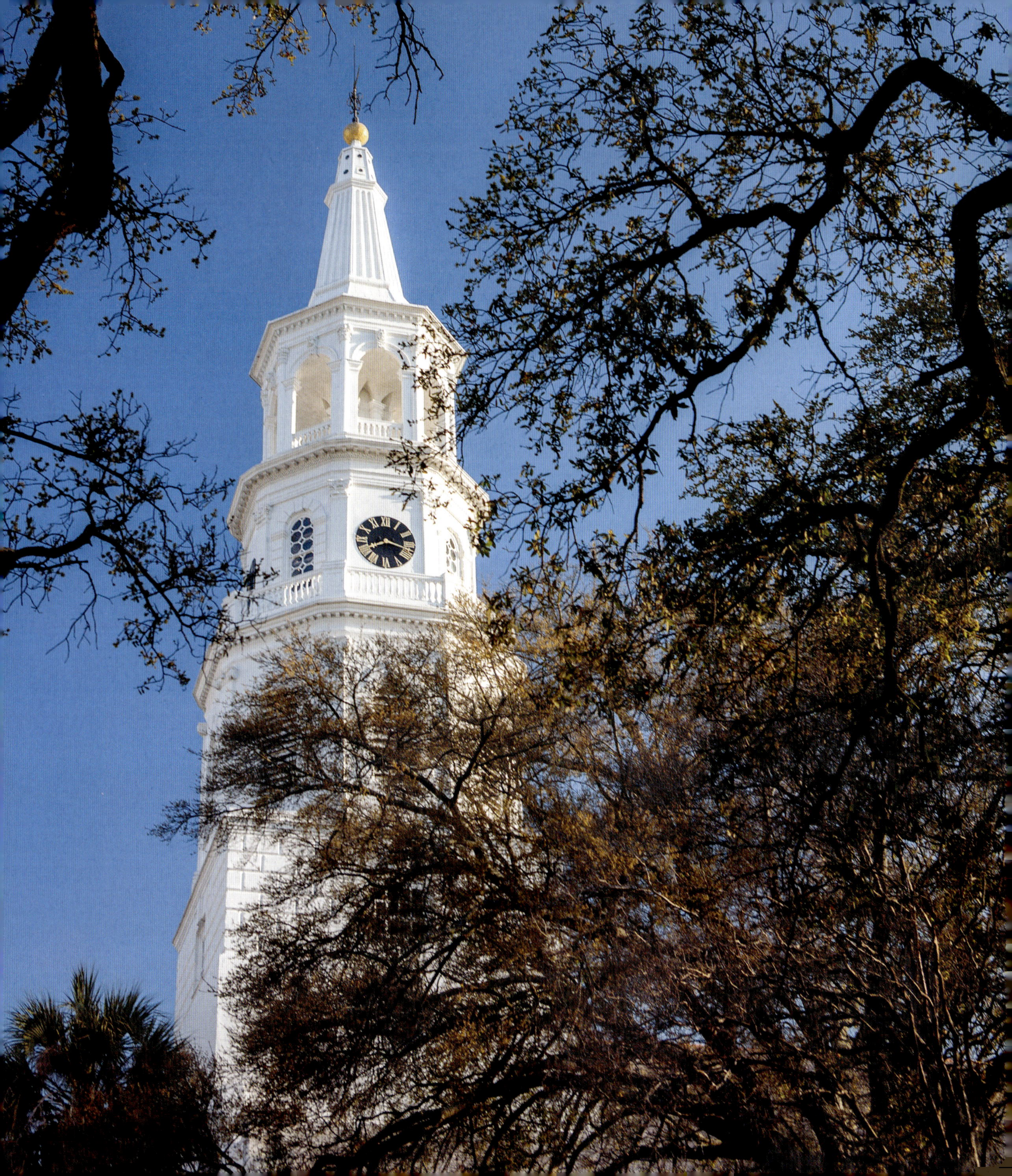

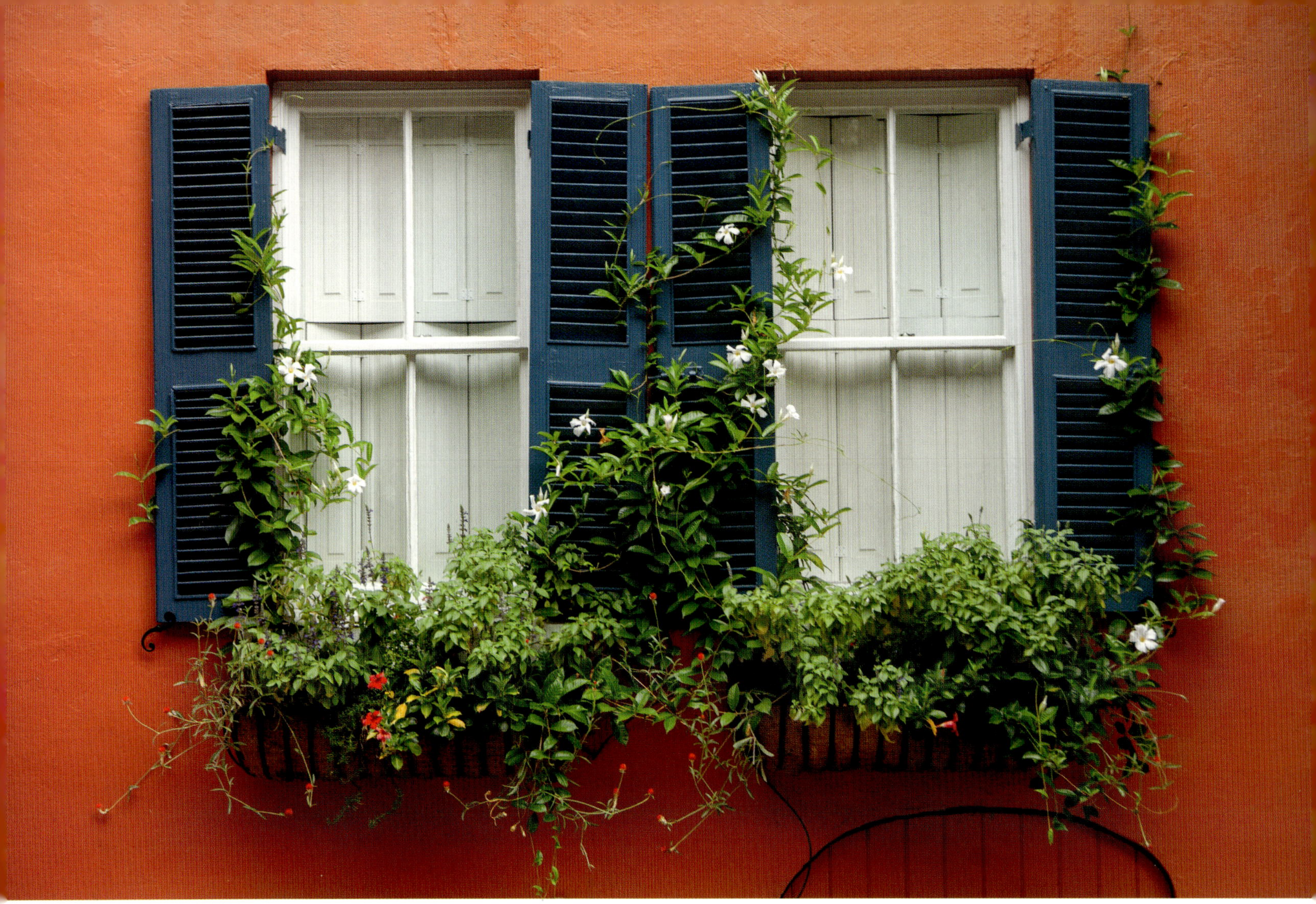

Charleston Window Box

Window boxes' flowering plants hold the eye in historic Charleston neighborhoods. They possess a distinguished history: ancient Romans grew herbs in terra-cotta boxes for medicinal purposes. They were a popular feature in colonial homes. Charleston Window Boxes have their own Facebook page. Are you a gardener without a garden? A fan of hummingbirds? Turn to window boxes. Stroll Queen Street and don't be surprised to see them on wrought iron gates.

Queen Street

For many years Charleston's streets had no names. Queen Street was among the early of Charleston's streets to be named. Looking a bit like Rainbow Row, Queen Street is central to Charleston.

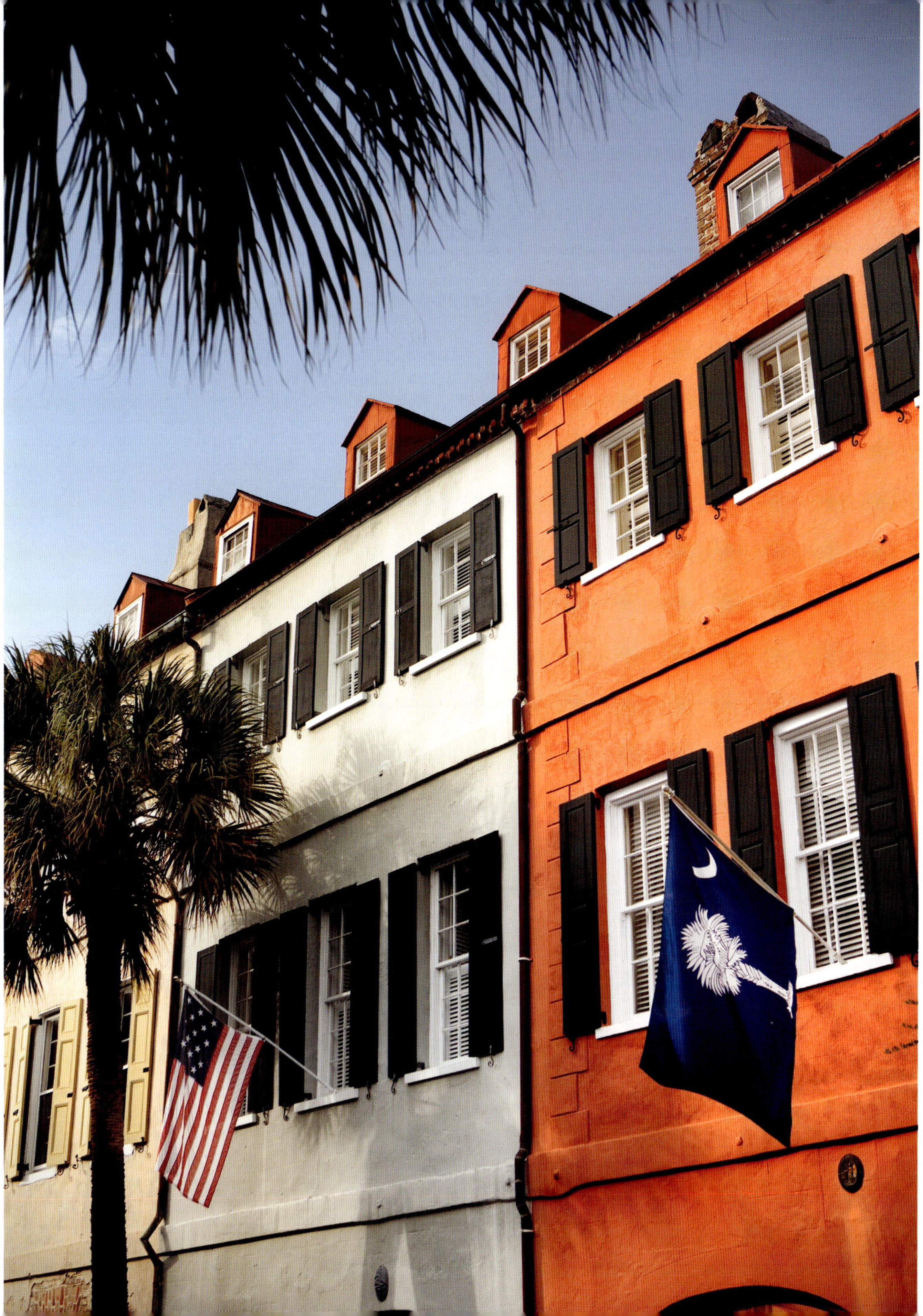

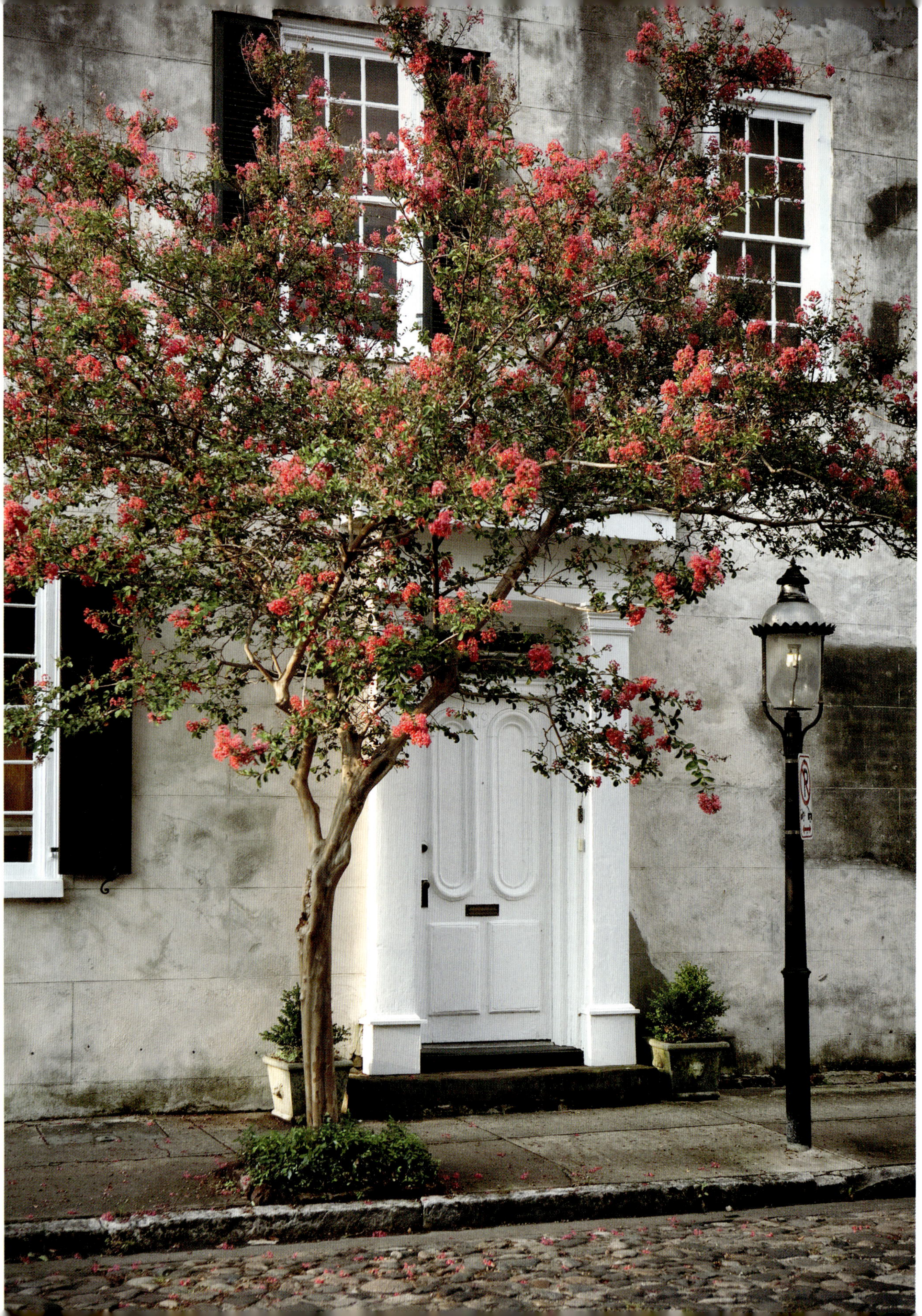

Crepe Myrtles and Cobblestones

Crepe myrtle (*Lagerstroemia indica*) blossoms rain down on a Charleston cobblestone street, the ballast of colonial sailing ships. French botanist André Michaux brought the crepe myrtle to the United States by way of Charleston in 1790. Michaux first grew crepe myrtle plants in his garden, and in time they spread across the city. Today they proclaim the arrival of summer across the South.

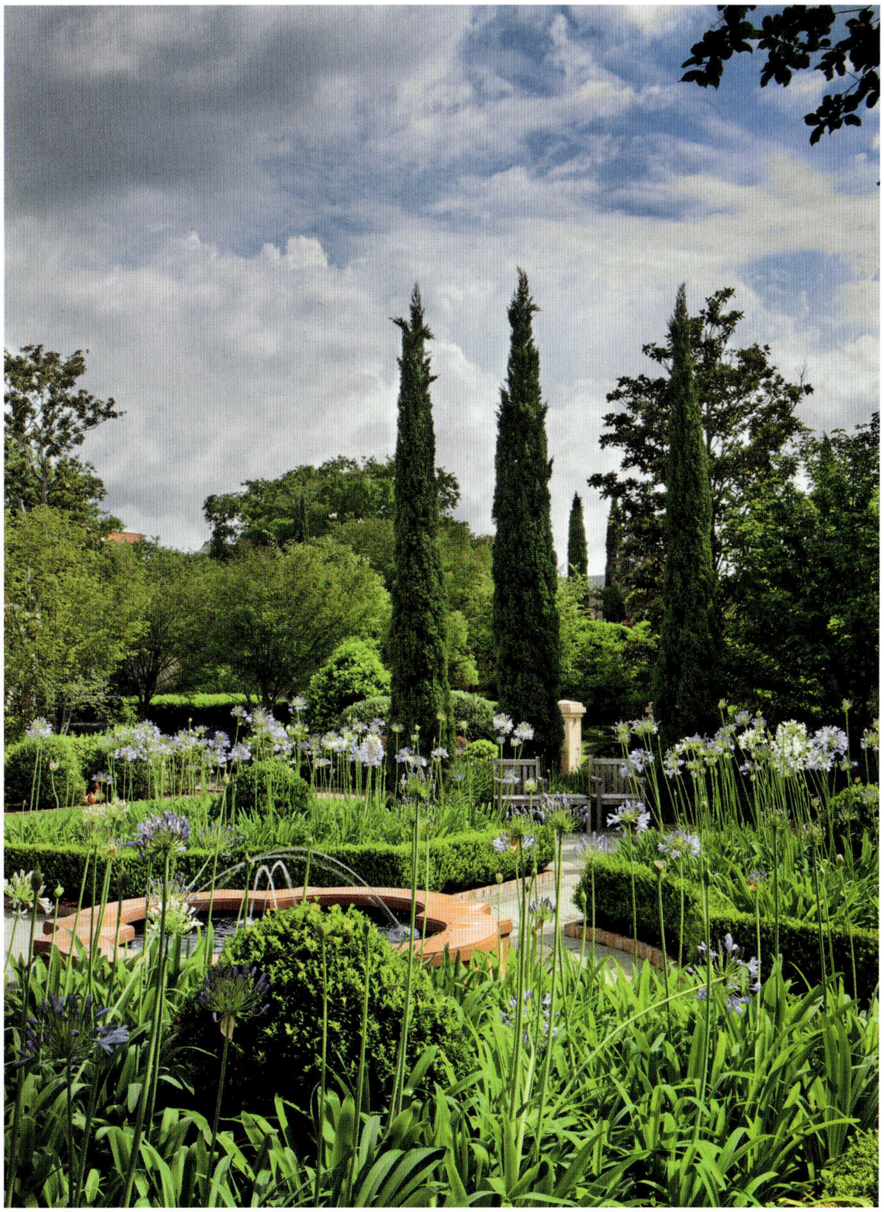

Gaillard-Bennett House Garden

Planter Theodore Gaillard Jr. constructed an Adam-style two-and-a-half-story frame dwelling ca. 1800 on high ground on three lots at the west end of Montagu Street, leaving ample room for a garden. Landscape architect Sheila Wertimer designed the present garden for Steven and Mary Caroline Stewart. The blue flowers are agapanthus, lilies of the Nile. In the background, Italian cypresses, grace one of Charleston's larger gardens.

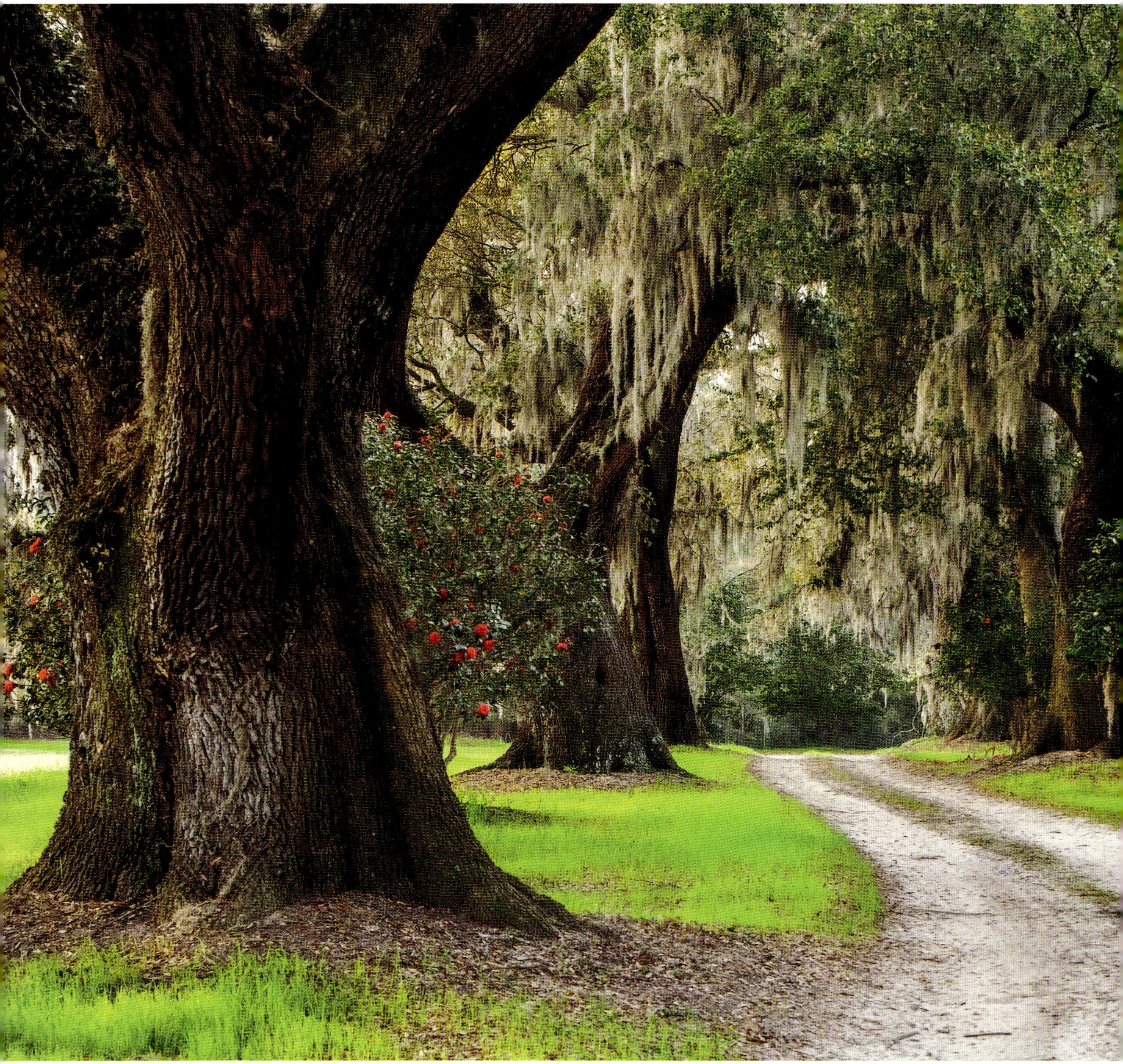

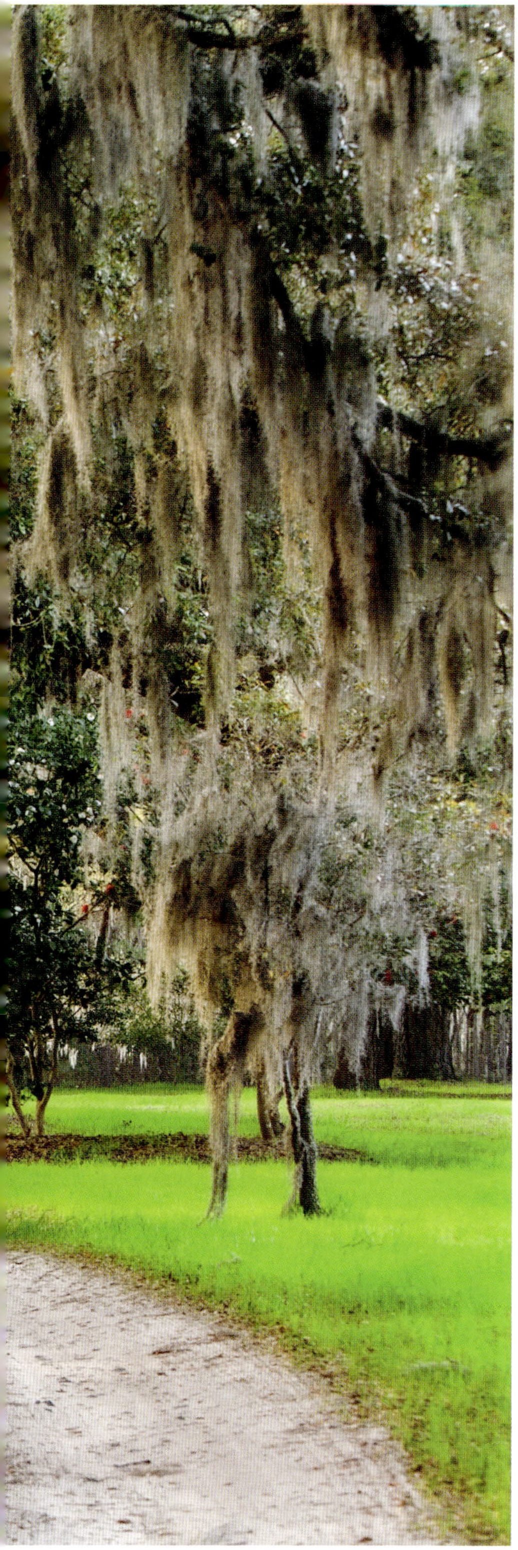

Thundering Down a Sandy Lane

Imagine sand flying as Benjamin Martin (Mel Gibson, *The Patriot*) gallops on horseback down a Lowcountry lane to confront the Redcoats. Action explodes amid a classic Southern setting of camellias, live oaks, and curtains of Spanish moss. Note the resurrection ferns that give oak limbs a green veneer and know that Gibson filmed key scenes here at a historic rice plantation.

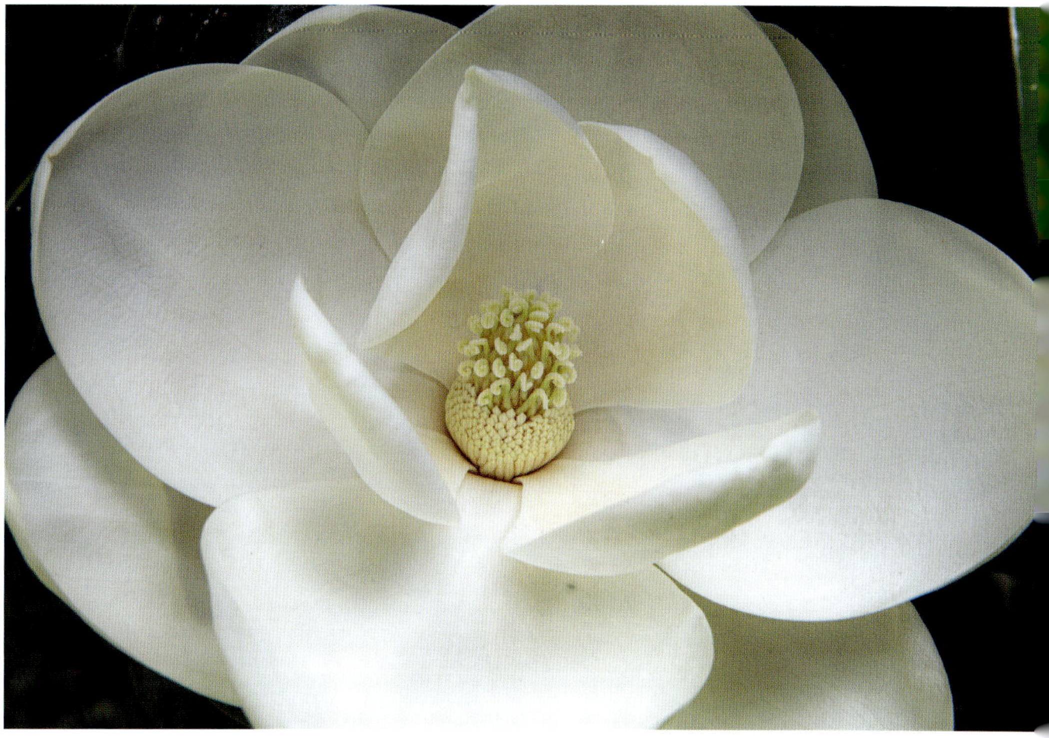

Symbol of the South

The magnificent magnolia (*Magnolia grandiflora*) symbolizes the South, and yet it somehow missed being South Carolina's state flower. When its showy blossoms send their aromatic scent into the air, it's a sign of summertime. One of the oldest plant species on earth, this native grows from North Carolina to Florida. A large tree with glossy dark green leaves and a skirt of dried dead leaves, it's known for its creamy white petals and sweet fragrance. It was named after the French botanist Pierre Magnol.

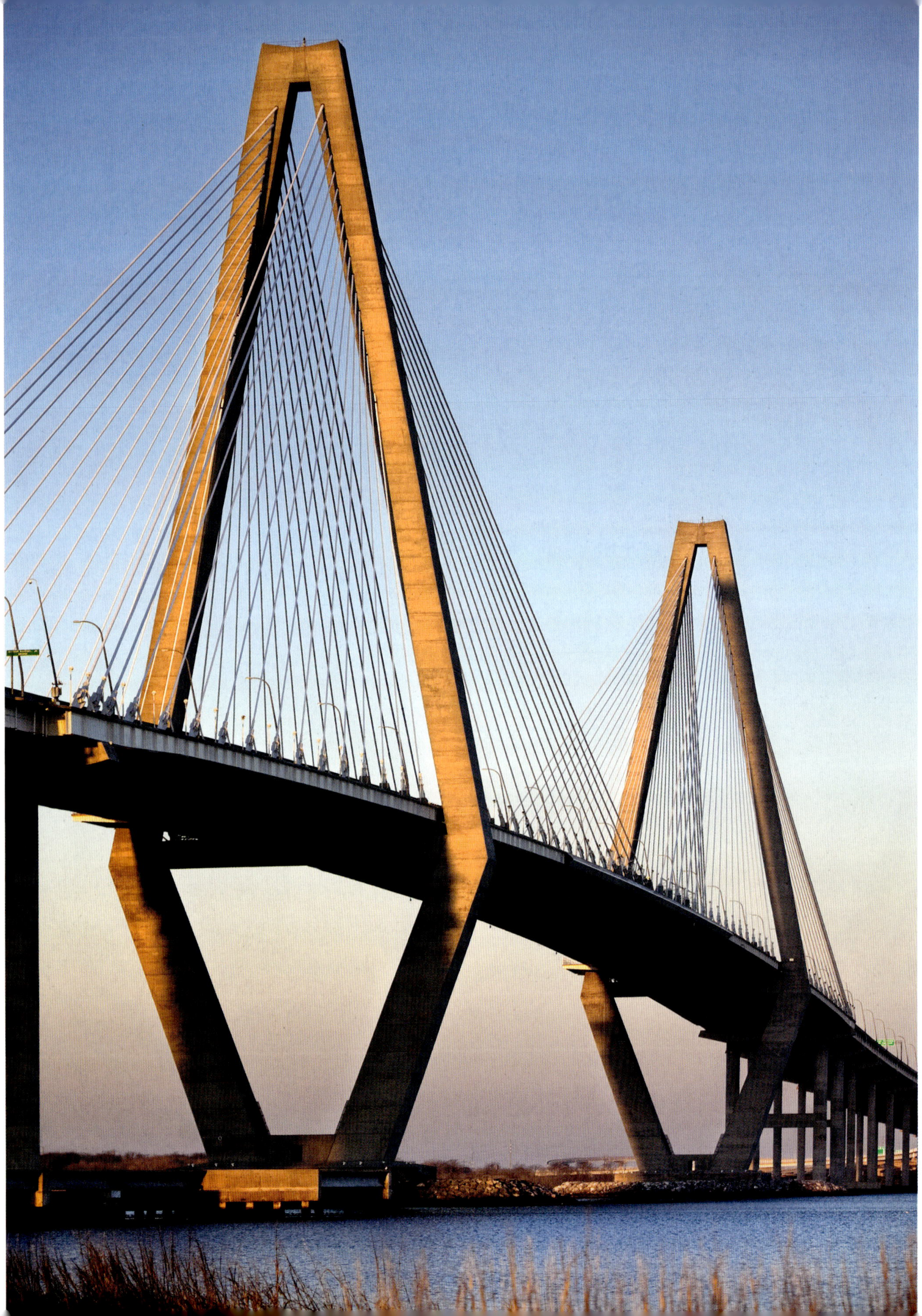

Arthur Ravenel Bridge

US 17 leads to a cable-stayed span bridge 1,546 feet long. Connecting Charleston and Mount Pleasant, the bridge's diamond-towers and cables can withstand earthquakes as powerful as the 1886 quake that struck Charleston. Old habits die with difficulty. Because the bridge crosses the Cooper River, some still refer to the Arthur Ravenel Bridge as the Cooper River Bridge.

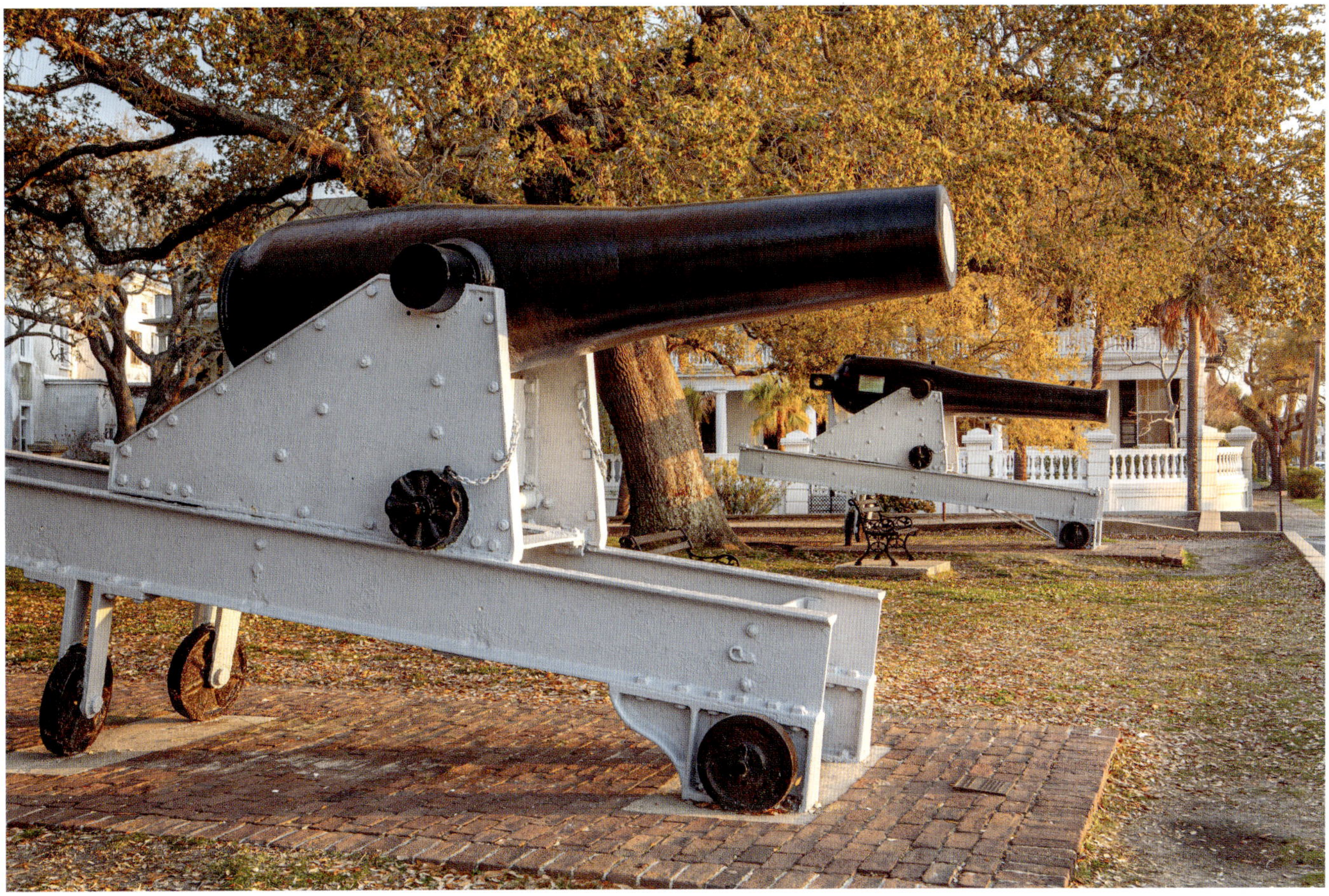

Battery Park Cannon

The USS *Keokuk* fired this eleven-inch, eight-ton Dahlgren on Fort Sumter in 1863. When Confederate artillery shelled the USS *Keokuk*, it ran aground off Morris Island where its crew abandoned it. White Point Garden in Charleston's Battery was first known as South Bay and later as Oyster Point. The name "White Point" came into play due to the sun-bleached oyster shells that piled up at the water's edge.

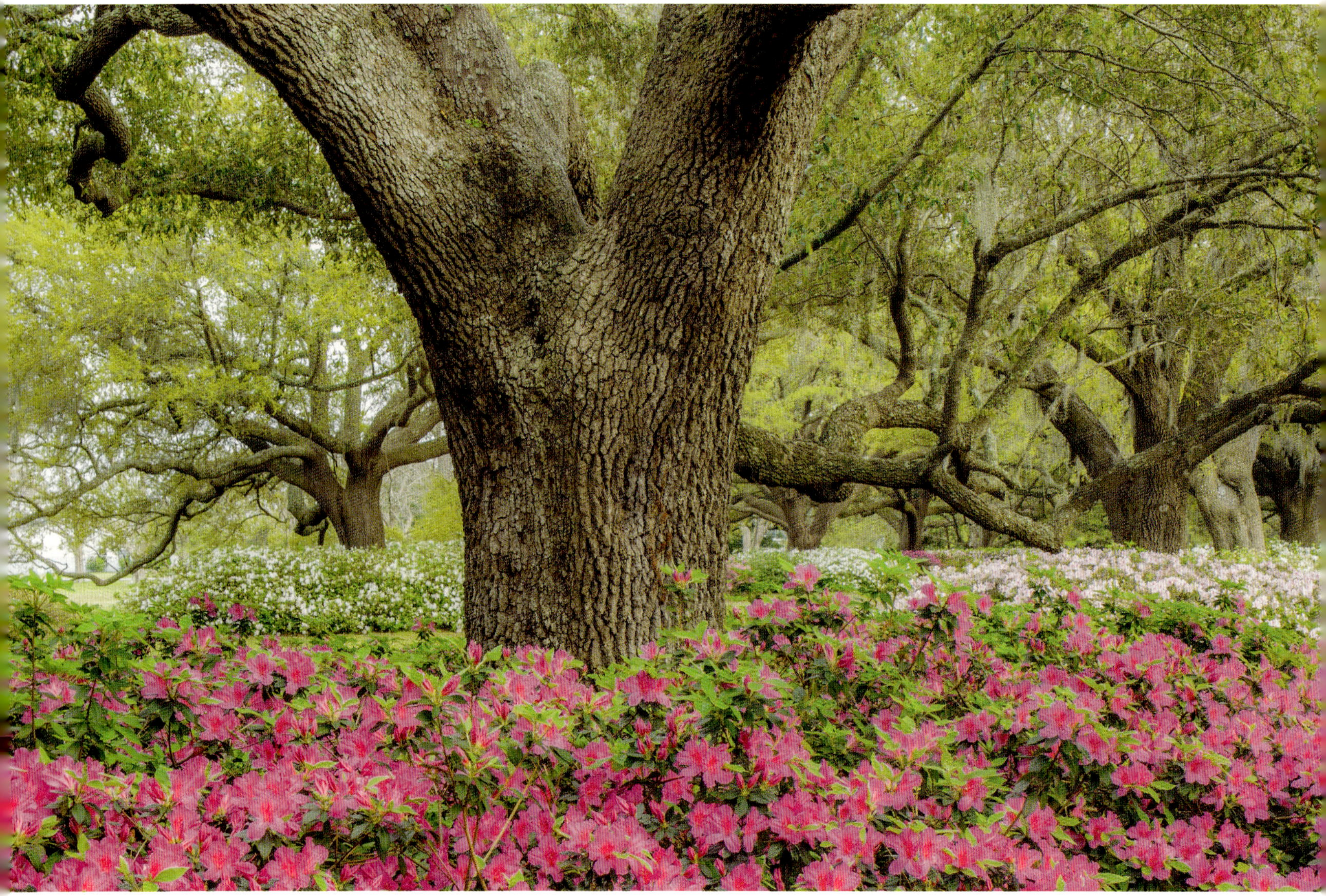

Signatures of the South

An icon of the American South, live oaks lord over Charleston County azaleas, flowering shrubs in the genus *Rhododendron*. First planted in Middleton Place Gardens, azaleas have been associated with Southern gardens ever since.

Great Blue Heron

You notice North America's largest heron's size right away, whether stalking the shallow edge of a pond or crossing the sky with slow wing beats. This great blue heron (*Ardea herodias*) stalks Hunting Island's surf. It is tall and long-legged, a bird built on stilts. When it flies you notice its long legs. With its neck curled into an S, it flies in a laborious way with its legs trailing well beyond the tail. It looks menacing, a bit like a pterodactyl.

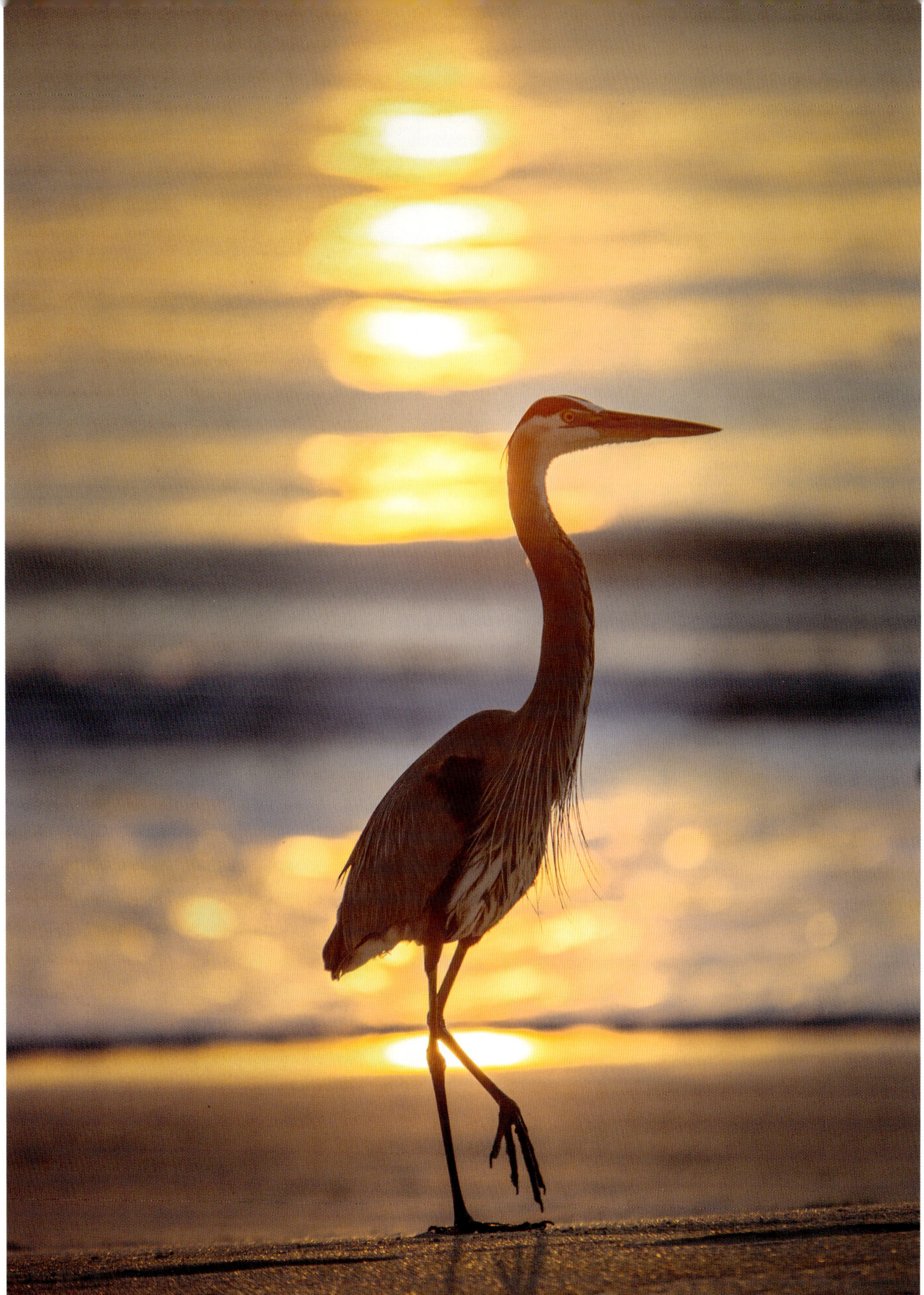

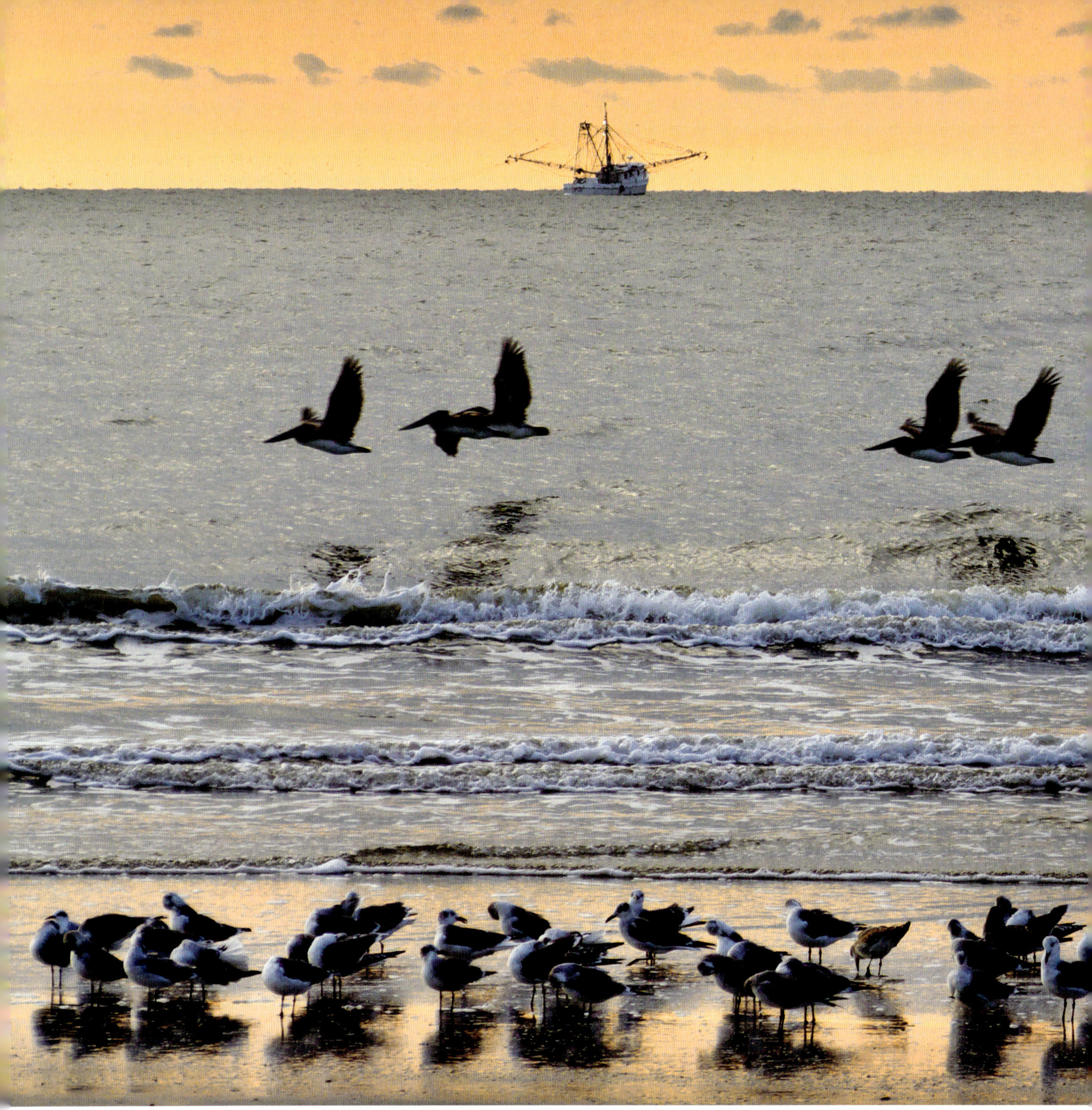

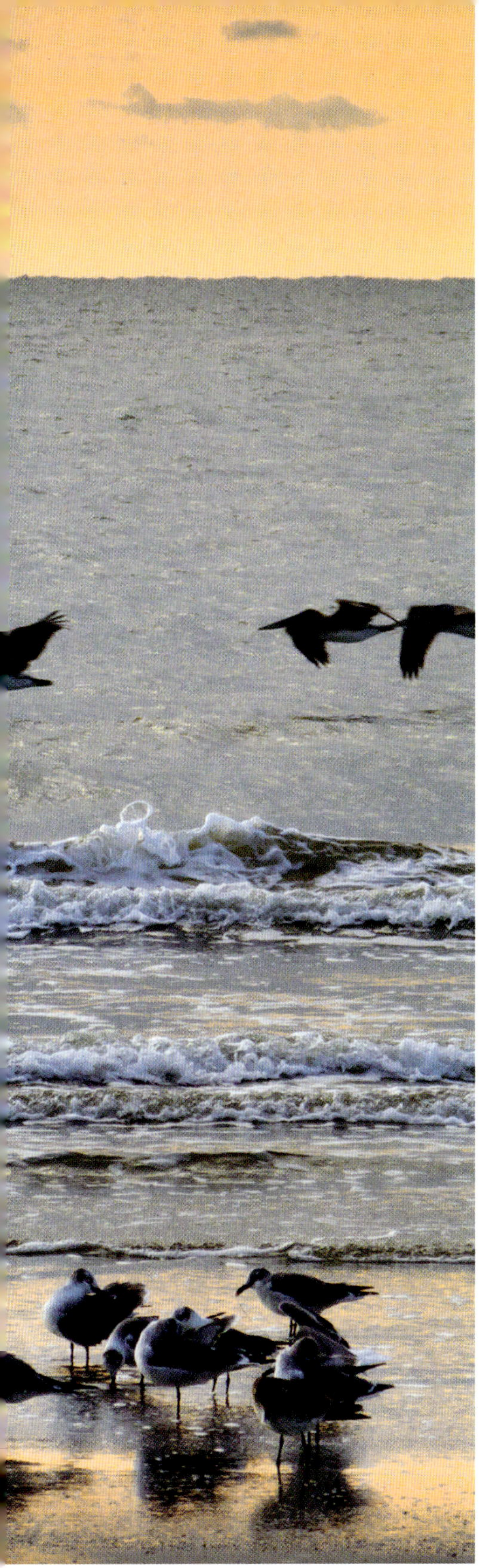

Foragers All

The quest for survival carries on at Folly Beach. Fishers and shorebirds alike seek sustenance from the Atlantic's generous bounty. You can't see it, but a maelstrom of gulls swirls about the trawler, seeking easy pickings.

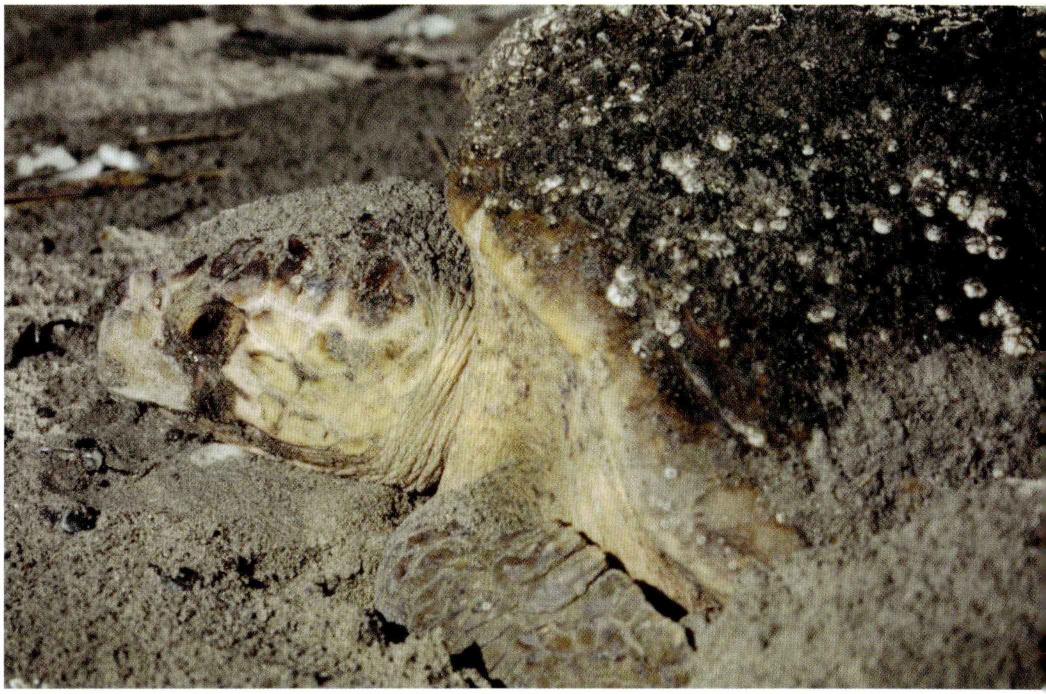

Nesting Time at Cape Romain

May through August ushers in the time when sea turtles lumber ashore under darkness to lay eggs in dunes. A single, wide scrape running up to the dune line indicates a female loggerhead sea turtle (*Caretta caretta*) is laying her eggs. A turtle always returns to lay eggs where she hatched. Once laying commences, she will not budge, behavior that makes female loggerheads vulnerable to poachers who prize the species' meat and eggs.

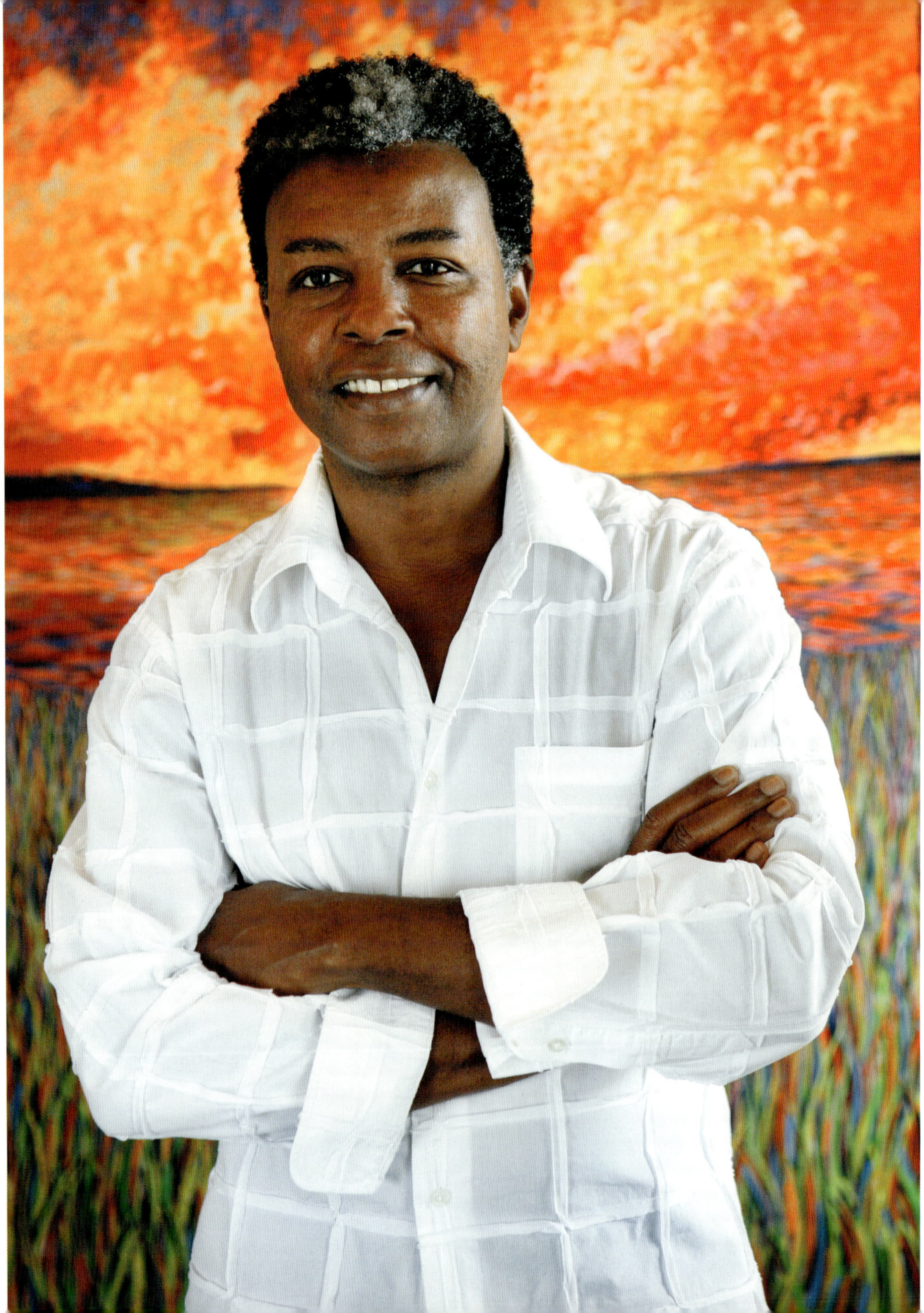

Jonathan Green

Jonathan Green, an internationally acclaimed and awarded professional artist, pays tribute to Gullah culture and its ties to rice cultivation in South Carolina. "Everything comes out of the rice culture." Being southern is of major importance to him as is his family's West African heritage. (Green traces his ancestry seven generations back to Senegal.) "Coupling the two, I try to take the angst out of art." Green's mastery of color and adroit use of the human figure let him preserve and share a deep sense of community and how people meet the life challenges of work, love, and belonging.

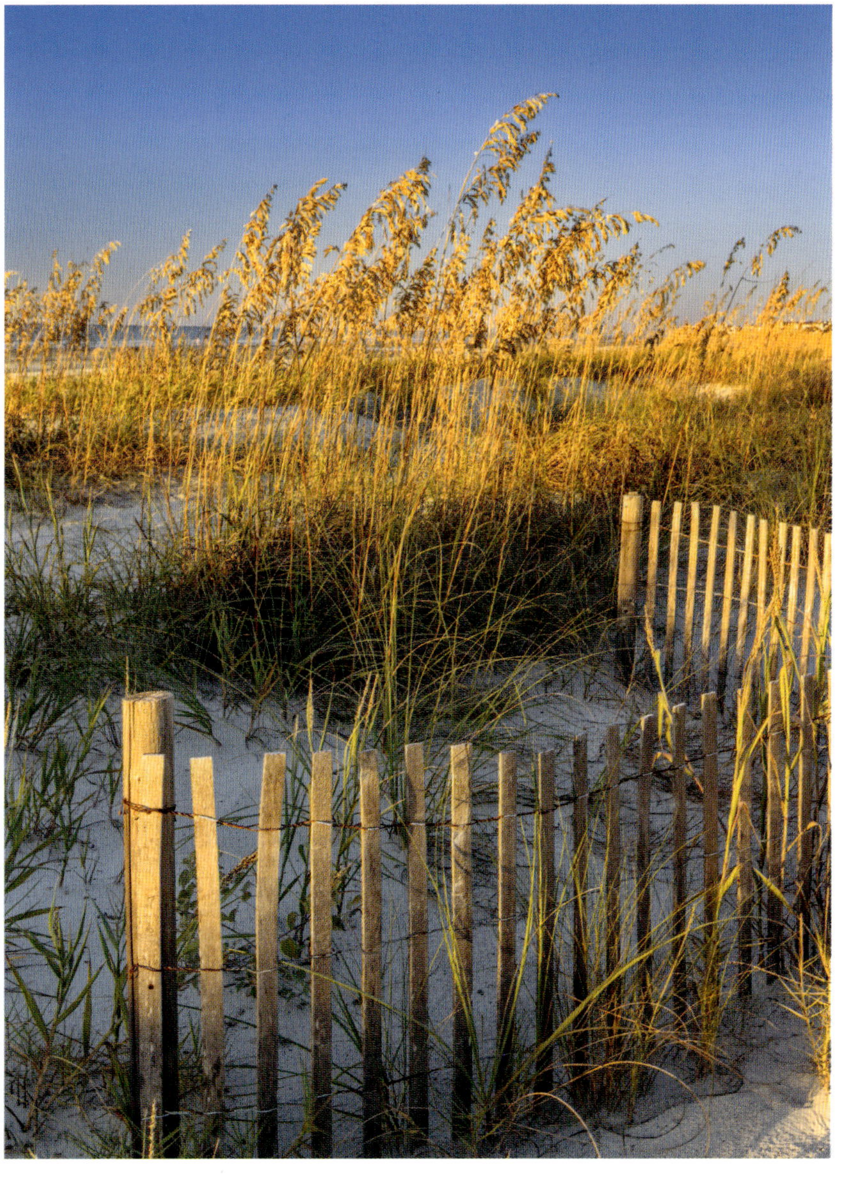

Dune Builder

Sand fences, known also as wind fences, slow winds carrying grains of sand. The sand falls, and a dune begins to form. Employed to fill gaps in dunes as well, consider it a form of wind engineering. The zone between the beach and dunes is an important habitat for nesting shorebirds and sea turtles. Cape Hatteras National Seashore and Cape Cod National Seashore use this simple method of reducing wind velocity to restore and nourish dunes.

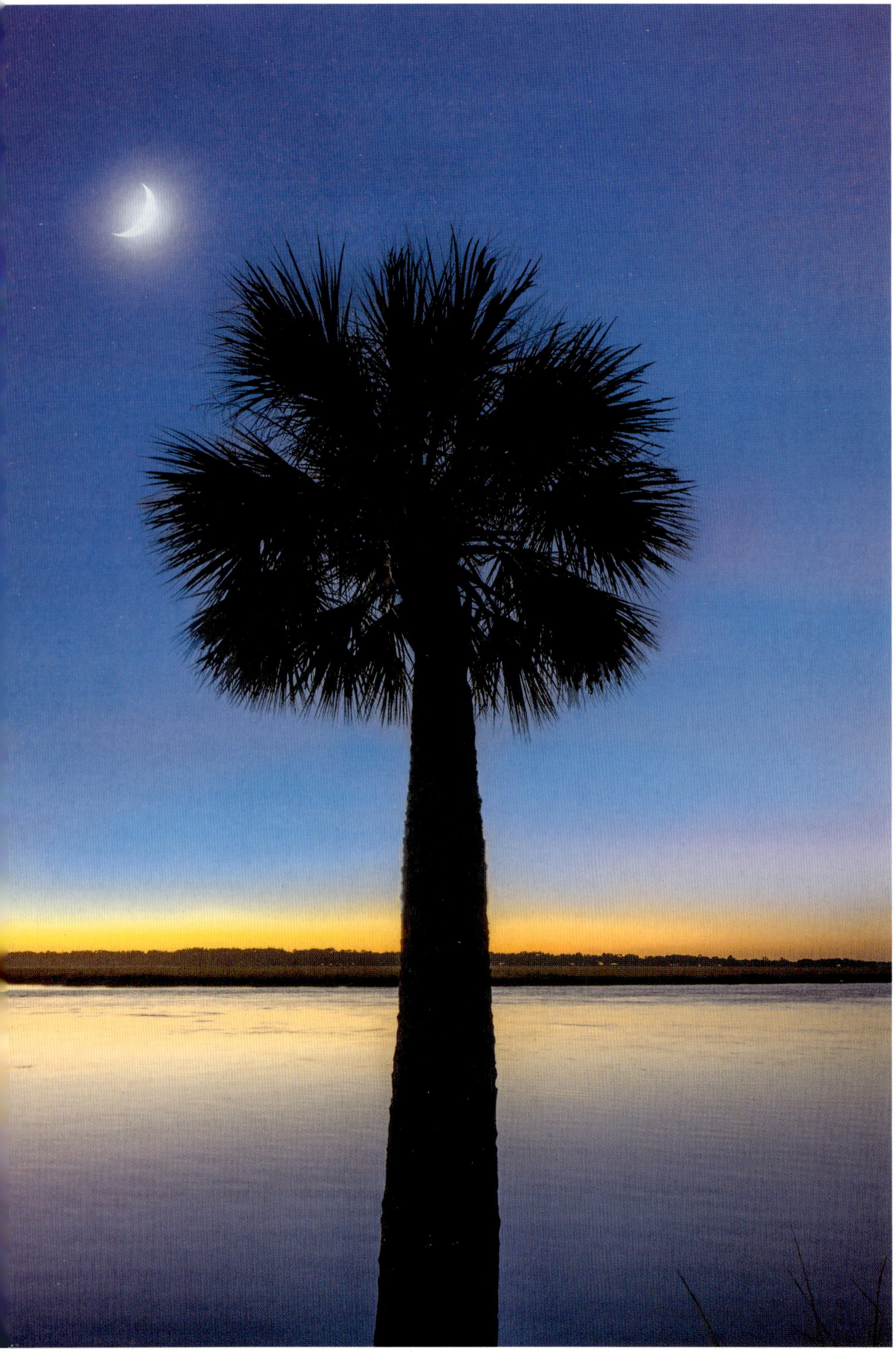

Our Journey's Debatable End

We close with a bit of mystery. The photo evokes the South Carolina flag, but is the crescent moon actually armor? Historian Rodger Stroup said Col. William Moultrie took the crescent shape from soldiers' hats. He also quotes Moultrie's diary, which says it's simply a crescent. As for the palmetto being a palm, it's not a tree. It's more closely related to grasses. Mystery aside, debate aside, the indigo flag with its white icons beautifully symbolizes freedom.

ABOUT THE AUTHORS

Robert C. Clark

Robert C. Clark's photography has appeared in *National Geographic* books, *Newsweek*, *Smithsonian*, and photographic awards annuals such as *Print and Communication Arts*. Specializing in architectural/interior photography, editorial, advertising, and fine art photography, he has photographed seven books on South Carolina, including *Carolina Bays* (University of South Carolina Press 2019). Clark is a member of the Professional Photographers of America. A native of Charlotte, North Carolina, he lives in Irmo, South Carolina.

Tom Poland

Tom Poland writes about the South, its people, culture, and natural features and gives talks throughout Georgia and the Carolinas. He is the author of several books including *Carolina Bays*. South Carolina Governor Henry McMaster conferred the Order of the Palmetto, South Carolina's highest civilian order, upon Poland for his body of work, stating, "His work is exceptional to the state." A Georgia native and graduate of the University of Georgia, he lives in Columbia, South Carolina.